THE ART OF
RUTH DRAPER

RUTH DRAPER

A Scottish Immigrant at Ellis Island

A portrait drawing by John Singer Sargent: London, 1914
(Inscribed 'To Lesley MacGregor', the Scottish girl in the monologue)

THE ART OF
RUTH DRAPER

❧❧❧❧❧❧❀❦❦❦❦❦❦

HER DRAMAS AND
CHARACTERS

❧❀❦

With a Memoir by
MORTON DAUWEN ZABEL

LONDON
OXFORD UNIVERSITY PRESS
1960

Oxford University Press, Amen House, London E.C.4

GLASGOW NEW YORK TORONTO MELBOURNE WELLINGTON
BOMBAY CALCUTTA MADRAS KARACHI KUALA LUMPUR
CAPE TOWN IBADAN NAIROBI ACCRA

PRINTED IN GREAT BRITAIN
AT THE UNIVERSITY PRESS, OXFORD
BY VIVIAN RIDLER
PRINTER TO THE UNIVERSITY

CONTENTS

꙳꙳꙳⟐꙳꙳꙳

PART I

PART II

THE DRAMAS OF RUTH DRAPER

LIST OF PLATES

✦

PART I

RUTH DRAPER

A Memoir by
Morton Dauwen Zabel

b 2 Dec 1884; d 29/30 Dec 1956 (72)

RUTH DRAPER

I

The art of acting provides its followers with many experiences that are charming, diverting, impressive, or memorable; it is not often that they are offered one that can be called unique. Nor is it often that the commemorator of an artist's life can rely on an advantage that promises at the outset to count for more than any others his task may give him—the mere act of setting down his subject's name. The talent that arrives at this kind of isolated distinction in its field, establishes itself as the archetype of a craft, and makes its name a virtual figure of speech or household word in its profession, must be recognized for achieving a form of success which has today become as difficult as it is rare and of which even the most distinguished careers in the theatre or elsewhere can easily fall short.

Ruth Draper's was a talent and a recognition of this order, and the present book is an observance of the fact. During the half-century of her career she not only made her name familiar throughout the English-speaking world and beyond it; she made it classic in her craft, a standard in her profession, the token of an art she carried to a point of mastery scarcely rivalled in her time. The particular art she practised was one she neither originated nor monopolized. She perfected it. The quality of uniqueness she gave it derived from no exclusiveness of practice or aptitude—she had numerous predecessors and contemporaries in the dramatic monologue and she will doubtless have successors—but from the fact that she made her work so completely and unmistakably her own that no one could take it away from her by rivalry or imitation, dispute the stamp of personal authority she gave

it, or fail to recognize her as its master. She made the name of
RUTH DRAPER the title of a chapter in the history of the
theatre of her time.

That chapter closed with her death in 1956, and today it is
only in the memory of her surviving audiences that her craft
and presence remain vivid. How vivid these were in her
actual performances no memoir, printed texts, or phono-
graphic recordings can hope to convey fully. In the end they
share the pathos that finally touches all practitioners of the
art of acting. The 'poor player' has always inspired as much
sympathy as affection in his audiences. His 'hour upon the
stage' casts its spell while he is there to 'strut and fret' it, but
he is always haunted by the fate of soon being 'heard no
more', his 'insubstantial pageant' fading even in the minds
that once responded to it as to a reality more acute than that
of familiar experience. It was one of the triumphant members
of the profession who pronounced its inevitable sentence:
'An actor is a sculptor who carves in snow.'

The spell Ruth Draper cast during her long career was
literally world-wide. It surmounted boundaries of language,
culture, and convention. Hardly another actor of her time
won a larger or more far-flung audience. She performed not
only in all the principal and many of the lesser cities of
America and Great Britain, but in most of the countries of
western Europe, in South and central Africa, South and
Central America, India and Asia, Australia and New Zealand,
and on ships at sea. She was often watched and listened to by
people unfamiliar with the language in which she spoke. It
would require a combination of vocal recordings and animated
photography even to suggest what she conveyed to them,
just as it would require more than a short memoir to suggest
all that her life held in friendships, travel, generous loyalties
and enthusiasms, and a restlessly varied activity—an energy
as tireless outside the theatre as within it.

Yet the pathos that closes down on the careers of most
actors is rebuked in her case. She did more than impersonate

the characters of her dramas; she created them as well. She wrote all the roles and sketches in which she appeared. Unlike most performers, she was not content to leave the creating of her men, women, and plots to others. She found at the outset that her talent was unsuited to interpreting the products of other imaginations. This bent of her temperament inevitably limited her opportunities. If it saved her from the inconsequence and triviality of the conventional theatre to which many members of her profession devote their lives, it also denied her the great roles of the stage. She never applied herself to Shakespeare or Racine, Ibsen or Shaw, classic drama or modern drama. What her gift required of her was an identification with her characters so complete that nothing short of her own imagined and created *personae* could elicit the feeling or sympathy she required for bringing them to life. She presented herself simultaneously as author and actress; and it is this fact that makes the present memorial of her work possible and that enabled her to make a contribution to the theatre that survives her performances and now takes the form of a printed record.

In her time she was described by many different terms—as monologuist, monologist, impersonator, mimic, reciter, 'solo performer', 'one-woman theatre', *diseuse*. The title she herself preferred was 'character actress', and her choice was sound. (She was likewise never satisfied with the names usually applied to her portraits—'sketches' or 'monologues'. She conceived them as 'dramas', and it is as dramas, however concentrated or miniature, that they are presented here.) It was as a master of the art of character that she showed her surest instinct, and it is as such that she lives in the memory of all who saw her. But since no writer, dramatist, portraitist, or serious actor becomes a master of character without having rich resources of personal character to draw on in himself, some radical capacity of human insight and compassion with which to respond to the life or truth he seeks to render, there necessarily existed behind all the personalities Ruth Draper created a force of personality of her own, a nature strong in feeling, sympathy, self-assertion, and generosity, which all who knew her intimately came to feel and all who saw her across the footlights sensed as the source of her charm and authority. It is her character even more than her 'characters' that finally accounts for her talent and her achievement.

Her name survives, however, and still evokes its spell for reasons less elusive than these, even as it did in her lifetime. The house-lights dimmed, the theatre darkened, the audience fell silent, a plain unfurnished stage was revealed against its background of simple curtains, with nothing but a chair or two or a table to indicate a setting, and often with no furniture of any kind to relieve its bareness. Upon that spare undecorated platform there presently appeared—striding or faltering, advancing hesitantly or sweeping abruptly—a figure alone. What the audience saw at first glance was a handsome American woman, simply garbed or scantly disguised, perhaps equipped with a peignoir, a rain-coat, or an evening cloak, sometimes with an odd hat, handbag, lorgnette, or umbrella, or most characteristically with one of the shawls that became her particular insignia: a peasant's cowl, a Scottish Paisley, a darned or knitted shoulder-cloth, a mantilla, a swaddling-cloth for a child—scarves of adroit and magical evocation. For that brief moment the figure was obviously and perilously alone on the empty boards. But in a flash the solitary woman was transformed into someone else —a young bride, a New York matron, an Irish countrywoman, a breathless débutante, a Balkan peasant, a tourist in Italy. In another moment a scene materialized—a ballroom, a boudoir, a country cottage, a porch in a Maine village, a busy office in New York, a crowded restaurant, a country house in France or England, a church in Florence. A few more moments and the scene began to fill with people; a background became all but visible; an atmosphere filled the air—of excitement, of teeming domesticity, of distracting action, of solitude or forlorn desolation. All these were fixed and held in the mind's eye for ten minutes, twenty minutes, or half an hour, while the performer surrendered herself to the character and world she concentrated in her voice, words, and gestures. Presently the words ended; the figure disappeared; and until another took its place the theatre was left to reverberate with the glimpse of life and destiny that had been made real. Only then was the spectator reminded that everything he had felt, heard, and 'seen' was the creation of a single person, a single voice and body, and of the fewest aids to illusion he was likely to witness in a lifetime of theatregoing.

Ruth Draper's art was based on many assets of charm, imagination, ingenuity, physical energy, technical skill and invention; but what they all reduced to in the end was the sorcery of her solitary and unaided skill in illusion. She made her body, voice, and temperament into an instrument of isolated and self-sufficient evocation. It was this power as much as anything that entranced her listeners; and it was in this that she revived on the modern stage one of the oldest claims of the actor's craft. Henry James was one witness who recognized that appeal in her work, as we shall presently see. Thirty years before he saw her act and made a friend of her, he had paid his tribute to the kind of acting his old age responded to in her performances:

It has often been said that the great actors who flourished in the times preceding our own gave a more striking proof of genius than their successors are called upon to give. They produced their famous effects without aids to illusion. They had no help from scenery and costume; the background was nothing; they alone were the scene. Garrick and Mrs. Siddons, wandering over England, and interpreting Shakespeare as they went, represented the visions of Hamlet and the sorrows of Constance with the assistance of a few yards of tinsel and a few dozen tallow candles. The stage was dim and bare, but the great artists triumphed, so that the tradition of their influence over their auditors has been sacredly preserved. For the most part, to-day we have changed all that...nothing that can delight the eye or touch the imagination has been omitted—nothing, that is, save the art of the actor.[1]

The words enforce a contrast and oblige the reader to recall an opposite tradition of the theatre that has become only too familiar in the past century. When Sarah Bernhardt died in 1923 a French writer said of her that 'her life was shot with thunder and lightning; it was a whirlwind of dates, titles, gleaming swords, fireworks, poets and prose-writers, men of genius and clever men, garlands, smiles, prayers and tears. A great clamour arises from it: applause, sobs, whistling trains, steamers screaming in the fog; a kaleidoscope of all countries; a babel of all tongues; shouts of enthusiasm, ejaculations of worship, cries of passion.'[2]

Ruth Draper's career carried her to cities, lands, and continents even beyond the range of Bernhardt's prodigious tours—but with a difference. She performed wherever her travels took her—in theatres, in halls, in drawing-rooms, in college auditoriums, in a country store in New Mexico, in a ship's salon. She carried none of the enormous equipment of scenery, lights, costumes, managers, impresarios, and paraphernalia the great Frenchwoman required. She travelled through five continents and over thousands of miles by land, sea, and air without retinue, staff, or company, carrying all the equipment she needed in a few dress-cases or hat-boxes and the most rudimentary of make-up kits. When she first went to see Lugné-Poe at the Théâtre de l'Œuvre in Paris in 1921 and struck up the alliance that sponsored her appearances in the French capital for many years, the veteran actor and producer watched her curiously as she scanned the auditorium, paced and measured the stage, and took stock of the dimensions and equipment of his theatre. Presently he

[1] Henry James, writing on Tommaso Salvini's appearances in Boston in 1883, in *The Atlantic Monthly*, March 1883; included in *The Scenic Art: Notes on Acting and the Drama 1872–1901*, by Henry James, edited by Allan Wade (1949), pp. 168–85.

[2] The French writer, unidentified, is quoted by Maurice Baring in his *Sarah Bernhardt* (1933), pp. 7–8.

asked her what she would require for her performances and how many players she would bring with her. '*Non, oh non*', she answered. '*Je suis seule... Ce sont des compositions de scènes écrites par moi... Je n'ai besoin de personne... Seule, moi... Un rideau, seul.*'

This '*alone*' which kept returning in her talk pleased me, put heart into me [Lugné-Poe wrote many years later]. There was something indefinably proud in it, something consolatory... Her '*alone*' had the accent of a challenge. I like that. I have always esteemed those who believe themselves alone. The solitaries have always captivated me. We must take heed of them.[1]

Every actor who hopes to survive in the memory of his auditors must add something of his own to what he portrays—some quality or element that adds a dimension of personal authority, conviction, or legend to his craft. Like any artist's, his work must carry his signature in all its parts—in its style, its atmosphere, its individual force and meaning. There are many who succeed perfectly in meeting the demands of the parts they are called on to play. There are comparatively few who are capable of adding creatively to those requirements, and fewer still who succeed in achieving a personal legend for themselves. The memorable actors of the past survive in terms of such qualities—Champmeslé, Siddons, Rachel, Salvini, Ristori—long after the audiences that once witnessed them have vanished. So, within the reach of living memory, do the fabled performers of a later day—Coquelin, Chaliapin, Caruso, Moskvin, or the illustrious women who had the fortune to have their genius commemorated by artists skilled in the language of praise: Duse in the last frail months of her life, moving like an ashen ghost through *Spettri*, *La Donna del Mare*, or *La Città Morta*, yet still evoking the 'illusion of being infinite in variety of beautiful

---

[1] 'Ce "seule" qui revient à chaque minute en ses propos me fait plaisir, me regaillardit. Il a un je ne sais quoi de fiérot, de confortable... ce "seule" a tout l'air d'un défi. J'aime ça. J'ai toujours estimé les gens qui se croient "seuls". Le solitaire m'a toujours séduit. Il faut y prendre garde.' Lugné-Poe, *Dernière Pirouette* (Paris, 1946), pp. 133-6.

pose and motion'; the two Irish sisters whose voices made
unforgettable the music of the poets who wrote their plays:
Maire O'Neill as Synge's Deirdre or Pegeen-Mike, Sara
Allgood as Maura in *Riders to the Sea* or later as O'Casey's
Juno and Bessie Burgess—the 'one all simplicity, her mind
shaped by folk-song and folk-story; the other sophisticated, lyrical and subtle', both of them 'players of genius'
who answered instinctively the 'need of the poet to be
heard'; Bernhardt as Phèdre or Camille, the *voix d'or* even
in its last dulled decade suggesting what it had been when
it 'boomed and crashed with a superhuman resonance
which shook the spirit of the hearer like a leaf in the wind'
and before 'the Terror and the Pity that lived in it and
purged the souls of mortals [had] faded into incommunicable
dreams'.[1]

It was to the art of these masters and magicians of her
craft that Ruth Draper's gift and ambition impelled her, and
it was in their company that she found her self-defined and
honoured place. Like them she brought a quality of individual
authority and legend to her work—the stamp of her protean
sympathy, her self-reliance, her responsive imagination, her
power of reducing the actor's art to its simplest essentials and
of achieving her effects and creating her 'company of characters' unaided and alone. Her life and her work were able to
draw on many resources in their fulfilment—on her background and tradition, her friends and encouragers, her personal stamina and dedication. In all these she was fortunate,
and in everything but her work no one could have been less
a solitary: her talent for friendship, society, and generosity
was as urgent and as much a part of her nature as her creative
need. But her greatest fortune and her success finally reduced,

[1] On Duse: Bernard Shaw, *The Saturday Review* (London), 15 June
1895, in *Our Theatres in the Nineties*, vol. i, pp. 148–54. On Maire O'Neill
and Sara Allgood: W. B. Yeats in his Nobel Lecture on 'The Irish
Dramatic Movement' in 'The Bounty of Sweden', *Autobiographies*
(1955), pp. 563–5. On Bernhardt: Lytton Strachey, 'Sarah Bernhardt',
The Nation and Athenaeum (London), 5 May 1923, in *Characters and
Commentaries* (1933), pp. 273–6.

as all achievement in the end is likely to, to something single, decisive, and resolving: *Je suis seule.*

II

She was born a New Yorker; New York City was her home throughout her life; it was there that she centred her work and her success; and it was there that her life and her career closed in 1956. But New England presided in the background of both the families from which she descended, and however far she ranged in her travels and activity, it was to New York and New England that Ruth Draper always returned as to the two homes of her spirit.

Her father, William Henry Draper, was born at Brattleboro, Vermont, on 4 October 1830. His family and ancestors had been Vermonters from early times and he found his first schooling there. His ambition in science became evident in youth, and when he left his native town for New York, it was in scientific studies that he specialized. Graduating from Columbia College in 1851, he went on to the College of Physicians and Surgeons, graduated in medicine in 1855, received in the same year his Master's degree from Columbia, and then went on to further studies in Paris and London. Being a skilful musician and improviser at the piano and organ, he paid his way through his medical course by playing the organ in St. Thomas's Church when it was on lower Broadway at Houston Street, and in several other churches. He had a fine voice, loved to sing, and was later to share in his family's musical enthusiasms. Medicine claimed his full professional life, however, and during the forty years of his practice he became one of the most active and honoured physicians in New York. He served on the federal Sanitary Commission during the Civil War; became an attending and consulting physician not only at the New York Hospital, where he served for almost thirty years, but at St. Luke's, the Presbyterian, Trinity, and Roosevelt Hospitals, and at the New York House of Mercy; was appointed to the faculty of the College of Physicians and Surgeons in 1869 and later became professor of Clinical Medicine there; became a trustee of the College and of Columbia University and one of the founders of Barnard College; and by the time he reached middle life was recognized as one of the most influential practitioners and teachers of medicine of his time. Two of his sons were to follow him into the medical profession and to make of it a family tradition that played its part in shaping the lives and characters of his children.

'I was born and grew up in the lap of the medical profession', his daughter Ruth said in May 1948 at a ceremony at the New York Academy of Medicine, the occasion being her presentation, in honour of her father, of a specimen of the original penicillin culture which had been given her in London two years earlier by Sir Alexander Fleming and the staff of St. Mary's Hospital following a performance she gave there for the staff and patients:

and I feel in a very definite way that my education and preparation for life were closely connected with it and deeply influenced by it. When I tell you that through the years of my childhood... [the] friends and colleagues of my father and my brother, Dr. William Kinnicutt Draper, were all familiar figures whom I looked on with awe and admiration, many of them with deep affection, you will understand what I mean.... I often drove with my father on his rounds of visits, and to the hospitals, the College of Physicians and Surgeons, and to meetings at the Academy, little dreaming that I should one day be making a speech before the Council and presenting a gift in his memory.

When Dr. Draper's long career ended with his death on 26 April 1901, one of his eminent colleagues wrote a tribute to him in the *New York Times*.

It has been given to few men to adorn the profession with greater graces of the head and of the heart [said Dr. (later Sir) William Osler]. He belonged to that rare group of men whose daily routine is a benediction, and whose very presence is a benison.... He had in full measure 'that wisdom which results from combining knowledge with the instinct and skill for its useful application'—words which he himself used in describing the modern practitioner of medicine. Of his generation it would be difficult to name a man more beloved by his patients or more esteemed by his pupils and his colleagues.... Rare grace of presence, with a quiet dignity and reserve, made him a marked man in our gatherings, and his genial and unfailing courtesy and sweetness of manner gave him an unrivalled popularity.

These were the honours and tributes that came to him in his later years. But half a century earlier, in the 1850's, he was a young doctor with his way to make and a place to establish for himself in Manhattan. He married, soon after his graduation from medical school, Elizabeth Kinnicutt of Worcester, Massachusetts, and of their union two children were born: Martha Lincoln Draper, who was to count for much in the lives of her brothers and sisters and to become a major influence in their careers, and William Kinnicutt Draper, who followed his father into medicine and likewise had a long career in medical practice in New York. But Dr. Draper's first marriage soon came to grief. His young wife died and left him to raise their two children. His life fell into sadness and loneliness. His work and responsibilities did what they could to ease his privation; he sought refuge in musical diversions among his friends; and it was at a musical evening in the home of one of these, a Mr. Haydock, that he met the young woman who was to become his second wife and the mother of his second family.

Ruth Dana brought a different character and background into his life. She was the daughter of Charles A. Dana and his wife Eunice Macdaniel, he from New Hampshire, she from Maryland, but the New England tradition that had shaped their lives was in sharp contrast to Dr. Draper's more sober Vermont ancestry. Born at Hinsdale, New Hampshire, in 1819, Charles Dana had gone to college at Harvard and became involved there in the intellectual ferment and Emersonian inspiration of the 1840's that had their upshot in the Brook Farm experiment at Concord. It was at Brook Farm that Dana became the friend and associate of Emerson, Bronson Alcott, Hawthorne, Margaret Fuller, and George Ripley during the five years of that rugged venture in philosophic socialism. He taught Greek to the Farmers, became head of their gardens, and shared the troubles that soon overtook the colony.

One of these was a smallpox epidemic that broke out in the winter of 1845-6. The management of the Farm had fallen largely on Dana, and when, in an improvised hospital that had been set up for the afflicted, he noticed the efficient nursing service of a young woman recruit, he felt a gratitude that soon grew into something stronger. Eunice Macdaniel had come from Maryland with her mother, sister, and brother to live at Brook Farm, but she was biding her time there. Secretly she was eager to go to New York and become an actress. As the winter of the epidemic ran its course Dana's responsibilities in the community increased. Beset by financial difficulties, its leader, George Ripley, asked him to go to New York to seek funds from sympathizers there. When Eunice bade him farewell she confided that she too was determined to leave the Farm and go to New York to study at a dramatic school. Dana seized the opportunity to propose to her. She accepted him on the spot, and by the end of February followed him to New York, where, a week after her arrival, they were married on 2 March 1846. The couple planned to keep their marriage a secret, but when Dana returned to Brook Farm to find that its largest building, the Phalanstery, had burned down and the colony in the process of disbanding, he saw that he would have to seek a livelihood elsewhere. With this turn in her fortunes Eunice Macdaniel abandoned her dream of a career in acting and devoted herself to her husband's future. (Almost eighty years later, in 1923, Ruth Draper, always remembering her grandmother as the single member of her family to have had an ambition for acting and the theatre, was in London, at the end of one of her earliest and most triumphant seasons in the British capital and with the English public and its critics eloquent in their admiration of her work. 'I feel quite sad to be leaving the Garrick tonight', she said in a letter to an old English friend: 'It has really been an amazing experience, and I have a strange awareness that it is probably the climax of my career. I feel too that Mother would have been thrilled by it all. And I think back to her mother, who as a young girl at Brook Farm dreamed of all that I am experiencing—and never attained it,—and I who never dreamed of or wanted it have the world at my feet! How strange it is!')

Dana took his first step toward his new career by finding work on the *Boston Daily Chronotype*, and thus launched himself in the journalism that was to become his profession for life. In 1847 his old ally at Brook Farm, Horace Greeley, called him to New York to become city editor of his recently founded *New York Tribune*, already in the vanguard of liberal and abolitionist journalism. By 1849 Dana became Greeley's managing editor, and worked with him throughout the following turbulent decade when the issues that were preparing the Civil War were mounting in crisis and intensity. On some of those issues Dana was to differ sharply with his chief, but throughout their association, and long after it ended, the two men remained allies in the cause of critical liberalism and became models for the editors and newspaper writers who were carrying American journalism into its most active and influential era.

In 1864 Dana was called to Washington by Lincoln's Secretary of War Stanton and was appointed an assistant secretary in Lincoln's Cabinet. By 1868, with the war ended and his government duties over, he returned to New York and became editor and part owner of the *New York Sun*. He now found his true vocation, and during the next thirty years, until his death in 1897, he became one of the most famous editors America has known, a leader and paragon in independent journalism, a stubborn defender of liberal and lost causes, the sponsor of a new style of newspaper writing, and the presiding genius of a paper that came to be known as 'the American newspaper-man's Bible'.[1]

Ruth Dana was twenty years younger than Dr. William Draper. By the time he met her at the Haydock house she had grown into a spirited, vivacious young woman, skilful at the piano, avid in her social and artistic interests, much favoured in the social life of the city. Surrounded by a circle of young friends and by several serious admirers, she at first gave little heed to the shy and handsome physician who paid his court to her—in fact she discouraged his attentions and on his first proposal of marriage she rejected him. But he persisted, summoned up the boldness to propose again, and so impressed her with his sincerity and courage that one day she abruptly accepted his hand. They were married on 7 December 1877, in her father's house at Glen Cove, Long Island, and set up housekeeping in the city. Ruth Dana now became the step-mother of his two children, but in the next nine years a new family of brothers and sisters joined them. The oldest, Charles Dana Draper, was born in 1879. Then followed George, Dorothea, and Alice. In 1884 the Drapers acquired a new home at 19 East 47th Street, off Fifth Avenue. There their two youngest children were born: Ruth on 2 December 1884, and Paul on 29 November 1886. And there the family remained until Dr. Draper died in 1901.

III

The 47th Street house was the home they knew in child-hood—'a forty-foot brownstone house on the north side of 47th Street between Madison and Fifth Avenues', as one of Ruth's sisters describes it in some memory-notes, in what was then uptown residential Manhattan. Dr. Draper kept his office on the ground floor. Around and above were the

[1] Dana's career has been recounted in every record of American journalism, most fully in *The Life of Charles A. Dana* by James Harrison Wilson (New York, 1907) and in *Dana and The Sun* by Candace Stone (New York, 1938).

PLATE I

(a) Ruth Draper in infancy: about 1885

Mrs. William Henry Draper (Ruth Dana Draper) with her
daughters Dorothea, Alice, and Ruth

(b) Ruth Draper as a child: about 1888

Photograph by Thomas, New York

PLATE II

(b) Ruth Draper at 15: New York, about 1899
Photograph by Miss A. F. Bradley, New York

(a) Ruth Draper as a schoolgirl: New York, about 1895
Photograph by Moreno, New York

living rooms, and on the upper floor the nursery and school room. There the Draper children came into consciousness of the life around them, received their first lessons, and banded together in the close-knit intimacy of a spirited family life and of a home notable for its free hospitality and its love of music and the arts. Martha Lincoln Draper, who was never to marry, was old enough to be the benevolent eldest sister of the clan and to show even in her early years the strong qualities of character and responsibility that made her not only Mrs. Draper's second-in-command in household affairs but in time a greatly respected and influential citizen of New York, deeply devoted to her family, liberal in sympathy and counsel, keenly interested in education, one of the founders of the Public Education Association and a member of the Board of Education of New York City. Her brother William soon entered on his medical studies; and since these two were older than Dr. Draper's second family, they watched with grave and responsible affection the growing-up of the younger children around them. 'The family divided itself, for nursery parlance, into "the four big ones and the children" ', one of the sisters recalls:

The children were inseparable companions and early showed the talents that developed into careers as time passed. My mother was proud of us as beauty specimens and provided everything to contribute to the development of each of us. She once told me that she had no possessive feeling about us; that she respected each one as an individual and a trust. There was great fun at home, strict discipline and affection without sentimentality. We had nurses as needed, help in the house, and plenty of room to play and run about. As time went on nurses were replaced by a German governess and teachers for subjects like music and dancing.... The day was busy. Family breakfast at eight; lessons from nine to twelve; a walk or play in the back yard till lunch time at one-thirty; with my father and mother out to the park for the after-noon and home by five to dress for six o'clock supper, and bed for us by seven-thirty or eight. I cannot recall that my parents were ever out for lunch. We had our supper early; they dined at seven-thirty but went out a great deal in the evenings or had dinner parties at home. These were great events for us children. Though we were supposed to be asleep, one eye waited for the flicker of gas-light in the hall to shine through an opening door; we knew Gustave would be coming in with ice-cream for all of us. On occasions I recall my mother bringing her guests to the nursery to see us all sleeping, while father smoked cigars below with the gentlemen.

Not far away was the house of 'Grandpa and Grandma', their Dana grandparents, in 60th Street, as well as the homes of Mrs. Draper's sister Mrs. John Brannan, her brother, 'Uncle Paul', and Dr. Draper's brother, 'Uncle Frank', and his sister, 'Aunt Julia Kent', with her six children. 'We were always in and out of 25 East 60th Street in the Winter, and in summer at Grandpa's place on Long Island.' With the elder Danas lived Mrs. Dana's maiden sister, Aunt Fanny Macdaniel. 'She was beloved by each one of us and her room was the best place to spend a rainy afternoon. She would have only one child to visit her at a time. She taught us to sew, to paint flowers and paste leaves on cards—a hundred ways to be careful and tidy, and to respect and appreciate beauty.'

The six younger children of the Draper household showed the contrasting natures that are likely to appear in any large family group. The oldest, Charles Dana, responsible and serious by nature, was the honoured senior brother who presently went off to Cutler School, then to Harvard, from which he graduated in 1900, and so entered on a long career in the business world of New York and in various public philanthropic activities that ended with his death in 1947. George, the second son, inherited his father's scientific bent as well as the imaginative temper of the family. From his school and college years at Groton and Harvard he proceeded to medical studies at the College of Physicians and Surgeons, to research work at the Rockefeller Institute, to studies with Jung in Switzerland, to specialization in heart disease and later in the psychological aspects of medical treatment that led him to become an initiator of 'psysomatic'—or, as it was later called by the term he promulgated, 'psychosomatic'—therapy, author of leading books in his field, and one of the pioneers of these branches of medical treatment in the United States. The older sisters also advanced into young womanhood, schooled in the public spirit of their father and older brothers and in their mother's musical and artistic enthusiasms. Dorothea, who first married Linzee Blagden and after his death Henry James, the oldest son of William James of Harvard, became an active citizen of New York and a participant in its educational and hospital work and public charities. Alice, after her marriage to Edward C. Carter, followed her husband to India, Burma, England, and France on the educational and international projects that occupied him during almost forty years of his career, while raising a family of six children and keeping in close touch with her own family in New York.

But it was in the two youngest members of the family, Ruth and Paul, that the artistic enthusiasms of their parents came to the liveliest expression. They were the juniors of the household. In nursery days they had their early supper together apart from the older children, conspired in games and amusements, and found themselves natural confederates in play and study. Even as small children they showed themselves to be the creative temperaments of the family, the artists; and all the instinctive feeling that throws imaginative natures into alliance sealed their sympathy with each other from their earliest days.

Paul, Ruth's junior by two years, was inventive, mercurial, quick to respond to fun and humour; it was he who collaborated with Ruth in nursery games and charades. Advancing into boyhood and young manhood he went to Groton School, then briefly to Harvard, where he discovered that his gift and ambition lay in music. He went to Europe after leaving Harvard to seek the advice of Leschetizsky in Vienna, but he found he was too late to embark on a serious study of the piano and turned instead to the training of his fine tenor voice. After his marriage in 1909 to Muriel Sanders of Haverhill, Massachusetts, he lived and studied in Europe—first in Florence under Isidore Braggiotti, then in London under Raimund von zur Mühlen, one of the foremost interpreters and teachers of German *Lieder* of the time. It was in London, in their house in Edith Grove, Chelsea, that the Drapers made their home and created one of the most celebrated salons of its moment, the eve of 1914. There they were hosts to the musicians, artists, and writers of the time, Casals, Thibaud, Kochanski, the young Artur Rubinstein, the Flonzaley Quartet, and other makers of music joining with such listeners as Henry James, Sargent, and older friends to make the night music of Edith Grove one of the envied pleasures of London's high Bohemia. The two small sons of Paul and Muriel Draper were with them in Edith Grove, Paul Junior and Raimund Sanders. Sanders, thirty years later, was to meet his death in the Royal Air Force during the Battle of Britain, leaving a young daughter, Anne Draper, to become one of Ruth Draper's best-loved grand-nieces; while Paul was to become, after studies in the arts and engineering in Europe and America, the brilliant dancer who developed the art of formal and interpretative tap-dancing to a height of style and elegance it had never reached before, to make himself famous in his art, and in time to share on occasion in his aunt's programmes in America, England, and Europe.

Paul Draper, in the midst of a many-sided social life, kept avidly to his voice and musical studies; and while his voice lacked the calibre and volume necessary for a full-scale professional career, the sensitive taste and instinct that joined with his love of song literature brought him the admiration of friends and critics who recognized in his renderings of Schubert, Schumann, and Brahms, of French and Italian art songs, and of English or Scottish ballads and American folk-music, an authentic gift and instinct. He sang Mahler's songs with the Boston Symphony under Karl Muck, appeared with

the Philadelphia Orchestra under Stokowski and with the
Friends of Music in New York, and on many occasions between 1915 and 1922 joined his sister Ruth in private and
public recitals. The First World War took him back to
Europe, first with the Presbyterian Hospital Unit in France,
then as a Second Lieutenant in the American Army with
whom he served as liaison officer and interpreter at the
American headquarters at Blois and Chaumont.

The promise of his high gifts was never fulfilled after his
return to America when the war ended; he died at the early
age of thirty-nine in 1925. But in youth and early manhood
the charm of his character, his natural sense of humour and
imagination, his vivid eloquence in story-telling, his gaiety
and zest for art, made him for his sister Ruth not only an
adored younger brother, 'always in tune' with her in matters
of invention and imagination, but a companion in her early
hopes and aspirations. She knew with a sister's sympathy the
charm of temperament that kept him buoyant in spirit and
cheerful in disappointment; she profited by his gaiety in her
own stricter temperament; and she never forgot the sympathy
that had existed as an instinctive bond between them from
their earliest years.

It was in these early years that Ruth began to show her
own irrepressible gift for fantasy and invention. And it was
in the upstairs nursery in 47th Street that another activity
than childish play and games was soon in progress. 'Do
Fräulein for us, Ruth!' sang the other children. 'Do the
Channel crossing!' 'Do the little tailor!' And Ruth, in her
nightgown, would stand in the middle of the floor, or sit in
her little rocking-chair, or perch on the edge of the bed, and
perform the feats of mimicry that came as naturally to her as
eating or sleeping. 'By the time Ruth was eight', one of her
sisters remembers, 'her individuality was recognized even by
the rest of us.... She began to pretend she was Mrs. Frost,
who came twice a year to make our clothes. While the nursery
was busy with blocks and steam engines, Ruth was in a

window with a shawl over her shoulders pretending she had
a cold in the head. She would sew and talk to herself. As
time went on she added her imitations.' The people she saw
during the day in her mother's parlour, in the streets outside, or on summer holidays were already falling under her
sharp childish observation. Soon she was called on to perform downstairs. 'Do something to amuse us, dear', she
remembered her mother saying after the evening guests had
left the dinner table; and she was always prompt to oblige.

There were governesses in the house for the boys and girls
until they reached the age of eleven or twelve. When she
was ten, in 1894, Ruth was sent to Miss Spence's School for
a year, and again briefly in the autumn of 1896. This venture
in formal education proved unsuccessful. She disliked the
impersonal order and discipline of the schoolroom; found
herself unable to follow the lessons; she protested, and
eventually her mother took her home. But not before she had
made her impression of independence and self-will on her
schoolmates. One of these, who was to become a lifelong
friend of Ruth and her sisters, was to recall, sixty years later,
her first glimpse of Ruth in the autumn of 1896. Most of her
memories of Miss Spence's regimen had dimmed, except for
the passion the schoolmistress put into her readings of
Shakespeare, the occasional recitals of the Kneisel Quartet,
or the splendour of great paintings in Mrs. Havemeyer's
mansion on Fifth Avenue to which the Spence charges would
be taken for special treats on Sunday afternoons. But one
moment of the schoolroom remained vivid:

There came a morning when, in the very middle of the school
singing class with... Frank Damrosch beating his rigid measure,
the door opened and Ruth Draper appeared! She couldn't have
been more than eleven years old—a thin, straight little figure, thin
pale face and great wonderful eyes. I've never seen such eyes....
She wore a stiffly starched white shirtwaist and a skirt of plain
wool—a big pattern—with *bretelles* going over her shoulders. She
looked about the room in a quiet way, not shy, not in the least

self-conscious, and then walked slowly to a vacant chair. She was
grave and simple and observant and with a look of cool appraisal,
not unkind but very keen! No more singing for me that morning.
I was absorbed in watching the fascinating child.[1]

Mrs. Draper now looked for a new governess, and by a
stroke of luck she found one who was to become one of the
memorable influences of Ruth's girlhood. She was a German
woman, small, eccentric, dedicated, who had the natural art
of kindling the minds and imaginations of her charges. Her
name was Hannah Henrietta Hefter, and for several years
she took charge of Ruth's schooling. Ruth now warmed to the
excitement of pictures, museums, and books; for the first
time became eager to learn; began to revel in the lore of
history and literature. For a time she attended classes for
young ladies that were held in New York in those days by
Miss Joanna Davidge; but it was Fräulein Hefter whom she
was to remember as the guiding spirit of her schooldays and
as the most inspiring of all her teachers. To what Ruth's
father and mother had given her in their devotion to science
and music, Fräulein Hefter added the enchantments of story-
telling and great painting, and Ruth was to carry it with her
in all her future explorations of literature and art. Years afterward, thrilling to her first discovery of the galleries of the
Prado in Madrid in 1922, she wrote in her diary: 'So many
pictures familiar from my studies with H. H. Hefter. Bless
her for what she gave to me!' 'She lit the spark', Ruth was
often to say, and she never forgot the debt she owed her in
the years when her imagination flowered into its first
responses to the world of art and books.

Languages had been subjects in the Draper schoolroom

---

[1] Aileen Tone, in *The Spence Alumnae Bulletin*, June 1957, p. 29.
Glimpses of R. D. in youth have been recorded elsewhere; one appears
in the autobiography of a childhood friend, later the distinguished
American sculptor Malvina Hoffman, *Heads and Tales* (1936), pp. 30–31.
Miss Hoffman met her husband, the English violinist Samuel B. Grimson,
through an introduction from Mrs. William H. Draper; her sister Helen
became the wife of Dr. William Kinnicutt Draper.

from early years, first German, then French. Meanwhile another horizon had widened. In 1890 Mrs. Draper took her step-daughter Martha and her own six children abroad for a summer in England, chiefly at Felixstowe. Another in England and Germany followed in 1891, and others in England in 1898 and 1901. Ruth proved to be a bad sailor at that age and became very ill at sea; she tended in these years to be delicate in health. But for the first time she tasted the enchantment of travel and foreign countries, and became infected with the virus of wanderlust and adventure that possessed her throughout her life. Other ventures overseas were to follow during the next decade. In 1897 a second home began to figure in the family's life: it was in that year that Mrs. Draper built a large rambling summer house in Maine, at Dark Harbor on the island of Islesboro in Penobscot Bay. Dark Harbor now became a summer haven for the family; there their happiest holidays were spent for many years; and there Alice Draper was married in 1908. When Mrs. Draper died in 1914, she left the Dark Harbor house to all her children jointly, but eventually Ruth bought it from the other heirs and made it her permanent summer home. She came to love it more than any of her other homes; loved the sea and became a skilled swimmer and sailor; returned to Dark Harbor year after year from her tours and travels in all parts of the world; became a familiar spirit of the local community and of her Maine neighbours, and came to feel herself as much a citizen of Maine as of New York.

IV

The years were now passing swiftly. In 1900 Ruth was sixteen; in 1903 she was introduced to New York society as a nineteen-year-old débutante; in 1904 she was twenty and her first decade of adult womanhood began. After her father died in 1901, the big house on 47th Street was sold. Mrs. Draper then bought two houses on 8th Street, off Fifth Avenue above Washington Square, threw them together and made a new home out of them, and there Ruth made her home until her mother's death in 1914.

The crowded days of a New York life engaged her—parties, dances, theatres, concerts, country visits to Long Island, Virginia, or New England, weddings of her girlhood friends— the round of diversions and duties of a popular young woman in the early years of an expectant twentieth century. Her childhood weakness was now put behind her. She discovered unsuspected resources of energy in her body and mind. The slight figure of girlhood took on strength and stamina. She became an enthusiastic walker, dancer, party-goer, explorer. Her social gifts flowered. Besides the old New York and New England friends she had inherited from her parents or made in childhood, she began to form a wider circle of friends of her own, not only in America but in Europe. Her intimate relations expanded. Inevitably her spirit and personal vitality attracted the attention of the young men she knew, and there were attachments of warm and friendly affection to claim her. Yet there persisted also an essential reserve in her nature. Those closest to her remember her in these years as 'keeping things to herself'. Even her own family was unaware of what secret thoughts or hopes were occupying her. It was not until after 1912 or 1914 that she became the active and outgiving personality of her later years.

It was during this decade that she first felt the stirrings of literary ambition, and soon she was trying her hand at self-expression in verse. There has survived a notebook of verses she wrote during the years between the ages of thirteen and thirty. The earliest stanzas in it are two droll childish poems she wrote in 1897 to her father and mother, but after another ten years the pages take on a more serious intention. Only once did she see one of her poems printed, a lyric of two quatrains titled 'Winter Flowers' in *Scribner's Magazine* for March 1913. Her other efforts remained secret, and once her verse-writing phase had passed she became too self-critical to take her work in this line seriously or to offer it as competent poetry. She would not wish it to be offered as such now. She wrote her stanzas at a time when American verse was still conventional, unawakened to the fresh impulse in language and style that was to come after 1912, and when the poetic efforts of young women observed the discretions and gentility of an earlier day. Ruth's, in fact, closely suggest those of the young Edith Wharton several decades earlier. Yet this notebook is perhaps the most intimate record that survives of Ruth Draper's inner life at this time, and as one glances through its pages one catches glimpses of the thought and emotions that were filling her intimate moments. There is a touching poem called 'To Two Boys', dated November 1911, in which she records her devotion to her sister Alice's small twin sons and her love of children. Another, untitled and dated January 1912, speaks to another child:

> Come to my heart, you little child,
> Come to my lonely heart,
> Subdue the storms and tame the wild,
> And heal the wounds that smart.
> For I have lost the safest way,
> I've gone too rough a road,
> And through the years by night and day,
> I've borne a weary load.
>
> .   .   .   .   .
>
> You turn? I understand. You fear.
> Though Love speaks, you hear pain.
> And I who thought that peace was near
> Must climb the rocks again.

An earlier poem, in 1909, had been addressed to 'Pain' as

> The all-embracing power that subdues
> Delight and jubilance and strength to live,

but it went on to say that pain's ordeal,

> if borne with patience and with prayer
> Leaves to the sufferer, when it departs,
> A wondrous gift:
> Of deeper insight into lovely things,

Of keener sympathies and kindly ways,
Of joyfulness and strength to help the weak
And a great love for life, and a deep faith
That all is right, that in the end God will
Explain his ways, and there will be no pain.

'O dull dark clouds that hang about my soul,' she apostrophizes in another lyric:

Go hang your burden on some lifeless thing,
Or climb too brilliant skies and cast soft shade
For tired souls to rest in, do not bring
To pure young hearts that yearn black doubt and fear.

And she pleads with love to 'lift the veil and show the vision far'.

These are evidently records of her innermost secret moments, her seizures by fear and doubt, her dread of missing the greater opportunities and fulfilments of life. Most of them are souvenirs of the quiet suffering that visited her in the intervals of her busy outward activity, and all of them suggest impatience with fortune, a waiting for life to show its face to her, a sense of suppressed and thwarted expectancy. For there also emerges a promise of what she will make of her life once it reveals its confidence, an ardour to embrace opportunity and enterprise, an eagerness for adventure and action. In a poem of 1910 she reveals the darker vision:

I came from out a heated room
Angry and hating all mankind.
The night was cool, I sought the woods
To see what solace I could find.

I walked along a lonely path,
The lake below, lit by the moon;
The soft scent from the sodden swamp,
The calling of a distant loon,

The lapping of the tender waves,
The gentle rustle of the trees,
A holy silence, full of sounds.
My thoughts swam through the mysteries.

'Distraught and sad, and full of doubt', the speaker lays her head on a cold stone, grasps at a pine, releases a groan of pain from her lips. Suddenly she finds herself struck by a different fear which turns her away from self-abandonment and despair:

> Startled I turned, I felt no more
> The aching heart, my one desire
> To flee the fearsome moonlit wood,
> To reach the warmth of glowing fire.
>
> .   .   .   .   .
>
> For after Nature ministered
> And tore from me that echoing cry,
> She did not crave my thanks and prayers.
> I heard her laughing silently.

But there are two poems of March 1912 which express something different: a release from fear and self-doubt and a turning toward faith in life and in herself. In one of them she addresses the spirit of life as a magnetic pole toward which 'All my lesser loves assemble / And in one force rush to thee!'

> All my love of dreams and fancies,
> And my love of pensive mood;
> All my love of gay abandon
> And my love of solitude.
>
> All my love of Nature's beauties,
> And the fair works man has wrought,
> All my love of books and comrades
> And the things for which I've fought.
>
> All my love of this world's pleasures,
> And the joys they bring to me;
> Last, my self-love and the vision
> Of the great things I would be.
>
> .   .   .   .   .
>
> Take them as the mighty ocean
> Silently accepts the stream.
> While I pray that thou wilt grant me
> The fulfilment of my dream!

And in the other she salutes the love that at last gives promise of embracing her:

SONG

My love and I sail on the wave,
The winds and sky are fair.
I press my lips to his cool brow
And play with his sunlit hair.

As I lie in his arms I sing
And steer for the sapphire sea,
And no two in the universe
Are happier than we.

My love and I ride in the wood,
The leaves like jewels glow.
The air like wine flows in our veins.
We clasp hands as we go.

And if from Nature's joyousness
We take more than our share,
We kneel together at a shrine
And pay our penance there.

My love and I climb mountain heights;
He helps me struggle on.
And hand in hand we face the gloom
Till what we seek is won.

And should death come to take my dear
I'd fall too in the strife,
For we two could not dwell apart.
My brave young love is Life.

V

The ten years between 1904 and 1914—between her twentieth and thirtieth years—were Ruth's decade of decisions. Her verses show that she was troubled by a sense of decisions delayed, chances missed, a confidence often severely daunted. Her old friends were setting up households and families. She herself turned in other directions—to new friends, to the charms and distractions of travel, or to the sketches she was now writing and training herself in. There were further trips to Europe in these years. Italy, France, and England reopened their doors to her, and all her romantic feeling for ancient cities, shrines of art, foreign scenes and places, and the ways of strange people expanded as she explored the older world.

Greater friendships also began to form. In Washington Henry Adams was advancing into extreme old age and slowly succumbing to the 'melancholy of declining powers', the pessimism of his earlier years now laying its chill on his solitude. In letters to old friends like Henry James or Elizabeth Cameron he could reveal his despairs, but he never lost his enthusiasm for youth and its generous expectations, and to young women like his nieces Louisa Hooper and Elizabeth Adams, or to Aileen Tone and Ruth Draper, he could respond with the charm and spirit of his other nature. 'I love Ruth Draper,' he wrote to Elizabeth Cameron in 1911; 'she is a little genius, and quite fascinates me.' And a year after suffering a severe stroke he wrote from Paris in the spring of 1913 to Henry James in London:

> Your letter reminds me that it is just a year since I again woke up, after an eternity of unconsciousness, to this queer mad world, ten times queerer and madder than ever, and what a vast gulf opened to me between the queerness of the past and the total inconsequence of the present. The gulf has not closed: it is rather wider today than a year ago; but I wake up every morning and I go to sleep every night with a stronger sense that each day is an isolated fact, to be taken by itself and looked at as a dance. Our friend Ruth helped me, and I am glad to think that she helped you. We need it.[1]

For in spite of her intervals of uncertainty and doubt, and against whatever fear she felt that life was passing her by,

---

[1] *Letters of Henry Adams: 1892–1918*, edited by Worthington Chauncey Ford (Boston and New York, 1938), pp. 560, 612–13.

there had continued to assert itself in Ruth a force of confidence that not only carried her forward but overflowed into the relations she struck up with others. At the basis of that confidence was her insight into the lives of people, her sense of their characters, the sympathy whereby she responded to them imaginatively, translated their thoughts into her own thoughts and words, and made dramas of their humours, griefs, and eccentricities. The magic of mimicry that had appeared in the nursery and family drawing-room now took on a richer sympathy. She discovered that she could not only mimic and imitate but act and visualize. To her aid came the tones and accents she caught from the voices around her, her unfailing skill in seizing the significance of gestures, habits, physical and facial traits, eccentric signs and motions. In childhood her mimicry had been simple and spontaneous. Now it became serious, studied, satirical, penetrating. Gradually, year by year, she began to cast her impressions into written form and to shape her miniature dramas out of what she saw in the streets or houses of New York, Maine, and Europe. Her monologues were coming into being. In long sessions of private rehearsal she wrote, revised, developed, and corrected her manuscripts. By the time she was in her early twenties she had developed a repertory of portraits and dramas—the seeds of what was to become her 'company of characters'.

Some of them were taken out of the social life of the New York houses she frequented—portraits of hectic society ladies, light-headed hostesses, ambitious mothers, culture-hungry yearners, giddy débutantes. She saw them all with a sharp critical eye, and satire of this kind was always to remain one of the staples of her repertory. But she also saw people of other kinds—the working-girls of the New York streets, hard-working telephone operators or factory wage-slaves, Jewish families from the Bronx or Brooklyn, secretaries in business offices, charwomen trudging through their labours in the night hours, harassed servants and governesses, provincial

wives and mothers from the Middle West or New England,
the old women of bleak villages along the Maine coast, immigrants at Ellis Island. Her avidity for all these curiosities of
human behaviour became endless. Her eyes and ears increasingly alerted themselves to every form of oddity, pathos, or
energy in the life around her. And when she went abroad her
camera-eye was no less sharp. She marked the tourists with
their Baedekers, awkwardly or earnestly exploring museums
and cathedrals of France and Italy, high-tempered dress-
makers in the Rue de la Paix, temperamental actresses of the
Paris stage, English hostesses and dowagers in their London
homes or country houses, waifs of the London streets, women
leading hard lives in country towns or mining districts, old
mothers in the by-ways of rural Ireland. Some of them she
saw with humour and sardonic amusement, but others she
saw in their dignity of toil, hardship, and grim endurance.
Year by year the range of response widened, and one by one
the members of her gallery took on form and existence.

'How did it all start?' she would be asked in after-years in
countless interviews. And she would tell of the nursery games
and exhibitions, the performances for guests in 47th Street,
later the requests that she perform for friends in their houses
or at parties, then the recitals for charity or other public
causes. The first sketch she worked out fully was of a little
old Jewish tailor her mother employed to do the family
sewing and suit-making. 'A pathetic and lovely little man',
she remembered him as being. 'I can see him now. "Its could
be fixed," he would say. "Its could be fixed. Little padding
on the shoulders. Pearl buttons here. Velvet collar. New
lining. Semi-fitting back. Box front." A lovely little man.'
To him and her other subjects she found herself responding
by a natural instinct.[1] The voice took on its appropriate pace

[1] Ruth Draper was interviewed scores of times during her career.
When she preserved these cuttings in her scrapbooks, with or without
correction, I have ventured to quote them as reliable. The above quotation and several following come from an interview in the *New Yorker*,
6 March 1954.

PLATE III

Ruth Draper as Débutante: New York, 1903

Photograph by Miss A. F. Bradley, New York

PLATE IV

Ruth Draper in London: 1913

Photograph by Dorothy Hickling, Ebury Street, London

and accent, the gestures materialized, the stoop of shoulders, stance and carriage of body, gait of walk, play of hands, flash of eyes and expression, all came to suit the occasion.

She never studied acting, never took lessons in elocution or exercises in timing and placement. All these seemed unnecessary. Something instinctive and spontaneous, natively ebullient, sympathetic, and image-making, served her instead. By means of long sessions of self-training, self-correction, and rehearsal, the sketches materialized, took on detail and body, and through the trial-and-error method of actual performance came to life. She had watched actors and actresses in their stage performances with acute attention from the time she began attending the theatre; many hints and suggestions were gathered from them. But her beginnings were never professional or methodical. They were entirely self-cultivated. She was in the exact sense of the word an *amateur* of her art. Her family, friends, and listeners caught the accent of a truth, a quality of authenticity, which no professional training could give. 'To have Ruth Draper perform' became an ambition among New York hostesses. By 1905 and 1908 she was finding her time increasingly occupied with afternoon or evening recitals in private houses, on country week-ends, or at summer gatherings and benefits.

At first it was all done freely and gratuitously, and it took many years before she ventured to offer herself as a professional. In cases of charitable occasions there was no question of asking a fee, and this rule was to continue into the later decades when she became world-famous and her performances for charities of all kinds in war-time or peace-time took up a major part of her working time. When fees eventually came into question it was also a question of what fees to ask. 'I used to perform at parties all over', she remembered. 'People took advantage of me really.' But such amateur status could not go on indefinitely. There did exist, after all, a tradition of the one-man or one-woman theatre, the professional sketch or monologue. Now that it was time for her to think of making a career she found herself also obliged to think seriously of making such a career pay for itself.

VI

Three suggestions, as she later recalled, were to prove decisive. 'I saw Beatrice Herford perform her monologues and realized what could be done. And I saw a Chinese play, *The Yellow Jacket*, without scenery—small steps that one went up and down, so, when one wanted to enact climbing a mountain—and I understood the extraordinary illusion that can be created with nothing. But Paderewski played a large part.'

Beatrice Herford was an Englishwoman, born in Manchester in 1868. She lived to a great age, dying in 1952 at eighty-four, and theatre-goers saw her perform her sketches or act in New York plays as late as the 1920's—now-forgotten entertainments like *What's in a Name*, *Two by Two*, *Cock Robin*, *See Naples and Die*, *Run Sheep Run*. She was the daughter of an English Unitarian minister, Dr. Brooke Herford, and a sister of Oliver Herford, born five years earlier than herself. She discovered her acting talent early, and by the time she was in her early twenties she was acting on the provincial stage in England. Both she and her brother were young people of great humorous gifts. Both found themselves bent toward comedy and satire at an early age. In Oliver this proclivity took the direction of comic and satiric writing and drawing, and of a verbal wit that was to make him one of the most admired humorists of his time—a figure in the journalistic and club life of New York in the early decades of this century, author of such whimsicalities as *The Rubaiyat of a Persian Kitten*, writer for the Broadway stage, a familiar visitor of the Players' Club, and for many years one of the leading contributors of humorous verse, prose, and pictures to the old *Life* magazine. Innumerable examples of his wit found their way into the hearsay of his time, the genial New York life of the early 1900's.

His sister Beatrice showed the same vein of humorous invention and ironic comedy. She had made her début as a monologuist in London in 1895 before an audience that included Shaw, William Archer, Ellen Terry and Henry James, and was soon counted a star in the genre and a fully qualified rival to such other wits and mimics of the time as Corney Grain, George Grossmith, Cissie Loftus, and Yvette Guilbert. In America she made her début at the old 39th Street Theatre in Annie Russell's Old English Comedy Company, acting Mrs. Hardcastle in *She Stoops to Conquer*. But she soon resumed her solo performances, and by the later nineties she was giving programmes of these at the Lyceum Theatre, the Waldorf-Astoria breakfasts, and other places of entertainment. She continued to perform them as late as the 1930's, sometimes in theatres of her own, sometimes on vaudeville programmes at the Palace, sometimes in Broadway revues. Her repertory was eventually assembled in two volumes of her sketches—*Monologues* in 1908 and *Beatrice Herford's Monologues* in 1937.[1]

Her wit and ingenuity are apparent in these books. What an early critic, John Corbin, said in an article in *Harper's Weekly* as early as 1899 shows as clearly as what another, Alexander Woollcott, remarked a quarter-century later: that 'all the monologues are studied with a minuteness of discrimination that is truly wonderful, they fairly bristle with wit, and brief as they necessarily are, and limited in scope by the very fact of their being monologues, they have a truly literary deftness and accuracy of effect'; and that 'all these horribly familiar characters of the American scene come magically to life when Miss Herford speaks'. Her types were gathered from many levels of American life—'A Sociable Seamstress', 'A Lady Packing', 'A Professional Boarder', 'The Complainer', 'The Book Agent', 'The Young Reciter',

[1] *Monologues* by Beatrice Herford (New York: Charles Scribner's Sons, 1908), and *Beatrice Herford's Monologues* (New York and London: Samuel French, 1937).

'Piazza Ladies'; and her episodes ranged from 'In the Art Museum', 'Choosing the Wall Papers', 'Marketing', 'At the Hairdresser's', and 'The Tale of the Train', to 'Changing the Wedding Presents', 'Telephoning the Doctor', 'The Country Store', 'In the Hat Department', and 'The Man with a Cold'.

It will be noticed at once that her subjects were very like those Ruth Draper later developed. Their difference from Ruth's lies chiefly in their comparative narrowness of range. All are humorous or satirical in key; most of them tend toward a gentle or indulgent malice of attitude. There are no moments of pathos, grief, or tragedy. In fact, Miss Herford's voice and mannerism did not lend themselves to these contrasts and variations. She was essentially a *comédienne* and always adhered to that vein. But in her time she was a brilliant exponent of the genre. It is easy to see why Ruth Draper found her stimulating, and saw in her work an encouraging example of what her own talent might become.

During the twenty years of her retirement Miss Herford lived between her homes at Wayland, Massachusetts, and her summer place Seaconnet Point, Little Compton, Rhode Island, where she died on 18 July 1952. She had married Sidney Willard Hayward in 1897, and with his help she established at Wayland an amateur playhouse in which she and her friends presented plays and benefits for charity. As old age overcame her she withdrew from the theatre and her old associations in New York, but Ruth Draper never forgot her or what she owed her. Not long before her death, hearing of her illness, Ruth wrote her a letter, told her what she had counted for in her own life, and received a grateful answer. She never hesitated to speak of Beatrice Herford as one of the decisive influences in her own career.

The Yellow Jacket, the play that told Ruth what nonscenic illusion could achieve on the stage, was in its day one of the most remarkable experiments of the New York stage. Long before Broadway saw the Chinese performances of Mei

Lan-Fang or the devices that Yeats and other poetic dramatists had taken from the classic Noh drama of Japan; well
before the 'little theatre' movement of Stuart Walker and his
followers in Greenwich Village made its mark, and a quarter-
century before Thornton Wilder's *Our Town* appeared on the
bare boards of an undecorated stage in 1938, *The Yellow
Jacket* had revealed what a complete rejection of conventional
décor and painted canvas could do for a play and its audience.
Written by two dramatists who never again achieved an equal
success, George C. Hazleton and J. Harry Benrimo, it told
a Chinese tale of simple pathos and tragedy in which a few
elementary properties took the place of rooms, furniture,
houses, mountains, streams, and landscape. The actors
created by voice, gesture, and suggestive movement all they
required in the way of settings. Its first production at the
Fulton Theatre in New York on 4 November 1912, brought a
new kind of imagination into the American theatre and
created so strong an impact that it was soon produced
throughout Europe.[1] It corrected the dependence on painted
sets and photographic scenery that Belasco and the realists
specialized in, and thus became a pioneer event in the
developments to which German Expressionism, Appia's and
Gordon Craig's inventions in scenery and lighting, and the
new school of American stage design were to contribute so
influentially after 1918. The play came to Ruth, as to all who
first witnessed it, as a revelation of a new order of imagination

[1] Following its original New York production in 1912, the play was
taken on tour in America for several years; was revived in a new production
in New York by Mr. and Mrs. Charles Coburn in 1916; was produced in
London in March 1913; by Max Reinhardt at the Kammerspiele Theater
in Berlin in March 1914 and later in Munich, Vienna, and Budapest; by
Stanislavsky at the Moscow Art Theatre; in a translation by Benavente in
Madrid; and subsequently in Italy, France, and other countries. Hazleton
had written earlier plays of a romantic sort, *Mistress Nell* (1900) and
Captain Molly (1902), and was later to adapt Pierre Frondale's version of
Pierre Louys's *Aphrodite* for a spectacular New York production in 1919.
Benrimo, a native of California, had used the Chinese influence of San
Francisco in an earlier play called *The First Born* and later collaborated on
another play of Chinese theme, *The Willow Tree*, with Harrison Rhodes,
in 1917.

in the modern theatre; and it added its encouragement to her ambitions.

Paderewski's advice was a more personal matter. The great Polish pianist had made his début in America on 17 November 1891, in the early years of his fabulous international career. Mrs. Draper became one of his patronesses, hostesses, and friends in 47th Street; when in New York he usually lived near by in the old Windsor Hotel on Fifth Avenue. He spent many evenings with the family then and in after-years in the intervals of his world tours and immensely attended recitals. His gentleness, humanity, and modest sincerity made it possible for him to be a man of intensely human needs and charm at the same time that the world at large knew him as a paragon and phenomenon, the continuator of the tradition of Chopin, Liszt and the other celebrated masters of pianism in the nineteenth century. Ruth always kept on her walls the copy of the Burne-Jones portrait he had affectionately inscribed to her. He had watched her as a child in the nineties; watched her with more serious attention when, after 1900, she began to develop her sketches more seriously. She had many talks with him about a future in the theatre, but as her private performances went on he became concerned that she was not making more of her gift. One day he spoke to her more pointedly. As she herself remembered it, it was about 1908, 'or perhaps 1909 or 1910'. 'You must do this professionally,' he said. 'Perhaps you should go to Paris to study. Mind you, I am not advising this. You may not need training. *You* must make the decision. It must come from you, from inside. And I will always help.'

One other piece of advice closely resembling this was shortly to come to her from another quarter, as will presently be seen. 'Everyone', as she recalled, was advising, flattering, encouraging, and promoting her in these years. It took the great professional musician to make something more impressive of such attentions. She knew his own story of long struggle, severe self-discipline, and resolution to become a pianist against earlier inclinations in other directions. She knew that when he spoke it was with the authority of a hard-won professionalism, of many years of personal rigour and self-denial, and of an artistic dedication that had successfully weathered all the clamour, sensationalism, and publicized inflation of one of the most dramatic careers in modern musicianship. He spoke to her not as a patron, flatterer, or friend, but as a fellow-artist, and for the first time she heeded the summons of a professional.

VII

From the time she was twenty Ruth had performed her sketches with fair regularity among her friends, relatives, and New York acquaintances, but with no attempt at making full-scale recitals of them. The themes that had begun in the nursery or during her school days were never abandoned; some of them provided her with germs that were now to develop fully. But by the time she was in her mid-twenties, in the years between 1905 and 1910, she was working hard at her manuscripts, putting herself through increasingly strenuous sessions of rehearsal, and cultivating a repertory. With the year 1910 she began to keep a record of her engagements. The book, leather-bound and hand-written, was to be kept with her for the next forty-six years, its pages growing denser with the decades. Now too she began to collect her press-cuttings and mount them in scrapbooks—a series of large portfolios teeming with notices from every variety of newspaper, magazine, and press report in America and Canada, later in England, France, Italy, and other continental countries, and ultimately in countries of Africa, Asia, South America. It is in these archives that we can begin to trace her activities chronologically.

In the winter of 1910–11 her engagements were in New York and the East, either in private houses or in performances for charity. Mrs. Robert Winthrop, Mrs. Jacob Schiff, Mrs.

James Speyer, Mrs. Mortimer Schiff, and Mrs. George Blumenthal had her to entertain their guests. The Colony Club, Briarcliff School, Miss Spence's School, the Comstock School, the Stockbridge Casino, and the Three Arts Club called on her to divert their members. Benefits for charities of the Ascension Church, the Incarnation Church, and the New York State Charities were performed. By the following year, in addition to evenings or afternoons in many private houses, there were engagements at Groton School, at the Broadway Tabernacle, at the Union Club in Cleveland, at the Princeton Faculty Club, and even for the benefit of the Norfolk Fire Department in Connecticut. In 1912–13 she performed for the Century Club of Philadelphia, St. Mark's School in Massachusetts, the Boston Settlement House, the Briarcliff-Ossining Hospital, as well as for Mrs. Franklin Roosevelt in Albany and Henry Adams in Washington.

In the spring of 1913 she was in England; and though on earlier visits she had shown her work to her friends there, the word of her talent had now reached a larger circle of society and she began her conquest of the great houses of London. She gave recitals at Lady Mountstephen's, at Lady Speyer's, and at Mrs. Waldorf Astor's; she gave a programme at a Suffrage Entertainment at the Hotel Cecil; and presently she received an invitation to a more illustrious house of the Edwardian era. The Princess Christian was now beginning the last decade of her long life. Born in 1846 as Princess Helena Augusta Victoria, third daughter of Queen Victoria and the Prince Consort, she had in 1866 married Prince Christian of Schleswig-Holstein-Sonderburg, and entered on her career as a hostess and patroness of philanthropic, hospital, and charitable institutions. Her house in Pall Mall became one of the centres of Victorian and Edwardian society, and her patronage almost indispensable to any movement in public charity. She was also an eager follower of the arts. Her invitation to Ruth Draper came as a climax of Ruth's first London success; and after her first performance for the Princess she returned to give two others. These were attended by a distinguished audience: King George V and Queen Mary accompanied by the Princesses Victoria and Marie of Schleswig-Holstein, the Duke and Duchess of Connaught with Princess Patricia, the Crown Prince and Princess of Sweden, Prince and Princess Louis of Battenberg, Prince and Princess Alexander of Teck, Princess Henry and Princess Louise of Battenberg, Lady Dufferin, Lady Stradbroke, Lady Essex, Lady Greville, Lady Mountstephen, the Marquis de Soveral—the royalty and nobility of the age. Queen Mary's first acquaintance with Ruth was to be the prelude to many later attendances at her London performances; to a command performance at Windsor Castle fifteen years later; and to many delightful exchanges of messages and talks after curtain-fall in the theatres. She became a devotee of the sketches; became curious that a girl of Ruth's origins should have found a career in acting; on one occasion became especially curious about the hat worn by the lady in 'Opening a Bazaar'; and expressed her interest in many words and messages of admiration.

Ruth's brother Paul and his wife Muriel had now settled in London, following his musical studies in Italy and Germany. Their house in Edith Grove became one of Ruth's centres. Here she formed friendships that were to survive for many years; and though her acquaintance with James, Sargent, and many other friends of the moment was of her own making, she was swept into the artistic life around Paul along with her other social and personal engagements.[1] She sped from one party or engagement to another; met her appointments; crossed to Paris to see Henry Adams and others who were sojourning at the moment in France. Adams came to her aid when the performances at the Princess Christian's were in prospect, and to celebrate the occasion

[1] The Drapers' years in London and their entertainments in Edith Grove are recorded in Muriel Draper's book *Music at Midnight* (New York and London, 1929).

he made her a gift of two dresses by Worth in which to perform.

We have had various passing [he wrote to Anna Lodge on 15 May], the last and most vivacious being Ruth Draper, who was staying with Looly Hooper for a week, to get a dress for to act before the Queen who has sent for her through Princess Christian. She has rushed my social secretaries about like a wild gazelle, but goes today, so I shall probably pass only part of my time at Worth's henceforward. The two lovely dresses I had made for her are of course too good for the Queen, but what could I do?[1]

By midsummer she was back in America, and the following months were occupied with many engagements in the East: at Mrs. Payne Whitney's, Mrs. Arthur Curtiss James's, Mrs. Stuyvesant Fish's, and Mrs. Archer Huntington's, in New York; at Greenwich, Southampton, Ridgefield, and Sea Bright; at Miss Masters's School and at St. Paul's. But by June of 1914 she was back again in England, once more swept up in a round of recitals, parties, and country week-ends. She entertained at Lady Sheffield's, at Mrs. Bruce Richmond's, at Mrs. John Astor's and Mrs. Waldorf Astor's; and on one memorable evening at 10 Downing Street, where Mrs. Asquith had bidden her to entertain her guests. This too was the summer of her last meetings with Henry James, of her sittings to Sargent in Tite Street, and of a rapid dash to Paris to see Henry Adams and his friends.

The months were speeding ahead now, drawing toward the crisis which was to bring an era to its end. The murders at Sarajevo in June had passed almost unnoticed in Ruth's

[1] *Henry Adams and his Friends: A Collection of his Unpublished Letters*, compiled with a Biographical Introduction by Harold Dean Cater (Boston and New York, 1947), pp. 754–55 (Letter to Anna Cabot Mills Lodge, from 6 Square du Bois de Boulogne, Paris, 15 May 1913). Adams was in France in the summers of 1913 and 1914 with his nieces Louisa Chapin Hooper ('Looly' or 'Loulie' Hooper) and Elizabeth Ogden Adams ('Elsie' Adams), and Miss Aileen Tone. In the summer of 1913 he rented the Château de Marivaux near Saint-Crépin in the Oise Valley, and in the summer of 1914 the Château de Coubertin. It is to the latter that Ruth Draper refers in her letter of 9 July 1914.

world, but by July the clouds over Europe were darkening. It was to be the end of a chapter in her life too. The four years of the world war were to prevent her from returning to Europe until 1918. She could look back afterward on the last happy summer of 1914 as so many were destined to look back on it—as the epilogue to the long Edwardian twilight of the Victorian age. That decade had brought her through her twenties. She had in a few years sprung out of her old New York life into a greater, international activity. She had arrived, as she later said, at the threshold of a new purpose, new decisions, a new conception of her future. Anxious news had followed her across the Atlantic from home. Her mother had now fallen into her last illness, and in August she was to die. The old family circle was to suffer its second loss, and to feel the end of one of the ties that had bound it most closely. But these public and personal crises still lay ahead when Ruth took the *Lusitania* back to New York.

On the ship she wrote many letters back to her friends in England and Paris, one of them to Henry Adams:

Dear Uncle Henry [she wrote on 9 July]: Now that I really have some time on my hands, it shall be spent in writing a letter long due to you. I cannot tell you how disappointed I was not to come to you in Paris, but as I wrote Aileen, various opportunities suddenly turned up. I felt I must stay in London. I have had a very full and interesting month, all too short. As usual I am regretting that I came away so soon. I did not have such a dose of Royalties as last year—none in fact, except for a pleasant call on Princess Victoria of Schleswig-Holstein, whom I like so much. I calmly refused to recite there again, preferring to run the chance of getting a real job, which I did. I had messages from Their Majesties of kind memory of last year, but they were frightfully busy, and could not find a free moment to see me, poor things. I had many delightful engagements, twelve in all, and met interesting people. I dined at Downing Street and recited afterward to a charming and distinguished company, and was duly thrilled to be in that beautiful house, so full of solemn and living spirits of the great nation's government. We dined in the Cabinet Chamber for the first time in history (as the entertainment took place in the dining-room) and it was really impressive. A lovely, dignified room, with double windows, and books right up to the ceiling— there I sat eating my little dinner in the great Council Chamber and later I scribbled out my program at William Pitt's desk. I saw Henry James many times, and we found the same happy combination. He looks and seems much better than last year. I had the great pleasure of seeing Mr. and Mrs. Lodge at lunch there just before I sailed. Sargent has done me again, twice, both in character, one as the Scotch Immigrant and one as the Dalmatian Peasant, very grim and unpleasant but as I look, I feel sure. I tell you all these items as I know you will be amused.... I think of you all settled by now, in your lovely château....

We are having a damp, grey sort of journey, and my spirits are in tune with the weather, but I suppose I shall revive in the baking heat that probably awaits me. I shall spend a lazy summer working in a garden, running a Ford motor, recounting my experiences to Mother, and I hope composing new pieces. Dorothea and Linzee sail on the 11th of July and perhaps will be fortunate enough to look in on you if they are motoring in France. My love to Loulie, Elsie, and Aileen, and much to you!

Always your affectionate niece,
RUTH.

VIII

One friendship during these years in London on the eve of 1914 was to count as particularly cherished in Ruth Draper's life and forms a separate chapter in her record. Henry James was now in the last decade of his long career. He had reached his seventieth birthday in April 1913, and he was to die less than three years later, in February 1916. In America the James and Draper families had been friends for many years. Sixty years earlier Henry James's father had known Ruth's grandfather Dana as a friend of Emerson and a member of Horace Greeley's circle at the *New York Tribune*; twenty-five years later Ruth's sister Dorothea was to bring the families into closer alliance when she married James's nephew Henry, the oldest son of William James, his father's biographer and his uncle's literary executor. The novelist was now living between Lamb House at Rye in Sussex, the shrine and haven of his last eighteen years, and his recently acquired flat in Carlyle Mansions, Chelsea. Near by in Edith Grove was the home of Paul and Muriel Draper, whose musical evenings he attended; and it was in Chelsea that Ruth's friendship with him ripened into a profound affection and confidence.

James had seen her perform her sketches in Edith Grove and other London houses. His avidity for the drama had persisted through his lifetime, against whatever discouragements he had met in the popular playhouses of New York, Paris, or London. Twenty years earlier he had portrayed the genius of a brilliant actress, Miriam Rooth, in his novel *The Tragic Muse* of 1890; and his old ambition to see his words come to life on the stage had been only temporarily rebuffed by his failure as a playwright in the early nineties and the fiasco of *Guy Domville* at the St. James's Theatre in January, 1895. 'I'm afraid you impute to me a more continued interest in the theatre than I am conscious of, or have been for long', he was presently to say to one of his American correspondents (Brander Matthews, in a letter of 2 February 1915): 'I am only now, and in a deeply obscured and discouraged way, interested in the drama—which is in our conditions so very different a thing.' Yet he had recently resumed the writing of plays, and he had never lost his curiosity about the special mysteries of the art of acting which had led him to write his searching studies of the players he had seen or known over half a century—Bernhardt, Ristori, Salvini, Irving, Ellen Terry, Coquelin, Elizabeth Robins.

Now, at seventy, he responded with delight to Ruth's miniature dramas, found himself charmed by her craft, and saw her sketches as a possible medium for his own dramatic skill. She in turn had revelled in his tales and novels, found them a treasure-house of the human insights and sympathies that were stirring her own imagination, and soon counted him not only a 'great-hearted seer, teller of rare tales', but one of the most sympathetic allies she had ever known.

In May 1913 she wrote some verses in tribute to him and sent them to Carlyle Mansions:

To H. J.

Great-hearted seer, teller of rare tales,
Humorous cynic, searching analyst,
Who weighs with niceness of a goldsmith's scales
Our frailties and our faults—all we have missed
Of greatness; and yet to redeem our loss,
In tender lights and shades you paint the soul,
Showing the truth and beauty with the dross,
Like a philosopher who knows the goal.
Brilliant interpreter of humankind,
Whose wit and humour mingle in a song.
Of English epicure, and to the mind
Revealer of new beauties in our tongue,
Creating phrase and picture that have proved
The skill and finish of an unmatched art.
Blessed be my fate that I have seen and loved
The all-embracing wisdom in your heart,
The piercing vision of your kind grey eyes
That look through clouds of knowledge to the skies.

James was sitting during these spring and summer weeks of 1913 to his friend John Singer Sargent in his nearby studio in Tite Street, where there slowly materialized the portrait (now in the National Portrait Gallery in London) which a large group of James's friends had offered him as a gift on his seventieth birthday. Sargent had also become a friend of Ruth's and had recently drawn a charcoal portrait of her, intended by Ruth as a gift for her mother. It proved to be a wholly conventional likeness, and Sargent was immediately chagrined by it. Seeing her act some of her sketches one evening at the home of the Yates Thompsons just before her return to America, he wrote her a note begging that the picture be destroyed:

31, Tite Street,
Chelsea, S.W.

Dear Miss Draper:

I feel on coming home from the Yates Thompsons' that I ought to have seen you do these wonderful things before drawing you—and that the drawing is *non avenu,* so please throw it overboard and let me have another try next year—don't send me a cheque for this one. I will return it if you do, with floods of sermons—this drawing is a present from me to your mother if there is anything in it that she likes—if not overboard with it.

Yours always,
JOHN SARGENT

The two portraits he eventually drew of her—as the Scottish immigrant and the Dalmatian peasant woman—were made during Ruth's next visit to England in 1914. ('I was sailing for America the next day, but the following year, in London, he came over to me at the opera one night and we made an appointment, and he did these two, in an hour and a half', she recalled forty years later. 'He would not take a cent for them, not a cent.') Meanwhile James, eager to see her commemorated by Sargent, had spoken of Ruth during his own sittings in Tite Street, and soon sent her a letter after her return to America and after he had received her poem. She was spending that summer with her mother in a house they had taken at Katonah, New York. Her mother was already gravely ill and Ruth had crossed the Atlantic in anxiety.

21, Carlyle Mansions,
Cheyne Walk, S.W.
[15 June 1913]

Dear and admirable Ruth,

How delightful to get such generously prompt news of you, both in prose and verse, and to get it so brave and beautiful. Odd as the statement may be it's a real relief to me to know thus that the situation at home was 'bad enough' to justify your return—unless your subtle little mind is simply putting it so to yourself and to others to defend itself from any more convulsions on the subject. *Of course* you are doing good by being there—only that isn't a particular proof of anything but that it's *you*. However, your farm of the queer name does just now sound like as right a place for the little fevered heroine I last saw as the transposition from those *alentours* in such a jiffy savours of the fairy-tale, and I wish you indeed a good stretch of weeks of quiet easy intercourse with your genius, out of which, the soil having been so fertilised by all you have lately seen, some fresh flower or two of character may happily spring. Mull it all over at your leisure and with the aid of a few cigarettes, and something good will surely come. I went to see your so genial and beautiful sister-in-law a few days after your flight (to exchange photographs with her, the one she gave me instead of the one I first had from you being now in the hands of the framer for the decoration of the most eligible of my poor walls.) Apropos of which Sargent, dear man, the very a.m. after your last appearance here, at which he had been present, expressed simple despair at having presumed ignorantly to do you before having seen you at work,—and only wants the result destroyed so that he may start on you afresh altogether. But I am not destroying *my* copy till something vivider and truer does take its place—and meantime have been sitting to him myself (for an image in oils,) with a success by what every one says that I am almost ashamed to boast of to you. He has been doing a slow and very careful portrait—I have myself greatly enjoyed the process and his company—and I judge he will really have done a fine and characteristic thing. I feel I am being hugely—and exquisitely— celebrated, dear Ruth, when on top of this I receive your slightly overgrown, but all the more luxuriant, 'sonnet'—a brave and liberal and charming thing, whose excesses I can only blushingly acclaim. If one *is* to be glorified I rejoice in the free hand and fine brave touch you do it with. Please believe I appreciate every word of your inspiration. And I am not less happy to think that by this time you will have had a good view again of my admirable Nephew. I can't say whether I shall most want now his news of you or yours of him. I earnestly hope at any rate for the former on his part. Please greet your Mother very faithfully for me and tell her I rejoice for her in your presence with her now and all your gain of impressions and visions for her beguilement. But good night—I am sitting up for you! And am yours, dear Ruth, all affectionately   HENRY JAMES[1]

---

[1] The first two of James's letters have been copied from the holographs

PLATE V

Ruth Draper in London: 1920

Photograph by Dorothy Wilding, London

PLATE VI

Ruth Draper in the early 1920's
Photograph by Dorothy Wilding, London

The beguilement Ruth had brought into James's declining
years remained with him during the autumn and winter of
1913, and he could not rest until he had tried his hand at
writing a monologue for her. His re-engagement in playwriting in recent years had stirred his old fascination by
'the scenic art'. Forbes-Robertson and Gertrude Elliott had
produced his play *The High Bid* in Edinburgh and London
in 1908–9; he had revised another, *The Other House*, in the
latter year; Gertrude Kingston had acted *The Saloon* in
London in 1911. Ruth was the last actor to call him back to
dramatic writing. She saw him often during her English
sojourns in these years. ('In memory of Henry James, my
friend and counselor in London in 1913 and 1914', she wrote
in a copy of James's plays for a friend in 1956.) He had
encouraged and advised her; listened to her plans and per-
plexities about her future; consoled her in moments of
trouble; they had attended the theatre and listened to music
together. By December he had finished his monologue and
sent it to her across the Atlantic with a covering letter:

21, Carlyle Mansions,
Cheyne Walk, S.W.
December 4th, 1913.

Dictated

My dear Ruth,

I am posting you herewith, separately, the Monologue stuff that
I wrote you a few days since that I was attempting. It has come
out as it would, or could; and perhaps you may find it more or
less to your purpose. I don't really see why it shouldn't go; and I
seem definitely to 'visualise' you and hear you, not to say infinitely
admire you, very much in it. It strikes me, going over it again, as
a really practical, *doable* little affair; of which the general idea,
portée and reference will glimmer out to you as you study it. It's
the fatuous, but *innocently* fatuous, female compatriot of ours let
loose upon a world and a whole order of things, especially this one
over here, which she takes so serenely for granted. The little scene

---

that survive among Ruth Draper's papers, the third from a typewritten
copy she made. From the third letter (of 5 January 1915) a personal post-
script has been omitted here. The letters are printed by the kind permission of Mr. William James, of Cambridge, Massachusetts.

represents her being pulled up in due measure; but there is truth, I think, and which you will bring out, in the small climax of her not being too stupid to recognise things when they are really put to her—as in America they so mostly are *not*. They are put to her over here—and this is a little case of it. She rises to that—by a certain shrewdness in her which seems almost to make a sort of new chance for her glimmer out—so that she doesn't feel snubbed so very much, or pushed off her pedestal; but merely perhaps furnished with a new opportunity or attribute. That's the note on which it closes; and her last words will take all the pretty saying you can give them. But I needn't carry coals to Newcastle or hints to our Ruth; who, if she takes to the thing at all can be trusted to make more out of it by her own little genius than I can begin to suggest. You'll see it's more of a little *action* than most of your other things; though I do greatly hope there won't seem to you *too* much awkwardness in the two supposititious presences with which she is in relation. They have only to be one off at the right and the other at the left of her, I think, for the thing to go easily. I have kept down her echoing of their supposed words as much as possible, or at least made these words as few; but the little action requires of course *all* of them. However, again you will understand better than I can tell you! And I cast my bread upon the waters. I don't really think the thing too long—for its interest; and won't pretend to say that I see you taking out of it anything you like, because it seems to me so *close* already, for comprehension and clearness; for adequate *expression*, I mean, of its idea. Of course if you find anything *can* be spared, you have complete license! But I hurry it off to you; only making this one little request, by reason of my not taking time, under pressure, to take a copy of it—other than my first rough draft. 'Henry James, Rye. Received.'—*that*, cabled off to me, will relieve my solicitude for the safety of my packet. Everything else, protest, disappointment, abhorrence, impossibility—can all come by letter. But here goes! Yours, my dear Ruth, all faithfully   HENRY JAMES

P.S. I don't so much as dream, for the moment, of a title. Anything in the world you think best! But again, an intense plea for *public* anonymity!

The subject of the monologue was as James described it in his letter—the comedy of a socially ambitious American woman in London negotiating for a presentation at Court. In the drawing-room of her London hotel she presses her importunities on the Secretary of Embassy, Mr. Lynch, and on an old English friend, Sir Robin; plies them both with her claims; and demands their co-operation with the announcement that she is only going 'the full length of the American woman's right' in demanding the patronage of the Embassy and the favours of the Court. Ambitious, spoiled, and ruthless, she forms a small footnote to James's study of the American woman abroad who had for years been a feature of his 'international subject'. The type had re-engaged his attention a few years earlier when, on returning from his visit to America in 1904–5, he had written his book on *The American Scene* (1907) and contributed two series of papers on the speech and manners of American women to *Harper's Bazar* in 1906–7. His present heroine was a sister of the Mrs. Headways, Henrietta Stackpoles, and Mrs. Newsomes he had portrayed in his tales—another 'acute case of Queenship' among his more predatory countrywomen. His sketch pictured the type in its cruder comic essentials: 'there is nothing the American woman socially less resembles than a second fiddle. It is before her, and her only, that the score is open, while, without any hesitation, and with a play of elbow all her own, she brandishes the bow.'

The monologue—it bore no title—was not printed until six years after James's death, in *The London Mercury* for September 1922; more recently it has been included in Leon Edel's edition of *The Complete Plays of Henry James* (1949). James 'liked the courage, independence, and individuality of the American woman', says Mr. Edel, 'but on the negative side of their new-found freedom he saw some of them as aggressive, demanding, masculine. Spoiled by doting husbands or parents, they walked across the American-European stage, hard and imperious, graceless and exacting'; and 'It is in this context, as in the context of *The Bostonians* with its ironical treatment of suffragettes, faddists, the "do-gooders" of James's time, the socially and politically ambitious female, that this little monologue must be read'.

Ruth Draper received James's manuscript with mingled pride and misgiving. She had by this time discovered that she could act only what she herself had written; and James's sketch 'bore his peculiar stamp' all too obviously. She also felt it impossible to obey his injunction to conceal its authorship. She must have found further that the speech of a Jamesian character, so brilliant in his novels and so unpronounceably verbose and stylized in his plays ('inhumanly literary' was Shaw's word for it), was as impossible to adapt to her tongue as most of James's other stage interpreters had.

Don't I miss our native pedestal and the lovely way we just float on? [says James's heroine at one point]. Well, no, Sir Robin—I don't think I miss anything with *you*, because I seem to recognise that you feel the *charm*—oh no...I don't mean mine more than any other, you poor dear dense delightful Englishman; I mean that of our beautiful response to the way we're treated in general—when we're really nice: the effect on us of being treated as Queens is that we have the grace and dignity and outlook of a class *expected* to receive homage sweetly. We get so much of it that we *have practice*—we know *how*; and that's why...I have the confidence just to accept all yours.

Faced with a style so totally at odds with the easy fluency and realism she gave her own characters, Ruth found the monologue wholly impracticable. 'I think he was disappointed', she said later, 'but I never learned it or tried it on anyone.' It remains James's tribute to her art and friendship, a last token of his old hope of bringing his art to terms with the elusive sorcery of the stage.

Whatever James's disappointment, it caused no disturbance in his affection. Thirteen months before his death, on 5 January 1915, he wrote what appears to be his last letter to Ruth. Her mother had died in August 1914; she was now becoming involved in war work and benefit performances;

and he responded to her sorrow from the depths of his own
affliction by the war.

Dictated
                  21, Carlyle Mansions,
                  Cheyne Walk, S.W.
                  January 5th, 1915.

My dear Ruth,

This deadly impersonal form (so far as appearance goes) has
small grace beside your pages so wonderfully pencilled under, or
over, the 'rhythmical rumble' of your touring train; but you have
kindly put up with it before, and, with the 'nervous wreck' our
unspeakable public situation makes of one (or would make of *me*
if it could) here, the nimble play of the pen is more than ever a
lost art. Thinking at all indeed of anything but what immediately
presses on us is a lost art too; in fact I feel the only art at all
acquired is that of feeling, and seeing, all 'outside' things, things
of the other time when life wasn't a nightmare, push in and make
their claim with difficulty through our thick and charged and
burdened air. One has to make a great effort to *connect*—with any
link of the past; the past in which every chain of interest and
relevance, no matter how silver or how golden we had thought it,
broke short off in a single night some five months ago and left us
staring at jagged ends on one side and vast abysmal voids and
blanks (since tant bien que mal more or less filled up).

You can take measure of this pretty well, I fear, from the fact
that I was condemned to hear of the great sorrow that had over-
taken you, the sorrow that makes *the* landmark, in the natural
order, of one's lifetime, without being able to hope or attempt to
express to you in any way my participating thought. I was paralysed for any such expression, and I still more or less am; so
please see me yourself as seeing everything *myself* through a glass
darkly and trying rather in vain to repair by a fumble here and
there the sad waste and drain and strain of attention and emotion
consequent on our dire conditions. I suppose I like to think, or at
least like to try to, of your all going about, beyond the sea, on your
usual errands and with your usual motives; but I conceive such a
state as of a lost paradise, the golden age that once existed for us
here too—in the mere form of not being a black oppression.
Clearly, all the time, in spite of your comparative public paradise,
you also need all your courage and faith, and I gather that you are
making the bravest assertion of these things in your own now so

changed life. You have my affectionate blessing on it—and indeed I have only to read your letter over, as I am just doing, to see how fully you understand everything that makes up the whole aching difference for us here. The great thing is to cling to the work that the old years have permitted us so far as we *can* do that; and not to let go thereby every spark of the fine light (for so fine it *was*!) by which we anciently walked. I say anciently because it seems a hundred years ago; the strange fact being that, crammed as the time is with anxieties and agitations, with every form of violence and incoherence, it still keeps the swiftest stride, the dreadful days succeeding each other so fast in spite of their dreadfulness. I mustn't speak as if they were dreadful *only*; they aren't, because they have a most interesting and uplifting side. But what I mean is that though there hangs about them the grave uncertainty of what they may at any hour bring forth they melt at once in the great gaping cup or crucible into which our destiny chucks them one by one, stirring them up and squashing them, so to speak, out of individual recognition. So it is that, rather blessedly, no doubt, they don't seem to hang back after the fashion of mere dreary times; they are ahead of us always, and yet we keep catching up with them—all of which is a superfluous way of saying that I have never known a dire dark damp drenching devilish month of December, and a little more, keep so headlong a pace. I see the War as long as 'long' still, long in the vital interest and by the (I trust) triumphant but complicated process of the Allies; and yet when I say to myself that it must, must absolutely *for us*, last a period of which we have already traversed only about a third, I cling to the idea of a certain crescendo of swiftness even for this—especially as I am helped thereto by the conviction that anything so drawn-out was never in the least dreamed of or desired by Germany, and that she has a hundred more reasons for fearing it than we have. Goodbye at any rate now, dearest Ruth; and don't be deterred by any vision of the impenetrability I seem to depict from attempting access again to your all affectionate old

Henry James

These abundant letters, the sympathy and admiration they brought her, James's expending of his genius on an effort to contribute to her repertory, the example he gave her of his creative faith, were to remain with Ruth Draper as one of her choicest memories. One day she had a talk with him that stirred her beyond all others. Though she had found and proved her gift, had met success before private audiences, and had won the enthusiasm of a large circle of friends, she still paused and doubted. She was approaching thirty. What would she make of her life? Should she attack the professional stage and attempt a career there? Or try to make something of her ambition as a writer and poet? Or should she apply herself anew to her monologues and make a career of these? Paderewski in New York had already given her his judgement. Now, talking with James by his fireside in Carlyle Mansions or strolling with him along Chelsea Embankment, she debated her hopes and doubts, groped her way to a decision, solicited his counsel. In an inspired moment James leaned toward her, measured his words with his most deliberate gravity, and gave her at a stroke the advice she needed and a motto for the career that lay ahead:

'My dear child...you...have woven...your own...very beautiful...little Persian carpet....Stand on it!'

IX

The coming of war, her mother's death in August 1914, the profound loss she felt with her passing, brought Ruth to a new phase of her life on her return to America. London had proved what she could do as a performer tested by the most exacting private audiences. The moment for a greater decision than any she had yet made was not quite ready, however: the war was to delay it for another five years. But she came back to New York not only with ten years of continuous amateur performance behind her, an already large repertory of sketches to her credit, and her imagination stirring with new themes and projects, but with the advice of Paderewski and Henry James firmly fixed in her mind. Her doubts, her hesitation before a great public challenge, her impatience for her great hour to strike, were becoming subdued to a new resolution.

Between the autumn of 1914 and October 1918 she was kept incessantly occupied in the States. Performances in New York and the East were soon extended. She became for the first time a seasoned trouper. Though her engagements were still mostly in private houses or before private groups, she now set out across the country. Chicago, Colorado, California, the Northwest, the midland States, and New England were attacked. She gave her programmes in a great variety of places, likely or unlikely—at Princeton University, at the Princess Theatre or the Hippodrome in New York, at a Polish benefit organized by Paderewski, in a grocery-store in Tyrone, New Mexico, and in towns that ranged from Kennebunkport and Narragansett to Kenosha, Colorado Springs, Silver City, Santa Barbara, and Pasadena.

By the autumn of 1915 she was deep in war-time causes and benefits. She performed for the French Hospitals Fund, for the American Ambulance Corps, for the Belgian Milk Fund, for the Red Cross, for the District Nurses Association, for the Canadian Hospitals Fund. In 1916 she went on tour with Elizabeth Perkins on a round of benefits for the American Fund for the French Wounded; in 1917 on a tour for the Red Cross; in 1918 on a series of Y.M.C.A. benefits. Presently, in October 1918, an even more strenuous war-time venture called her. But meanwhile there had been several interruptions in these activities.

One of them came in the spring of 1916 when she met the English actress Marie Tempest, then on one of her many tours of America. Miss Tempest had seen Ruth's sketches, was amazed at their adroitness, and presently offered Ruth a part in one of her frequent new comedies. It was thus that Ruth played her single role in a Broadway play. She cancelled twelve engagements of her own and in May joined Miss Tempest's company in Cyril Harcourt's comedy, *A Lady's Name*. Two weeks of rehearsal were followed by try-out runs

in Montreal and Atlantic City, and then by an opening at
Maxine Elliott's Theatre in New York. Though the thought
of taking part in a full-scale play had teased Ruth's mind for
many years, she was never sure her talent or ambition lay in
that direction. She was quickly confirmed in her doubt. It
was an experiment she had to try at least once; and once
proved enough.

The play was a triviality devised along conventional comedy
lines by a professional contriver of star-pieces and routine
commodities for the successful actors of the day. Harcourt
made successes for himself with comedies like *A Pair of
Silk Stockings* and *A Place in the Sun*—artifices in a semi-
farcical, semi-serious mode that had their vogue in New York
and London before the wind of a new experimental drama
struck the stage. *A Lady's Name* dealt with a lady novelist
who, in search of material for a new book, advertised in the
newspapers for a good husband, counting on the replies to
supply her with the oddities of human behaviour she was looking for. Marie Tempest was an old and brilliant hand at artificial situations of this kind. One of the New York reviewers
said, 'Had it been anyone but Miss Tempest, perhaps the
ridiculous situations in which she found herself as a novelist
in search of material might have made the audience say "It's
hardly likely to happen"; but there she was doing it and
making it highly plausible and natural.' But not sufficiently
plausible, apparently, to make a success of the play. It was
taken off after its six-week run. One of the five victims of the
lady's device was a servant of unctuous self-importance, 'half-
butler, half-valet', who asked the lady to tea in his master's
kitchen. There she made the acquaintance of the cook, the
scullery drudge of the house, and the lady's maid.

Ruth Draper took the part of the maid in this episode, and
had as her fellow-servants two veterans of comedy, Daisy
Belmore and Beryl Mercer. The role was slight almost to the
point of invisibility: 'I had almost nothing to do', she said of
it. All three of the servants' roles were 'drawn in broadly

humorous strokes, and each [was] provocative of a round of laughs', remarked one of the critics; and Ruth received compliments on the deftness of her style. But that is all that her single venture in play-acting came to. She never again undertook a part in a full-length play.

She experimented that winter with some shorter efforts in drama, however. On the afternoon of Tuesday, 6 February 1917, she put time and money into staging a programme of three numbers at the Comedy Theatre—Strindberg's one-act play *The Stronger*; a 'pantomime in three scenes' invented by herself and called *An Old Story* (its three characters were Pierrot, Pierrette, and Death); and her own 'solo play', 'The Actress' (also called at that time 'Mlle. X. of the Comédie Française'), in which, taking the part of a European actress in Paris, she was to reach one of her highest points of virtuosity—it remained one of the most brilliant numbers in her repertory during the next forty years. The critics rated the programme 'ill-advised', 'singularly misguided and tedious', and Ruth wrote it off as 'A loss!' in her record-book. Only 'The Actress' won the applause of the reviewers, as if to confirm her in her *métier*. This matinée was her last attempt to hold the stage with other actors. Apart from a few scenes she contributed to benefit performances in later years—on one occasion in 1929 as Juliet in an all-star programme of great dramatic scenes arranged by Winthrop Ames for the Duse Fund—she never played with a company again.

By the autumn of 1918, with the end of the war in sight, the restrictions against women in army entertainments for the Allied troops in Europe were lifted by the military authorities. Ruth's war work in America had netted many thousands of dollars for war-time causes. But her three brothers were serving overseas; she longed to get back to old scenes in France and England and to share more closely in the struggle. She now made arrangements to go abroad with her friend Harriet Marple, a singer from Bexley, near Columbus, Ohio, to entertain the troops in a series of Y.M.C.A. programmes.

She sailed on the *Baltic* on 12 October and immediately launched with Miss Marple on a round of performances that lasted into June of the following year. The autumn and winter were spent staging shows at army centres and base hospitals in England—at Dartford, Oxford, Cliveden, and Lancaster—and it was there that they saw the war end and victory come in November. By February the two women moved on to France and appeared before troops, officers' clubs, and hospital patients in Paris, Auteuil, Neufchâteau, Liffol, Chaumont, Joinville, and Bar-sur-Aube. In March, after four strenuous months of work, they took a leave and went on a short holiday in Paris and the south of France— Avignon, San Raphael, Nice, Cannes, Menton. By April they were back at work in camps and army bases of the Third and Fourth Divisions in France and Germany. They stayed on in Europe during the spring and summer and were in Paris during the exciting weeks of the Peace Conference. Ruth had now renewed her old ties in France and England after an interval of four years and she was to remain in Europe into the winter of 1919–20. But in August she and Miss Marple were ready for a longer holiday.

It took the form of a two-month bicycle trip through Ireland, and became one of the happiest vacations she was ever to know. From Dublin they cycled south and west to Killarney and County Kerry, on to the Aran Islands, so into Galway and Sligo, then northward to Antrim and the Giant's Causeway, and so back to Dublin. Ruth was enchanted by Ireland. The green secluded country was a world away from her hard-pressed war-time years in America and from the army posts and encampments she had recently visited. She grew to love the villagers and country people, the brilliant lakes, purple mountains, and soft-hued distances, the silent valleys and sea-buffeted coasts. They came to her, even in what was then an uneasy and militant island, as a restoration of peace after strain and violence. At one wayside stop the two cyclists spent an hour or two resting in the cottage of an old Kerry woman who had lost a son at Gallipoli, and there Ruth found the drama for the monologue 'In County Kerry', which remained her tribute to Ireland and her Irish holiday during the remainder of her career.

Back in London that October she resumed her private appearances. There was one great occasion, on 20 October, when she appeared at a large party in the house of Lord and Lady Curzon and found the King and Queen of Spain among her listeners, thus forming a friendship that was to be renewed during the following decade in Madrid. There were performances at Mrs. Asquith's, at Mrs. Keppel's, at Mrs. Greville's, at Lady Pollock's and Lord Lathom's and Sir Philip Sassoon's. There were country visits and week-ends with the John Astors, the Yates Thompsons, the Sassoons, with Lionel Curtis and with Sibyl Colefax, as well as with Paul and Nora Phipps and their children and with Wilfrid and Jane de Glehn, painters and disciples of Sargent's and close friends of Ruth's for many years. In February 1920 she returned to America for two crowded months of recitals, family duties, business problems, and her American friendships. But before leaving London she had made a significant decision and arrived at a new milestone. On 10 April she was at sea again, bound for England. The nineteen-twenties had begun. The most eventful decade of her life lay ahead. Amateurism, free-lance work, private programmes and benefits, were now at last to give way to a new career. She had decided to cast her lot with professionalism and to accept the hazards of the public theatre. A new and greater challenge was about to be risked.

X

On Thursday afternoon, 29 January 1920, a week before she sailed to America, Ruth Draper gave a programme of her 'character sketches' in the Aeolian Hall in London. After returning from three months in the United States she reappeared, again at the Aeolian Hall, on 27 May. These two dates she underscored in her record-book. They were her first fully professional appearances as a monologuist in a public theatre.

They were followed, in the intervals of a round of private recitals at the Mansion House and for Lady Northcliffe, the Duchess of Norfolk, and other London hostesses, by eight further programmes at the Aeolian Hall during the summer and autumn, a two-week engagement on the variety bill at the Coliseum, a week at the Alhambra in Glasgow, one at the Palace in Manchester, another at the Hippodrome in Brighton, and single programmes in Norwich, Cambridge, Edinburgh, Bath, and at the London Palladium.[1] By the time she sailed back to America in mid-December she had established herself as a professional actress, at the age of thirty-six. The nineteen-twenties, the decade during which 'she was discovered everywhere', had opened by launching her on the climactic phase of her life. Her success in London was immediate. The *Observer* called her the 'hit of the season'; another critic announced that 'Miss Draper has established herself as an institution'; and for years to come variations on these phrases were to figure in her press-notices wherever she appeared.

From now on she was in continuous passage between America and Europe, crossing and re-crossing the Atlantic every year, interspersing her theatre seasons with countless engagements in smaller cities or university and college communities, sweeping from one end of the United States and Canada to the other and to most of the countries of western Europe. In London at the Coliseum she once shared a programme with Grock, the great European clown, but she became equally familiar in Oxford, Cambridge, Edinburgh,

[1] Throughout this chronicle of R. D.'s engagements, of which only a small number are mentioned, as in earlier references to her private and war-time activities, her own record-book is followed. Many of the dates and places have been further verified by consulting American and European newspapers or her collections of programmes, press-cuttings, and letters. Such verification has not been possible in all cases however; where impossible, the record-book has been relied on.

Brighton. Her London theatres now and in the future included playhouses both large and small—Palladium, Haymarket, Vaudeville, Criterion, Duke of York's, the New, the St. James's, the Garrick, St. Martin's, Apollo, the Wigmore Hall. In New York she staged recitals or longer engagements at the Princess, the Comedy, the Selwyn, the Times Square, the Broadhurst, Bijou, Ritz, Vanderbilt, Playhouse, and Empire. America gave her little rest; barely had she filled a New York engagement than she was off to Montreal or Pittsburgh, Chicago or Minneapolis, Detroit or Salt Lake City, Philadelphia or Denver, Boston, Dallas, or San Francisco, weaving tirelessly north, south, east, and west to her bookings. She became celebrated for her punctuality and strict observance of her datings. It was an event of special importance when she contracted the flu in February 1926, had to postpone a programme in Stillwater, Oklahoma, from 9 February to 5 March, and marked it in her date-book as 'the only engagement I ever missed!'

Scanning the list of her engagements during these years, one catches the contagion and energy of her movements. When she was not performing she was busy with her friends and affairs at home; when not busy she was snatching short late summer or early autumn vacations in Maine; when not week-ending with old or new friends in England or France she was off on motor-tours in France and the Pyrenees, holidays in Normandy, explorations of Spain and the Mediterranean, rovings among her best-loved shrines and landscapes in Italy; with incessant public or private engagements to draw her abruptly back into the current of her professional life.

There were high moments to punctuate the rounds of her work and holidaying. Ruth had known the White House in Washington from the earlier years when she had been invited there by President and Mrs. Theodore Roosevelt and later by the Tafts and the Wilsons. Now, on 6 December 1921, President and Mrs. Harding called her there to give an evening programme for their guests in the Blue Room. Another red-letter day came a few years later, in May 1925, when she appeared at the American Embassy in Brussels before the King and Queen of Belgium and Cardinal Mercier. Still another—the climax to her success in England—came on 18 June 1926, when she was commanded by the King and Queen of England to appear before the Court at Windsor Castle, the first of other Windsor command performances to come in the future and anticipating by two years her presentation at Court at Buckingham Palace on 28 May 1928. The night she spent in the castle was starred in her record-book and letters as one of the high romantic experiences of her life. In Madrid in 1922 she appeared at both the Teatro della Princesa and the Ritz Hotel and was invited to appear at a reception at the Royal Palace. Italy was never missed on these journeys if her schedule allowed her a return. She gave performances at the Teatro Fidenti in Florence, at the Palazzo Pisani in Venice, at the Quirinetta and the Odescalchi in Rome, at the American and British Embassies, and at the Palazzo Doria-Pamphili. There was one extraordinary occasion—14 March 1928—when it was arranged that she give a private recital for the *Duce* himself, Mussolini in his belligerent and precarious glory, at the Palazzo Chigi, startled him out of his pomposity when she entered the immense *sala* with her bundle of shawls (a concealed bomb?), and ran through several of her sketches before his puzzled and incredulous eyes.

Amsterdam, The Hague, Stockholm, Oslo, Gothenburg, Copenhagen, Geneva, Lausanne, Siena, Warsaw—they flash in succession through her schedules. But two particular climaxes of her continental record came in 1921 and 1928, when she was sponsored in Paris and in Germany by two of the illustrious men of the European theatre.

One morning in the early autumn of 1921 she walked up the Rue de Clichy in Paris and knocked on the door of the director of the Théâtre de l'Œuvre. Paris had for a decade

beckoned her as a world capital of the theatre. She had performed there frequently in private. But when the moment
came for making her siege of its public theatre, an instinct
told her that there was one *régisseur* above all the others then
working in France who should be her sponsor. Aurélien-
François Lugné-Poe was now fifty-two, and at the height of
his fame. It was almost thirty years since he had inaugurated
his Maison de l'Œuvre at the Bouffes-Parisiens with Maeterlinck's *Pelléas et Mélisande* on 17 May 1893, and so opened
a new chapter in the French drama.[1] His early productions of
Rosmersholm and *An Enemy of the People* made him the leading exponent of Ibsen in France and made Ibsen himself the
guiding-star of the Œuvre, his name and medallion printed on
Lugné-Poe's programmes and letter-heads throughout the
career of his theatre. In the decades following, Ibsen,
Björnson, Strindberg, Hauptmann, Wilde, and Maeterlinck
alternated with the classic drama of Shakespeare, Musset,
and Gogol to set a standard for the new dramatists he took
under his wing. The Œuvre rapidly became one of the centres
of literary and experimental drama in Paris, joining the succession of the Cercle des Escholiers, the Théâtre d'Art, and
Antoine's Théâtre Libre, and so preparing the way for
Copeau's Vieux Colombier and the experimental companies
that rose after 1918. From plays by Henri de Régnier,
Tristan Bernard, Villeroy, Rolland, and Alfred Jarry's sensa-
tional *Ubu Roi*, Lugné-Poe moved on to his patronage of

---

[1] Lugné-Poe wrote the record of his career and productions in a series
of books: *La Parade: Le Sot du Tremplin, Acrobaties, Sous les Étoiles,
Pirouette, Quatre Ans et demi dans un deuxième Bureau, Henrik Ibsen*, &c.,
concluding with *Dernière Pirouette*, published in 1946, six years after his
death on 19 June 1940, at Villeneuve-lès-Avignon, in the month of the
invasion of France. The last-named volume tells of his first meeting and
friendship with Ruth Draper, whose file of his letters to her has also been
drawn on here. The earlier years of his theatre are described in an
American study, *Adventure in the Theatre: Lugné-Poe and the Théâtre de
l'Œuvre to 1899*, by Gertrude Rathbone Jasper (1947), as well as in many
French accounts of the modern Paris theatre. R. D. remained a close
friend of Lugné-Poe and his wife Suzanne Desprès throughout the years
following her first appearances at the Œuvre.

PLATE VII

Ruth Draper: portrait by Wilfrid de Glehn

PLATE VIII

Ruth Draper about 1935
Photograph by Karsh, Ottawa

Samain, Gide, Claudel, and Lenormand; moved too from one Paris playhouse to another—Bouffes-Parisiens, Bouffes du Nord, Comédie-Parisienne, Cirque d'Été, Renaissance— until he settled in his own house in the Rue de Clichy. He was to remain active in the French theatre as producer, director, performer, and film actor until a few years before his death in 1940. When Ruth Draper approached his door in 1921 she was drawn by her sense of a fellow-spirit. Within an hour she made a friend who remained a devoted ally for the nineteen years that remained of his life.

After she had inspected the house and he had taken his account of her, they came quickly to terms. 'I will give you the hall, sixty per cent. of the receipts will be yours, forty mine.' Ruth was astonished at the speed of his co-operation. (*'Elle paraît stupéfaite.'*) 'But you don't know me!' she protested. Lugné-Poe answered that she had 'interested' him: her *'seule'* had caught his admiration. 'I am not risking much,' he assured her. 'You will appear here three or four times. If I lose I shall not do it again; if we make a profit, so much the better: we'll continue.' And he told her that what had persuaded him more than anything else was what he had seen in her eyes: *'une lueur de bon théâtre.'*

Ruth made her first appearances at the Œuvre on 24, 26, and 28 October 1921. She returned for four further recitals the next June, and was back for other programmes intermittently during the following decade. Later she was to appear in other Paris theatres—the Daunou and the Champs-Élysées—but the Œuvre was the house she called her home in Paris. When she appeared there for the last time in May 1950, it was in tribute to Lugné-Poe's friendship and the immediate sympathy they had struck up at their first meeting. Paris gave her some of the keenest critical appreciation she received. Gérard d'Houville in *Figaro*, Tristan Klingsor in *Le Temps*, Maurice Rostand in *Le Soir*, H. Pierrot in a detailed analysis in the *Cahiers de l'Étoile* in 1929—she counted these among the critics the artist values for keeping him to the highest pitch and standard of which he is capable.

Another impresario of Europe was struck by her work later in the twenties. In the late summer of 1927 she met Max Reinhardt at Salzburg and was invited to his baroque palace in the nearby countryside, Schloss Leopoldskron, where he was then reigning as the overlord not only of the German and Austrian theatre but of the dramatic productions of the Salzburg *Festspiele*. A compact was soon drawn up between them, and when she returned to Europe the following winter it was Reinhardt who sponsored her first appearances before German audiences—at the Komödie in Berlin where her hosts were Sir Ronald and Lady Lindsay at the British Embassy, at the Schauspielhaus in Munich, the Neues Theater in Frankfort, and at Reinhardt's own Theater in der Josefstadt in Vienna. Even Vienna was not the easternmost point of her European conquests, however. In the following year she ranged as far as Warsaw and appeared there in the Philharmonic Hall, with friends like Paul and Zosia Kochanski, Artur Rubinstein, and Karol Szymanowski to make her welcome in their Polish homeland. She took this opportunity to make her one excursion into Russia after her Polish weeks in June 1929. She spent a week in Moscow and several days in Leningrad, but these were tourist excursions; she did not perform in the Russian cities.

With these far-ranging tours her posters and programmes took on an exotic appearance. The titles of the monologues, so long familiar in English, blossomed into a polyglot variety of translations. '*Dottori e Regimi — Una Contadina dalmata — Un' Istitutrice tedesca ed una Classe di Bambini.*'   '*I en italiensk Kirke — Åpningen av en Basar — Tre Generasjoner i en Rådhusrett.*'   '*De Opening van een Fancy-Fair — Drie Onbijten — Een Dalmatische Boerin in een Ziekenhuis.*'   '*I grevskapet Kerry — Hennes första bal.*'   '*Een Fransche Coupeuse — Liefde in de Balkanstaten.*'   '*Inauguração dum Bazar de Caridade — Uma Governante alemã — Tres Gerações perante um Tribunal.*' '*Dans une Gare du Far-West — Dans un Village de la Côte Nord-Est de l'Amérique — L'Émigrante écossaise à Ellis Island.*' '*Señor Clifford y tres Mujeres — A la Puerta de Casa en un Pueblecito costero.*' '*Trzy Pokolenia — Na Stacji Kolejowej na Dalekim Zachodzie.*' '*Pariser Schneiderin und ihre Kunden aus U.S.A. — Hellenische Körperkultur — Drei Frauen und Herr Clifford — In einer Kirche in Italien — Am Hofe Philipp IV — Doktoren und Diät.*' So the changes were rung as the monologues were taken from country to country and over five continents.

Greater journeys were yet to come, the longest of them after Ruth Draper had reached her fiftieth year. Meanwhile, during these teeming years of the nineteen-twenties and thirties, however far she ranged it was in America and England that she most fully gained her institutional status. Her American tours and seasons became prodigious, reaching something of a climax when she played the two longest runs of her career and broke all records for solo performance in America. On Christmas night of 1928 she opened at the Comedy Theatre in New York and played eight performances a week for nineteen weeks before she closed on 28 April. The following year she opened her New York season, again at the Comedy, on 26 December, and played continuously, again with eight performances a week, until 4 May 1930.

In England none of her seasons was as long as these, but they became an almost annual feature of the London and provincial theatres until the Second World War interrupted them in 1940. Great though her popularity became in the States, it was possibly surpassed in Great Britain. Ruth said on occasion that she never performed anywhere else quite as she performed before British audiences; and the British audience in turn made of her what it is no exaggeration to call a cult. Something in her lifelong sympathy with the English character reached across the footlights the moment she appeared in an English theatre. The English love of portraiture, satire, humour, eccentricity, studied neatness and finish of execution, responded avidly to her portraits. Her regularly scheduled appearances, her name in the Court Circular, her generous services to English charities, her respect for the technical and stylistic traditions of English acting, her uncannily accurate rendering of the English, Scottish, or Irish voice—all these combined to make her as much at home among the British as she was in her own country. Certain critics of the London and provincial newspapers made a yearly business of studying her art and writing extended appraisals of it. She also soon won the accolade of *Punch* and became the subject of a series of tribute poems that appeared in that weekly during these decades.

> She crowds the stage with airy shapes,
> Puppets of which she pulls the tapes
>   With such address that none can ape her;
> All by herself does all the parts,
> And, scorning aid of outward arts,
> With just her fancy's genius drapes
>   The drama's scene. Ah, what a DRAPER!

This bouquet came from *Punch*'s own editor, 'O. S.' (Owen Seaman). But other contributors chimed in:

> Let others celebrate the skill
>   Of Hagen (not the Wagner person),
> Of Bobby Jones, or tune their quill
>   In praise of Gish or Billy Merson;
>
> Let them wax lyrical upon
>   The stalwart nymphs at whom one gazes
> In wonder, as at Wimbledon
>   They bang the bounding ball to blazes;
>
> Let them exalt Stravinsky's Muse,
>   Explosive, sombre, and barbaric—
> I find it easier to enthuse
>   About RUTH DRAPER at the Garrick....

Another began and ended, under the title 'The Lady of the Voices':

Many magicians have I heard or seen
  From Jefferson and Sothern and Trebelli
Down to Karsavina and Chaliapine,
  From Liszt and Joachim to Grock and Jelly;
But one with special force my fancy fetches,
Ruth Draper in her multilingual sketches.

She comes and goes, she never has outstayed
  The welcome her Protean genius earns;
Laurels like hers endure, they never fade,
  But are renewed, each time that she returns.
By fresh proofs of a study that embraces
Two hemispheres and half-a-dozen races.

        .   .   .   .   .

If the 'gigantic daughter of the West',
  America—as hymned by Alfred Tennyson—
Does not at all times give us of her best,
  Here she deserves our very warmest benison,
For we forget the talkie and skyscraper
In the magnetic presence of RUTH DRAPER.

On 24 February 1932, A. P. Herbert devoted a lyrical-
humorous panegyric in prose to her; and at the end of
another London season *Punch* bade her farewell in further
quatrains:

'Babe Ruth', the Pitcher, leaves me cold,
  Though featured in my picture-paper;
Another Ruth takes stronger hold,
    RUTH DRAPER.

Most entertainers who unbend
  Distress or make me hot all over;
But you can keep me hours on end
    In clover.

Mistress of many tongues, you shine
  In satire, pathos, wit, and *bonhomie*,
Yet practise in your 'words' a fine
    Economy.

Your going casts us into gloom,
    And yet we feel less sad and sober
Since you were able to illume
    October.

So *Punch*, though loth from you to part,
    Cuts this admiring doggerel caper
In homage to your perfect art,
    RUTH DRAPER!

XI

Through these crowded months and thickening successes
Ruth moved with inexhaustible zest, response, and gratitude.
The exciting air of the twenties exactly matched her energy,
her inveterate romantic expectancy. The hard persistent
effort of so many years, the sense of purpose that had been
prepared through years of apprenticeship and patience, her
stubborn confidence in her vocation—all these came into
triumphant resolution between 1920 and 1930 and were
never to spend themselves in the quarter-century of work
that still remained to her. She met her success with unflagging spirit, determined never to fail the audiences that
gave it to her. The world was at her feet, and she accepted
its homage with gratitude and a half-incredulous amazement.
    The highest masters of the theatre became her tribute-
bearers.

Dear Ruth Draper:
    I'm more delighted than I can tell you that you should like
being at the dear old Coliseum, and that you should write and tell
me so. Of your success I was absolutely certain. *I'm just glad!*...
If you are acting anywhere round about London let me know
your whereabouts for I'd like to be able to go and see you again—
for I am ever your admiring and affectionate
                                                        ELLEN TERRY

One such letter must here stand for scores. Ruth's letter-
books take on, year by year, the character of a comprehensive
Who's Who of the theatre of her lifetime.

There were two occasions of which too little survives in the way of written record: one when she had an interview with Sarah Bernhardt in Paris and performed for her in private; another when she had several long talks with Eleonora Duse in Milan and gave her glimpses of her repertory. She brought her profoundest homage to both the great rival queens of the European stage, and both sent her away with blessings that she counted among her greatest memories.

Ruth seldom kept a systematic diary. She had too many letters to write every day of her life, to her sisters and brothers, to her business associates, and to friends in every part of the world. Thus many of her most intimate moments and memories were never put on record. But several of her journals exist, one of the year 1922, most of it written not day by day but in a headlong, retrospective chronicle in the last week of the year while she was sailing back to America on the *Majestic*. Its pages convey as well as any she wrote the excitement of her life during these years, and we may take it as typical of what they meant to her. After a few rapidly jotted entries on 8 May ('Lunched with Paderewski, wonderful as ever'), 10 May ('Sailed on the *France*', with 'Calvé, Cavalieri, Muratore, de Luca, Aileen Tone, and George Blumenthal' among her fellow-passengers), and her arrival in Paris on the 18th for programmes at the Œuvre, she begins again on the following page, but now writing on 31 December:

I stopped writing this diary 'way back in March. It is now December 31st, at sea! I cannot let the old year die without scribbling down the sketchy memories of the past eight months, for this whole year has been perhaps the most wonderful that I've ever lived yet! I've filled in roughly the gaps in April and May, and I begin here with Paris, where I was so happily fixed for the end of May, all of June, and until July 6th, in the enchanting little flat in rue Jacob. Léa Dessay, Raymonde Glaenzer's maid, stayed on, did all my work,—cook, maid, companion—and became my dear friend. She is one of the rarest souls I know—beautiful, intelligent, with such charm and distinction.... I will never forget those weeks. Every morning such a joy to wake, look out on to the trees in the garden—always flowers, sunshine, delicious breakfasts, writing, telephoning, friends to lunch and to dine...seeing to things at the theatre, rehearsing the Spanish sketch, which gave me a good deal of trouble; fittings; looking up friends; doing the hundreds of things that seem to fill the days in Paris.

Rounds of visits follow; evenings performing in the houses of friends; programmes at the Œuvre; tours of the Louvre and the galleries; an excursion to Chartres; dinner in Montmartre with the Jo Davidsons; a recital at the Embassy. Then:

I had the very amusing and interesting experience of going to see Sarah Bernhardt and reciting for her. I shall not soon forget it. Such a scene as her house—her room, dogs, parrot, *objets d'art*, dust of ages, photographs, autographs, etc. She marvelous, vital, keen, enthusiastic, full of force! She was exceedingly kind and said charming things.... She urged me to go on the stage, which left me quite cold, but the experience of watching and listening to her, and the whole picture of myself reciting in that room, three feet away from the great old lady, was humorous to a degree. She is superb in her youthful spirit, her vigor and vitality. I was deeply impressed by her.

Then on to dinners at the Princesse de Polignac's and the Princesse Murat's; evenings at the Diaghilev ballet; a 'great Venetian Ball at the Opera'; a *soirée* at the Rothschilds'; music by Casals, Thibaud, and Cortot.... Soto London in July for three weeks of public and private recitals while living in Halsey Street, 'the sweetest place I ever saw'; the Royal Garden Party; a round of new plays: *Loyalties*, *The Dover Road*, and of old ones: *Dear Brutus* and *The Second Mrs. Tanqueray*; a recital at Lady Violet Astor's that made nearly £600; Lenglen's tennis at Wimbledon; an evening recital at Lady Bathurst's with the Princess Christian, Sir Edward Carson, the Duc de Guise, and Kipling among the guests.

In August came a holiday in Normandy, at Houlgate, with her sister Alice and her husband and four children in 'a ridiculous little villa which I had taken'.

Then began five weeks of a very real holiday, a regular un-
eventful life: bathing every day, walks, enormous delicious meals,
a little tennis, a few expeditions, reading and sewing, playing....
The days flew—a happy and restful existence, talking and walking,
playing with the boys.... Read an interesting history of Spain,
some poor novels, and a great deal of Baudelaire.... It was a
delicious holiday, and I loved the place, but I began to get restless with such peace, wanted to work again, and worried over lack
of ideas for the new monologues. But after the children left I at
last got started. Worked over 'The Children's Party', the 'Charwoman', and 'The Switchboard Girl', and made 'Five Imitation
Folk Songs'. It was an exciting two weeks when these things suddenly took life and shape. I heaved a sigh of relief when I felt that
they were at least started.... I took long walks along the beach and
through the country, beautiful in the autumn, with wonderful
sunsets and moonlight, long hours of peace, the crowd having
departed by the middle of September. There is little to relate in
detail of the quiet days, so I'll stop and jump to September 28th
when I left for Paris to begin again a more variegated existence.

Paris was followed by visits in eastern France at Nancy,
Chantillon, and Tonnerre, with old friends and families.
Then on to London again from 11 October to 6 November
for studies in voice production and breathing with Raimund
von zur Mühlen ('a strange loveable personality who I'm sure
knows more of the art of song-singing than anyone in the
world: I loved him and the rare privilege of working with
him').

The days flew, London in autumn at its most enchanting... a
recital in Cambridge and one in Oxford at Balliol Hall, a great
success, while I stayed with Lady Osler.... I recited at Winchester
College and that was wonderful—such a beautiful place—and had
two very successful recitals at Wigmore Hall... an evening at
Sibyl Colefax's, a delightful dinner with unusually interesting people, Edmund Gosse, George Moore, Strachey, Mrs.
Hunter...'to the British Museum, the Wallace Collection, the
National Gallery... went to see *Secrets* and heard Kreisler.

On 8 November she crossed again to Paris to spend ten
days with friends, have dresses made, and see plays, until,

after engaging a maid, she left on the 19th for Spain: 'a comfortable night followed by a long interesting day through the amazing country of northern Spain, barren, austere, beautiful, mysterious.' In Madrid a welcome awaited her from her Spanish friends and those at the American and British legations:

I spent the first week arranging things at the theatre, rehearsing, deciding the performances, interviewing, seeing people, presenting cards, and paying calls. I felt rather poorly, fighting a cold and having misgivings about my success.... Everybody was so kind. My shows went very well...I went often to the Prado. That in itself is sufficient reason to go to Spain. Overcome by the Velázquez and at last I realize the wonder of El Greco. Superb Titians, Rubens, Van Dycks, and Goyas. A little Mantegna and a little Veronese ('Death of the Virgin' and 'The Finding of Moses' respectively) impressed me particularly. A wonderful Angelico 'Annunciation' and that beautiful Titian of Isabella. So many pictures familar from my studies with H. H. Hefter. Bless her for what she gave to me!...I spent one unforgettable day in Toledo, coming back by moonlight—unspeakably beautiful, the impression of the whole strange scene. The choir of the Cathedral and Greco's 'Burial of Count Orgaz' are two *events* of my life!...The evening at the Palace was perfect. Luncheon with the Duc d'Alba, seeing his beautiful things.... Met many of the critics, all of whom gave me splendid notices. Made 3000 pesetas! Every day was a glory of sunshine and cold clear air....

She left Madrid on 5 December for Cordoba; then on to Seville ('saw the Cathedral and drove about the city, went to a cabaret with Lafita, took a long walk in the Santa Cruz district. Full moon!...Saw the great fête of the Virgin in the Cathedral with the dance of the *seis*, and went to a wedding. Saw gypsys dancing the *Triana* late at night. All marvelous beyond words.') Thence to Granada on an all-day journey— 'fascinating, strange, barren country; white villages; olive orchards; lakes at Locha.' Granada becomes a list of names and exclamation points—'Generalife!—Alhambra!' 'Albaicui! Falla!' 'Moonlight, music, and poets—Federico Garcia

Lorca, René Chalupt.' Thus on to Ronda ('Wonderfully beautiful and interesting old town') and to Algeciras ('a most beautiful journey through wonderful mountains'); so to Gibraltar to sail past the Balearic Islands to Toulon and Marseilles, then a 'glorious journey along the Riviera on a perfect day' to Ventimiglia, where the train for Milan awaited her:

> Hôtel Cavour... Sent a letter to Duse... Went to a superb performance of *Falstaff* at the Scala with Toscanini, and in the evening saw Duse in Ibsen's *Ghosts*: she beautiful beyond words... Talked with Duse the next afternoon... Recited for Madame Duse and had a long talk... Went to the Brera, the Ambrosiana, saw the Leonardo and the lovely church of San Ambrogio (H. H. H.)... Recited again for Duse in the evening... Saw Duse in the evening in *La Via della Croce*.... Talked with Duse for a last time and said goodbye....

The meetings with Duse are as sketchily recorded in this diary as the one with Bernhardt, but Ruth's letters of that month give further details. In one dated from the Hôtel Cavour in Milan, 20 December 1922, to her old friend in England, Mrs. Yates Thompson, she said:

> The culmination [of my journey] has been here, seeing and meeting Mme. Duse. I saw her play *Ghosts* the night of the day that I arrived, and she plays a modern piece called *Così Sia* tonight. I have talked with her and recited for her (she is in this hotel), and I have been so moved by her beauty, and her wonderful acting. It is like nothing I've ever seen, because it is not in the least like 'acting'. She is the most tragic personality I've ever seen, but her beauty is amazing still, though she looks old and ill. Her hair is white, and she uses no make-up, but her movements, gesture, voice, the line of her throat, and her whole expression move one to tears. She has been dear to me, so interested in my work; it seemed really to give her pleasure, and she said such beautiful things that I should like to remember them forever. She seems poor, tortured by all the business end of her work, the Union working against her—it seems there is a Theatre trust, and she does not wish to belong, so in every way they are blocking her

success. She may come to America. It seems a hideous tragedy that such a great person, with such a beautiful thing to give to people, should be balked and defeated. The public flock, theatres are crammed, but after a few performances in each place, they refuse to lease her the house! I am so thankful that I came. It has been a great experience, a very personal one, for I felt a deep sympathy with her and an understanding of her ideal.

And one of Ruth's friends in Italy recalls her telling that while Bernhardt, finding herself oppressed by the sombre sketches, remarked sharply *'Pourquoi ne faites-vous la comédie?'* Duse counselled her *'Mon enfant, ne faites jamais la comédie.'*[1]

The days in Milan ended on 21 December. The night-train took her north to Paris for a day of shopping and fare-wells; another carried her on the 23rd to Dinard in Brittany for Christmas with a family of old American friends ('recited for a party on Christmas night. Wrote a difficult letter in Italian to Duse and one to Lugné-Poe'); and a motor whirled her to Cherbourg and the *Majestic* for a rough winter cross-ing back to New York, with Coué and Stanislavsky among the passengers. ('Fine visits with Stanislavsky of the Moscow Art Theatre. *"Un dieu!"* as L.-P. says.') And so, with America drawing near once more, the year ends on New Year's Eve on the last page of the book: 'This awful diary is finished!'

XII

Throughout these years her friendships continued to play a major part in Ruth Draper's life and to figure as an obliga-tion second only to her work and her family affections. In her girlhood she had found her ties chiefly in New York, New England, and Maine, and had inherited from her parents a large circle of their associations. As she advanced into her maturity friends of her own age and generation were added to these, and as her public career developed she made

[1] Iris Origo, 'Ruth Draper and her Company of Characters: An Ap-preciation', *The Cornhill Magazine*, No. 1014 (Winter 1957–8), pp. 383–93 (reprinted in *The Atlantic*, October 1958).

countless others. They grew in number wherever she travelled, so that while there always remained a central circle of long-tested personal intimacies, with her own family as its nucleus, her enthusiasm and generosity responded to countless other calls and appeals.

To turn the pages of her letter-books is to become aware of the scope of these sympathies, the range of her emotion, the fund of feeling she brought to her personal contacts and loyalties. It is also to become conscious of the difficulty—and the invidiousness—of singling out names from the long list of those who came to figure in her life. It would require more than a short memoir—it would require a lengthy collection of her correspondence—to give any just account of what her friendships counted for in Ruth's career. Any life which is divided, as hers was, between the private and the public self shows these accretions of interest and *rapport*. The actor more than any other artist is likely to number his friends and well-wishers by the hundreds or thousands where most lives count them by the score or the handful. And when the actor performs alone as she did, there rises a sense of contact and affection between the stage and the spectator which can make a hundred new friends in an evening.

Her genius for friendship was instinctively democratic— avid, eager, responsive, open-handed. She could count the old servants of her parents' home, the dresser she employed during her many London engagements, her maid and *lingère* in Paris, a faithful correspondent in Oklahoma, or her fellow villagers in Maine as giving her something as important to her life and imagination as what she received from her old schoolmates, her colleagues of the New York and London theatres, her hosts in American and English homes, or her old friends in France and Italy. With all of them she kept in touch; remembered them on birthdays and holidays; remembered them in times of war or trouble with the help that always remained secret and in many cases anonymous. No compilation of names, even of those closest to her, could do justice to the wealth and warmth of her affections. They are an essential part of her record but the slightest indication of them must stand here for the scores of lives and loyalties that came to figure in her experience:

From Kate Douglas Wiggin in 1914: 'I simply glory in you as an American product! You were wonderful at the Club yesterday; more finished, more versatile, more authoritative than ever and that is saying a good deal. Your command of your peculiar resources seems now absolute.'

From Charles Dana Gibson in 1920: 'Your splendid success is close to my heart. Just a line to say I love you.'

From Compton Mackenzie in 1920: 'I had the great good fortune to reach England in time to see your last performance at the Aeolian Hall. And now a week later in cold blood on a wet night I write to tell you that I have never enjoyed—I won't say anything of the kind, because there never has been anything of the kind except in the pages of a book called *Sylvia Scarlett*—but really I don't think I ever enjoyed sitting in a stall so much. It was perfect.'

From William Archer on the *Majestic* in 1923: 'Though you must be tired of praise, I cannot deny myself the pleasure of telling you how immensely I enjoyed your sketches this evening.... The subtlety of your observation and the width of your range are, in my experience, unique. It is a great joy to see *anything* done with such mastery—and this is no slight thing either. The humour of some sketches and the humanity of all are beyond praise.'

From Eddie Cantor in 1929: 'May I now thank you for the most wonderful evening I have ever spent in the theatre? I wish it were possible to send every young actor and actress to witness your remarkable performance.'

From Henry Ainley in Yorkshire, August 1939: 'Your beautiful work is the peak of perfection; you make me very proud to be an actor.'

From John Gielgud: 'This is only a word of grateful thanks for the great pleasure you gave me, and a tribute to the fresh and exquisite variety of your brilliant work. I hope it gives you some of the joy you give the audiences who adore you. The test of concentration and self-criticism which it must involve is something to marvel at.'

From Helen Keller on the *S.S. America*: 'This is to tell you how happy I was to receive a note from you so overflowing with your lovely personality. Not only have I many dear associations with you as a great woman and a friend, but I also feel close to you in your freedom of spirit and independence of thought. It is wonderful that you, Polly and I are on the same boat....Truly it has been a magnificent storm! As I lay idling in bed my spirit rejoiced in the might of the tempest, its solemn organ-like rhythms interrupted with menacing reverberations. With our love until we clasp your hand again.'

From Laurence Olivier: 'Vivien and I both experienced an unforgettable two-fold joy in the miracle of your work, and the enchantment of meeting you personally. Apart from my own cup being so full with that Elysian feeling of entire satisfaction that watching you always brings to one, it quite overflowed with the sweet emotion of sharing Vivien's experience of seeing you for the first time.'

From Walter Starkie in Dublin, 1932: 'I am very glad that W. B. Yeats is coming up from the West to see you. Your visit to Dublin has been a revelation to Ireland. There has been nothing like it. You have reached all the sensitive souls and brought before them the most intimate drama imaginable. Not only have you appealed to their intellect and to their emotions but you have opened up new vistas of technique, of gesture, of plastic rhythm, and voice modulation....You are one of the only people except Duse who can produce drama by your immobility as well as by your movement.'

From Otis Skinner: 'Neither age nor custom can take away my amazement at you....But I have one serious quarrel with you. You carry one of the largest supporting companies I have seen. In each of your sketches you have surrounded yourself with a group of actors whose art is perfect and whose presence is compelling and hypnotic. And yet you pay them *nothing*!! Do you think that is fair?'

From Gilbert Murray, Boars Hill, Oxford, 1946: 'How good to have you back with us again! It makes us forget these six long years of fear and dread, and tells us that your return was one of the things we were waiting for during all of them.'

From Bernard Berenson at Settignano in 1946: 'Yesterday morning I read a most enthusiastically appreciative account of one of your performances; I thus learned that you already were in England. An hour later the post brought me a long and dear letter.

I am delighted to learn, but not a bit surprised, that you have been welcomed everywhere. It would not be otherwise with an artist, a woman, and a character like your so very dear self....Darling Ruth, while I am alive you must think of *I Tatti* and *Casa el Dono* as homes where you will always be eagerly welcomed....'

Such are a few of the sentences that appear as one turns the pages of Ruth's letter-books, a scant indication of dozens like them. Two of her friends, however, require fuller report, not only for what they contributed to her life but for what they added to her creative activity. Edward Sheldon of New York was one; Lauro de Bosis of Rome the other.

Ruth first made the acquaintance of Edward Sheldon—always 'Ned' to his inner circle of intimates—in the years around 1910 when, on first coming to live in New York from his boyhood in Chicago and his brilliant career at Harvard, he swept all before him with his astonishing early success as the author of *Salvation Nell*. A youth of irresistible charm, wit, and enthusiasm, he had discovered his literary gift while still a student in the courses of his favourite professors at Harvard, Charles Townsend Copeland and George Pierce Baker. The theatre had been his realm of romance from boyhood, and when Mrs. Fiske, then a reigning actress of the American stage, accepted his second effort in playwriting, staged it with resounding success in New York, and made it a forecast of a new and more serious day in the American theatre, Sheldon found himself famous overnight, at the age of twenty-two. *Salvation Nell* at the Hackett Theatre in 1908 marks a date in the emergence of a modern American drama. What Eugene O'Neill said of it two decades later—that 'along with the work of the Irish Players on their first trip over here, [it] was what first opened my eyes to the existence of a real theatre as opposed to the unreal'—suggests what it counted for in the theatre of its time. During the next five years Sheldon wrote six further plays, four of which—*The Nigger, The Boss, The High Road,* and *Romance*—became out-

PLATE IX

Ruth Draper about 1936

PLATE X

Ruth Draper, with Gaetano Salvemini and her grand-niece Anne Draper

In her summer home at Dark Harbor, Islesboro, Maine, 1945

Photograph by Robert Bolaffio, of New York

standing successes. *Romance,* with its star Doris Keane, carried his fame from coast to coast in America, throughout Great Britain, and to countries as far afield as France, Russia, Norway and Sweden, South America, and Australia during its forty-year history of productions, revivals, and translations into every possible form of theatrical, film, or radio adaptation. Its author became a man of mark among his contemporaries: a skilful hand at every variety of theatrical work, inexhaustible in his energy and generosity, the devoted friend of everyone who touched his charmed life.

On this rich achievement in public success and social amenity a destiny that would have been crushing to anyone without Sheldon's moral and mental stamina was fated to close down. He was not yet thirty when, in 1915, the first symptoms of acute arthritic paralysis overtook him. Within three years he was an immobile cripple; in another twelve he was blinded; his body became rigidly confined to its bed. He passed through successive phases of incapacity, suffering, and physical prostration that deprived him of all power of movement. From this appalling affliction he fought his way back to a second life. His old friends became closer than before. His new ones became his passionate devotees and the recipients of loyalty and counsel that counted as a major force in their lives. He collaborated in writing a further series of plays or adaptations, most of them successes. His correspondence became world-wide. During the almost thirty years of his affliction his character, heroism, and counsel became a living legend in New York and in the wide circle of his acquaintance, and his penthouse blue room, high above Madison Avenue and 84th Street, became a mecca to everyone who knew him.[1]

Ruth was only one in the great circle of his friends, as he was one in hers; but everything in her personality that

[1] The story of Sheldon's life has been told, admirably, by Eric Wollencott Barnes in *The Man Who Lived Twice: The Biography of Edward Sheldon* (New York, 1956), some of whose details have been followed here.

responded to his feat of solitary heroism joined with all she represented to him as a creative force in the theatre to make her and Sheldon fellow-spirits. Through more than three decades she was one of his faithful visitors. When distance separated them their letters kept them close across the wide areas she covered in her journeys. She performed her mono-logues for him; he reacted to them with delight and with the keen advice in which his practical theatrical sense had made him an expert.

In 1923, before blindness overcame him, it was decided between her and Sheldon that they would collaborate on a play. During the summer months of that year they carried on long discussions out of which a subject emerged. The subject, unpromising in the practical terms of the theatre, was the personal life of the three Fates. Looking down from the height of heaven or chaos, they find themselves stirred by envy of 'mortal womankind'. One envies 'the woman en-grossed by mother-love'; the second envies the woman given to 'the love of man'; the third envies 'the eternal feminine that most nearly touches God'. They rise, leave their loom, spindle, and shears, and decide to descend to earth as mortal women. In the three acts and nine 'pictures' that follow, the outcome of their experiment unfolds, in scenes ranging from New England, the open prairie, and a Pacific city in America, through eighty years of life in Paris, to imperial and war-time Russia. At the end the Fates return to their 'high place beyond the stars', old women now, 'weary, exhausted, beaten', life having proved 'too much for them'. They take up again their loom, spindle, and shears, and resuming their godhead become young and eternal once more. But when the children of the earth call them as mothers they rise in-voluntarily, knowing now what the ordeal and suffering of humanity mean, and one by one descend again to the world of the living.

The Three Fates survives as a 42-page scenario. It was Ruth Draper's longest effort at dramatic invention. It appears

that Sheldon was mainly responsible for its general conception and structure, she for many of its specific episodes and
characters. The play was never produced or even (since the
dialogue was never fully worked out) carried as far as a pro-
ducible version. Its effect is cinematic, and in its combination of supernaturalism, fantasy, and panoramic geography
it would probably have offered every possible obstacle to
successful production on the stage. Sheldon made other
attempts at fantasy—*The Garden of Paradise, The Lonely
Heart, Bewitched*—but these met no success on Broadway.
His talent lay in the social or sentimental realism that made
Salvation Nell, The Nigger, and *Romance* effective; and in his
later collaborations the realism took over bodily and made
pieces like *Lulu Belle* and *Dishonored Lady* full-throated
melodramas of a tougher era than the one in which he had
found his first fame. Ruth, as her sketches show, had little
gift or proclivity for fantasy. Both writers were trying their
hand at an uncongenial medium, and its uncongeniality is
what remains most striking in the surviving scenario.

The collaboration was a stimulating experience for Ruth,
however. She seems to have seen *The Three Fates* as a possible extension of her writing talent, perhaps as an opportunity for enlarging her scope as an actress. Sir James Barrie
thought so when she showed the play to him in England in
1927. 'I see you appearing in all three parts yourself and
growing at once, as you do in your sketches', he wrote her on
26 December. He advised her to get rid of the prologue and
epilogue in Heaven, retain the three individual adventures of
the Fates, and make 'a capital one-act play' of each of them:
'if you could work them out in your own inimitable way for
yourself and with no one else on the stage, I believe you
would triumph exceedingly. This though you did only one,
any one of the three, though of course the contrast is so great
that the three in one evening would be masterly. Your mind
dwells on contrasts—so right for your individual entertainment but so wrong I think for the author setting forth on a

long play. This is all probably wrong-headed and to be disregarded, but is how I see it.' When Ruth wrote to Sheldon,
she emphasized Barrie's esteem for the theatrical force of the
manuscript ('in my opinion it has the unusual quality of
being too dramatic', he had added; 'you never have your
finger off the public pulse'.) 'I am sure that Barrie's estimate
of the sustained, tremendous dramatic quality will please you',
she said. 'That is all yours and I am proud to think I kept
it alive with you. What fun we had anyway, working on it
that summer!'

Through the twenty years that followed she was never out
of touch with Sheldon. In New York she visited him in the
blue room. On her travels she sent him her vivid letters.

She appreciated as no one else his intense feeling for color [says
Sheldon's biographer] and her letters brought not only the forms
and sounds of remote places, but every tint that crossed her
consciousness, from the 'peach-colored velvet jacket' which she
happened to be wearing when she once wrote, to the 'bright red
jacarandas' on the shores of the Indian Ocean. She knew well the
spots that he had loved as a young man; she made him see again
the fresh green of London parks, the snow on the Cotswolds, and
Florence with its 'blue sky [and] that row of tiny yellow houses
that lies along the Arno beside the Ponte Vecchio; the green
shutters, brown-tiled roofs, broken stained walls....'

From Australia in 1938 she sent him a promise of reunion
from one of the farthest distances she ever reached:

I shall have so much to tell you—so many things, places and
people. My thoughts leap to my chair beside you—and the silence
and intimacy of your room, and I hear you laugh and see you
smile and know that you will understand and feel everything as
if you had been with me everywhere....I'll book my first evening
with you when I land.

When Sheldon's death came on 1 April 1946, she found it
as impossible as all his other friends did to believe she would
never see and talk to him again. 'Somehow I never thought
he might die,' she wrote in a letter; 'he seemed so a part of

the things that never die—the things by which one lives,
believes in, clings to as secure and beautiful forever.'

In 1928 Ruth made another of the major friendships of her
life, perhaps the one that was to bring her personal and
emotional experience to the most intense crisis she ever
experienced.

The years 1927–8 were a time of incessant activity for her.
From the closing weeks of her New York season at the
Selwyn Theatre early in 1927, she had gone on a trans-
continental tour of America that took her from coast to
coast; then back to New York for further recitals at the Times
Square Theatre; then to the Mediterranean on 10 May on
the *Conte Rosso* for a long tour through Italy; thus to summer
seasons in Paris and London; and finally back to America in
September for the autumn at Dark Harbor. But by 5 November she was at sea again, bound for Europe on the *Majestic*.
The twelve months that followed were to prove if anything
even more eventful than those she left behind. Her five-week
London season at the Criterion was followed by her appearances in Germany and Austria in January and February
under Max Reinhardt's sponsorship. When they ended late
in February she moved southward again, over the Brenner to
Italy. There were programmes in Florence and Rome, and
on 14 March her 'command performance' for Mussolini at
the Palazzo Chigi, an episode that was soon to take on a more
curious and sinister significance than she could then have
anticipated.

Italy, now under the heel of the Fascist dictatorship, seemed
more beautiful than ever during the two months she spent
there that spring. Its beauty struck her as all the more appealing, perhaps, because she now found herself challenged by a
divided allegiance. Her old love of the land and its people,
her devotion to her Italian friends and her gratitude for their
reception of her programmes, was troubled by her instinctive
American dislike of the régime which, now in its seventh

year, had slowly blanketed the country with its curtailments of freedom, suppression of civil and intellectual liberties, coercion of literature, press, and other forms of creative expression. Ruth Draper had never taken an active or even a serious interest in politics, either at home or abroad. In Europe she was aware of political events chiefly in terms of what the war had done to alter the face of European life, shift the familiar frontiers of countries, and produce the restless conditions which made the fate of nations more a matter of casual scepticism than of serious critical scrutiny to the average travelling American. She was too busy with her work to devote any systematic attention to the forces that were shaping a sinister future. She lingered on in Italy until early May. Before she sailed for home on 20 June she was to give performances at the Athénée in Paris, the Haymarket in London, at Oxford, and at Stratford; and on 28 May she was to be presented at Court at Buckingham Palace. But in Rome that April she unexpectedly found herself drawn into the current of the forces that were shaping the time, and into a participation that had not yet figured in her serious activity. A meeting in Rome was to prove in the sequel of even greater significance to her than her successes on the Continent or in London.

At a luncheon party in a Roman house she met the young Italian poet Lauro de Bosis. They met as members of a pleasant gathering of old Roman friends. He was introduced to her as the brilliantly talented scientist, writer, and translator he had already become at the early age of twenty-seven. Born in Rome in 1901 as the son of the poet Adolfo de Bosis and his wife Lillian Vernon, daughter of an American Protestant clergyman who had come to Italy in the second half of the nineteenth century, Lauro became by birth the heir of two national traditions that were united in the ideals of intellectual liberalism and an idealistic political faith. He grew up with his brothers and sisters in a home—a large apartment in the Via dei Due Macelli—in which democratic humanism was a living ideal. His mother, though fully dedicated to the country of her adoption, instilled into her children a knowledge of American principle and history. His father, born in Ancona in 1863, had early become one of the outstanding poets and critics of the generation that took D'Annunzio as its poetic spirit, De Sanctis and Croce as its intellectual leaders, and the future of Italian liberalism as its political doctrine. Though he had graduated in law from the University of Rome and practised it for some years, and though he later supported his family in commercial ventures, Adolfo de Bosis was a writer by vocation. He became editor of the journal *Il Convito* at thirty-two, translated Homer into Italian verse, published his most famous collection of poems, *Amori ac Silentio*, in 1895, became the '*amico intimo*' of D'Annunzio and other artists, and was honoured on his death in August 1924 as one of the men who had done most to guide the younger Italian writers out of the romantic and nationalistic conflicts of the nineteenth century into the tests and promise of the twentieth. He was a lifelong devotee of Shelley. His translations of Shelley had begun as early as 1898 with a version of *The Cenci*; his version of *Prometheus Unbound* appeared in 1922; his collection of Shelley's *Liriche* posthumously in 1928.

It was doubtless the spirit of Shelley that hovered over Ruth Draper's first meeting with Adolfo de Bosis's son. Her own lifelong love of the English poet joined with Lauro's Shelleyan inheritance to create an immediate bond between them. After they left their lunch party they spent a long afternoon in the gardens of the Villa Medici and the Villa Borghese. All Ruth's feeling for Italy, her romantic sense of its past, its art, and its people, were answered in the voice of the poet who walked and talked with her that day on the Pincian.

The crisis in his country's history had already become a crisis in Lauro de Bosis's life. Like so many young Italians of his generation he had found himself swept into the violent cross-currents of Italian patriotism and Fascist enthusiasm.

His career had been marked by precocious brilliance from boyhood. He had attended the University of Rome, achieved his doctorate there in chemistry, and won honours in theoretical science. He had begun to write verse as a boy. In 1923 his translations of Sophocles and Aeschylus were performed in the Greek theatre on the Palatine. He made a three-volume Italian translation of Frazer's *The Golden Bough*. Barely twenty at the time of the march on Rome in 1921 and still unaware of what the new régime would mean to academic and intellectual freedom, he had been seized by the surge of Fascist action and prophecy. But as his imagination was divided between science and poetry, his thought became equally divided between the theory and the reality of the new nationalism. It was during these years that there shaped itself in his mind a long poetic drama on the myth of Icarus. He wrote the poem in 1927—*Icaro: Una Tragedia*—and dedicated it 'To my brother Valente and to all those who have shared the spirit and the destiny of Icarus.' It received the Olympic Prize for Poetry at Amsterdam in 1928 and was published in Milan in 1930. It was a remarkable portent of the course his life was to take.

That life, begun in extraordinary promise and inspired by a genius for friendship equal to Ruth's own—'impetuous, generous, brilliant, imaginative in all it touched', as one tribute expressed it—inevitably found itself caught, as the headlong aggressions of Fascism showed themselves during the 1920's, in the conflict that was to bring so many young Italian careers to grief and tragedy. It took the Matteoti murder in 1923 to show what Fascism meant in ruthlessness and violence. By 1928 he resolved to leave the country to find his opportunity abroad. By a combination of tact and diplomacy he secured a semi-official appointment as secretary of the Italo-America Society, with its headquarters at the Casa Italiana in New York. This post involved him in the work of official Fascist propaganda, but De Bosis turned his American opportunity to other uses. Through friends in England and

the United States he made contact with the supporters of
Italian liberty. On journeys back to Italy he joined forces with
the opponents of Fascism and helped to organize the Alleanza
Nazionale, the secret society which hoped, by merging the
doctrines of liberalism, monarchism, and Catholic Action, to
consolidate the opposition to Mussolini into an effective
resistance. He wrote leaflets and pamphlets for the Alleanza;
circulated them secretly up and down the country; and soon
became known both inside and outside Italy as one of the
most inspired critics of the dictatorship.

Between 1928 and 1931 Ruth Draper found herself
progressively involved in this activity. She shared in the
enthusiasm and the peril of Lauro's work; became deeply concerned with Italian events; made friends with other workers
in the cause; gave hospitality, now and later, in New York
or at Dark Harbor to refugees from Italy; and contributed
generously to Lauro de Bosis's undertakings.

In late November of 1930 the leaders of the Alleanza
Nazionale, Mario Vinciguerra, Renza Rendi, and their associates, were arrested in Rome. In December they were put
on trial. The printing machine on which their pamphlets had
been printed was found under a mattress in the home of
Lauro's mother. Signora de Bosis, old and ill, was confined
in a prison hospital. The trial before the Fascist Special
Tribunal was swift and perfunctory. Signora de Bosis, after
writing Mussolini a plea for the pardon of her erring son and
hoping to protect her other children and grandchildren, was
released. Vinciguerra and Rendi were sentenced to fifteen
years in prison.

Lauro de Bosis's part in these tragic developments brought
his life to its crisis. At the trial in Rome a letter he had
written to the Italian Ambassador in Washington applying for
the post at the Casa Italiana was read, and it threw his whole
participation in the resistance into question. His plight was
desperate. Across the Atlantic in New York he heard of the
arrest and sentence of his confederates. 'Constantly haunted

by the thought that his friends in Italy were exposed to physical risks while he was at a safe distance,' as one report of the time put it, 'he determined to give them a sign of his undimmed enthusiasm in the cause by a flight over Rome.' By summer he was in England laying his plans. He had printed a new stock of leaflets defending the Alleanza and Italian freedom and appealing to the Italian nation to rid itself of an ignominious tyranny. He took lessons in flying at Hendon. Early in July he set off for Italy from southern France with his first plane-load of leaflets. His first flight came to grief; he crash-landed on Corsica and abandoned his damaged plane there. His resolution redoubled, he returned to England, had half a million new leaflets printed on India paper, and laid plans for a second flight. By early October he had secured a new plane and was ready for his desperate venture.

On the afternoon of Saturday, 3 October 1931, he left the Marignan airport near Marseilles, planning to reach Rome in the early evening when the streets were crowded. He reached the city by nine o'clock, flew low over the Garibaldi bridge, and so circled over Rome. 'He remained about half an hour over the city,' Ruth Draper wrote two years later: 'and eye-witnesses have described the raid as a feat of great skill and daring. He flew very low over the streets, and in places it seemed as if snow had fallen, so thickly were the leaflets strewn. He dropped them into the laps of spectators at an open-air cinema, and among the tables of cafes in the squares. One spectator recounted that the plane seemed to be mounting the Spanish Steps.' Planes of the Fascist Air Force were swiftly alerted and sent in pursuit. No official report was ever issued on their success in overtaking Lauro as he sped westward over the Mediterranean, and no trace of him or his plane was ever discovered. He is believed to have run out of his scant supply of fuel and to have crashed and drowned in the sea.[1]

[1] The accounts of Lauro de Bosis's life and work at the time of the

To Ruth Draper these developments, followed so anxiously throughout their crises of desperation and danger, and intensified by her love for Lauro de Bosis and her sympathy with his heroic dedication, became a crucial experience in her life. She was in France that autumn. It was in Paris that she kept vigil during Lauro's flight, awaited its outcome, waited for the word of his return to Marseilles, and waited in vain. When it became certain that his flight over Rome had ended in death, she felt it not only as a disaster for his cause but as a personal crisis to herself. While the world rang with the news of his heroism she could share in its tribute:

How much of Shelley was in the poet's thoughts when he planned this flight and sacrifice, and what dreams out of all the beautiful treasuries from which he had stored his mind, magnificent poetry, thought and action, who shall say? Behind his act lies the Mediterranean genius for finding the great symbol, which can both express the idea and satisfy the imagination, and by doing so takes on to itself its own life and power. Whatever may have been his determination and devotion, it was his poetic mind after all that enabled him to give to the world his own private splendor.[1]

But his death came as the end of one of the greatest emotional experiences and one of the most complete dedications she

---

events in Rome in 1930 and of his flight over Rome in October 1931 are extensive in the European and American newspapers of the period. Among the reports followed here are those in the London *Times* of 15 October 1931, and in the *New York Times*, 30 and 31 May, 4 and 8 October 1931. A more recent view of the controversial aspects of his activity and death is in Giuseppe Prezzolini's *Italiano Inutile* (1954).

The place and date of Ruth Draper's first meeting with Lauro de Bosis have been differently given in other accounts of their friendship. Exact evidence on these details has been difficult to determine; they are given here as remembered by those closest to R. D.

The two friends of R. D. discussed above are commemorated in the dedication of an American novel, *The Ides of March*, by Thornton Wilder (1948): 'This work is dedicated to two friends: Lauro de Bosis, Roman poet, who lost his life marshalling a resistance against the absolute power of Mussolini; his aircraft pursued by those of the Duce plunged into the Tyrrhenian Sea: and to Edward Sheldon, who though immobile and blind for over twenty years was the dispenser of wisdom, courage, and gaiety to a large number of people.'

[1] Editorial: 'Icarus', in *The New Republic*, vol. lxix, p. 33 (25 November 1931).

had ever given herself to. For months she felt the shock and desolation it brought her. She had shared Lauro de Bosis's passionate faith, his moral courage, his creative resolution, and the desperation that had driven him to his heroic exploit. These were emotions already familiar to her in her own career; now they came as a reinforcement of her life's purpose and of her character. In the months and years that followed she entered on one of the most intense and productive creative periods of her life. She worked at her performances with a renewed zeal; she wrote new monologues; she undertook the longest journeys of her career—to Africa and Asia, to Australia and New Zealand and the islands of the Pacific. Her sixth decade was to become even more eventful than those before it.

But first she applied herself to commemorating the name and memory of Lauro de Bosis. In 1933 she published through the Oxford University Press her translation of *Icaro*, with a preface by one of his and her old friends in England, Gilbert Murray. Later that year she issued her translation of *The Story of My Death*, the testament he had written in French during the night of 2 October 1931 and posted at 3 a.m. on the day of his flight to Rome. That year also saw the publication of his critical anthology, *The Golden Book of Italian Poetry*, with a foreword by another old friend in England, G. M. Trevelyan of Cambridge. She kept closely in touch with still another friend who counted Lauro de Bosis as one of his 'heroes'—Romain Rolland in France, to whom she sent memorial relics of the poet together with copies of *Icaro* and *The Story of My Death*. It was at Ruth's instigation that Rolland wrote his introduction, titled 'Euphorion', for the French translation of *Icaro* that was made by Ferdinand Hérold (*'C'est mon honneur et mon devoir de raviver la flamme du souvenir sur la tombe in-connue du jeune frère de Shelley et de Mazzini'*). A further tribute to Lauro's memory came from Ruth Draper when she established at Harvard University the Lauro de Bosis

Lectureship in the History of Italian Civilization, first by an annual gift during the years 1933-8, but in 1938 with a permanent endowment. The first holder of the lectureship was Gaetano Salvemini, who now and later became one of Ruth's greatest friends in America and Italy: the distinguished historian who was one of the leaders in the cause to which Lauro de Bosis gave his life and who in New York became a member of the circle of friends of Italy in which he, Arturo Toscanini, and other exiles from Fascism were leading spirits and in whose work and faith Ruth was to participate for the remainder of her life. Gaetano Salvemini was the sole occupant of the chair at Harvard until his retirement in 1948, then succeeding himself as Lecturer Emeritus until 1954.[1] He remained one of Ruth's closest counsellors and confidants until her death. (His own was to come eight months after hers, on 6 September 1957.) She saw him last when she visited him in his retirement at Sorrento on her last trip to Italy in April 1956, and together they paid their final tribute to the poet who had been a source of love and inspiration in both their lives.

[1] Gaetano Salvemini, born Molfetta, Italy, 8 September 1873; teacher and professor successively at Palermo, Faenza, Lodi, Florence; Professor of Medieval and Modern History, University of Messina, 1901-8, University of Pisa, 1910-16, University of Florence, 1916-25; member of the Parliament of Italy, 1919-21; arrested by the Fascist authorities in 1925 and spent 36 days in prison; acquitted but resigned his professorship on 5 November 1925; exiled in France and England, 1925-30; Visiting Professor Harvard University, 1930; Yale University, 1931; naturalized as an American citizen 1940; Lauro de Bosis Lecturer in Italian Civilization, Harvard University, 1933-48, Emeritus, 1948-54. Returned to Italy 1954.

'This fierce spirit...a man quite without fear....But mere fearlessness that makes some men bravos was joined in him with a rectitude, a childlike innocence, a gaiety, a spontaneity, which never let him hesitate for even an instant between right and wrong; he simply didn't know that a choice existed. He was incapable of restraining himself in the presence of smugness or error. Ruth Draper, who died last winter, was largely responsible for the fact that Salvemini found physical sustenance here when his own country drove him out. She founded the Lauro de Bosis Lectureship at Harvard, which Salvemini held for some fifteen years. But intellectually and morally he would have survived without help anywhere and under any conditions. We must not forget him, one of the historians who live and make history as well as write it.'—Hamilton Fish Armstrong in *The New York Times*, Sunday, 15 September 1957.

XIII

The tragedy of October 1931 was a decisive crisis in Ruth Draper's life, perhaps its final turning-point. It was to be many weeks before she overcame the shock of it; she lived with the memory of it for years; but there could be no submission or surrender to it. Work became more urgent to her than ever. During the first three months of 1932 she moved with little rest from England to Scotland and Ireland on a new circuit of engagements. By May she was in Switzerland for programmes at Lausanne and Geneva; by June in Paris for a week at the Daunou; by July in England again. She returned to America in August by way of Canada for the autumn at Dark Harbor. In November and December she was in New York for two seasons at the Ritz Theatre and a series of benefits. By January she had returned to England, playing almost continuously until the end of May from Edinburgh and York to the St. James's Theatre in London. The next eight years were to be even more strenuously occupied and *mouvementé* than the twenty that had preceded them. Her characters had now become an inseparable part of her existence and consciousness. She enriched the old ones with new detail and feeling; she created new ones. Her repertory had expanded to almost forty items, all of them sealed in her memory as they had been from the beginning. It was many years before she reduced her texts to full manuscript form.

By this time she was established in her last permanent home in New York. In November 1928 she had moved to the apartment at 66 East 79th Street, between Madison and Park Avenues, which she now bought and made her residence for the remainder of her life. The Sargent portraits were hung between the windows of the long living-room; Paderewski's portrait by Burne-Jones faced them from the opposite wall; her books, with those that James, Adams, and other friends had inscribed to her, were assembled; keepsakes and tokens of her travels crowded the rooms; the piano, sofas, deep chairs, and fireside made a gathering-place for her friends. On the inner wall of the living-room there soon appeared a mural map of the world, painted by Stanley J. Rowland, thickly punctuated with stars for every city, country, and continent she had visited or played in. During the next quarter-century the stars were to cluster more thickly or spread to farther corners of the two hemispheres as her journeys carried her to continents, lands, and islands she was now to explore for the first time.

In early December of 1933 she sailed from New York for South Africa. Johannesburg welcomed her for a week of performances. Christmas was spent at Pretoria with the Governor General and Lady Clarendon. Engagements took her to Durban, East London, Port Elizabeth, Pietermaritzburg, and Cape Town. She flew from Johannesburg to Zambesi to see the Victoria Falls; gave performances at Bulawayo and Salisbury; flew northward into Kenya for a show at Nairobi; then on to Uganda and Khartoum; and so by steamer down the Nile to see the temples at Luxor and thus advance to Cairo, where she entertained at the British Embassy at a party for the King of Spain. A swing to Alexandria, Jerusalem, Baalbek, Damascus, Palmyra, and Beirut followed before she took ship for Marseilles, went on to Paris, and so arrived in London for a season at the Haymarket. After three months in England she sailed once more for America and Dark Harbor.

The next three years were divided between America and Europe on her usual round of engagements, but they too carried her afield: in February 1935 to Mexico and Cuba; in the spring of 1936 to Sweden, Norway, Denmark, Holland, and Belgium, with recitals all the way from Stockholm, Gothenburg, Malmo, Oslo, and Copenhagen, to The Hague, Amsterdam, Rotterdam, and Brussels. In March 1937, after her American tour had carried her across the country to California, she sailed to Hawaii for a month, then working her way back across the States to New York. By November she was back in London for a month at the Vaudeville Theatre. On the last day of the year she boarded a ship at Marseilles with her friend Mary Erdman for eight of the most spectacular months she had yet undertaken.[1]

Ceylon came first, with performances at Colombo and Kandy and motor-trips, picnics, and excursions through the island and its mountains. On 24 January she sailed across to India and Madras. Performances (invariably marked 'sold out' in her notebook) followed in Madras and Mysore, at Bombay and Agra, at Delhi, Benares, Calcutta, and Darjeeling. The local Governors were often her hosts; there were trips and excursions almost every day—to the Seven Pagodas, to the great dam at Krishnarajasagara, to Bangalore and Jaipur. She dined with the poet Sarojini Naidu, visited and thrilled to the Ajanta Caves and their sculptures, and on 25–27 February, while at Darjeeling, 'saw the whole Kanchenjunga range in magnificent morning sunlight' and 'Mount Everest incredible and overwhelming at dawn from the terrace of the Tiger Hotel'. On 1 March she flew from Calcutta to Burma— Rangoon and Mandalay—to perform in theatres, for local charities, or 'for the 61st Rifles'; thence to Bangkok; on the 12th by train and motor to Angkor and its ruins; on the 17th by air to Penang; on the 20th by boat to Singapore for four performances; again by boat to Java and Batavia for several more; then by air along the arc of the Netherlands Indies to Surabaya and to Bali for still others in the intervals of her 'indescribable enchantment by the Paradise of these islands'. On 7 April she returned to Surabaya and set sail for Australia, where she landed on 20 April.

[1] R. D. kept a consecutive journal of her travels during the first eight months of 1938, beginning with Marseilles and Egypt, and so through Ceylon, India, the East, Australia, New Zealand, and her homeward passage across the Pacific to California. It is amplified by quantities of more fully descriptive letters to her family and friends. The present brief account of these journeys has been drawn from these, but with very slight indication of the explorations she made, the people she met, her programmes and audiences, and the impression the eastern and south Pacific worlds made on her. The 1922 and 1938 diaries appear to be the most detailed journals she kept.

PLATE XI

Ruth Draper as Honorary Doctor of Laws
University of Edinburgh 6 July 1951
Photograph by Vandamm, New York

PLATE XII

Ruth Draper with her costumes: 1951

A photograph taken in her dressing room at the Theatre Royal, Brighton, summer 1951,
after receiving her decoration as Commander of the British Empire from
H.M. King George VI

Her three months in Australia began at Brisbane with a week's performances ('Lovely country, unattractive city, kind people, cozy hotel, beautiful drives, fine audiences'). On 29 April she flew along the coast and over the mountains to Sydney for two weeks at the Theatre Royal ('Sold out every night and matinée, fine reviews, many hundreds turned away'). Newcastle came next, followed by a month at the Comedy Theatre in Melbourne, three weeks at the Theatre Royal in Adelaide, a visit to Canberra where she stayed at Government House with Lord and Lady Huntingfield, and a return for two weeks to Sydney. The eager freshness, hospitality, and enthusiasm of the Australians were inspiriting; she loved the great reaches of the open country and grazing lands, where she walked over the soft grasses or roamed for hours by the sea. On 27 July she sailed from Sydney for New Zealand; landed at Auckland on the 29th; and spent three weeks on its islands, exploring the wonders of landscape and mountains, making excursions in many directions, and performing continuously in Wellington, Christchurch, Dunedin, and Auckland until she sailed away on the *Mariposa* on 22 August.

The fortnight's crossing of the Pacific brought a pause at the Fiji Islands, where a matinée had been arranged at the Suva Town Hall; but since the single performance had been sold out for a month in advance, the director of the Fiji Broadcasting Company asked her permission to broadcast the programme over Station ZJV, so that it was heard, as her hostess Lady Ellis later told, by 'people living on lonely coconut and sugar plantations, in isolated island homes, in Tonga and Samoa, and even [on] yachts and ships at sea', with half the takings going into a Ruth Draper Benevolent Fund for needy cases in the islands and the other half to the Suva Cottage Home for the Aged. There was a stop at Pago Pago, another at Honolulu, a landing at Los Angeles on 5 September, a flight homeward, and by mid-September Ruth was back at Dark Harbor for the autumn once more.

1939 began at the Little Theatre in New York and was then divided between England, Paris, London again, and Islesboro for the autumn. She had lingered in England until August and reached America within a few days of the outbreak of the war. For six years the world catastrophe was to close Europe to her, but the six years meant continuous tours back and forth across the States and Canada, her theatre engagements alternating with scores of benefit performances for the American and Canadian Red Cross, for the French-Canadian War Relief, for the British Red Cross, and in camps, canteens, and hospitals. The war and its havoc consumed her mind and emotions during these years. She kept in touch with her many friends in the stricken countries and sent them food and help continuously. It brought the death of her nephew Sanders Draper in the Royal Air Force in March 1943. She made Dark Harbor a refuge for as many friends and exiles as it would hold during her summer and autumn sojourns. The news of the invasion of France and the siege of Britain reached her at a great distance, for she opened the decade of the 1940's by making her first trip to South America in the late spring of 1940, sailing from New York on 4 May with Artur and Nela Rubinstein and Professor and Mme Henri Focillon as her shipmates. May, June, July, and early August were thus spent in another newly discovered world—in Brazil and Rio de Janeiro; at Montevideo in Uruguay; at Buenos Aires, Rosario, and Cordoba in Argentina; thus over the Andes by air to Chile for programmes in Santiago and Valparaiso; up the coast to Arequipa and Lima in Peru, and to Quito in Ecuador, and finally, in mid-August northward and home-ward once more, by way of Barranquilla, Panama, and Miami, to New York and to Maine.

In December 1944 she reached her sixtieth birthday. The thought of easing her life and retiring from her work had begun to cross her mind or appear in her letters. But it no sooner appeared than it was dismissed. Her work was her existence. There were more calls on her help and aid now than ever, with so many of her friends in England and Europe to think of. Her energy hardly knew a moment's flagging or uncertainty. She became eager to see Europe again as soon as it should become accessible to travellers. She felt as strong as she had thirty years before, and she began to count on the end of the war to reopen the larger scene of her work and travels.

XIV

Her friends and family, her travels, her social activity, her public interests—these filled her days, but at their centre there remained from first to last her work: the characters she had created and the art by which she made them the focus of her existence. She carried them with her in her memory wherever she went, ready to spring into visible, audible life at a moment's notice, a living part of her conscious experience and perhaps its most vital reality.

In several of her last interviews she was asked what she counted as the essential elements of her work. She gave them as three: curiosity and energy in herself, and imagination in her audience. On the first she said:

What I had as a child I've never lost—the child's ability to *pretend*: to *be* what he imagines he is. If you give yourself completely to what you pretend you are, you will convince other people that it exists, and only then. Children do this spontaneously, without self-consciousness. Most people lose the power as they grow up, but a few do not. You must believe so thoroughly and instinctively in what you imagine that there cannot possibly arise the question that it is something imagined. Your curiosity must take you outside of yourself so that you cease to exist and the thing you pretend you are takes your place.

And on the second: 'It simply happens that I've been very fortunate. I've always had very good health and vitality. One *must* have vitality to project one's self into an imagined life and then to project this across the footlights into the minds of the audience. Happily I've always had it. Without it my work would have come to nothing. It must somehow always be there, to draw on at a moment's notice, so that any fatigue, distraction, or other preoccupation can be disregarded and the thing to be done becomes the only thing to do. All actors must have vitality. The moment it fails them they lose their power to transform and project themselves.'

But [she continued] it is the audience that must supply the imagination. All I can do myself is to make the audience give it to me. I suppose my work needs more of this than most acting does, for I give people no help in the way of scenery, lighting, or stage effects. Long ago a man who knew a great deal about the theatre told me that the old advice to actors 'You must put it over' was wrong. What is really important is not to put anything 'over', but to bring the audience up onto the stage and into the scene with you. It is they who must give you even more than you give them in the way of imagination and creative power. Once this was the great fact of the drama. It needed no artificial effects; it simply brought the actor and the audience together and fused their minds and feelings in an imagined reality. The great trouble today is that so much entertainment—cinema, radio, television—makes people passive, deadens their imagination. It gives them so much that it leaves them with nothing to give in return. In the older drama—Oriental, Greek, Medieval, Shakespearean—the audience had to supply what wasn't there. The poet or dramatist gave the cues, and of course his genius lay in giving the right ones; but it was from the audience that the experience of truth had to come. What has encouraged me most in my work these later years is that young people who have never seen anything but films or television find, when they see me, that they are expected to share in what I create, and to their amazement they discover that they can do so. They find a thrill in discovering that they too can create, that they too have imaginations. They give me the credit for it, but they are not right when they do so. What holds their attention most is what they themselves are able to give.[1]

[1] Several of R. D.'s interviews are drawn on here, particularly a lengthy one she recorded for Station WFMT in Chicago in February 1955. The above quotations are based on this recording and several printed discussions, supplemented by further notes of conversations with her.

Ruth Draper never analysed her art in terms much more elaborate than these; she wrote no essays on her work. But she frequently singled out the essentials of her craft and knew they were what she had relied on from her nursery beginnings. Her craft was inevitably much more calculated and complex than she allowed. Into it went years of study, self-training, self-criticism, rehearsal, revision, and scrupulous testing of her effects. She calculated her words, phrasings, accents, movements, and gestures tirelessly. Frequently a telling phrase or detail would occur to her unexpectedly, in the midst of a performance. Some of these might be caught and retained; some of the most effective, she discovered to her dismay, would be completely forgotten and lost by the time the next performance arrived. Her sketches grew and enriched themselves as she acted them. On the basic idea or outline she played innumerable variations of wording and phrasing to the end of her life. Even as now printed the monologues are only approximations of what she made of them when she spoke, acted, and spontaneously elaborated their texts in actual performance. 'I have to live with a sketch for two, three, or five years before I am sure it has something in it,' she said. 'That is probably why I have added so few to my programmes these later years. Once they used to come to me more rapidly. Now I have to be content with those I've already written and performed. I'm always surprised that people want to see them over and over.' Yet she was undoubtedly right when she said that all her sketches rested on a few essential elements and most of all on a simple, instinctive ability to 'pretend'; and that this instinct was something she had been born with—unaccountable, inexplicable, unanalysable, but always and unfailingly there. 'I know no way of explaining it. One must simply *become* the person one depicts.'

Her feat of 'becoming' her characters was achieved long before modern theories or disciplines of acting had advanced into their present science and complexity, and well before the

modern stage had taken over the 'method' promulgated by
Stanislavsky and his disciples: the principle by which the
actor derives 'his characterization from his own personal
experience', imagining 'a given situation so strongly that he
can "feel" himself in it'.[1] Ruth Draper certainly never conceived of herself as an exponent of 'method'; she would
doubtless have repudiated the term. But she was a pioneer
in this style of modern acting long before it became a cult
in the contemporary theatre, and she would certainly have
agreed to another of its tenets: that the actor's 'experience
being necessarily limited, he must also feel it legitimate to
derive at second hand from the real experience of other
people, but [never] from other acting'. Of the two major
traditions of acting—the stylistic or rhetorical, which derives
from long-established, formally evolved principles of mannerism and technique, and which emphasizes devices
external to the actor's personality; and the naturalistic, which
issues empirically from the inner constitution of the character portrayed and from the actor's identification of himself
with that character—she represented from the outset of her
career the second. Her doing so could never have been a
matter of choice. It was dictated by her instinctive response
to the life and people around her, her natively unconscious
powers of sympathy and *rapport*. However conscious her
skill became in its later evolution, it was on that original
instinct for 'becoming' that her artistry relied, and it was her
special fortune that she never lost it.

The instinct was native, intuitive, ineradicable. It was the
factor that held and transfixed the attention of her audiences;
and her ability to set it into convincing operation with the
first words she uttered and in the most unlikely of circumstances—on a stage, in a drawing-room, in theatres small or
large, on a table in an Oxford dining-hall, on a ship, or in
an army barracks—provided at least half the fascination of

---

[1] So defined by Tyrone Guthrie, *The New York Times Magazine*,
15 September 1957, pp. 23 ff. The following quotation is also his.

her performances. But there was inevitably another source of
fascination in them: the factor of paradox which has always
figured in the actor's art or in any theory of it. Diderot gave
it its classic definition in the *Paradoxe sur le Comédien* when
he discussed the discrepancy between the actor's own feelings
and those he is assigned to portray—between real emotion
and simulated emotion. Every conception of histrionic action has had to admit the problem, whether in terms of style
and rhetoric or in terms of naturalism. Certainly one of
the sources of Ruth Draper's peculiar magic was that she
reduced the problem to its essentials—gave it the most concentrated of possible demonstrations. 'I suppose it is the
speed of my transformations that impresses people', she
once remarked; and anyone who remembers the lightning
quickness with which she changed, in a work like 'Three
Generations in a Court of Domestic Relations', 'An English
House-Party', or 'Three Women and Mr. Clifford', from an
immigrant Jewish grandmother to a life-broken daughter and
then to a fervent, life-loving young granddaughter; or from
an eager young girl out of an English parsonage to a bored
aristocratic horsewoman; or from an efficient secretary to a
cynical wife and thus to the world-wise grace of Mrs. Mallory,
must recall the startling force of these transformations. Any
one of her programmes offered these tests of physical and
emotional legerdemain. The silly débutante was as authentic
when Ruth Draper was sixty as she had been when she was
thirty years younger; the old woman in Maine, Ireland, or
Italy was transformed in a moment into the Parisian actress
or dressmaker; the New York matron at her Italian lesson
dissolved into a miner's wife in Scotland, the lady of the
Spanish court into the girl in a railway station on the
Western plains. The tongue that spoke Bronx slang, highland Scots, cultivated English, or a plain New England
accent became, incredibly, the tongue that two minutes later
shaped the dialect of an old Italian beggar, a French that
passed muster with an exacting French audience, or the

convincing gutturals of a totally imaginary Slavic, Swedish, or Corsican dialect. This was paradox made actual, physical, audible. And it was never so impressive as when, at curtain-call, all these imagined roles and realities were suddenly dropped, discarded, put away, and the actress who had created them appeared to take her bow—the lame, bent, or life-worn woman, or the eager and passionate girl, reckless of the pathos, absurdity, or indignity she had been called on to embody, becoming the dignified, self-possessed figure of Ruth Draper herself.

It is a commonplace among singers that a programme of songs or *Lieder* is more difficult to sustain than a performance in opera, however demanding. The opera singer has a single role to portray, a continuous and consistent effect to achieve, other singers to support and collaborate with him, scenery and lighting to enhance his effort, an orchestra and a conductor to carry him forward on the enveloping tide of the music. The interpreter of *Lieder* has his accompanist but is otherwise alone with the poem and the song, taxed by the subtlest gradations of meaning and emotion, and obliged to change the mood and colour of his voice from moment to moment. Ruth Draper worked in an even greater isolation: she had no accompaniment to rely on. Her voice, incredibly unworn by decades of incessant use on the stage or off it, had to make meaning and music simultaneously—had to communicate and express, speak its lines and conjure its atmosphere, at a stroke.

No one who ever saw or heard her can forget this astonishing fusion of effects she achieved; no one who, like the present writer, watched her from the wings, saw her take an exit and then, hardly drawing a breath, make a new entrance in a totally different role, physically and vocally transformed, can overcome his awe at the speed and pace of her transformations. A lifetime's training and expertise went into their effectiveness, of course. But that never lessened the sense of the miraculous they conveyed, or of the unflagging energy by

which they were conjured. This is what Ruth Draper meant
when she spoke of 'vitality' as the physical and psychological
basis of her achievement. And a further factor of the incredible
appeared in the thoroughness with which she dismissed the
fact of time and age. 'The dramas of memory', Aldous
Huxley has said, 'are always Hamlet in modern dress.' The
Ruth Draper who portrayed the 'Débutante at a Dance', the
young wife in 'Three Breakfasts', or the young girl in 'Three
Generations' was obviously an older woman in 1956 than she
was when first seen in these roles in 1921. The early frock by
Worth, Chanel, or Lanvin had changed into the graceful
brown gown by Valentina; the face, coiffure, and figure of
young womanhood had altered to the firmer and maturer
(though still remarkably youthful) appearance of seventy.
Yet the lapse of time seemed to count for nothing. The
moment the voice, the laugh, and the gestures were summoned up, the intervening thirty-five years dropped away
and the listener saw once more the girl of 1921. Equally there
seemed little difference between the old Irishwoman of
County Kerry or the hostess at the English bazaar or the
Dalmatian peasant of the early sketches and the same characters of almost four decades later. There have been many
astonishing feats of time-obliteration among actors. This,
certainly, was one of them; and it is doubtful if any actor of
Ruth Draper's time or any other has been able to maintain
so complete and remarkable a continuity of physical and
illusory effect over so long a span of years.

She was heard at times to express dismay or vexation at
her inadequacy in a given performance. 'I didn't do at all well
tonight,' she would say; 'the right thing didn't come.' The
inadequacy was more likely to be felt by herself than by her
auditors; but inevitably she was as subject as any actor is to
the abeyance of the *grâce* on which he relies for his success
and whose occasional failure led a great French actor to say
'*Ce soir le Dieu n'est pas venu.*'[1] Yet few members of her

[1] Mounet-Sully, quoted by Michael Redgrave, *Mask or Face:*

profession, and perhaps none of those who worked in isolation
as she did, could have felt as confident of the god's punctual
descent. This too was part of her vitality—of her power of
spontaneous response to the moment, her virtuosity of mood
and emotion, her unhesitating willingness to take on every
assignment her working-life called on her to take. Once, in
an early moment of doubt or fatigue in Madrid in 1922, when
she faced a series of particularly taxing performances, she
wrote to a friend: 'I'll write again after the rest of my shows
are over. I shall be glad when they are. I don't know what
strange power drives me to make such a terrific test of myself. I hope it all serves some good end, for it can't be termed
unalloyed pleasure!' Such moments are rare in her letters
and they must have become rare in her life. She was too
dedicated to her work to permit them often. What lay at the
basis of her success was more than her confidence in herself,
her faith in her work, even her sense of vocation. It was the
fact that her romantic feeling for her *métier* existed in combination with an unquestioning sense of the seriousness of
her work and with her unflinching refusal to shirk its
demands. Like all successful artists she was more than a con-
juror, an exhibitionist, or a temperament. She was what the
force of her character and ambition made her: a thorough-
going professional.

XV

The monologues themselves were fairly defined in their
range and contrasts from their earliest years. Humour and

Reflections in an Actor's Mirror (London, 1958), p. 95, who says further:
'Surely it is persuasion which comes first in the actor's armoury. He must
persuade the audience to suspend its disbelief....It is not that when the
God does not come and there is no dispensation of grace the performance
is necessarily bad. It may be good, even exciting, and it may have wonderful
moments, but it can lack that essence which Stendhal, writing on the
subject of love, called crystallization. We therefore do not fall in love
with it, we are not swept off our feet, however much we may admire.
The responsibility for creating this love affair must, of course, be the
actor's.'

satire were prominent at the outset ('A Class in Soul Culture', 'A Quiet Morning in Bed', 'A Board of Managers Meeting'), but pathos and hardship, the grim and sombre aspects of life, were equally so ('A Dalmatian Peasant', 'A Miner's Wife', 'Three Generations', 'Vive la France! 1916'). Their spectrum ran from farce to tragedy, from absurdity to violence, and Ruth Draper was to maintain these contrasts throughout her career. Most of her followers among monologuists were to emphasize comedy, as Beatrice Herford had done; few were to venture into Ruth's essays in starker drama and realism.

It appears to be a tradition in this form of entertainment that comic effects are more viable than serious. The American humorists or monologuists of the nineteenth century—Artemus Ward, Josh Billings, P. V. Nasby, Mark Twain—specialized in them; so did the Englishmen who worked as solo performers—Corney Grain, Little Tich, George Grossmith, Arthur Roberts, George Robey. This was in its day a venerable and standard line of humour; it had its valid connexions with folk wit and satire; descending to the twentieth century from the popular minstrel, variety, or vaudeville stages of the pioneers, it has been kept alive chiefly in vaudeville and revue wherever these now debased or adulterated forms of theatre survive. There was, however, another tradition—the elocutionary exhibitions of the Victorian reciters in both England and America; and here the business was usually debased to the bogus ventriloquism and rhetorical bombast of the old melodramatic theatre. Dickens was probably the Victorian 'reader' who, following such pioneers as Charles Mathews and Albert Smith, combined both traditions in their classic proportions. It took his particular combination of popular literary texts, comic genius, histrionic eloquence, and lurid or sentimental appeal to make the dramatic 'reading' a huge success in his age; and in America Mark Twain and his fellow-humorists soon rivalled him on their own ground. But what these vogues of humour and melodrama descended to in the vaudeville, Lyceum, or

Chatauqua circuits of a later day easily accounts for the disrepute into which the solo reading or recitation fell by the time the twentieth century opened. It had become either an elocutionary stunt or a form of humorous exhibitionism. It continued to have its talented exponents on the popular stage, but they survived either as singing performers like Marie and Alice Lloyd or Alfred Chevalier, or as satirists and yarners of the day's news or public events and foibles—Grossmith, Grain, Roberts, Will Rogers.

The dramatic monologue was in doubtful repute when Ruth Draper set out on her career; even in vaudeville its vogue was waning; and she must have begun her work convinced that something new in the way of taste, skill, and refinement was needed to make a serious art of it. She evidently began her cultivation of the genre as its conscious critic. It may be allowed that she did not entirely repudiate its Victorian ancestry. There is a visible line of descent from 'Mugby Junction' or a popular thriller like 'Asleep at the Switch' to her own 'In a Railway Station on the Western Plains'. Her 'Miner's Wife' is in the Dickensian tradition, and so are some of her satires of society and 'culture'. But most of her sketches are explicit in their repudiation of exaggerated caricature and melodrama; she early found the knack of applying irony or understatement to the elements in which she dealt. No artist works in a void. She knew very well that she had her popular appeal to make, and that her predecessors had defined its essentials. But she was fortunate to arrive on the scene when certain performers had prepared the way for the refinements she was to cultivate. Beatrice Herford had done something to span the gap between Victorian extravagance and modern irony. So had a mimic like Cissie Loftus, with her brilliant caricatures of stage types, and so on an even higher level of dramatic and vocal impersonation had Yvette Guilbert, with the rich tradition of the Parisian *café-concert* and sardonic revue to support her genius in realism and comedy. These can be counted as Ruth Draper's immediate predecessors; and at times, in her folk-song *pastiches*, Balkan parodies, or broader caricatures, her derivation from them is clear.

She drew at the outset, however, from sources quite different from these. Her childish versions of the little Jewish tailor or the German governess derived from no theatrical source. A direct, intuitive observation of life and character was her original impulse; and though she was often to say that she never based her monologues directly on living originals—that whatever hints or cues she took from actual people, she always developed her sketches independently of their models—her art was essentially one of acute empathy, insight, and recognition, not (except in a few obvious *tours de force*) of deliberate invention or fantasy. She was at heart a realist, a recorder of social and moral fact, a reader of the common human destiny. This curiosity must have been fundamental and continuous in her imagination. It accounted for the accuracy of her detail, the keenness of her verbal and oral fidelity, the sharpness of her wit and compassion. Even these might have remained matters of surface notation and record, as they usually are among monologuists, had it not been for her extraordinary means of conveying and realizing them in her speech and action. Her sharpness of eye and ear were obvious; her sincerity of personal insight could be read in her words; but neither of these was enough to produce the final reality of her portraits. That reality was physical—in the superb mobility of her face and body, in her spontaneity of gesture and movement, in the art with which she could discard her own dignity and take on without self-consciousness or embarrassment the poses and motions of her characters; above all, in the authenticity of her voice and of the spectacular range of accents and intonations through which she could carry it.

Often she spoke in her own voice—the cultivated American or New York speech she was born to; and her skill in tuning that speech to humorous or ironical uses was as impressive as her critical skill in treating the life most familiar to her— New York manners, caste attitudes, snobbery and social pretension—with satirical or destructive effect. But New York speech could equally mean the talk of working-girls, Jewish families, or Slavic immigrants; her American voice ranged from New England to the South or the western plains; her English speech shifted without hesitation from the aristocratic voice to the Cockney, Scottish, or Irish; her French from the Rue de la Paix or the Théâtre Français to the Breton peasant. Remarkable as her realism of body and gesture could be, it was above all her voice that expressed her essential insight and produced the accent and atmosphere of truth for her dramas. It was one of the most astonishing instruments of expression in the theatre of her time. It became supremely effective in such passages as the American tourist's earnestly rambling pedagogy in the 'Church in Italy'; in Mrs. Clifford's selfish vacuities; in the English lady's effect of summarizing her whole life's history in 'Opening a Bazaar'; in the stifled anguish of the wife in 'Le Retour de l'Aveugle'. It became superb in what may certainly be singled out as one of her masterpieces, 'On a Porch in a Maine Coast Village', where the old Maine woman, stationary in her rocking-chair, slowly spread around her the living atmosphere of a long life's rigour and endurance, its idiosyncrasy as well as its classic fortitude, with the rocky coast, the bleak village, the patience of hardship, the sea air and sea wind, blending in an effect of irresistible truth. And from such passages it was only a step to those that said almost as much—the moments of dumb suffering or silence: the young Frenchwoman of 1916, the mother in 'Three Generations', the Dalmatian peasant in the New York hospital, the silent woman at the end of 'In a Church in Italy'.

One of Ruth Draper's strongest admirers among the New York critics, Brooks Atkinson, once said that 'The surface of her art is not distinguished. Her quality comes from within.' The impression of her surfaces, now emphasized by the printed texts, may be what he says of it. As a dramatic writer Ruth Draper was neither a stylist nor a discoverer of original situations, neither a creative imagination of strong inventive powers nor 'an expert in the psychological wilderness'. There is a sense in which her portraits were simple, basic, primary, even—like so much in drama—primitive. Their appeal was the appeal of the familiar, the casual, the average and the recognizable. When Henry James wrote his monologue for her he tried his best to sketch in broad strokes, but the strokes were involved and entangled in stylization and literary effects—obviously unactable by a person of Ruth Draper's selective and simplifying intuition. That intuition was what was particularly unerring in her own monologues. It must be remembered, in reading them now, that they were never conceived or written as literary compositions. They were vehicles for acting, and specifically for her own kind of act- ing—inseparable from what she made of them in the living form of her physical and vocal impersonation. Their art lay in their accuracy in cutting to the quick of experience. This may at times have resulted in the simplification that produces the ludicrous cartoon or caricature. Oftener it resulted in the crystallization that produces a classic insight, penetration, and essence.

It was then that Ruth Draper revealed the fundamental import of her work—her compassionate feeling for life and experience under whatever appearances they present them- selves, absurd or noble; her inclusive sympathy with the humanity that is vital, inexplicable, persisting under the doom of its mere existence, and therefore to be recognized, valued, and loved. 'It is comparatively easy to debunk the rich and the luxurious,' said Mr. Atkinson, 'but Miss Draper does not leave them destitute. For even her satirical sketches... have a tone of forgiveness running through them. She has a heart, and she never closes it completely.' And he added that 'the simple people who appear in her sketches she endows with a certain divinity'. It was this unforced effect of divinity, glory, transcendence, that crowned her work. It was her highest tribute to life.

She kept a series of notebooks in which she wrote down her favourite poems and prose passages—the poems by Shakespeare, Keats, Shelley, and Baudelaire she took most to heart; *aperçus* or paragraphs of prose that had seized her attention. One day she took down one of these books to show a visitor, opened it, and struck the page. 'That', she said, 'is one of the greatest things that have ever been written about art.' It was Conrad's preface to *The Nigger of the 'Narcissus'*, copied out in longhand. It was easy to understand why it had become one of her cardinal texts. Its most famous sentences are a concentrated statement of the principles that had guided her in her own work. 'My task which I am trying to achieve is...to make you hear, to make you feel—it is, before all, to make you *see*. That—and no more, and it is everything':

> To snatch in a moment of courage, from the remorseless rush of time, a passing phase of life, is only the beginning of the task. The task approached in tenderness and faith is to hold up unquestioningly, without choice and without fear, the rescued fragment before all eyes in the light of a sincere mood. It is to show its vibration, its colour, its form; and through its movement, its form, and its colour, reveal the substance of its truth—disclose its inspiring secret: the stress and passion within the core of each convincing moment.

She had found the rule of her art even more briefly and classically stated elsewhere. When an English admirer asked her, in 1931, to contribute an inscription to his autograph-book she wrote:

> 'To hold, as 'twere, the mirror up to nature.'
> I always hope that my work interprets these words.

It became the opinion of her witnesses, as nearly unanimous as such things can be, that her work did so. One day in the early twenties Mrs. Patrick Campbell persuaded Ruth to

PLATE XIII

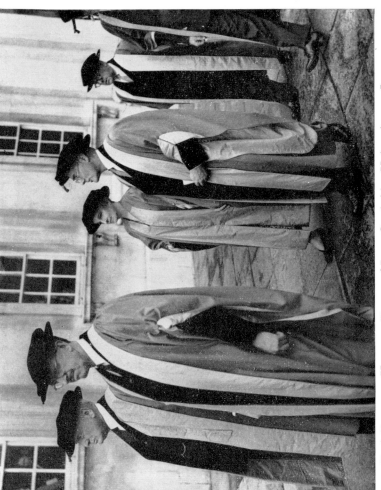

Ruth Draper as Honorary Doctor of Law, Cambridge University: 10 June 1954
Others in the procession are, from left to right: Lord Goddard, The Marquess of Salisbury,
Sir Edward Bridges, and Professor Sir Charles Dodds

Photograph by Reuter

perform some of her monologues for Bernard Shaw. 'Have
you ever seen such acting?' she demanded when Ruth had
finished. 'That's not acting,' Shaw replied. 'That's life.'

XVI

The year the war ended, 1945, kept Ruth Draper busy in
America, touring her old circuit from the East coast to the
West, down the Pacific states from Vancouver and Victoria
to San Francisco and Los Angeles, and through the South.
But early in 1946, after a six years' absence from Europe, she
sailed on the *Queen Elizabeth* on 28 February, bound for
England once more. She opened her London season at the
Apollo Theatre in March, and found her English audiences,
still faithful after their six years of hardship and devastation,
as eager to welcome her as ever. 'All the people who are Ruth
Draper returned to London last night', said one of the
reviewers. 'To see the familiar parade again was rather like
flipping through the thumbed pages of a well-loved book.'
The welcome rang wherever she appeared, from Cambridge
and Oxford to Edinburgh and Glasgow. It sounded anew
when she went on to the Continent in mid-summer—to
Switzerland, down to Italy to visit her old shrines and friends,
and so by October up to Holland for performances in six
cities, to Brussels, to Paris for a week at the Théâtre des
Champs-Élysées, and to London for another month at the
Apollo in November. Back in New York she opened at the
Empire on 28 December and ran through February. She was
now sixty-two; the last decade of her life had begun. There
was to be no abatement of her work or travels. Once more she
crossed the Atlantic every year, as much an 'institution' as
ever, her transatlantic world still held in the palm of her
hand whenever she took the stage and cast her spell.

Whatever her triumphs in the twenties or during her
world-circling tours of the thirties, this final decade perhaps
brought her greater. Communities that had not seen her for
years discovered that she was someone they had missed and

greeted her like a long-lost friend. Audiences that had come
to believe she had retired and had made her a subject for
nostalgic reminiscence were amazed to find that she could
still be a girl of seventeen as convincingly as when they had
seen her thirty years before. In America, where the increasing difficulty and expense of staging seasons in public
theatres had prevented her from visiting certain of the larger
cities for a decade, she was reclaimed as a classic. What
delighted her most was to discover that young people who
had not been born when she came into her first success and
who had grown up schooled in tastes for wholly different
forms of amusement became her spellbound 'fans'. There
was an autumnal touch in her appearance now. Her hair had
slightly silvered; she fell into the poses of her older women
more naturally than she once had; her figure had taken on an
air of patrician dignity. But the 'magic' every reviewer unfailingly found in her art was as punctual as ever, and the
young girls of her sketches, still speaking the language of an
earlier generation, came to life as easily as they had when she
had been only twice, instead of four times, their age. 'Miss
Draper is discovering,' said one New York reporter, 'that
grandmothers from her audiences of the past are being taken
to see her by their grandchildren—as somebody new!'

A new generation of critics now saluted her. Many of her
old admirers in the newspapers and magazines—Woollcott,
Percy Hammond, Stark Young, Robert Littell, Heywood
Broun in America, Desmond MacCarthy, E. V. Lucas, James
Agate, Owen Seaman, S. K. Ratcliffe in England—had
retired or disappeared, but their successors took up the
applause. One of them, Kenneth Tynan, writing in the
London *Evening Standard* on 23 May 1952, spoke for most of
them when he said:

I am sure that what happened to me at the Criterion Theatre
on Tuesday night was happening to very few other people in the
house. I was seeing Ruth Draper for the first time. The rest of her
audience were annual loyalists, ancient friends of her art; for

some of them, I afterwards discovered, she had all but ruined the pleasures of normal playgoing, since her large supporting cast, which exists only at her mind's fingertips, is so much more satisfactory than any which makes the vulgar mistake of being visible.

I cannot content myself with a few perfunctory references to the familiar, inimitable *etcetera* with which she presents her well-loved gallery of *etceteras*; she must have enough notices of that kind to paper a palace. I want to declare Miss Draper open to the new generation of playgoers, and to trample on their suspicions, which I once shared, that she might turn out to be a museum-piece, ripe for the dust-sheet and oblivion. She is, on the contrary, about as old-fashioned and mummified as spring, and as I watched her perform her thronging monologues the other night, I could only conclude that this was the best and most modern group acting I had ever seen....She works her miracles benignly and unfussed....I have an idea that, at the back of her mind, Miss Draper is hoping still to find a company of actors skilful enough to stand up to comparison with the accuracy, tact, and wisdom of her technique. She is actually doing her contemporaries a great kindness by not exposing them to such a hazard.

So the years turned in their familiar grooves. In New York she had seasons on her old stages—Empire, Vanderbilt, Bijou, Playhouse. In London she was back at the Criterion, the Haymarket, the Globe, the Duke of York's, the St. Martin's. Her nephew Paul joined her in both America and England for some of these seasons, and their programmes were divided between his dancing and her sketches. In May 1950 she returned to the Œuvre in Paris, ten years after Lugné-Poe's death, and paid her last tribute to their old association. Holland welcomed her in 1946, 1948, 1950; the Scandinavian countries in 1950; Italy in 1946, 1948, 1950, 1954.

Dark Harbor invariably called her back for the end of summer or the brilliant weeks of the early Maine autumn, and the beloved house was filled with friends, American and European, children of all ages, travellers from distant countries, survivors of the war, members of her family. For the children or her young relatives her affection and energy overflowed in every direction. For one of them, a few years earlier, we find her drawing up a list of *Things To Do!* during the long Dark Harbor summer days; it runs through more than fifty items, from 'Reading', 'Writing letters', 'Drawing', 'Painting', 'Scrabble', 'Bagatelle or ninepins', and 'Picking balsam for pillows', through 'Western jetty, rowing', 'Canoeing, sailing, or bathing', 'Swinging in the hammock', 'Do exercises for back and shoulders', 'Walk to Village for mail and papers', 'Pick raspberries and blackberries', to 'Pick flowers', 'Get tidy for meals', 'Clip twigs off trees and paths', 'Put away croquet mallets and balls', and 'Go to bed!!!' A war-time letter from Dark Harbor to Miss Martha Draper in New York begins: 'Little John Salmond is practising Bach so beautifully in the next room that I want to cry,' and continues with detailed reports on the other children then under her roof and wing. Now, in the years of peace, the old Maine haven continued to call and comfort all who came to it during Ruth's sojourns or during her absences. It had become more than ever her own haven of peace and comfort, her closest tie with the distant past when her mother had built it and gathered her clan around her more than fifty years before.

Twice, in 1951 and 1954, she was billed as giving her 'farewell season'. The critics and reviewers protested in a body; interviewers pressed her for a retraction; and she followed a classic tradition of the stage by exercising her right to change her mind: 'Well—possibly not.' The moment she secretly dreaded could be deferred: 'It hasn't quite come yet!' she told an old friend. Like her ancestors of the profession—Mrs. Siddons, Bernhardt, Duse, Ellen Terry, Nazimova, Mrs. Fiske—she reserved a right as boasted among actresses as among their more stalwart *confrères*. Her audiences could rest assured. Her bookings went on. The word 'farewell' was dropped from the placards of her 1954 seasons at the Vanderbilt in New York and at the Duke of York's Theatre in London. It did not reappear when she began 1955 with Paul Draper at the Bijou or opened her 1955 London season in

June at the St. Martin's. There would be no retirement, no 'farewell season'. Not yet.

An extra-curricular activity much engaged her during these post-war years—one that served as her tribute to one of her oldest literary devotions. On her return to England in 1946 she had been approached by Mr. Neville Rogers, then a young R.A.F. officer, to see if she could do anything to revive interest in the Keats-Shelley Memorial Association and contribute to its work in restoring the graves in the Protestant Cemetery in Rome and the Memorial House in the Piazza di Spagna. She responded to his appeal at once, sought the help of Arthur Houghton on her return to New York, became President of the Keats-Shelley Association of America, and gave her support to its allied societies in England and Italy. In collaboration with her colleagues, Lady Crewe, Dorothy Hewlett, and Mr. Rogers in England and Mabel Steele at Harvard, she shared in the work of the *Keats-Shelley Memorial Bulletin*, helped raise an endowment for the maintenance of the graves and the library in Piazza di Spagna, and raised a fund for the Keats house in Hampstead. The Roman house and graves had suffered seriously during the war and German occupation. The library had been reinstalled after its sequestration at Monte Cassino by the faithful custodian, Signora Vera Signorelli Cacciatore; but the building required restoration and the future of the Memorial called for maintenance. The two poets were sacred names to Ruth; they had also become inseparably linked with another of her loyalties in Rome. She summoned help and funds from their American devotees, wrote reports on the activity of the American Association, corresponded with her English and American colleagues, and on the late afternoon of the day in June 1954 when Cambridge University honoured her she sped from the ceremonies to London to join the dignitaries who attended the dedication, by Ambassador Aldrich and John Masefield, of the memorial plaques to the two poets in

Westminster Abbey. Her work for the Association—her one official service to literature—brought into combination her lifelong reverence for the poets and her affection for their shrines in Italy and England; and it became the last public cause to which she devoted herself.[1]

Honours now descended on her from other quarters than the press that for more than forty years had given her a continuous largess of praise on both sides of the Atlantic. They had in fact begun some years earlier. As far back as 1924 she received her first honorary degree of Master of Arts from Hamilton College at Clinton, New York, where her sponsor was the college's most infatuated alumnus and one of her own rapt admirers among the New York critics, Alexander Woollcott, who was likewise given an honorary degree at the ceremony. In 1941 the University of Maine honoured her as both the 'master of a delicate and sophisticated art' and a 'public-spirited and admired summer resident' of the state, by conferring on her its degree of Doctor of Fine Arts. In 1947 Smith College gave her its degree of Doctor of Humane Letters. But her crowning honours in these later years came from Great Britain.

In April 1951 she was notified by the British Ambassador in Washington, Sir Oliver Franks, that King George VI had 'been pleased to confer upon [her] the Insignia of honorary Commander of the Most Excellent Order of the British Empire'. Ruth was about to leave for Europe on the *Liberté*; the conferring of the Order through the Embassy in Washington was impossible; in England she was put in touch with Buckingham Palace; once more she was invited, as a quarter-

---

[1] Cf. *Keats, Shelley and Rome: An Illustrated Miscellany*, compiled by Neville Rogers 'on behalf of the Keats-Shelley Memorial Association' (London, 1949 and 1957). The volume includes histories of the House and graves; literary studies by Edmund Blunden and Dorothy Hewlett; accounts of the Memorial, the war-time havoc in Piazza di Spagna, and the sequestration of the library at Monte Cassino, by Mr. Rogers and Signora Cacciatore; and an essay, 'Shelley Epilogue: Lauro de Bosis', by Mr. Rogers.

century earlier, to give a command performance before the
Court at Windsor; and later that autumn, returning to
England for a second time within the year after her autumn
at Dark Harbor, it was arranged that she be received in
private audience by King George and Queen Elizabeth at
Buckingham Palace and that the decoration be conferred on
her in person.

That summer the University of Edinburgh summoned her
to its Graduation Ceremonial on 6 July. The Scottish actor,
Alastair Sim, was Rector of the University that year and
joined her in receiving the honorary Doctorate of Laws,
along with seven other scholars, statesmen, and men of letters.
In his Laureation address the Vice-Chancellor of the University, having noted that 'her ear is tuned to catch "the still
sad music of humanity", and her touch is unerring', concluded with classic gestures:

> Pindar, in his eulogy concerning Theron of Akragas, used
> words which may well be adapted to today's occasion, and we
> may say of Miss Draper: 'The sea-sand none has numbered; and
> the joys that [she] has given to others—who shall declare the tale
> thereof?' As Theron for his performance was given an Olympic
> crown of wild olive, let us now give to this great creative artist our
> academic crown.

The summer of 1954, one of the most brilliant of these
later years, brought her the high honour of Cambridge University and its degree of Doctor of Law *honoris causa*. Ruth
was to play her London engagement that summer at the Duke
of York's Theatre, but four days before her opening on
14 June she went up to Cambridge, stayed the night with her
old friends Professor and Mrs. G. M. Trevelyan, and the
next morning marched to the Senate House in procession
with her fellow-graduands the Marquess of Salisbury, Lord
Goddard, Sir Edward Bridges, Sir Edward Charles Dodds,
and Professor Patrick M. S. Blackett of London, Gertrude
Caton-Thompson, the archaeologist, and Edgar Lobel of

Oxford, to hear the Orator of the University present her to
the Chancellor, Lord Tedder, in resounding Latin:

Unus homo, ut ait Vates noster, *Unus agit multas vitae per
tempora partes*. Rarus autem qui non vicissim solum, ut voluit
poeta, sed simul, ut ingeniosa haec femina solet, complures suo
Marte personas sustinet....Quod si nullis fere partibus ingenium
tam versutum deesse dixeris, restant tamen quas ego saltem
quamvis assiduus studiosusque eius auditor neque agentem vidi
neque unquam egisse suspicor: num, quaeso, mulieris academicae
adhuc personam induit? Nunc igitur, ut fabulas etiam togatas
ceteris addere discat, purpura nostra vestiendam curemus,
minime dubii quin in nova hac persona tuenda aeque et in aliis
animos nostros lepore et venustate nativa delectare possit. Duco
ad vos RUTH DRAPER.[1]

'The great day is over,' she wrote her sisters the next
morning, 'and *what* a day! I wish I could live it over again.'
But there was a month's season to play at the Duke of York's;
Paris to visit in July; visits to make in Italy—Florence, Siena,
the Origos at La Foce, Berenson at Vallombrosa, Milan,
Lugano—before flying home to Dark Harbor in August. And
in 1955 another year to divide between America and England.

When 1956 began she set out on a tour through the Middle
West that kept her on the road through January and

---

[1] The Orator's full speech was translated in a leaflet accompanying the
programme of honorary citations:
' "One man," says the Bard, "One man in his time plays many parts".
Still, it is unusual to find someone who not only plays his parts one after
the other—which is what the poet meant—but several at once, as does our
talented guest. When, for example, she—author and actor at once—is
telling us of the beauties of last month's flowers or extolling the virtues of
the latest system of diet, do we not see, in the words of Lucretius,
"wondrous shapes and figures" crowd the stage, conjured out of nothing
into the realms of light solely by the witchcraft and magic of her art?
Such is her versatility that one would suppose her equal to any part whatsoever; yet there is one which I at least have never seen her play, though
I suspect that she has still to try it. Has anyone, I wonder, seen her in the
character of Academic Woman? It is surely time that she added *fabulae
togatae* to her repertoire, so let us clothe her in our scarlet gown, in full
confidence that she will sustain this new role, like the others, in a manner
to delight and captivate us with her native elegance and charm. I present
to you Ruth Draper.'

February. 'My wonderful life goes miraculously on', she wrote to a friend of thirty years.[1] Late in March, after a pause in New York, she flew from the Idlewild Airport straight to Italy. She went at once to Sorrento to visit Gaetano Salvemini. 'I flew over last week', she said in a message to America, 'and I am in this lovely place once more, but going next week to Sicily, and later to Rome, Florence, then Paris, Holland, Vienna! It is so beautiful here—still cold, but as enchanting as ever.' A New York friend presently joined her and together they made the circuit of Sicily during the *Primavera Siciliana*. By mid-April she was back in Rome for performances at the Eliseo and the Sala Cherubini before going on to another at the Fidenti in Florence. ('*Per due sere*,' reported one of Rome's critics, Nicola Chiaromonte, '*il pubblico romano ha ammirato e applaudito Ruth Draper... con la sua* Company of Characters, *che è una formula felice per indicare la numerosa folla di personaggi che essa è capace di evocare da sola sulla scena, con una precisione mimica e fonetica che hanno del prodigioso*.') In Vienna she reappeared, after an absence of a quarter-century, at Reinhardt's Theater in der Josefstadt, with his widow Helene Thimig to welcome her in memory of their association in the days of her husband's theatrical empire. ('*Man soll Ruth Draper nicht versäumen: Ein Weltstar gastiert in der Josefstadt*', ran one review, while another concluded: '*Sie ist eine Menschendarstellerin großen Formats mit Herz und Geist, mit Schärfe und Wärme. Begeisterter Beifall dankte.*') By June she was appearing in four cities of Holland. ('*De Amerikaanse voordrachtskunstaktres Ruth Draper heeft gisteren in Diligentia laten zien welke grote mogelijkheden het solotoneel als kunstvorm te bieden heeft.*') In Ireland, Dublin and Belfast greeted her 'with crowded houses'. ('The matchless...' 'The incomparable...' 'The magical...' 'As inimitable as ever.')

Her London season that summer was at the St. James's

---

[1] Iris Origo, op. cit., p. 383.

Theatre in King Street—the scene of so many of London's famous first nights and soon to be doomed against the protests of its embattled defenders. Terence Rattigan's *Separate Tables* had just ended its two-year run; Ruth's four weeks began on 2 July, and she was elated at the luck that gave her a month in one of the London theatres she loved most. 'What newly spotted marvels can one enumerate?' said the *Observer*, expressing the general admission that critical superlatives had long been exhausted: 'This is one of the great actresses of the world.' 'There is nothing else that need be said', added the *Daily Telegraph*. 'She has many imitators but no equals'— 'Miss Draper is unique, unchallenged'—'Triumphant'— 'Undiminished'—'Redoubtable'—'Consummate': the press echoed its salvoes of thirty-six years. One afternoon she went to Holloway Prison to perform before an audience of women prisoners—it proved to be her last recital in England—and ended by thanking her audience for 'their share in the work of bringing her invisible characters to life'. It was left to a suburban paper to sum up the verdict by saying that 'London has long ago worn its most extravagant adjectives, clichés, and superlatives to tatters in its attempt to cope with her achievement'.

She flew back to America in August and went immediately to Dark Harbor. 'I don't think it was ever lovelier than this year,' she told a visitor in 79th Street on her return to New York on 26 September. 'I could have stayed until winter. This morning I took a last walk through the woods and along the shore and thought how impossible it was that I should be leaving. What a blessing that Dark Harbor is always there to go back to.'

In October she was off to the Middle West; by 1 November to South Carolina; by late November back to Chicago; in early December to Pennsylvania and Baltimore. On Christmas night she opened at the Playhouse in New York. There were people in the audience who were seeing her for the first time and who were left amazed by the youth and gusto of her performance. She had spoken of fatigue several times in recent weeks, and the holiday weeks were crowded with extra performances. 'My season started last night,' she wrote on the 26th, 'and I have two shows today, which I dread! But I hope to gather strength as the season proceeds and I get in the stride of the work again. The public will help me to continue with zest. All went well last night.' On Wednesday, the 26th, there were both matinée and evening programmes, as again on Saturday, the 29th. She carried them through unflaggingly, and told a visitor to her dressing-room that her fatigue of the earlier part of the week had completely dropped away.

She left the Playhouse on Saturday night at 11.30. The city glittered with its Christmas lights and decorations. For many years she had been used, during her New York seasons, to engage a car to take her to and from the theatre. On an impulse of delight and excitement at seeing the sparkling town she asked her driver to make a little tour of the streets before starting home—through Broadway and Times Square, east to Fifth Avenue, and so up the Avenue, past the Plaza, and along the wintry reaches of Central Park. The festive city—of her childhood and youth, of her many Broadway seasons, of countless memories and old associations, and of the seventy-two years of her life—passed the windows of her car as it moved northward to 79th Street.

Her maid had laid out her midnight supper. She ate it and went to bed. When the maid returned in the late morning of Sunday—30 December 1956—the apartment was quiet. The drawing-room waited as if expectant of holiday visitors; the long map with its stars glowed in the morning light along the wall. No sound came from the bedroom. When the servant entered it she found her mistress lying as if in calm repose. She had died in her sleep sometime in the early morning hours.

To her family who were quickly summoned, to her friends up and down New York, to the unbelieving spectators who had seen her on the stage of the Playhouse only a few hours earlier, to the countless audiences she had enchanted during more than fifty years and to the world to which the news was sped by radio and newspaper, the shock of her death was intensified by all she had meant to them of life in its keenest energy and purpose, its inexhaustible zest and generosity. It was almost as quickly alleviated by a second thought: that she had died at the height of her career, the applause of her audiences with her to the last, her achievement sustained and undiminished. None of the things she would have dreaded most came to her—incapacity, retirement, the abandonment of the work she loved and of which she had never tired. She had not only stood, firmly and resolutely, on her Persian carpet; she had made it a carpet of authentic magic that had carried her and her contemporaries into a self-created region of vision and delight. The response to her death was grief, shock, incredulity, a sense of personal loss to thousands; but with them came a sense of exultation and fulfilment. She had been able to enhance the life of her time to the end, and she had done it alone.

On Wednesday, 2 January, at noon, her funeral was held at Grace Church in New York. Eight days later there was a memorial service at St. Martin-in-the-Fields in London. The press of the world, reviving the phrases it had lavished on her during almost five decades, produced a flood of tributes that spoke in a single voice: 'There will never again be anyone quite like her.' In the autumn of 1957 a memorial exhibition of her career was held in the Museum of the City of New York—her portraits and photographs, programmes and posters, letters and souvenirs, and, in one corner, the simple well-worn properties and costumes that had helped her create her company of characters. Among them hung what she had always hoped would serve as the mantle for her bier and what at the final rites in Grace Church had covered it—her shawls.

MORTON DAUWEN ZABEL

PART II

THE DRAMAS OF
RUTH DRAPER

FOREWORD

It was not until the last eighteen months of her life that Ruth Draper decided to put her monologues into definitive manuscript form. Apart from the original working drafts she prepared at the time of first creating them, she had kept her entire repertory of dramatic sketches in her memory throughout the more than fifty years of her performances; and it was this memorized repertory that she carried, without recourse to prompt-books or rehearsal notes, on her tours and travels around the world.

The monologues now printed were written from about 1910 to about 1947. Her method in inventing them, once the idea of a character had taken shape in her mind, was to prepare successive trial versions which, through a process of gradual revision, development, and refinement of detail, and with much testing through private rehearsal, self-correction, and occasional suggestions from relatives or friends, became the finished monologues she performed in public. Several of those that follow—'The German Governess', 'A French Dressmaker', 'A Scottish Immigrant', 'A Charwoman', 'A Débutante at a Party', 'On a Porch in a Maine Coast Village', &c.—grew out of sketches she first developed and performed among her family and friends in her early years. The first twenty in the sequence belong roughly to the years before 1925; the next thirteen were developed at various times between 1915 and 1935; the last three she wrote were 'A Cocktail Party', 'Vive la France! 1940', and 'The Return'. Since Ruth Draper did not attach dates to her manuscript of these monologues, her theatre programmes and other information have been relied on in arranging them in an order approximating to that of their composition or performance.

In preparing the monologues for publication, no word of the spoken text as Ruth Draper prepared it in manuscript in 1955–6 has been changed, except for the correction of incidental usages and inconsistencies. For the making of that manuscript she performed the monologues in her apartment in New York and had them taken down in shorthand. This shorthand version she then emended and corrected before having it copied in an original typescript and several carbon duplicates. It is from this typescript, as approved by her, that the present texts derive.

Among Ruth Draper's papers were found partial drafts of fifteen sketches, the earliest dated 1903, the latest 1955, which she either never completed or had performed on early programmes, then dropped from her repertory, and never wrote out in complete form. 'The Seamstress' (1903) was one of her very earliest monologues, first devised in childhood and included in some of her earliest performances. (Of another very early sketch, 'A Jewish Tailor', the only one in which she assumed a masculine role, and which was also included in the early programmes, no copy has been found.) Three others—'A Quiet Morning in Bed' (1910), 'A New York Factory Girl' (1918), and 'A Class in Soul Culture' (1926)—were likewise given in the early programmes. Ten further sketches—eight in English: 'Seeing off the Ship' (1914), 'In a Munitions Factory' (1919), 'Two Voices', subtitled 'A Post-War Episode' (1919), 'A Deaf Lady' (1922), 'The Wedding Bells' (1924), 'In the Ruins' (1927), 'The Picnic' (1935), and 'A Children's Hour' (1920); and two in French: 'Un Poilu' (1916) and 'Un Voyage' (1920)—were apparently never finished and never performed. There exists further an unfinished and untitled draft of a monologue in three parts, dated 8 November 1955, and portraying three women—a wife who speaks to her husband Gerald about her wish for a divorce, his mother who cautions him against the divorce, and his young daughter Geraldine who consoles her father and promises to take care of him. Since it has been impossible to reconstruct these fifteen monologues or to print them here in a form which Ruth Draper would have approved, they have had, necessarily and regretfully, to be omitted.

PLATE XIV

On a Porch in a Maine Coast Village
Photograph by Trude Fleischmann, New York

PLATE XV

A Débutante at a Party
Photograph by Trude Fleischmann, New York

Unlike the thirty-five monologues now published, these incomplete drafts were dated in the manuscript, and so can be listed in a chronological order which has been found indeterminable for those that follow.

Readers familiar with Ruth Draper's performances, perhaps with repeated hearings of them in the theatre, will doubtless notice that the present texts do not always agree strictly with their memory of her words, or even with the wording of the three monologues ('The Italian Lesson', 'Three Generations in a Court of Domestic Relations', 'A Scottish Immigrant at Ellis Island') which she recorded for the RCA-Victor Company in 1955. Her performances were never rigidly identical in all details. While the basic wording of the sketch and its sequence of sentences were generally followed, certain words were likely to be shifted, parenthetical phrases transposed, some incidental details altered, new phrasings or spontaneous remarks incorporated, as the moment or spirit suggested. The language of the monologue was thus kept fluid and spontaneous at the same time that it adhered to its established text, theme, and character. The editor, like everyone else who now reads the text, remembers various details of the stage performances which do not appear in these printed versions; occasionally some memorable turn of phrase or meaning may be missing; and the various unpublished recordings to which he has had access show a considerable number of minor or incidental alterations. However, it has not been considered prudent to insert or indicate these variants. The present versions follow Ruth Draper's text as she herself authorized it.

That text, however, contained only the slightest indications of setting, costume, gesture, and stage action, or of other characters evoked or involved in the action of the dramas. Those who saw Ruth Draper's performances will recall how meagre her properties and costumes usually were; in some monologues none were used at all; and it will be equally recalled how adequate the properties (or the lack of them) became as soon as she began to speak and act. But those who never saw her perform will require some indication of the appearance she evoked for her characters; what she was able to create by means of a shawl, a hat, an apron, a mackintosh, an umbrella, or a rain-coat; what rooms or scenes she made real on the bare stage and against the background curtains. The editor, who saw twenty-eight of these thirty-five sketches in performance, some of them many times, has therefore ventured to amplify the very brief indications of setting and costume in Ruth Draper's manuscript. The preliminary descriptive paragraphs are his; the parenthesized references to action, persons addressed, entrances and exits, are partly his, partly Ruth Draper's. All such interpolations have been kept at a minimum. The monologue itself must be trusted, here as in the theatre, to create its own character, setting, and drama. The punctuation has been left largely as Ruth Draper herself inserted it, though an effort has been made to regularize it throughout the monologues. The running periods and dashes were used by her to indicate pauses for gesture, action, listening, or other details in the only way such details can be suggested in printed form.

Matters of dialect, accentuation, and emphasis are only approximately suggested, particularly in such sketches as 'A Charwoman', 'A Dalmatian Peasant', 'A Miner's Wife', 'On a Porch in a Maine Coast Village', 'A Scottish Immigrant', 'Christmas Eve on the Embankment at Night', 'In County Kerry', and 'The Actress'. Nor can spellings and grammar suggest the wide range and authenticity of voices or intonations Ruth Draper employed in her renderings. Three of the monologues—'Vive la France! 1916', 'Le Retour de l'Aveugle', and 'Vive la France! 1940'—were given in French; several others—'A French Dressmaker', 'The German Governess', 'At the Court of Philip IV', 'In a Church in Italy', 'The Actress'—include passages in French, German, Italian, and Spanish, languages with which Ruth Draper was familiar or skilful. The Slavic passages in 'A Dalmatian Peasant' and

'The Actress' are composed of imitated or synthetic versions of Slavic speech which she devised and made convincing by her intonation, one of the most remarkable features of her linguistic skill. These pastiches are left as she invented them, as are the imitated languages she devised for the 'Five Imaginary Folk Songs'. (Her other sketch of this kind, 'Love in the Balkans', does not exist in manuscript.)

At the end of the monologues is printed a list of the stage properties Ruth Draper used in her performances, as well as an enumeration of the characters portrayed and evoked by the speakers of the different sketches. Her properties were never standardized; she used such chairs, tables, or benches as her managers or local sponsors could supply. Her only consistent equipment was the articles of dress and jewellery, and the various canes, umbrellas, and handbags, which she carried with her on her travels. (Most of them are shown in one of the photographs in this book.) The performances were usually presented on an empty stage and against neutral-coloured cyclorama curtains. All but one of her sketches in a given programme were performed in a single gown, usually of brown, beige, or neutral colour, changing its fashion over the years, but adaptable to all the characters she created; with this gown she wore the scarves, shawls, coats, evening wraps, hats, gloves, jewellery, or other articles the successive characterizations required. Only one character—the Spanish court lady in 'At the Court of Philip IV'—was garbed in a complete and elaborate stage costume, adapted from the Velázquez portraits of the seventeenth century.

I am indebted to Ruth Draper's sisters, Mrs. Henry James (Dorothea Draper) and Mrs. Edward C. Carter (Alice Draper), who first proposed the preparation of this book, and who gave help and advice freely on many of the details of the memoir and the monologues. Without their assistance in matters of Ruth Draper's early and family life, public career, and friendships, and without the access they gave me to her papers, letters, and diaries, the undertaking would have been impossible. They have also provided the illustrations from their own or their sister's collections. I am obliged to the Radio Corporation of America, and to Messrs. George H. Grau and Warren Ling of its RCA-Victor Record Division, for generously supplying me with trial disks ('reference lacquers') of ten of the recordings made in their New York studios by Ruth Draper but thus far not published. These recordings (of 'A Class in Greek Poise', 'The German Governess', 'On a Porch in a Maine Coast Village', 'A Débutante at a Party', 'In a Church in Italy', 'A Southern Girl at a Dance', 'In a Railway Station on the Western Plains', 'Vive la France! 1940', 'Opening a Bazaar', and 'At an Art Exhibition in Boston') have supplemented the three ('The Italian Lesson', 'Three Generations in a Court of Domestic Relations', 'A Scottish Immigrant at Ellis Island') published by Victor Records on Record No. LM-1859 under the title *The Art of Ruth Draper* in 1955, now unfortunately discontinued, in revisualizing the performances. I am grateful to Dr. Leon Edel for advice on this project, and to my colleagues, Professors Jeanne M. Brochéry, H. Stefan Schutz, Hannibal Noce, Wells F. Chamberlin, and Bernardo Blanco-González for advice on foreign idiom. From friends of Ruth Draper in America and England, or from my own who were long familiar with her performances, many incidental suggestions have come and are gratefully acknowledged; the most important of them are mentioned in the memoir. The photographs in the book are acknowledged wherever it has been possible to determine the photographers who took them. Special acknowledgement is made to Miss Trude Fleischmann, of New York, who was Ruth Draper's chief photographer in the last ten or fifteen years of her life.

Throughout the preparation of both the memoir and the monologues I have relied continuously on my memory of conversations and discussions with Ruth Draper herself: on what she told of her friendships, travels, and professional life; of the development of her work, career, and stage experience; and on many other details of her personality and experience. When such details are not otherwise credited they usually come from what I recall of these talks and reminiscences.

It must be kept in mind in reading the monologues that there was never more than one speaker on the stage. Whatever other characters figure in the action, however many other people are named or addressed, it was Ruth Draper alone who evoked and brought them to life, whether a single listener or a crowd that at times could be made to fill the scene.

The monologues will be read by two classes of people—those who saw Ruth Draper's performances on the stage, and those who did not. The former will find their reading continuously supplemented by their memory of her voice, appearance, gestures, and action. It is hoped that the latter will be able to visualise, with the help of the photographs, what these texts became when they were given life by Ruth Draper's art, presence, and evocative powers. The texts may serve another purpose. They may define what the art of the monologue requires for its successful achievement and so establish the working principles of the genre for those concerned to continue the kind of dramatic art of which Ruth Draper made herself the master in our time.

M. D. Z.

THREE BREAKFASTS

※◈※

THE FIRST: IN A SUBURB

A young, newly married wife runs gaily into the dining-room laughing. She wears a light blue sweater over her dress. She is apparently being pursued by her young husband and seizes a chair to ward him off. She laughs uncontrollably, then suddenly stops breathless and takes her place across from him at the breakfast table.

Harry! Please—no! *Please*, Harry! (*Laughs*) Oh! I'm all out of breath—you chased me so fast I nearly fell downstairs.... (*She sits at the table*) Isn't it the most *lovely* day!... Darling, how long is it going to take you to get to the station?... Oh! Harry, that only gives us five minutes for breakfast!... But, darling, let's get up earlier!... It's awfully bad for you to hurry so—and I love getting up early!... No, really—I do—I *love* getting up early these nice cold mornings—I can hardly wait to start the day!... And there's *so* much to do! (*The maid enters with the coffee*)

Mary, will you bring everything in, please, as quickly as possible?... Yes, we are a little late—we'll have to hurry.... (*The maid leaves*)

Isn't she nice?... Oh! I hope she stays.... Aren't we lucky?...

Will you have your coffee now, darling?... It's nice and hot.... (*Pours coffee*)

Oh! I'm going to have such fun today! I'm going to accomplish so much with you out of the way!... You don't want me to do too much without you?... All right, my sweet.... (*Passes the cup*) Does that look right?... I'll just do lots of little things that don't concern you very much, but which are very important just the same.... You know—all the kitchen things, and the linen, and the china and glass and groceries and everything, to put in order.... (*The maid returns with breakfast*)

Oh, thank you, Mary—isn't it a lovely day!... (*Helps herself to the oatmeal*) Thank you.... (*Mary leaves*)

Then I'm going to unpack, and put away all my things, and get everything in apple-pie order.... *Then* I'm going to do something for *you*! I'm not going to tell you—it's going to be a surprise.... Would you rather know? Well, I'm going to unpack all your bags, darling, and put everything away, so when you get back it will be just as though you'd always lived here! I'm going to fix all your cupboards, and your closets, and the bureau drawers, and the desk, and all your papers, and get the bags out of the way, so that.... What? Why? Oh! darling—*let* me!... But I'll tell you where everything is!... You'll love the way I fix it—I've got the most wonderful plan! I'm going to put your collars and your ties and your handkerchiefs in that nice little piece of furniture that Aunt Aggie gave us.... You don't want me to touch anything?... (*She pouts*) Yes, I'm disappointed. (*Drinks*) Because I thought that was one of the (*Drinks*)—look out, my sweet, it's hot!— duties, (*Drinks*) and privileges, (*Drinks*) and pleasures, of being a wife! In fact, I thought that was why you married me,—*one* of the reasons you married me!—to take care of you!... Don't you want to be taken care of?... Don't you want me to keep things tidy so they'll be easy to find, and you'll know where they belong?...

Well, will you put them away the way you want them, then let me keep them tidy that way?... Because you see, darling— you happen to be *very* untidy. I just happen to be very tidy.... But I like you the way you are, because it gives me something I can do for you.... You mean you want me to leave everything in the middle of the floor, the way it is now?... All right! I won't *touch* your old things, and some day you'll be sorry—some day, you'll come and ask me where something is, and I won't know...and I won't care! (*Drinks*).... (*Laughs*)

Listen, darling—if I can't do anything for you, will you please do something for me?... You'd better write it down—you might forget.... I want a roll of copper wire—picture wire, best quality, and some nails—different sizes—and three dozen picture hooks.... But we have at least three dozen pictures—don't you want to hang them?... Then, will you please bring some kind of a tool—that will do for *everything*?... Now, don't laugh at me—there *are* such tools! We have nothing to open anything with.... We've got about thirty boxes, and crates, and barrels—wedding presents—and we can't open them! I want to see what's in them! Haven't you *any* curiosity?... I hate to tell you, but I broke the point of your penknife last night, opening a crate.... No, I didn't get it open—that's why I want a tool.... I'll get you a new knife, my sweet—I promise I will.... I know I'm impatient, but I want to get settled.... It is lovely, now, but it's going to be lovelier when we get all our pretty things about....

What shall we do tonight when you get back? Shall we put down the stair carpet, or shall we put away the books in the library, or shall we hang the pictures? Which would you rather do?... (*Laughs*) Darling—you're *hopeless*! We cannot sit on the sofa in front of the fire—no, because that's the only time I have you to help me, between then and dinner. And we have to work hard and get everything in order....

I know *one* thing I'm going to do for you today, and I'm not going to tell you what it is! (*Drinks*) You needn't guess—I'm not going to tell you.... More coffee, my sweet?... (*Pours coffee*) You might as well learn that I've got a very strong will, and I'm not going to tell you everything, anyway.... No, I'm *not*!... Well, you are not going to get this out of me, so you needn't guess—I'm *not* going to tell you.... (*Laughs*) Don't look like that, darling—don't look like that!... I can't bear it —I'll tell you.... If you really want to know—I'm going to make you a pudding!... I certainly *can* cook!... I can make seven things, and they always turn out.... Well, I *can* make a few that don't!... But seven *always* do, and this is the best pudding you ever tasted....

You know, I'm much cleverer than you think I am....You are never going to find it all out.... Well, I was told once, by a man who knew a lot about life, that I must keep you guessing to the end!... (*Eats*) You must never know it all, he said. I must always be something of a mystery! I must always keep *surprising* you!...

What? Go to the theatre next week? Oh! Do you *mean* it? Ummm! Shall we spend the night in town?... Shall we go to your mother's?... Well, I think she would love to have us— I mean, I think it will give her a lot of pleasure.... And it will save us a lot of money!...

What are we going to see?... I don't care, darling—anything amuses me as long as I'm with you.... You know, Harry—that is the only thing that worries me a little about being married, that the more I love you, the sillier I get! I'm definitely sillier than I used to be!... Well, there's an example: the theatre. I used to be *very* particular, I hated anything that wasn't first-class, I was bored by anything that wasn't awfully good. And now, I don't care what I'm looking at.... It can be the worst show in the world, if I'm sitting next to you, I'm perfectly happy!... Is that the way *you* feel?... Then *why* do we go to the theatre? (*Drinks*)

(*Laughs*) You know, Harry, lots of people have told me that it only lasts a little while...feeling like that.... I think it's going to be rather exciting when it begins not to last.... Do you want me to tell you the brutal truth right away? Or do you want me to keep it a dark secret, (*Drinks*) and pretend?... What are you going to do?...

I don't believe it's going to be true about *us*!... I don't know—I just have a feeling that it is always going to be more and more—and never less and less!... (*She suddenly breaks off in alarm*)

Oh! Darling, you must *go*! You'll have to hurry, and you've had a wretched breakfast.... The eggs weren't cooked and the bacon was burned.... (*They rise*) Will you please get a glass of milk in the middle of the morning?... Now, Harry, don't laugh—you're much too thin, everybody says so, and if you get one of those nice little bottles of milk and keep it on your desk, nobody will notice!...

I *love* you in that tweed—I like *all* your clothes. You have very good taste—but I'm sorry to tell you that you have a little egg on your tie!... Oh, it doesn't show—it wasn't your fault—the egg was too soft.... It's very hard to get boiled eggs just the way you like them.... And you were an angel not to say anything about the lumps in the oatmeal.... Weren't they *awful*? One thing I can *not* abide is lumps in oatmeal!... But it will *never* happen again as long as we live, because that is one of the things I know how to cook—oatmeal without lumps.... I can tell her how not to put them in!... (*In great haste she helps him put on his coat*)

Goodbye, my sweet.... Are you coming back on the four-thirty-two?... Well, you might call me in the middle of the morning.... Oh—just to ask me how I'm getting on...tell me how *you're* getting on.... It's going to be *desperate* without you.... (*They part at the door*)

Goodbye, darling—don't go too fast down the hill, it's slippery.... Goodbye!... (*She waves goodbye to him*)

(*The maid has entered*)

Mary, I'll help you clear away. Everything was *delicious*—breakfast was *wonderful*, and the coffee was simply *marvellous*! I wonder if you could cook the eggs a little more?... They were very nice, but we happen to like them a little more—(*She breaks off as she sees husband reappear in the doorway*) What, darling? Forget something?... No—you did'nt—you didn't forget anything!... I did? What did I forget?... Something important?... What are you talking about?... What?... Oh!...

(*She rushes into his arms in the doorway as the curtain falls*)

THE SECOND: IN THE CITY

It is about fifteen years later. The wife comes in, looking very cross and ill-tempered. She wears a green woollen scarf around her shoulders and carries the morning newspaper. She pulls her chair out crossly, sits down at the breakfast table, and begins to read her newspaper. Suddenly, looking over its edge, she sees her husband come in, carelessly watches him sit down, then goes on reading. Presently she speaks, curtly and dryly.

Morning.... (*She pours the coffee and hands it across*) Here.... Got it? (*Pours coffee for herself. Chin on hand, she looks about the room. Then she helps herself from a platter handed by the maid. Eats and drinks in silence*)

Harry—did you telephone your mother last night?... I said, did you telephone your mother?... Oh, *Harry*—I *did* tell you!... While we were dressing for dinner. She called up, and wanted you to speak to her before you went out, and I *told* you so. I naturally thought you'd done it.... I don't know *what* it was about. She *never* tells me—how should *I* know?... (*A silence*)

Pamela? She's not coming down.... I told her to stay in bed—she has a bad cold.... (*Another silence*)

By the way, what happened to you yesterday afternoon?... Do you mean to say that you *forgot* it was Pamela's birthday, and that you'd promised to take her out?... Harry! How *could* you forget? She spoke of it only at breakfast. You promised you'd take her out on her birthday afternoon—she'd been looking forward to it for days.... I *did* telephone your office— I telephoned twice. You were not there—I naturally assumed you were on your way uptown.... I had to go to a meeting— I left her at the front door, waiting for you.... Oh, well... she'll get over it.... Just explain something.... It doesn't make any difference.... (*There is a long pause while they eat. The maid serves and goes*)

I had a telegram last night from Mr. Porter saying that

Bobby is being sent home from school.... (*She breaks off, startled*) Harry! Will you *please* not use such language before Mary?... Well, of *course* she heard you—she was just at the door.... Now, don't get so excited—he's not done anything wrong! Why should you immediately jump to the conclusion that he's done something wrong?... He's been getting exceedingly high marks lately. He's been standing at the top of his class for over three months—which is more than *you* ever did.... He's got something the matter with his eyes.... No, not serious.... Well, he had the measles, you know.... It has left him with some inflammation in his eyes, and the Headmaster thinks he ought to see a specialist, so he's coming home for a few days.... I thought if you had nothing particular to do, you might take him out. It isn't going to be much fun for him....

Harry! Please don't push your plate away like that—you nearly knocked it off the table....

Why isn't it fit to eat?... Tell me what's the matter and I'll see what I can do. Don't behave like an angry child!...

What?... Lumps in it?... Well, how do you expect *me* to know unless you tell me? I don't eat oatmeal—I've not eaten it for about fifteen years—horrible stuff. I never could see why you wanted it, anyway.... Well, I'll tell the cook. I'm sorry....

You're going up to the farm? (*Laughs sarcastically*) Excuse me if I smile.... Well, the idea of you on the farm in the middle of winter just makes me laugh, that's all.... How long do you think you're going to stay?... Ha! I bet you'll be back within twenty-four hours. You could no more stand the country in the middle of winter.... You'd simply *hate* it!... I bet you I'd stand it a great deal better than you would.... Because I really love the country! (*Munches*) I sometimes think I'd like to go and live there. (*Mumbles*) I sometimes think...anything would be better than this! (*Munches and mumbles*).... Oh! Never mind what I said.... Want some more coffee?... Hold out your cup....

You're not dining at home tonight? Oh, *Harry*—I think

you're awfully *mean*! But I *begged* you to save tonight.... Yes, I *did*, Harry—I told you at least three times that we had a box for the opera tonight.... The Andersons and the Millers are coming, and it's the chance of the winter to have a box tonight, because it's for *Tristan*.... *Tristan and Isolde* with that wonderful new singer.... Oh, *stop* talking like that! It's so silly to say such things—because it's one of the most beautiful things in the world.... Well, a great many people think so, and *always* have thought so, and *always* will think so—very intelligent people, too!... You're the person I'm sorry for! You're just so deliberately *deaf*—so deliberately *blind*—and you've never even tried to enjoy the things that I enjoy....

Oh, well, never mind—it doesn't make any difference. I can easily enough find somebody who'll be only too thankful to go.... I'm disappointed, that's all—and I thought we would all have a very nice evening....

Look at me a minute—*look* at me!... Disgusting! You have some egg on your tie. Look out! It's all over it—here. (*She points*).... Take your knife.... Disgusting!... (*Another long pause*)

Well, no wonder you're tired!... What time did you get home last night?... It's so silly, Harry—this dancing.... Everybody's laughing at you.... I was lunching with some women yesterday, and they were all laughing about you and that little Watson girl.... *I* don't care—why should *I* care? It doesn't make any difference to *me*.... It's just so silly— that's all. She's only about two years older than your own child.... Well, she may be a wonderful little dancer—but that doesn't make it any less ridiculous....

Harry—I wish you'd stop wearing that old grey suit.... Not the old grey suit?... Will you please tell me *why* you go and get a new suit exactly like the one I've always hated?... It's so drab and unbecoming.... And for heaven's sake, get a haircut— it's all down over your collar.... (*He rises. She remains sitting*)

Don't forget to go up and see Pamela....

Goodbye.... (*She does not look at him. Then she calls*)

Harry! Come back a minute, will you?... Listen: would you come to the opera late, and bring me home?... That new Isolde is singing—and there's a wonderful tune at the end.... You'd probably recognize it—you've heard it before.... It only lasts five minutes, and it won't kill you.... I really think you'd enjoy it.... It's called the '*Liebestod*'.... Are you going to be at the Club?... Well, I'll send the car at a quarter to eleven.... But don't be late, or you'll miss it.... Right. Goodbye....

(*Eats. Drinks. Sighs. Reads paper. Picks teeth. Hums tune— the 'Liebestod'. The maid comes to announce someone on the telephone*)

Come in! Who is it?... Mr. Who?... Oh! (*She folds her newspaper, rises, and moves toward the door*) Mary, will you please tell the cook I shall not be home for luncheon today, and send something up to Pamela....

(*She bends down as a puppy rushes in*) Hello, Raggles! Oh, you *sweet* puppy! Have you heard the news? Our Bobby's coming home—yes, he *is*—our Bobby's coming home! Come along—we'll go and tell Pamela, Bobby's coming home!... (*She walks off backward, waving the folded newspaper at the dog*) And who do you think *I'm* going to lunch with today? I'm going to lunch with your old master. Yes, I am—with your *old master*! Come on—we'll talk to him on the telephone!... Come on, come on, come on!... (*She leaves the room*)

THE THIRD: ON A FARM

It is forty years later. The wife enters, now an old lady. She wears a soft grey shawl over her shoulders. Her grandchildren are already crowding around the breakfast table. She beams lovingly on all of them, and after calling to her husband to come down, she speaks in a warm, cheerful, affectionate, grandmotherly voice to them.

Breakfast, Harry!... Hal, darling—go and tell your grandfather that breakfast is ready.... I don't think he heard us....

Come on, children—those lazy mothers of yours are not coming down.... They prefer breakfast in bed, which is something I *don't* understand.... (*She moves towards the table*)

Wait, children—don't rush at your grandfather like that!... You'll knock him over—six of you is a great many!...

Thank you, Bobby—my nice, polite Bobby—always remembers his grandmother's chair.... Thank you, darling.... Hal—quickly, dear! Pull out grandfather's chair....

Now, how are we all going to sit?... Molly, it's your turn to sit next to grandfather.... Come on, Tommy—you can feed the goldfish after breakfast.... They can wait.... You sit there, dear.... Bobby, here.... No, little girls, don't quarrel.... Peggy was next to him yesterday, and it's Nancy's turn.... And Hal here next to me.... *There* we are! What a *lovely* party!... (*She sits down at the table*)

Do you know, children, your grandfather and I were saying last night that we think it's great fun having you children here all to ourselves every morning, without your mothers—just *all* to ourselves.... (*Louder, to her husband across the table. He has grown very deaf*) I say we think it's great fun having the children here all to ourselves every morning....

Now, who's going to give grandfather his coffee? I think it's Nancy's turn.... Now, Nancy, darling—remember what I said about keeping your mind on what you are doing, and pay no attention to *any*thing or *any*body. Just think about the coffee-cup.... Have you got it, darling?... Now, watch the coffee, watch the surface of the cup.... Oh, oh! That's very nice! Didn't she do that nicely?... You little rascal! I saw what you intended.... I saw it in those blue eyes! You meant to make your sister giggle just as she took the cup—didn't you?... (*The maid enters to serve breakfast*)

Good morning, Mary—isn't it a lovely day?...

Well, children—what are we all going to do this lovely, lovely day?... I suppose you will be skating on the pond....

I saw the lovely black ice from my window and I *envied* you
so.... *Not* skating?... Coasting?... On the big hill?... Oh, we
must ask your grandfather.... I am not at all sure.... (*Loud,
to her husband*)

Harry, dear—do you think the boys should coast today on
the big farm hill, with the toboggan...and all the schoolchildren? You know, it froze again last night, and I'm afraid
there will be a sheet of ice on the track.... You *do*?... (*To the
children*) Well, if your grandfather says you may, I suppose
you may.... But oh! That hill makes me very nervous....
Well, perhaps I *am* foolish—but you see that is the hill where
your dear father was very badly hurt when he was a little
boy.... He never told you? Isn't that funny?... (*Louder*) Isn't
that funny, Harry—the boys never heard of Bobby's accident
on the hill.... Well, you ask him—I'm sure that he'll remember. He'll tell you all about it....

(*She suddenly turns to one of the little girls*) My darling
child—not so much in your mouth!... Don't eat it, darling—
wait—put it down again!... Why, you've got half the saucerful
in your spoon!... Now, begin again.... Take just a little
spoonful! That's it!... And you've got far too much sugar!...
(*Louder*) Harry—don't let that child take so much sugar....
She has more sugar than oatmeal.... Darling, you *mustn't* take
so much sugar.... And you must remember your table-man-
ners when you have breakfast with grandfather and me....
That's better!...

Let me see—your father was away at boarding-school, and
he had had measles, and it left him with some trouble with
his eyes, so he was sent to the city to see a specialist. The very
day that he got here, that night, your grandfather and I went
to the opera.... Now, what *was* that opera?... I've entirely
forgotten.... We'll ask your grandfather. He will remember—
he has the most remarkable memory.... You see if he doesn't
know, the minute I ask him....

(*Loudly, across the table*) Harry, dear—what was the opera
we were so fond of, that we went to the night of the fire?...

Tristan! It *was*—*Tristan and Isolde*! It comes back to me now —how beautiful it was! What a voice she had! What a wonderful evening! (*To the children*) *Tristan and Isolde*—a very famous opera.... I hope that you'll see it some day.... What was it about? Oh! It was just about two people—two people who loved each other....

I remember, now. Your grandfather did not go *with* me to the opera.... Well, he was a very, very busy man, and he couldn't always go.... But he came late, to bring me home, as he always did!... As we drove into our street—(*Louder, to her husband*) A little more coffee, dearest? Hold out your grandfather's cup, darling....

As we drove into our street, we realized something very exciting was going on, because there were crowds of people and policemen everywhere! Then, we heard bells, and whistles, and sirens. Then our car suddenly drew to one side, and a fire-engine went tearing round the corner, and then, a hook-and-ladder!... We realized, of course, that there was a *very* bad fire. And then, to our horror, we found that the fire—What darling?... Was in *our* house?... Quite right— you *guessed* it! It *was*! Oh! It was a *dreadful* fire!... Nobody was hurt.... They discovered it in time, and your father and your mother were carried across the street to some kind neighbours, and your grandfather and I had to go to a hotel for the night.... We never got into the house again.... Oh! Everything was burned—our books—our clothes—our furniture—our carpets and rugs—and pictures.... All our precious things—our linen and silver—all our wedding presents— everything that we cared for most was burned—burned to cinders and ashes!...

But fortunately, you see—very fortunately, we had the farm. So we decided—though it was in the middle of winter —we decided to come up here.... (*Louder*) Harry, will you *ever* forget the cold of that journey, and arriving here at night?... It makes me shiver to think of it, still.... But we soon got all the fires lighted, and the children were thrilled

to be in the country in the middle of winter, without any
school....

The next morning was a beautiful sunny day, with snow
on all the hills, and your father went off to coast with a lot of
schoolchildren.... Nobody knew whose fault it was exactly,
or what happened, but somebody steered very badly, and the
sled struck the big oak tree—you remember, at the foot of the
hill—and it glanced off and all the children were thrown into
the snow! Nobody was hurt except your father.... In some
way he was caught, and the sled dashed into the stone wall,
and your father was thrown against the wall, and he was
brought home to me unconscious!... He lay unconscious for
days, and we didn't know.... What, darling?... I don't quite
remember.... (*Louder*) The boys are very anxious to know
how many days their father was unconscious. Wasn't it
nearly two?... Wasn't it Thursday?... Didn't we come up on
a Tuesday?...

Nearly two days, he was unconscious.... What?... What's
what like?... To be unconscious?... Darling—that's not a
very intelligent question. You know what it's like to be conscious. You are conscious, now. But when you are asleep,
you are unconscious—so it's rather like being asleep.... To
be unconscious is to be *not* conscious!...

Then he woke up, and he was put in a plaster cast, and
it was *months* before he was really well, and able to walk
again.... He was very badly hurt! In the midst of it all, your
grandfather got pneumonia, and he nearly died.... Then,
your mother was very ill.... Then, I slipped on a bit of ice,
and broke my arm in two places.... Then, all the pipes burst,
and one of our cows died—and one of our beautiful old elm
trees blew down! Oh! What a winter!—What a winter!... It
was one thing after another, till I thought we would never
get away.... (*Louder*) I was telling the children about that
dreadful winter and our series of accidents.... But we all got
well in the end.... (*Louder*) I say, we all got well in the end....

Have you finished, dear? Shall we go by the fire?...

Children—have you all had enough?... Nancy—you've not eaten your breakfast!... Why couldn't you eat it?... What?... *Lumps* in it?... I've not noticed any. Harry—had you noticed any lumps in the oatmeal?... Grandfather hadn't noticed any.... But even if there were, darling, they wouldn't hurt you, because lumps—lumps are good for us. (*Drinks*) Lumps make us *grow*!...

Now, run along, children. Say good morning to those lazy mothers of yours. Then we'll decide what we're all going to do.... (*Louder*) What, my love?... Take the little sled, and watch the children coast from the top of the hill?... Yes, I'd *love* it! You don't think the wind will be too cold?...

Children—your grandfather and I are coming out to watch you coast from the top of the hill....

One moment, my dear—you've got a little egg on your tie.... It doesn't show, dear—it's not your fault.... The eggs were a little soft this morning.... It's very hard to get boiled eggs exactly as you like them....

Shall we go by the fire, and will you read me the paper?... You know, Harry—I've not told you yet, and scarcely admitted it to myself—but my eyes are *not* what they used to be....

(*She goes out slowly with her hand on his arm*)

A SCOTTISH IMMIGRANT AT ELLIS ISLAND

❧❦❧

The scene is Ellis Island in New York harbour, for many years the station of entry for immigrants coming from Europe to the United States. A young girl from the Highlands of Scotland has just landed and is seen among a throng of fellow immigrants in the hall of the Immigration Building. She wears a shawl over her head. She speaks in a pure Highland accent, here only roughly approximated in the spelling of her words. She speaks eagerly and excitedly at first, bidding farewell to the friends she has made on the ship, then turns to another fellow passenger, Mrs. Kelly.

Goodbye, Annie. Goodbye.... Aye—I have yer address—and as soon as I'm settled, I'll write ye, and ye'll come and see us!... I will—I promise.... Good luck to ye.... Goodbye!...

Are ye coming, Mrs. Kelly? It seems I have to speak to a gentleman here—one of the officials, they told me.... Oh, there's Mrs. Brown, and Charlie, and Nora.... Goodbye, Mrs. Brown! Goodbye, Nora! Goodbye, Charlie!... Oh, I hate to say 'goodbye'.... I'll miss ye all.... It'll be verra strange not seein' ye every day.... Aye, I'll write ye, Mrs. Brown—as soon as ever we're settled, and ye'll come to see us?... I want ye to know Sandy and I want him to know you!... I promise I will.... Goodbye, and thank you for everything!...

(*Calls*) Oh, goodbye, Jamie—I'm sorry I didn't see ye.... Aye, I have your address—I'll write ye, as soon as ever we're settled.... Goodbye!...

And d'ye think that's the gentleman I must speak to, Mrs. Kelly—that one over there? Should I go, now?...

(*She moves forward and stands before the desk of the immigration officer*)

Good morning, Sir—good morning.... My name?... Lesley MacGregor.... Lesley.... L—E—S—L—E—Y.... That's all.... It is. My only name.... Just Lesley. It's a Scottish name.... I come from Crianlarich.... Crianlarich. It's a small place— it's part way between Loch Katrine and Loch Awe in the Highlands of Scotland.... Spell it?... Ye spell it C—R—I— A—N—L—A—R—I—C—H. Crianlarich....

I'm twenty-one years old.... I have come oot to marry.... Oh, he's here.... Oh, yes. I know 'im.... His name?... His name is Mr. Alexander MacAllister.... He comes from Crianlarich....

Well, d'ye see—he left home three years ago, and when he had enough, he was to send for me. So now I have come.... Aye, he knows I'm coming.... He'll be here the day to meet me. I'm sure he will.... I beg your pardon?... Polygamist— am I a polygamist? Whatever is that?... Am I married?... Oh, no, Sir—I'm not married.... Anarchist? Is that a religion?... I am a Presbyterian.... In prison? Have I been to prison?... No, Sir—we have no prison in Crianlarich.... Asylum? De ye mean where the puir daft people go?... No, Sir—we have no asylum in Crianlarich.... Contagious diseases?... Well, I had a cold on the steamer coming over, but it's gone now—would that be a contagious disease?... No, Sir—I've never been ill; only in the wintertime, sometimes I have a wee cold!... Come out under contract?... No contract—only to Mr. MacAllister!... Three pounds, ten, and tuppence.... Three pounds, ten shillings, and two pence.... Not enough?... (*Turns to Mrs. Kelly*) He says I have no got enough.... (*Turns back to the officer*) Well, I'm sure Mr. Mac-Allister will have plenty with 'im. If not, my friends would help me.... Oh, I'm sure he will, because he's well off now, he has been verra lucky! He has a wee farm in New Jersey— a place called Far Hills, New Jersey.... He says it is—a verra pretty place. He likes it awfu' well!... He has thirty-five acres, he has fourteen cows, and he has chickens, pigs, and a few sheep—to remind him of home—only a few! But he has a beautiful apple orchard—a very large garden—and he has a new Ford car.... Oh, yes, Sir—a very nice house, and barns—and everything is ready.... Oh, no, Sir—I'm not going there! I'm going to his neighbour, Mrs. Allen, and I'm going to stop with her until we've filled out all the papers. It seems there are a great many papers to be filled out. But when they're all done, we'll be married, and then I will go to his house.... Is that all?... Thank you.... Oh, thank ye—I'm sure I will.... Goodbye!

(*She turns back to Mrs. Kelly*)

Whit wey would they be askin' ye those peculiar questions? Did ye hear what the man said to me? He asked me if I'd been to prison. I was fair affrontit. And if I was a poly-some-thing.... But he was a verra nice man. He said he hoped I wud be happy in my new home....

(*She speaks to some children*)

Oh, laddie, whit wey did ye come over here? Where's your fayther? Ye hadn't a right to leave go his hand. It's terrible dangerous here—you'll be lost in the crowd!... I canna show 'im to ye—I dinna see 'im yet mysel'!... Run along, now—haud on yer fayther's hand.... Aye, I'll post-card ye as soon as ever we're settled, and ye'll come down.... Aye, and ye'll see the farm 'n everything.... Goodbye, laddies—an' ye'll no forget Lesley?... Mr. Thompson, haud on yer bairns!... I'm all right, thank ye!... Goodbye!

(*Turns to speak to an Irish immigrant whom she has met on the ship*)

Oh, Mr. Muldoon!... Aye.... Oh, ye mustn't talk like that, sir.... But whit wey should we no meet again? Whit wey, no?... Aw, but ye must come down and see the farm. I want ye to know Sandy. I want Sandy to know you. He wud be awfu' pleased to make your acquaintance. I know he wud be verra, verra grateful to ye fer being so good to me on the ship.... Oh, ye were! Ye were awfu' kind!... Well, ye helped me

with my luggage, and ye gave me books to read, an' ye told
me many things aboot America, so that I don't feel strange—
and I'm awfu' glad to have a friend in this great country!
An' I hope ye'll surely come down.... Aye, well I will never
forget you!... Well, I wish ye great success with yer work,
and I hope ye'll have health and happiness always.... Aye,
I promise. Aye, I have your address and I'll write ye.... I
will.... Goodbye—I'll no forget.... Goodbye!

(*Turns to take the hand of a young girl*)

Oh, Annie, haud on me hand!... Ye'll get lost in the
crowd.... Mrs. Smith, yer bairn's here!... She's greetin' at
my skirts and says she'll no leave me.... Lassie, I canna tak' ye
wi' me.... Lesley is goin' to be married, dearie, an' ye maun
run along with yer mother.... Goodbye.... Now, yer not to
greet no more.... I'll see you again.... As soon as ever I'm
settled, I'll write ye, and ye'll come down wi' your mother
and pass the day!... I promise. Run along, now.... Goodbye,
ma doo! Haud on yer mother's hand.... I'm all right, thank
you. Mrs. Kelly is bidin' wi' me till he comes! (*To Mrs. Kelly
again*)

Can ye wait, Mrs. Kelly?... However am I goin' to find
him in the crowd?... I never saw so many folk thegether in
me life before.... An' look at the way they're all pushin' each
other aboot!... They're rather rough.... And are those Ameri-
cans?... Are they no rather peculiar looking people?...
They're awfu' small.... Oh, Sandy is far taller nor anyone
there! He's verra, verra tall—wi' grey eyes, and dark hair.
He's awfu' bonny lookin'. If only ye knew, Mrs. Kelly, ye
could be lookin' too!... Do ye suppose we've changed?...
Three years *is* an awfu' long time—but I'm sure I'd know
Sandy. I remember now, he told me to stand in one place,
and not move aboot, and he'll find me. So I'll stop here.
Don't wait, Mrs. Kelly. I know he'll come soon!...

(*Suddenly she becomes excited and cries aloud*)

Oh, I see him! He's there!... With a red tie, smiling....
And he sees me!... (*Shouts*) Sandy, I'll meet ye this side—

by the gate, here. Goodbye, Mrs. Kelly—oh, I hate to say goodbye, ye have been so kind—like m'ain mother—an' I'll never forget ye!... Aye, I promise.... I'll write ye as soon as ever we're settled. I want ye to know Sandy, and I want him to know you.... Thank you. God bless ye.... I'm all right, now.... (*Rushes towards the barrier shouting*)

Sandy! My Sandy.... I'm here!

ON A PORCH IN A MAINE COAST VILLAGE

*An old woman comes out through a doorway on the porch
of her house facing a road in a village in the state of Maine.
She wears a black crochet shawl around her spare shoulders.
She speaks first to her husband inside the house. Her voice
is a 'down East' Maine voice.—This sketch is a souvenir
of the many summers Ruth Draper spent in Maine, at the
house her mother built in the 1890's at Dark Harbor.
In later years Ruth Draper bought the house from the other
members of her family and made it her summer home
whenever she was in America. She spent the last autumn
of her life there, on her return from Europe in August,
1956. She knew and loved the Maine country people,
and for more than fifty years some of her happiest months
were spent among them.*

All right, William—I'm just goin' out on the porch to get a
mite of air.... Well, I'll come back if you want me—I ain't
goin' far. I'll be settin' right out here—if you call me, I'll
come in.... (*She sits down in an old rocking-chair on the porch*)
(*She looks down the road*) Hello, Hettie—hello!... Say,
Hettie, how's your papa?... Was it true he fell off the hay-
mow?... Did he crack his head open?... That's good!... I
was down at the store last night, and Jimmy Parker said he'd
hurt himself real bad.... Un-huh—I'm glad!... Aya.... Might
a' ben!... Aya—mighty lucky.... Tell your papa I'll stop by
to see him Sunday, after church.
     Lovely bright day, ain't it?... The wind's comin' out o' the
nor'-west.... I guess we're goin' to have a spell of nice bright
weather.... Good night! (*Hettie passes down the road. Sally
now approaches*)

Hello, Sally!... Is that you?... Say—when did you get back?... Won't you come up and set a spell?... Oh, what's your hurry? It's early yet—come on up!... I just come out to get a mite of air! I ain't been out o' the house all day.... Won't you set right down?... (*Sally takes a chair on the porch*)

Well—you're lookin' pretty smart! I suppose you was up to the funeral.... I wish I could a' gone.... It must ha' been lovely.... No, I couldn't get away—Will was feelin' mighty poorly, and I didn't like to leave him.... He's layin' in there on the couch, feelin' awful sorry for himself—he says he feels like he's all tied up in knots.... Oh! Jes' the rheumatism.... We've been havin' so much wet weather lately—it kinder gets in his joints....

Oh! There's nothin' much to do for him.... I rub him—I rub him mos' all night and mos' all day.... I don't think it does a mite of good, but he likes it, so I keep right on rubbin' —my arms are just about paralysed.... He's an awful heavy man to rub.... His leg's just like a log of wood....

I use the horse liniment.... Oh, I don't use it full strength —that'd take the skin right off.... I take a little saucer and I put in about a tablespoon of olive oil, and then I take the liniment and drop it in gradual—drop by drop—an' you keep a-stirrin', and it makes a kind o' creamy paste.... It's nice for rubbin' and it has a pleasant odour.... Will likes the smell of it —he used to work around a livery stable when he was a boy, and he says the smell o' that old liniment brings back his youth....

Oh, he did go to sea—when he was about fourteen, but when he was a little feller he lived on a farm.... He always liked horses better'n boats, and he'd a' liked to a' been a farmer.... But his father wanted him to be a sailor, and he was to sea most all his life....

Thank yer—I am pretty smart, Sally. I keep a-goin'.... I have one o' my spells now and then.... I felt sick as a cat last Tuesday, but I was so busy I forgot about it.... I always say, when you feel miserable, the only way is to keep a-goin'... and then forget yer misery....

We can't complain—we've had wonderful health in our family.... Will and I was sayin' last night how lucky we'd been.... We have seven children and sixteen grandchildren and four great-grandchildren, and there's nothing wrong with *any* of 'em.... That seems enough to be thankful for.... And there's a lot of other things besides.... Aya—we've had a good life, and lots o' good times....

They're all married...only my boy, Henry. He's my youngest—he's my pet—he stays right here with his Dad and me.... I hope he'll marry some day.... But my, we'd miss him.... It's awful lonesome when he's away. He's always laughin', an' singin', and knockin' things over, and it seems so quiet when he goes.... He's away, now.... Well, he takes a job every summer down the coast, with some o' these wealthy city people that come summerin' along the coast.... He's been with the same family now about eleven years, an' he enjoys the work.... He does all kinds of odd jobs.... He helps the help, mostly—them rich folks needs a *lot* o' help!...

Then, he's with the children mos' all day—when they're playin' round the shore with the boats.... Henry's a wonderful sailor—he's taught 'em all to sail.... They win all the races.... There's eight children in the family.... He enjoys the children—seems to know just how to handle 'em....

I know the lady thinks a lot of him.... She wrote me a letter last Christmas, an' she said, 'My husband and I would like to tell you that we think your son is the finest young man we know.' I was pleased....

Well, he's a nice boy.... He's a bright boy—he's the brightest of all my children.... I wish I could a' sent him to college, 'cos it seems like he's got brains.... I don't know where he got 'em—he didn't get 'em from me, and he didn't get 'em from my old man.... But I believe my grandfather was a brainy man.... He was a sea captain, and used to go off on those long voyages—round the Cape, and out to the East.... And my mother said she recalled her mother used to be so put out when she was packin' up his things—'cause she

never could find no place to put 'em—every shelf and corner
of his cabin and his sea-chest was always full o' books! He
was a great reader—and that's the way with Henry, always
readin'!... He goes to the library every week and brings back
a pile o' books 'twould take me a year to read! He keeps a
book in the barn, an' in the shed, an' in the kitchen, an' every
room in the house, and when he's got a spare minute, he's
got his nose right in a book.... He reads at night, after supper
and after he gets to bed.... Well, he's partial to history....
And he likes the lives of great men.... And he likes poetry
real well.... He's read all them Shakespeare plays three or
four times, and learned pieces out of them. Winter evenings,
when we're settin' round the stove, and Will gits out his old
pipe and I'm darnin' or knittin', Henry comes in and says,
'Now, Mother, I'm goin' to do you a piece.'... He does
Othello, Hamlet, Macbeth, King Lear.... And he does a piece
about a horse...yells out, 'My kingdom for a horse!'... Ye'd
think the roof was comin' off, he says it so loud. He's got a
strong voice.... He enjoys the dictionary—likes lookin' up
words—and he knows a heap about the stars.... Well, he
comes by that natural.... All the men folk in my family and
Will's family has done a heap o' lookin' at the stars—naviga-
tin' them vessels.... Now, he's got a mind to learn French....
There's a young lady in the family who helps raise the children—they call her 'Mamselle'. She and Henry struck up
quite a friendship. She give him a book, and she told him
how to pronounce the words.... It's a pretty language....

He writes a beautiful letter.... I had one last week, and I
was readin' it again to Will.... It was a long letter tellin' us all
about the weddin'.... Well, it seems the young lady daughter
got married.... She's nineteen years old—she's a wonderful
little sailor, and he's real proud of her—and o'course he's
known her since she was a little bitty girl.... He says she's
quite a beauty, very tall, with dark eyes.... He said she had
on a white satin dress, an' three yards of it was layin' right
on the grass—she was draggin' it around.... An' he said she

had a veil on her head that looked like mist—the material was so fine. It was blowin' against the blue sky. She was standin' under a big spruce tree, an' there was white birches all around her, an' her arms was full o' lilies.... He said, 'Her eyes was shinin' like stars, Mother, an' she looked like an angel to me.'... An' he said they carted away eighteen barrels o' swill—he said it was the swellest swill he ever saw—thrown right out.... He said he'd a' liked to send me a barrel!... O'course he was only jokin'—he likes to make me and his Dad laugh....

Aya—it's kind o' hard here alone, with Will so poorly—an' so much to do around the house.... Then, our old horse went lame an' I have to rub his leg.... We don't use him any, but we've had him twenty-seven years.... We just turn him out, an' he eats clover all day an' I make him a bran mash every night—an' he enjoys it.... When I rub his leg he licks my neck when I stoop over—like he was sayin' 'Thank you!'... Oh! We couldn't part with him—he's like an old friend....

I've had awful poor luck with the garden, this season.... My apples have all got the rust—I ain't got an apple. An' my beans have got the blight—I ain't got a bean.... An' I lost all my sweet corn—cutworms. They bit it right off at the root, and the whole lot of it laid right down an' died.... An' my tomatoes have some kind of a pest—they're hangin' on the vines like they was sick.... Then, the potato bugs is awful bad this season.... I put Paris Green on my potatoes last week, an' the rain come down an' washed it all off, so the bugs is thrivin' an' I got to do it all over again....

Well, there's been a lot goin' on here since you went away, Sally.... I never seen such a place—if it ain't one thing it's another.... Well, Saul Smith sold his point—he got a big price, they say.... Them summer-people has always been tryin' to buy that point as long as I remember.... Funny— can't see why anyone wants to live there.... There's nothin' to see only the ocean, an' I wouldn't want to look at the ocean all day.... Then, you know that little cove, this side o' the point?... Well, they stand there on the old bridge at ebb-tide an' they say, 'Oh—smell the delicious salt breezes!'... Salt breezes! T'ain't nothin' but a stench o' rotten old seaweed an' a few dead fish!... I wouldn't take that place anyway, if you gave it to me, because it's haunted, you know—ever since Uncle Zeb choked Aunt Maria there....

Why, Sally—where have you been? You never *heard* that story?... I was raised on that story.... Well—you're a younger woman than I am....

Don't you remember old Capt'n Zeb Hawkins—Uncle Zeb?... He was a first cousin o' my grandfather's. He was a great old character in these parts—he'd had an interestin' life.... Well, his mother died when he was seven years old and his father was so lonesome, he took the little feller right along with him on his whalin' vessel to the South Pacific.... When he got out there, he found harpoonin' whales was no life for a child, so he set him ashore on an island. It seems it was a cannibal island, an' he was raised by the cannibals, an' he says they was lovely people!... They raised him good.... His father'd go an' see him now and then.... Saw he was gettin' along fine, so he left him there an' he never come home till he was fourteen years old.... He told me, when his father took him away, his heart most broke!...

Of course, he'd learned the language o' them islanders, and he never forgot it. We children used to love to hear him talk. He was a rough man, but he was beautiful with children, an' we all loved Uncle Zeb.... I can remember sittin' on his knee when I was a little mite of a girl an' he'd tell us stories about the little children in Hongkong, Canton, Singapore, and all the islands in the Pacific, an' he'd tell us about shipwrecks and hurricanes.... He always kep' his pockets full o' presents, an' one time he gave me a little ivory box.... It come from Ceylon, made of an elephant's tusk,—I still got it to this day! I keep my buttons in it!... Aya, he was a great old sailor, an' he was master of his ship before he died.... An' he'd brought a lot of treasures home, ivory and amber beads, porcelain and coral, and a handsome ebony chair.

He married late in life—don't you remember Aunt Maria Hawkins?... She was a *peculiar* woman.... She had black hair that hung clean down to the top of her shoes.... It was black and heavy—just like a horse's tail. They said she was part Indian and that accounted for it.... An' she was awful proud of her hair.... Every Saturday night she used to put whale-oil on it to make it shine, an' I can remember the stench o' that whale-oil in church!... We sat in the pew—right alongside her.... She wore it in braids round her head, like a coil o' black snakes, an' a hat settin' on top....

Well, I was goin' to tell you. One Saturday, Uncle Zeb went out fishin'.... Come up thick a fog, and a north-east gale, an' they got lost out in the Bay an' couldn't make the harbour. Round midnight, the storm abated, an' the moon come out, an' they got in all right; but they was exhausted—drenched to the skin, cold an' hungry. He started home across the fields, an' seen a light in her window.... An' when he got in, he couldn't find nothin' to eat.... She'd let the fire go out.... An' there was Aunt Maria puttin' whale-oil on her hair.... She didn't have no supper for him—seemed like she didn't care whether he come back or not.... Well, he got mad—he was 'most froze an' starvin', ye see.... An' she didn't pay no heed at all—kep' right on combin' her hair.... An' it seems he went up to her, took hold of her hair—it was jes' like a rope, as thick as yer fist, an' she had one of them long jaws, hung down on her chest, like a hook—an' he caught her hair right under her throat.... Gave her a yank, an' she fell over—she was one o' them top-heavy women with small feet.... He was awful strong, the biggest man you ever saw—an' he started to drag her around the floor.... He drug her round three or four times, an' he looked back, an' he found he'd choked her dead.... Aya—he was sorry when he done it.... But he choked her.... (*She pauses, then listens to her husband's voice from the house*)

What is it, Will?... (*To Sally*) Will says it ain't so.... (*Louder, to her husband*) Well, I guess my grandfather knew

PLATE XVI

The Grandmother, the Mother, and the Daughter
in *Three Generations in a Court of Domestic Relations*
Photograph by Trude Fleischmann, New York

PLATE XVII

Vive la France: 1916

more about it than you do, old man!... Well, it seems her
ghost haunts that place. They say every night she comes
around the house, combin' her hair, and holdin' on to her
throat.... (*Her husband calls*)

What did you say?... All right—I'll come in.... (*To Sally*)
He wants me to rub him again.... I guess he hears us talkin'
an' he don't like to hear us havin' such a good time without
him.... Well, it's kind o' hard when you're miserable, to
know that other folks is enjoyin' themselves.... (*She rises*)

Well, Sally—it's been nice to see yer.... I'd like to hear
more about the funeral.... Must a' been nice—she was a
pretty woman.... Did you see my old Uncle David?... Does
he still wear them old green pants?... He wore them pants
at my weddin' forty-seven years ago.... I never seen anything
like 'em!... I asked him where he'd got 'em, an' he said he
bought an old billiard-table at an auction, an' it fell apart on the
way home, so he ripped off the cloth, an' had him a pair o' pants
made.... He's wore 'em to weddin's an' funerals ever since!...

Did yer see Polly Thresher?... Has she fleshed-up any?...
She don't flesh-up much, does she? She's awful scrawny....
I used to tease her when we was young.... I used to say,
'Polly, if it weren't fer yer face, you'd never know whether
you was comin' or goin'.'...

Well, good-night, Sally—I'm awful glad you're back....
I'll see you down at the store in the mornin'.... I'll be comin'
down 'round ten o'clock to get me some eggs.... My hens
ain't been layin' lately.... An' I got to git some apples to
make my old man a pie for Sunday....

It's a lovely bright day—the wind's comin' out o' the nor-
west, an' I guess we're goin' to have a spell o' fine weather....
Make us all feel better! Good-night!

Yes, Will—I'm comin' right along.... Aya—I'll rub ye....
I'm comin' as fast as I can.... Can't you have a mite o'
patience?...

(*Drawing her shawl about her shoulders, she walks slowly into
the house*)

A DÉBUTANTE AT A DANCE

→»→ ✖ ←«←

*A young girl enters, laughing in a high rippling girlish voice
and pretending to stagger with exhaustion. She carries a
white handkerchief which she waves, twists, strings out, rolls
up, unrolls, and flourishes throughout the conversation that
follows. She talks to the boy who has partnered her in the
last dance. She moves forward into a smaller room off the
ballroom, towards a large armchair which stands in the
middle of the stage. She gazes earnestly at the boy whenever
not otherwise occupied with her words or her laughter.*

Oh! Please don't make me laugh—I'm absolutely *exhausted*!...
Shall we sit down here and have a little rest?...
(*She turns to speak to another man*) Yes—I'd love to....
You'll have to give me five minutes, because really...I've
been dancing steadily for about three-quarters of an hour,
and I'm *absolutely exhausted*!... Well, I'm just going to sit
here, so do come back.... No, I promise.... I won't move....
I won't dance with anybody else.... I'll wait for you!...
Thanks....
(*Turns back to her partner*) Oh—what a *wonderful* party!
I've never seen so many nice people and the music is marvellous and isn't the floor absolutely perfect? Sometimes
it's too slippery—sometimes sort of sticky—but tonight you
just sort of *glide*—simply *divine*!... Oh! Let's sit down...
I'm absolutely *dead*.... (*She falls into a large roomy armchair
and remains there during most of her conversation but with much
wriggling and movement*) No, thanks—I don't want to smoke....
Now, please don't tempt me—*help* me!... Because I've
sworn off!... No, I have *not* been bribed.... I've not bet with
*any*body.... I just decided.... No—I just decided of my own

free will that I'd give it up…. Well, I'll tell you why if you promise not to laugh…. But I know you will…. Well, I decided that I had to find out whether I had any *character*…. I don't know if I have or not, and I think everybody *ought* to know, because you never can tell *when* you're going to need it!… Somebody told me that if you give up something you care about terribly, you mustn't tell anybody about it!… The whole point is, you mustn't get any reward—you mustn't get any praise…'cause lots of people do things in order to get praise, but *nobody* must know…. That's the point…. You just sort of make a pact with yourself—and then, if you succeed…that shows you've got a lot of character!… (*Laughs*) I knew you'd laugh…. Now I've told you, I've probably spoiled it all!…

Where was it I saw you last?… I remember—we had the most wonderful conversation…. And I decided you were one of the few men I knew who—well, I don't know, but… (*Laughs*)… Don't you know what I mean?… No, but I thought you were *marvellous*, because you were nearly as silly as I was…. Remember? We got the giggles—and we didn't either of us know what we were laughing at…. And it was such fun, because generally when you get the giggles, the other person makes you feel like an absolute *idiot*…. And then, we got frightfully serious—and I thought you were wonderful…. Because you made *me* feel quite intelligent!— and that was a new experience!… Well—I mean… I heard myself saying quite intelligent things…. But *you* made me say them…. Yes, you *did*…you *must* have—because you can't be intelligent alone!… Well—anyway I thought it was fun… because we had the same ideas about things….

I know—but I think that's the whole trouble about this business of going out…. I go out every night…. Yes—I just came out this winter and I was so excited—because I felt that at *last* I was really on my own…. I was going to meet so many people…and I was going to find out a lot about life, and about people, and about myself…and I don't think you *do*!…

Exactly! I know.... I literally go out night after night....
I meet *hundreds* of people.... And I talk and talk—I absolutely talk my head off.... And half the time people don't
even listen!... And the rest of the time they don't seem to
understand!... That's what I *mean*.... You sort of come up
against a kind of stone wall.... You don't sort of get anywhere.... I know—I've always thought people are the most
interesting things in the world!... I think that everybody has
something in them—*something* to give—and the point is to *get*
it.... And most of the time you don't, and you come away
sort of discouraged.... Do you?... Absolutely!—that's what
I mean....

Oh, I think that's *so* true!... Well—that's what I've always
felt.... I think you *have* to be—but of course, my friends
laugh at me.... Oh, they say I'm much *too* serious-minded—
I don't think I am—do you?... Well, anyway—I always have
been.... I don't think you can help it if you're *made* that way....
And I don't think it spoils your having a good time.... Nobody has more fun than I do, but I think a lot. Do you?...
I think practically *all* the time...and they say you shouldn't....

Yes, because I think the whole point is...there's so—*much*
—*more* in life than just all this!... And I want to find out
what it is!... After all, when you come right down to it—...
I think that life *is* serious—terribly serious....

(*Turns suddenly as she sees a friend*) Oh, *hello*! When did
you get back?... My! It's grand to see you—you look wonderful!... *Crazy* about your dress!... Did you have a divine
time?... When am I going to see you?... What? You mean
tomorrow?... Wonderful! Who's going?... Oh! What fun!...
How are you going to get 'em all there?... Do you want my
car?—do you want the family's car?—do you want my
brother's car?... I'll *try*—you'll need an awful lot of cars if all
those people are going, because everybody hasn't got cars....
Well, listen: call me up in the morning if I don't see you
again tonight.... Isn't it a *marvellous* party?... What?... Sure
—you bet I will!... I'm game for anything.... Fine!... Where

are we going?... Oh, *wonderful*! And the lilacs must be out....
Bye!

(*Turns back to her partner*) And the trouble *is* that so few
people realize it.... Well, that's what I mean.... And I don't
think you get *anywhere* in life unless you realize things—do
you?...

Absolutely! I think you've simply *got* to.... I *know*—and if
you don't...well—where *are* you?... You know—you're the
most wonderful person.... I don't know—the way you understand...and so few people understand!... Well, I always have
an idea back of everything I say...but sometimes it's terribly
hard to sort of.... Exactly! And you seem to catch my
point.... And we both get there together and it's such fun!...
Absolutely!

(*During what follows she becomes immensely serious, grows
feverishly involved in her effort at argument, even as the argument progressively wanders and disintegrates*)

What?... Do I believe in Platonic friendship? I certainly
do! I think it's the most *wonderful* relation between a man
and a girl.... I mean—to begin with.... I mean—you know
where *you* are—and I like knowing where *I* am!... The trouble
is, when anything else is coming...half the time you don't
know where you are...but in friendship you *do*...and I think
you get so much further if you know *where* you are.... Absolutely! It's *so* much safer.... Exactly—and anyway, I think
it's much better to be somewhere before you start!...

What?... Why, no—I don't think I have any more brains
than anybody else...but I *use* what I've got! I like to think—
and I like to talk.... Absolutely!... Anyway, I always sort of
feel that...(*Suddenly she breaks off*)

Oh! *Listen*! Do you hear what they're playing?... The
'Blue Danube'... Can you *bear* it?... Well, *I* can't!... I've
simply *got* to dance!... (*She rises*) I know I did, but I'm not
going to wait any longer.... Five minutes must have passed....
I'd rather dance with you, anyway....

You know, sometimes I get *so* discouraged about society,

and meeting people, and not sort of getting anywhere...and then suddenly you meet somebody.... Exactly—I feel as if I'd known you for *ages*!... Absolutely!... And I could talk to you about *everything*!... Come on—let's go!

(*Swaying to the waltz music, she goes off with her partner to the dancing*)

THREE GENERATIONS IN A COURT
OF DOMESTIC RELATIONS

⇢≫ ⊛ ≪⇠

*Three Jewish women come into the court-room of a Court
of Domestic Relations in New York City. The first is
the grandmother, eighty years old; following her are her
daughter, forty-seven, and her granddaughter, nineteen. The
grandmother advances, first to the clerk's desk, then to the
Judge who sits above her on his bench, while the two others
fall back and take chairs.*

THE GRANDMOTHER

(*She is old, bent, and rheumatic. She wears a black shawl over
her head and holds it tightly about her as she speaks broken English in a gruff voice and heavy Jewish accent*)

Come on, Sadie.... Rosie, come on.... (*She beckons to her
daughter and granddaughter to hurry and sit down. Then she
walks forward and peers at the clerk of the Court*)
What you want I do? (*She raises her right hand*) Yes, I
always tell the truth—always. (*She turns to the Judge*) Good
morning, Judge—good morning!... Eh?... My name? My
name is Anna Abrahams. Anna Abrahams.... I'm seventy-nine
years old.... Seventy-nine—yes...next week I am eighty....
I live at One Sixty-four Orchard Street, New York City...
with my daughter and my granddaughter.... Twenty-five
years—always the same place.... That's my home....

I come here this morning, Judge, please, to ask you to tell
my granddaughter she got to stay home and work!... She
wants to marry...and go to the West...and leave her mother
and me to starvation.... I'm an old woman—you couldn't
expect me to work—I'm too old to work. And my daughter,

she's got heart-trouble and can't work.... We couldn't live without Rosie.... She keep us now for two years—now she wants to go away and get married.... And we go on the street and starve.... She don't care.... (*Pauses*) She needs to be told by the Judge she must stay by us.... We give her good education—she should keep us.... She's a bad girl, Judge—she run around crazy and think only have a good time.... She go to the movies every day—she go dance every night—she come home late.... She waste her money—she waste her time.... She buys all those silly things...thinks only of herself...runs around with all those wild girls and boys.... Eh? This young man? Oh, he's no good.... He don't work and don't try to work—he has no job.... How he keep a wife?... And he drinks.... He make a very bad husband.... If she wait she will get a better man.... I'm an old woman—I find her a good husband when she get a little older, and bring him to the house, and we all be happy.... She's too young to get married—she don't understand nothing.... Eh? Sit down?... (*Mutters*) He don't listen to what I say! (*To the Judge*) You should listen to me, Judge—I'm an old woman.... I know what's right.... Rosie—she should stay by us.... We got a nice little home—why she want to go away? (*Muttering, she sits down*)

THE MOTHER

(*She rises from her chair. The shawl is dropped to the shoulders. She is wan and tired and speaks in an exhausted voice, and with a slight Jewish accent. She raises her right hand and takes the oath*)

Yes, Sir.... Good morning, your Honour. (*She speaks in a very weak voice*)... My name? Sadie Greenman—Sadie Greenman, yes, Sir.... I am forty-seven years old.... I am twenty-five years married.... I have three children—two sons and one daughter.... Well, one son has got tuberculosis...he couldn't work—he's in a sanatorium.... My other son—he left me.... I don't know where he is.... He ran away.... He doesn't write—and I don't know where he is....

My husband? He's dead—fourteen years dead.... Me, work? Yes, Sir, I did work.... For twelve years...in a box factory, but now I couldn't work no more.... I have a very bad heart-trouble and my arm is paralysed.... I couldn't work.... My daughter, Rosie, supports me and my mother—for two years now she has kept us.... I did all I could for my children—I sent Rosie to a business college when she finished public school...so she could have a profession....

Yes, Sir—she has got a wonderful job—she has a very fine salary.... She's getting along so well, and she likes her work. ... But now, she only wants to go....

Yes, Sir—she wants to marry and go to the West.... And then, my mother and me, we would have to go to a home for old people.... Well, I don't want she should leave us.... We got a nice little home.... So I come here this morning, Judge, please to ask you to tell my girl she should stay by us.... No, Sir—I have no money saved. We couldn't live without Rosie....

No, Sir—I don't like this young man.... He don't work regular—he don't seem to *try* to work.... And he drinks.... I'm afraid he would make a very bad husband.... I know it's hard for Rosie—but I think it's worse if she marries this fellow....

Oh, yes, Sir—that's right.... You should speak to her.... But please, Judge—tell my girl she should wait.... She's so young...and she don't understand what is life.... And she owes me something after all I have done for her.... Thank you. (*She sits down*)

THE DAUGHTER

(*She rises briskly from her chair. The shawl is now discarded. She advances and speaks in the fresh, alert voice of a young New York Jewish girl. She smiles and addresses the Judge eagerly*)

(*Takes oath*) Yes, Sir—Good morning, your Honour!... My name?... Rosie.... Rosie.... Oh, I beg your pardon—my name is Rose Elizabeth Greenman.... I always forget—everybody calls me Rosie, so when anyone asks me my name, I generally just say Rosie!...

Oh, yes, Sir—I do—I like my name.... I think it's a very pretty name—Rose Elizabeth—but I never use it.... Everybody calls me Rosie.... I'm nineteen.... Well, I'm going to be twenty next week.... Yes, Sir—the very day my grandmother's going to be eighty, I'm going to be twenty.... It's funny—we got the same birthday—we celebrate together every year.... She's exactly sixty years older than I am....

Yes, Sir—we live at One Sixty-four Orchard Street....

I do—I support them. For two years, now, I have kept them—I'm a stenographer....

Oh, I *have*—I've got a very nice job.... Yes, I have a good salary.... Oh, I love my work.... I think it's very interesting work....

Happy? You mean home?... Oh, sure—we get along just fine.... I'm always happy!...

Oh, yes, Sir—I *am*. I'm devoted to my mother, and my grandmother, too.... We have—we've got a very nice little home....

Yes, Sir—that's true too.... I do.... I want to get away from here and get married and go to the West—and I want that my mother and my grandmother should go to a home for old people.... And they don't want to go!...

Well, I made all the arrangements, you see—and now, they say they won't go.... So we come here to get your advice.... I went to five or six different places and I didn't care for them, and then I found this place and it really is just perfect, and I think they'll enjoy it when they get used to it.... It's not so very far away—it's only about forty minutes.... You can go three ways.... You can go on the Sub and the El and the Bus.... And when you get up there, it's beautiful—because the house has got four sides to it.... There's windows all around and the sun seems to be coming in everywhere.... They got a couple of trees in front and some grass—and in

the room they're going to give my mother and my grandmother, the window looks right straight into a tree—you can
see the sky through the branches, and I imagine it's like in the
country.... And they got some geraniums in the windows....
And the place is fixed up beautiful.... They got cretonne
drapes, cretonne sofas and chairs, and they got cushions in
the chairs.... They got rugs on the floor, and they got books
and magazines layin' around.... They got a piano, they got
a radio and a Victor, and they got a lot of records....

How many old ladies?... I guess there's about thirty....

Oh, they seem to be very contented.... Yes, Sir—they were
sitting around—some of them was knitting, sewing.... One
of them was singin' and playin' the piano.... And they take
them for a ride to the Bronx Park once a month.... And
there's a 'Five and Ten' and a movie only two blocks away....
And they got beautiful pictures hanging on the walls.... Yes,
Sir—somebody give them a gift of pictures and they hung
them all over the house....

You want me to tell you about the pictures?... Sure, if you
care to hear. I was looking at them for half an hour.... The
lady was very kind—she showed 'em to me.... My mother,
she likes beautiful things, and I know she'll enjoy them pictures just like I did.... Well—in the front hall, they got
Niagara Falls.... You'd think the water was there. It seems
to be coming down from the ceiling to the floor.... Then, in
the sitting-room they got a picture of a cathedral—I believe
it's in France.... It's got two spires, very tall.... And one is
different from the other.... And the lady was telling me the
walls is mostly glass.... And it's been there for about eight
hundred years.... And the stone is all carved by hand—they
didn't have no machines in those days.... And they got saints
and angels walking all over the doors...and flowers and everything carved right out of stone.... It's beautiful!... Then, they
got a picture of George Washington in the dining-room.... And
they got a picture of a garden in England—it's all in colour—
beautiful flowers—and there's a little house on a hill and it's

got a straw roof and smoke coming out—and there's some sheep.... My! It must be pretty over there—I'd like to see them flowers growing.... Do I love flowers? I certainly *do*.... I go uptown sometimes—see them in the florists' shops.... But those flowers grow in glass houses, and I guess in England the flowers grow out doors.... No, Sir—I was never in the country. I was to Coney Island, but you don't see no flowers growin' down there....

Well, you see, Judge—I can't give him up.... I got to go. He has got a wonderful job out in the West.... Well, my grandmother didn't tell you about it—she don't want that I should go.... But he's got a wonderful opportunity and we're looking forward to it.... Well, I'll tell you how it is. You see, my young man has got an uncle.... He's not personally acquainted with the uncle, but he's got a letter from him.... It seems he heard he was going to get married, so he wrote him a letter saying he would like to have him come out there and bring me, and live with him on his ranch....

Oh, it's very far away—yes, Sir.... But he's goin' to send us the money for the ticket.... All we got to do is go to Grand Central station, buy a ticket, get on the train, and go!...

Oh, you go for two days and two nights, steady going. Then, you get to a big city, but that ain't it.... No, Sir. You got to get out and cross the city and get in another train. Then, you go for two more days and two more nights.... Altogether, you go for four days and four nights.... But in the end, you get there.... And he says when you get out there's absolutely nothing to see—only land and sky. He says you can see very very far....

No, Sir—I never did.... I seen a lot of ocean down at Coney Island, but I never seen a lot of land....

Afraid? Why would we be afraid?... No—we'll be together and we'll be working.... We think it's a wonderful opportunity, and we're looking forward to it....

No, we don't know nothing about it—but we can learn.... Well, we're both young...and my young man's very bright.

Well, I won't be much use being a stenographer.... But I can cook.... Yes, Sir—my mother taught me.... I sure *am* glad, now.... Well, I think when men work hard all day, they like to come home and find a girl waiting for them with supper ready.... I'm going to do my best.... And I'm going to take out some cretonne and some pictures and fix the place up pretty—like that home I was telling you about....

Oh, I *will*—I'll miss my mother something terrible!... I never left my mother before.... I know I'm going to miss my mother.... I'd take my mother with me if she would go—but she won't leave my grandmother.... And I couldn't take the two of them—there wouldn't be room for two.... It's just a little bitty house and a lot of land.... But they couldn't sleep out of doors.... And I don't think it's right to take three, when they're just looking for one.... (*The Judge questions her further and she now becomes desperate and angry*)

Well, you see, Judge—there's not a word of truth in what my grandmother says.... Well, it's *not true*, because he's a *very fine* fellow.... That's why it's not true.... He's a very *fine* fellow.... He's twenty-three years old.... He ain't always had work—there's a lot of fellows ain't had work.... He tried very hard, but he never could seem to land a job....

No, Sir—he don't drink.... He does *not* drink!...

Well, he drunk some because he was so discouraged.... You know how it is, Judge—there's a lot of boys like that.... They go to look for work and they can't find work, and it seems that nobody wants them.... Then, they get discouraged, and then they get drinking.... He won't drink no more when we get married—he told me.... He told me he was never going to drink when we was married.... Well, he'll be working, you see, and he'll be happy, and somebody told me that men don't drink so bad when they're working and when they're happy.... (*Pauses and listens*)

Well, that's not true either—because I'm not that kind of a girl.... I do *not* run around and waste my time, and think only of myself.... They get everything I earn.... Every penny

I've earned for the last two years.... Only just what I have to
have to keep myself respectable for my work and buy my
lunch and a few little things. I ain't had no holiday in them
two years.... Oh, I never took no holidays—only them legal
ones.... I always got extra work.... I was lucky—and I'd
rather make the money.... (*Pauses*)

No, Sir—I do *not*.... Well—sometimes I am very fond of
dancing.... Maybe once or twice a week, I go to a dance—but
mostly I'm so tired, I come home and go to bed....

No, Sir. I do *not*. I have *not*.... No, Sir...., *No*, Sir!

Please, Judge!... I guess I can't talk and make you see....
I suppose you think I'm terrible selfish and ungrateful and all
that kind of stuff.... But don't make me stay!... Can't you see
—they're different?... They can't understand—that's all...
and you can't *make* them understand.... I want to get out
of this.... (*Cries*) I want my own life.... (*She stops suddenly.
The Judge has reprimanded her*)

I'm sorry.... (*There is a long pause as the Judge speaks and
she listens*)

You want me to come back?... Wednesday, ten o'clock?...
And bring him?... Oh, yes, Sir—he can come.... He'll be
pleased to come.... Yes, Sir.... And you want us to bring the
letter?...

Yes, Sir! And we can talk it over? And you'll tell us then?...
Yes, Sir—we'll be here—ten o'clock, Wednesday morning....
Thank you.... (*She steps back; then, heavy-hearted and half-
sullen she turns to her mother and grandmother*)

Come on, Grandma—come on home.... Oh, Mama—
stop!... Come on!... What's the use of talking now?... We
got to wait till Wednesday, anyhow.... Come on home....

(*She motions impatiently to her mother and grandmother and
follows them out of the Court*)

A CLASS IN GREEK POISE

→»» ✦ «««

The instructress enters, a tall, lanky woman of a certain age. She bows smiling to the assembled ladies, and takes out her notebook. She wears a loose garment designed for the exercises. She speaks in a flat, nasal, American voice with a good deal of perfunctory 'uplift' and 'inspiration' in it. There is a desk at one side of the room. On the other a pianist, Miss Mullins, presumably sits at a piano waiting for her cues.—This satire was one of the earliest in Ruth Draper's repertory, and since 'Classes in Greek Poise' are hardly a fashion any longer in America or elsewhere, it now takes on the character of a period piece, the period being circa 1910 or 1915.

Good morning, Ladies—good morning.... Now—if you will kindly give me your names and your most recent weights, I will inscribe them in my class-book, and we will begin at once!... (*She moves towards the desk, and sits down at it*)
Mrs. Jefferson?... Two hundred and fourteen pounds?... You have your bloomers, Mrs. Jefferson?... Madame Martel?... One hundred and ninety-nine and a half pounds?... A bathing suit?... Oh, no—it will serve beautifully. Many people use them, and I'm sure yours is very chic!... Miss Carpenter?... Two hundred and sixty-four pounds?... Green bloomers?... Oh, no—green is a lovely shade. Any shade that is near to nature is dear to me.... And I would like to call your attention, ladies, to the charming little tunic that Miss Carpenter is wearing.... A perfect Grecian garment—high-waisted tunic, and bloomers to match!... You've given some thought to your costume, I see!... Mrs. Foster?... Two hundred and thirty-five pounds?... Black satin? Very smart!...

Now, if you will all kindly line up on the chalk line, we will begin at once....

(She rises and stands before the line of women)

Ladies, I will not repeat to you what I said in my preliminary talk last week, on the underlying principles—the permanent value—of the study of Greek Poise! But there are two or three little thoughts which I would have you always carry with you. This course is based entirely on my own personal observations of Greek Art and the attitude of the Greeks towards the human body. These bodies of ours are, after all, the homes of our souls. I feel therefore that we should live to be beautiful—to attain bodily perfection as nearly as possible; and to express the spirit—the personality that lies within each of us—not only through our minds and the words which we utter, the thoughts we convey, but by our bodies, by gesture, action, and, above all, by our poise!... Poise is harmony—rhythm, control, posture, grace; and once you've got it, it will stay right with you. You'll never lose it, you'll never be awkward or ill-at-ease. You'll never be tired—you'll walk like goddesses—and when you sit, you'll sit *(She sits)* as if on a golden throne—be it merely a camp-stool, a soap-box, or a stone at a picnic. And when you lie down, your bodies will take beautiful, sinuous curves, relaxed as if on clouds— like the famous Fates on the Parthenon frieze. They look so graceful and yet so comfortable—relaxed and controlled at the same time!...

Now, ladies, if you will kindly take up your positions on the dotted line, we will begin with an exercise in deep breathing.... We all have to breathe, but very few people know *how* to breathe!... *(To the pianist)* Miss Mullins, will you please give us those slow minor chords?... Make them very *slow*, and *very minor*.... *(To the ladies)* Stand with the weight poised forward on the balls of your feet—arms relaxed, head up.... Then inhale deeply, rising on the toes, and raising the arms simultaneously in time to the music...*(She makes motions accordingly)* and keep on breathing until I tell you to stop!...

PLATE XVIII

The Children's Party
Photograph by Trude Fleischmann, New York

PLATE XIX

A Dalmatian Peasant in the Hall of a New York Hospital
A portrait drawing by John Singer Sargent: London, 1914

Ready!... Rise on the toes—breathe!... (*She claps her hands suddenly*) Don't strain—there should be *no effort* whatsoever....

Let me give you a little hint that will help you!... Will you imagine yourselves in a garden?... Full of pretty flowers— and just concentrate your minds on the odour of your favourite flower.... Mrs. Jefferson, will you take a lily?... Madame Martel, a rose?... Miss Carpenter, a violet?... Mrs. Foster, a piece of heliotrope?... That's *lovely*!... Now, ladies—just imagine you're smelling the sweet perfumes.... Rise on your toes, breathe—smell your flowers!... (*She rises on her toes*) Smell your flowers!... That's better! You see, you were breathing and you didn't *know* it!... Your lungs were filled with no effort at all!... Then, exhale gently, as though you were cooling a hot drink.... (*She exhales*) So!... Until the lungs are empty. A vacuum is created—then they fill up of their own accord. This is a natural phenomenon and we don't have to bother about it.

Now, ladies, we will do an exercise which I call 'prancing' —all my pupils enjoy this.... Will you just line up on the dotted line—about four feet apart so as not to interfere?... We're going to *prance*, like those youths and maidens on the friezes of the temples—with which I'm sure you're familiar— those lovely processions.... And to make it seem more realistic, I suggest you each carry a musical instrument.... Would you care for a flute, Mrs. Jefferson?... Just put your fingers on the stops, and play your little flute!... Madame Martel?... Cymbals? Just lovely!... Miss Carpenter?... Oh! They didn't have violins in those days.... How about a trumpet? A *long* silver trumpet?... Mrs. Foster?... A drum? Perfect!...

Miss Mullins, will you give us Schubert's 'Marche Militaire', and make it snappy?... Ready, ladies—on the first beat of the music, left foot forward.... Ready.... Go!... *Way* up with the *knees*, ladies—there's nothing more beautiful than the mechanism of the hip joint!... (*She acts out the motions*)

Blow your trumpet!... Beat your drum!... You're all out of time, Mrs. Foster—follow the music!... Breathe! Don't forget to *breathe*!... Play your flute, Mrs. Jefferson! Throw your head up and smile—put some *verve* into it!... Spirit is what I want to see—we're prancing along through the forest for the pure joy of living!... Keep on.... No, you won't explode. ... Once more around!

(*She stops suddenly*) One moment, Miss Carpenter—something is falling!... Careful—don't trip! Hold on to her!... Steady—just let them go—better step out.... Oh! That's all right—we're all friends here.... That might happen to anyone.... Elastic is of a very poor quality these days.... Just leave them on the table, and we will go on with the lesson.... Just pause a moment.... Thirsty?... Will you have a sip of water?...

Now, ladies, we will not do any more violent exercises— I don't want to tire you on your first day—but I would like to recall the exercises which I described last week, and have you practise them assiduously in the privacy of your rooms.... Remember the exercises based on my personal observations of all our little animal-brothers?... We can learn so *much* from them—even from the lowest forms of life we can learn. Nature has many lessons for us, if we would but hearken!... Do you remember, Mrs. Jefferson, what is one of the lowest forms of life?... The earth-worm—exactly! And what does he teach us?... Miss Carpenter?... To *stretch—precisely*!... He's probably the greatest stretcher in the world!... It is good for us all to stretch, so I suggest that every morning, when you alight from bed, just let yourselves fall carelessly upon the carpet—and pretend that you are *earth-worms*!... Stretch to your *fullest* extent from your finger-tips to your toes—then roll over and repeat on the other side, and so work your way across the room in this manner.... Then, pretend you're fishes, and swim... (*She demonstrates*) raising the head high above the floor and extending the arms in a swimming motion.... Then, leap like frogs around the room. (*She leaps*)...Crawl on all fours like Brother Bear. Climb imaginary trees, like monkeys.... And *fly* like the *birds*!... Every morning, when I go to the telephone, and move from room to room, I wave my arms rhythmically, like wings (*She waves her arms*), and it limbers me up for the day!...

Another beautiful exercise—though rather violent and exciting—is to pretend you're nymphs and dryads in a forest, being pursued by *satyrs*!... Open your windows wide—scatter your chairs and tables—and just *race* around the furniture in a *frenzy*!... It's like a wonderful game, and doubly efficacious, for it stimulates the imagination at the same time!...

Now, ladies—we will close with the walk.... The beautiful human walk. Very few people know how to walk—and we must *learn*!... Miss Mullins, may we have Mendelssohn's 'Spring Song'?... Will you please take up your positions on the chalk line?... The weight poised forward on the advancing foot—the left arm thus, as though you held a lily (*She demonstrates*)—the right thus, as though you were leading a lamb....

Now, let us paint you a little word-picture: imagine yourselves in a meadow on a beautiful morning in May.... The sky is blue above us. I see a little lake glimmering through the trees, sparkling in the sun.... There are flowers at our feet. The birds are singing merrily in the branches, and the air is soft and sweet.... We're going to enjoy our little walk, to the accompaniment of the famous 'Spring Song' by Felix Mendelssohn.... Ready—left foot forward, now.... In time to the music.... (*She walks accordingly*) We stroll along—breathing the soft sweet air—holding our lilies, and leading the lambs.... *Breathe*, ladies! Heads *erect*!... And smile!... Don't *wobble*, Mrs. Jefferson—don't take your weight off one foot till you've got it firmly on the other!... *Smile*, Miss Carpenter—we're enjoying our little walk!... Now, here by the silver birch, let us turn and change.... (*She turns*) Change the lily for the lamb!... And back we go to the mossy stone—

here, by the running brook.... And here we pause.... A fit closing to our lesson!

(*She stops and relaxes*)

Now, ladies—if you will go and get your showers and your rub-downs.... And just a word before we part. Will you *try*, between now and Thursday, *not* to soil your *lips* with *rich food*?... Remember, eat *nothing* but what I call nature's foods —fruit, nuts, and water, and I shall expect three pounds off each of you by Thursday!... I hope you're not exhausted.... And I wish you a very good morning, and *au revoir* until we meet again!

THE GERMAN GOVERNESS

→»»⊛«←

*She sits in a straight chair before her pupils in the class-
room of their family home, an elderly, thin, worried woman,
worn and harassed by her years of teaching, and nervously
aware of her unruly charges. She speaks in a strong German
accent, and is constantly sniffling and coughing as the lesson
proceeds. She wears several thick shawls around her shoulders, clutches a pocket handkerchief in one hand, and holds
her book closely before her near-sighted eyes with the other.*

Quiet, *please*, children!... And go to your places.... Stop this
laughing—this whispering and giggling!... Remember, when
I come in, I want you to be quiet.... Stand by your desks and
say nicely, 'Guten Morgen, Fräulein'.... Say it!... *Guten
Morgen, Kinder*....
Sh! Sh! Sh! (*She coughs and sniffles*) Shut that window,
Charlie! Shut it down! I have a very bad cold, *und* a very bad
headache.... I don't want any draughts.... Sh! Stop laughing,
please. What is so funny? I also like to laugh—but not now.
We are here to learn German.... Quiet, *please*! Remember,
the more quickly we begin, the more quickly we are through....
So everybody give me your attention.... Please turn to page
forty-eight.... Will you translate, Walter?... The top of the
page.... Go on, darling.... The hat?... Whose hat?... Whose
hat are we talking about?... Sh! Don't tell him. He gets it....
We are studying the possessive case.... Everything we talk
about belongs to somebody else. The hat belonged to somebody. Who did it belong to?... No—*not* my father.... Something belonging to my father.... My father's gardener—
exactly!... Where was it?... Sh! Don't tell him. He gets it....
Oh, I know you know it—you always know everything. Give

someone else a chance.... Nellie, will you please stop scratching your head with the pen!... You ruin the pen.... It's very vulgar. Put it in the desk. Go on, Walter.... The hat of my father's gardener was hanging.... Where was it hanging?... On the grapevine. Very nice—hanging on the grapevine.... The hat of my father's gardener was hanging on the grapevine.

Annie—will you take the second sentence?... It's all about flowers.... Now begin.... The lilies—what else besides lilies?... (*She notices more disturbance*) Sh! Stop it!... Go on, darling.... And roses—exactly! The lilies and roses.... Now, where were those lilies and roses?... Where would you *think* they would probably be?... You could almost guess where they were.... It's like in English, only with a 'T'.... *Garten*—exactly—garden. Whose garden?... Sh! Sh! Children, don't laugh at her. It's very mean of you. She's doing the best she can.... Go on, darling.... The lilies and roses in the garden of who?... Morris—will you please use your pocket-handkerchief!... You haven't got a pocket-handkerchief? What did you do with it?... You gave it to Louise? Louise, will you please give Morris his pocket-handkerchief.... You gave it to Harry?... Harry—give Morris Louise's pocket-handkerchief.... Children, how *many times* must I ask you—every day in this cold weather—*please*, everybody, bring your own pocket-handkerchiefs! I can't have always this mixed blowing going on.... Stop laughing!... Go on, darling. Who did this garden belong to, where the lilies and roses were?... *Schwager*, *Schwester*, or *Schwägerin*?... Sister-in-law.... The garden of my aunt's sister-in-law.... That is the sister of the husband of the aunt—or the wife of the brother of the aunt. You see?... Now, we come to the verb. What were the lilies and roses doing in the garden of my aunt's sister-in-law?... What were they doing?... Don't cry, darling. Just concentrate and you get it.... We must have a verb—everything must be doing something or else it isn't!... Just think a little. It was summer.... Perhaps the sun was shining, and it had been raining in the night. What would the lilies and roses probably be doing?... What? A little louder—we don't hear you!... Blooming! The lilies and roses were blooming—that's quite right. That's very nice! You see, you got it!

(*She turns suddenly in irritation*)

Charlie—will you please stop snapping your garters!...

Now, children—I want the rule for prepositions that we have been learning for ten days.... And I hope somebody knows it.... Do you know it, Bobby?... Well, tell us what it is. Go on!... Listen, please—children: *aus, außer, bei, mit, nach, seit, von*, and *zu*.... Stop it! You know very well that I mean it—now, stop it!... Annie—come and sit here and don't let him tease you.... It's your fault—don't look at him.... What case follows the use of those prepositions?... What case comes after?... No, they don't take the genitive.... No, they don't take the accusative.... (*In despair*) Oh, children!... No —you're just guessing. Does *nobody* know what they take?... They take the dative! Please remember: *aus, außer, bei, mit, nach, seit, von*, and *zu*, take the dative. *Durch, für, gegen, ohne, um*, and *wider*, take the accusative. *An, auf, hinter, in, neben, über, unter, vor*, and *zwischen*, take the dative for position and the accusative for motion. It's so simple. It is absolutely important that you know these rules. You never will speak German without them. They are fundamental to the understanding of the language!... If I go *out* of the house—*by* the fire—*with* my dog—*after* the cow...it's the *dative* case. You must learn the rules!...

Now, children, I am going to read you a beautiful little poem!... One minute! Harry—get up from under the desk there!... What have you got in your blouse?... What?... Guinea-pigs?... Those baby guinea-pigs?... Children, where do you get these ideas? There is absolutely nothing funny about it—it is outrageous! Cruelty to animals! They don't need to be kept warm, because they have fur on, and they have their mother. Go back and put them in the garden—and shut the door.... Now—quiet, please!... Now, children, please turn to page sixty-six.... You will enjoy this. It is a very famous poem called 'Die Lorelei', and it tells a story about a beautiful lady, and some sailors. Now, you will see what is going to happen to those poor sailors!...

DIE LORELEI

Ich weiß nicht, was soll es bedeuten,
Daß ich so traurig bin;
Ein Märchen aus alten Zeiten,
Das kommt mir nicht aus dem Sinn.

(*She breaks off, startled and angry*) Who threw this dead fly?... *Who threw it?*... Children—I can't stand it any longer! I come here every morning—I give you my life and my time. I try so hard to make you happy, and I have only insults. I will control myself, now—but mind you—you will hear of this again. It is by no means the end—your parents shall hear of it! It's outrageous! I can't stand such treatment any longer!... I will go away and leave you, and when I am gone you will see how you miss me!... And—listen to me—unless this fly is explained, every one of you gets punished!... (*After an ominous pause*) I will finish the poem.

Die Luft ist kühl und es dunkelt,
Und ruhig fließt der Rhein;
Der Gipfel des Berges funkelt
Im Abendsonnenschein.

Children!... Nellie—come back!... (*She looks about distractedly as the children disappear*) Where have they all gone to?... But you can't run away like this!... I don't care if it is a fire-engine.... Don't you know you cannot leave this room until I give you permission to go? My word is *law* here! (*She sighs and gives up hopelessly*)

Well, it is time to stop now, anyway.... Will you tell the other children the lesson for tomorrow—on page fifty-two?.... The second declension, and ten of the new words, and the rules over again.... *Ach! Ach! Wo werde ich enden mit den Kindern?... Es ist ganz abscheulich!... Ich kann's nicht länger aushalten....*

    (*She pulls her shawl about her, moans and mutters, and shakes her head dolefully as she leaves the room*)

A BOARD OF MANAGERS MEETING

✦

A New York lady comes hurrying into her drawing-room where her fellow members of the Board of Managers have already assembled and have been waiting some time for her late arrival. She greets them breathlessly and rather hectically, apologizing for her tardiness as she takes her place behind a table to preside. She is smartly dressed and hatted.

Good afternoon, ladies. I am *so* sorry to be late. I have been to a stupid luncheon party....

How do you do, Mrs. Walker!... How sweet of you to come!... Hello, Emily, dear!... Crazy about your hat.... How much? I don't believe it!... My dear—do let me have her address....

Where's our secretary? We must begin.... Oh, how do you do, Mrs. Barton! Sweet of you to come.... I hear your little girl had appendicitis.... Oh, it's *such* a relief to have it out.... I have had all mine out—I mean, my children's!...

(*To a servant who has come in*) Who's wanted at the telephone?... Alice, dear—you're wanted at the telephone.... And do hurry back.... We shan't have a quorum without you.... Where's our secretary?... Oh, there you are, Fanny dear!

Ladies—the meeting will please come to order!... We will have the minutes of the last meeting.... (*To Fanny*) *What?* You have *forgotten* the minutes?... You outrageous person! Really, Fanny, that's *too* careless. You must take this thing more seriously—it's a *very* important meeting.... I beg your pardon, Mrs. Walker?... *Send* for the minutes?... Oh, how sweet of you!... Your motor's outside?... Oh, that's too kind!... Oh, Eleanor—will you press the bell, please!... Just there, by the table.... No—that's the electric light.... Just

below that picture frame—to the right—near the table....
Have you got it?... Twice.... Thanks!

Ladies—the minutes have been unavoidably delayed, and
we will begin the meeting without them.... (*To the servant*)
Oh, James—will you please tell Marie to put on her coat and
hat, and take Mrs. Walker's motor.... Are you *sure* you don't
mind, Mrs. Walker? It's perfectly sweet of you!... (*To James
again*) And go right to Mrs. Preston's house, number one,
East Eighty-ninth Street, and go right up into her boudoir....
You're sure you don't mind, Fanny?... (*To James*)—Second
floor, in front.... (*To Fanny*) Back? Oh, have you moved?
Like it better?... Sunny, isn't it? (*To James*)...—and on her
desk, by the window, is a pile of books—sort of notebooks—
red.... And the second from the top—she thinks it's green—
with some yellow papers in it... (*To Fanny*)—You mean to
say you never *copied* them? Fanny, you *are* the most!... And
those are the minutes of this meeting!... (*To James*) And
bring them back here as quickly as possible.... Of course,
keep the motor!... Well, better bring *all* the books—the
whole pile.... Thanks, James.... Marie is out?... Oh, Lord!...
Well, is there somebody you can send?... All right! (*James
goes*)

Oh, he's very intelligent—he'll get them!

Now, ladies—the meeting will please come to order!...
Ladies—the most important business that we have to trans-
act this afternoon is to decide how we are going to raise four
thousand dollars for the furnishing of the Board Room in the
new Day Nursery.... Now I, being in the chair, it's not for
me to speak—and I want suggestions!... What do you think
of Anna's engagement?... Of course, I think she's mad.... I
think for a woman of her temperament to marry and rush off
into that country, now, is absolutely....

Ladies—please come to order! We must decide about this
money!...

I beg your pardon?... A dance?... Well, personally, I think
there is a great deal too much dancing.... And I think the

responsibility of it, and all.... I beg your pardon?... Tableaux?... My dear, do you think we've gone back to the Nineties?... Well, I always thought that tableaux are perfectly *deadly*.... One of the many things that should never be revived.... I think to pay five dollars to see a lot of women dressed up in clothes that never really fit—or are in the least becoming.... Oh, I beg you pardon?... Yes, I have an idea.... But as I say, being in the chair, it is not for me to speak!... Well, it's just this: here we are—a body of twenty women.... Why isn't it by far the simplest thing for each one of us to write twenty letters to twenty friends, asking for ten dollars?... Now, nobody minds slipping ten dollars in an envelope.... And there we are!... At the end of a week with four thousand dollars.... And no trouble to anyone!... You *do* agree with me?... Well, will somebody please put that in the form of a motion?... Oh, never mind! I think they heard what I said!... It has been moved.... Go on!... And seconded.... That we raise the money for the furnishing of the Board Room in this way.... All those in favour say 'Aye'.... Contrary, 'No'.... Motion is carried!

My dear Josephine, you can't object *now*!... I am very sorry but everybody else feels that it's the best way, and the vote has been taken.... You had your chance to discuss it.... Well, I'm sorry, but really you will find that it is very simple....

Now, ladies.... (*The children appear at the door with their governess*) Go away, children!... Children—I said *not* to come in! Mother doesn't want you! Mademoiselle, *why* did you...? No, children—go back!... Oh, well, come in, then!... Come in, darlings! Come to Mother!... Cecily, make a curtsey, and Bobbie, make your bow!... Cecily—won't you tell Mother that little French poem that you knew on Monday?... Go on, darling—stand up straight and tell us!... '*Au clair de la*....' What was the name of his friend?... And what did he ask for?... Well, sing it, darling! Remember the little tune?... (*To the ladies*) She knew it perfectly on Monday!...

Oh, yes—they speak French better than English! I always have my children begin with French.... Go on, Cecily—don't be silly!... But you *do* know it, darling.... You knew it perfectly on Monday—didn't she, Mademoiselle?... Well, never mind, then.... Don't cry!... No, you don't have to say it. Run along to dancing school now!... Yes, Mother's coming in a moment! (*The children and the governess leave*).

Y-e-s.... She *is* pretty.... But they are *so* naughty!... I have no control over them!... Pretty little dress, isn't it? Just came out from Paris.... She's a doll to look at, I must admit.... But they are just as *bad* as they can be!...

Now, ladies—we must decide about the milk.... Well, it's just this: I found that we can save five hundred dollars a year in our budget if we give the children condensed milk.... Now, some doctors think it's *poison*, but I think it's worth the risk.... Well, exactly! It does fatten children splendidly, and it does agree with some.... And we will just have to hope that it will agree with our babies.... I feel that five hundred dollars is not to be thrown away lightly!... Well, I am glad you all agree with me!

Oh—who told you about Dorothy?... Well, she had no right to!... But, my dear—if that sort of thing gets about town, you see where.... Exactly! I think we ought to do something about it....

Ladies—please come to order! We must get on with the meeting!... Well, the next thing we must consider seriously is the building of a car line.... Oh, you don't understand?... I forgot.... None of you were here when we discussed it before.... Well, it's just this: do you realize that we've built our Day Nursery at a point in the city where there are no cars to bring the mothers and babies to and fro?... Well, I realized this, but I went ahead—having all the time in the back of my mind the plan that we should influence the City authorities to build a car line at that section of the city.... In this way we will be doing the community—the entire community—a lasting service, and our little Board will go down in history as having accomplished that public benefit.... To me, that's where a woman's power lies.... You see, New York is laid out all wrong, anyway. It's a long, narrow island, and there are not half enough cross-town lines.... You didn't know New York was an island?...

Well, now—to come back.... Who do you suppose lays car lines?... Oh, no—the Street Cleaning Department has nothing to do with it!... The Public Service Commissioner! *That's* the man!... You know his wife?... Oh, my dear!... She knows the wife of the Public Service Commissioner!... She has influence with her husband?... Oh! How marvellous! Then we can go right ahead. Don't you see? You can have us all to luncheon, or something.... Isn't it extraordinary— there's *always* the opening wedge in a body of women like this!... We'll give him a wonderful lunch—make ourselves very agreeable—and there it is!... And as I said, we can push this thing through and do something for the city that will be of lasting value! I think it's marvellous—really!... What women can *do*—if they go about it in the right way.

Oh, dear—I have forgotten those wretched children! I promised to take them to dancing school, so I must run along now.... But I can meet you almost any day next week.... We have got a lot more important things to decide.... How about Monday? No, I am going out of town.... Tuesday? I am going to the dentist.... Wednesday? Having a permanent wave!... I am afraid I will have to telephone you, but I think we have accomplished a great deal today.... Don't you?... At least we have got the four thousand dollars, and I am awfully glad you agree with me about the milk!... And you know, I can just see those cars running to and fro across the city!...

Oh, here are the minutes!... If you don't mind, I think I will just omit the minutes until the next meeting....

Oh, goodbye ladies! Thank you all for coming!... And you will excuse me, won't you, if I run along?... Goodbye!...

Yes, children.... Mother's coming!

(*She hurries out distractedly, leaving the ladies to themselves*)

A CHARWOMAN

An elderly Irish charwoman enters an office in a large business building in New York City. She is in her working clothes and carries a dust rag. She finds another charwoman already there at work and greets her cheerfully. She speaks in an Irish-American brogue.

Good mornin', Mary—nice mornin'!... Indeed it is—a beautiful day.... Well, what's been goin' on here since I was away?... Did ye miss me?... I just thought I'd drop in and give ye a hand with the dustin'. I'm just through the other rooms and I'm goin' upstairs to scrub the floors.... Ha!... Ye hurt yer wrist?... Oh!... Liftin' that old marble gentleman.... He weighs a ton.... Sure, I squashed my thumb onc't with him.... Wonder who he is?... Oh, Mary, I'm sorry.... Did ye soak it good?... I'll bind it up for yer before we go....

Well, how have ye been gettin' on at home?... Pat's been drinkin' again?... And ye'd be leavin' him this time, would ye?... Well, I'm real sorry for ye, Mary—I am that.... Wasn't I through it all myself?... But I believe I'd do it again to have Jim back now.... Here—don't you be liftin' them heavy books.... I'll see to thim.... Ye're cold?... Ye must be ailin'.... I think it's grand and warm here!... We're lucky to have a place like this to clean.... A cousin o' mine, Mary Flynn, works down to the Tombs Prison.... *That's* a cheerful hole!... Ye need to have a warm heart and a good circulation to keep goin' at all in that place, I'm thinkin'.... Ah, and to be seein' the poor creatures in their cells!...

Mary, ye certainly giv' a grand polish to thim brasses.... Don't they look lovely!... What?... Your Mamie's got the measles?... Oh, now—ain't that a shame!... Oh, ye needn't fear.... No, she won't die.... Why, the rest'll do the child good.... It's the scarlet fever that's bad.... Then they take 'em away—put 'em in the hospital.... I lost two girls that way.... Oh, that's more than twenty years ago, now....

Here—I'll give ye a hand...hold on, now! (*She lifts a chair*)... I don't see how the gentlemen can do any work at all... sittin' in them comfortable chairs.... Ain't that elegant leather?... Your landlord's after ye?... Ain't he a terror, that man!... Oh, don't let him scare ye.... *Sure* he'll wait.... Ye'll get the money all right.... Christmas is comin'.... I guess they'll remember us here!... Why don't ye send him to Pat to collect?... Maybe the shock would keep him sober....

Ye're lonesome for yer girl?... Why, Mary, you're a fool.... Sure an' she's far better off in the country—in her own little place.... You should be thankful to have her so happy—instead of workin' her life away in this city!...

You ain't got no supper home, and Pat'll be beatin' ye, do ye think?... Mercy, Mary! Troubles is thick on ye.... Well, I'll tell ye what I'll do.... I've got a little piece of meat home—and half a pie.... Somehow, I don't feel much like eatin'.... I'll be leavin' 'em at your door, and you get back early and cook Pat a good supper, and tell him your hand hurts ye real bad...and you'll be keepin' him home.... Don't worry, now....

Listen till I tell ye a funny story.... Mary Flynn, my cousin, got it off one of the prisoners in the Tombs.... It seems there was a drunken man in the train.... He says to the man next him, 'What day of the week is this?' And the man says... 'Thursday!' And the drunken fella jumps up and sez, 'Goodness me! That's my station!'... Now, isn't that good!... I had to laugh when I heard it!...

(*She turns to speak to a janitor who has come in*)

Harry, will ye tell 'em to hurry up with them new demijohns of water for these rooms.... And are ye goin' up? Will ye take these pails o' mine up on your next trip?... I'll be scrubbin' on the next floor.... I'll be obliged if ye will....

(*Harry goes*)

(*A gentleman, the man whose office it is, enters*)

Good mornin', Mr. Jones.... It's early ye are!... Oh, we're just through here now in five minutes.... We be just after finishin'.... Yes, Sir.... The next room is all ready.... It's a grand day indeed!... (*Mr. Jones goes into the inner office*)

Mary, it seems to me them windows is awful murky.... Have ye got yer Bon Ami?... I'll polish 'em up a bit.... There —*that's* better!... Oh, look, Mary! Look! See the sun, shinin' on them windows up there.... Makes 'em like gold and diamonds!... I'll tell yer, Mary...we'd be rich if we could scrape that off the glass.... Ain't that lovely, now!... Just beautiful!...

Well, I guess I'll be goin' up to the next floor.... Hey?... What have I been doin' these five days?... Did ye hear tell of that big fire?... (*She now speaks slowly and brokenly*) Well, my boy, David...my only son...he was a fireman, you know.... Well—he was in the cellar...when the wall fell in.... Well, I was to the hospital with him for three days.... And then.... I took him up to the cemetery...and laid him beside his father.... Why didn't I tell ye?... An' how could I be tellin' ye and doin' me work?... How can I work?... An' what would I do—but work?... Well, good mornin', Mary!

(*Her voice becomes cheerful again as she goes out*)

AT A TELEPHONE SWITCHBOARD

⟫ ❦ ⟪

*The girl comes in briskly and cheerfully to take her place at
one of two switchboards in a public telephone office in New
York City. Her fellow worker, Carrie, is already seated at
the other switchboard as the girl greets her. It is early morning of a hot summer day. The girl, in spite of her friendly
good humour, is troubled by anxiety. After putting on the
neck-and-head piece at the board, she begins to manipulate
the instrument at which she sits, alternately using the plug
and handle of the board to put through the calls she receives
or sends out. An office-boy, Walter, is sitting nearby. There
are telephone booths in the room for private calls, and during the conversation that follows various customers come up
to the desk in front of the switchboards to order their calls.
The girl divides her speech between these customers, the
operators she talks to over the telephone, and Carrie and
Walter who are in the office with her; but throughout what
follows she is continuously busy manipulating the devices on
her switchboard. She talks in the broad, friendly accents of
a New York working-girl, and in an inflexion of the Bronx
or Brooklyn. The time of the action is around 1920–25.*

Good morning, Carrie!... Warm, ain't it?... It's going to be
a scorcher all right!... Oh, thank you, he's about the same....
Had an awful bad night.... No, I never went to bed at all—
just lay down on the couch now and then. (*She puts on the
neck-and-head piece*) Oh, I'm all right, thanks.... Katie, my
sister, you know, is a-watchin' him today.... She's goin' to
call me up soon.... The doctor said if he got through today
he'd give us some encouragement....
   (*She talks into the mouthpiece*)
   Hello, Central.... Morning!... Feeling pretty cheerful?...

Nice an' cool, ain't it?... Say, is that New Rochelle wire cleared up?... Oh, all right.... Hanover 6939.... Hanover 6939.... (*To the office boy*) Walter, just step over to the newsstand and get me some Wrigley's, will ye?... Here's a nickel!... Yes, sir, it is, *very* warm!... Hello, Hanover—Booth 2, please.... Hello—room 15?... I will connect you.... (*She pulls a hair off her shoulder*) Carrie, is your hair falling out?... Mine is—something terrible.... Herpicide?... Guess I'll have to try it.... Minnie was telling me about something made hers grow like weeds, only I forgot the name.... (*She plugs*) Broad 994?... Hello, Broad 994.... Good morning.... Flushing 32 party J.... (*Plugs*) Flushing 32 party J—forget something? (*Handle*) Hello—Broad 3920 has been changed to Broad 0994. One moment, please.... Hello...yes...I (*Plugs*) will call him.... Walter, go tell Mr. Apples there's a call for him.... Hello—Flushing (*Handle*).... All right, Mr. Hall— Booth 7.... I won't listen!... Broad—No. 3....

You see, Carrie, what worries me is the doctor says my brother—... Hello... (*Plugs*) One moment, please.... I will connect you.... (*To Carrie again*)—can't go back to work for ever so long.... (*To a customer*) Telegram? No, sir, in the far corner over there.... You're welcome.... (*To Carrie*)—and that he should go to the country and eat lots of nourishing food.... (*To Mr. Apples*) Your (*Handle*) call's in No. 1, Mr. Apples.... (*To Carrie*)—milk, eggs, everything.... Now, how am I going to manage to get him there?... (*Into the mouthpiece*) Vanderbilt 9547?... Hello.... (*Plug*) Vanderbilt 9547.... (*To Carrie*)—and Katie and I can't keep the flat without he helps.... You see, he earned twelve dollars a week.... We've (*Plug*) got—... Hello—the line is busy... —we've got a lovely little flat.... Gee! I'd hate (*Plugs violently*) to leave it.... Yes—that's just it.... Well, I know, but what are you goin' to do about it?...

(*Into the telephone*) I'll ring them again. (*Plug*) Try Vanderbilt 9547.... Long distance—yes, sir.... Hello.... Long distance.... Where to?... Chicago?... Chicago, please.... What number?... Main 3300.... Right.... (*To a customer*) Will you take a seat, please, and I will call you. (*Plug*)...Hello... (*Handle*).... Hello.... Murray Hill 6021 (*Plug*)...Hello—Murray Hill 6021...Hurry, please (*Plug*) John 3676.... Hello.... Hello—John 3676.... Hello—Murray Hill?... One moment, please. (*Handle*)...(*She looks around for the customer*) Where is he?... He was in such a hurry.... (*The man comes up*) Take Booth 14.... Hello...I will try them again, sir.... Hello—Central, can't you come in on this wire?... Can't you get Vanderbilt 9547?... (*Plugs hard*) Still busy?... Hello, John? No. 9. (*Handle*) Spring 2474?... Hello.... Spring 2474. (*Plug*) Hello.... Plaza 9000?... Hello.... Plaza 9000? (*Plug*) New Rochelle 53, party W. ...Hello (*Plug*) Say Central, is that New Rochelle wire clear?... Then give me 53, party W.... Plaza 9000.... (*Handle*) They do not answer!... Spring—the line has been temporarily discontinued. (*Plug*) Patterson 373?... Hello.... Patterson 373!... Wrong number—excuse it, please.... Hello. (*Plug*)... One moment.... Sorry sir, they do not answer....

(*She rings her home number*) Hello.... Hello.... Katie, is that you? (*Handle*) How's Billy?... Patterson? No. 3 (*Plugs with pencil*) Seems better? Good!... Brightened up some?... Try him on a little of that chicken jelly I brought in last night. (*Plug*) Hold on.... Lenox 7878?... Hello, Lenox 7878!... Katie, are you there?... Doctor been in yet? (*Handle*) Wait a minute.... Lenox—Booth 6.... I'll see, sir.... Hello.... Central?... How about New Rochelle? (*Handle*) All right?... No, sir—I'm sorry, sir, but the line is only just mended.... It was down in the storm.... I got it as quick as I could.... Hello—Katie?... Did he ask for me?... How long did he sleep after I left?... Good! Well, call up again later, will ye? So long.... Oh, Katie—fan him a little!... And there's some Cologne on my bureau.... Maybe he'd like some on his head...or a wet cloth, you know....

(*She disconnects Katie*)

Hello.... My lines are all busy.... (*To a customer*) You

(*Plug*) want to be connected with room 27?... One moment please.... There you are!... (*Plug*) Rhinelander 6600?... Hello.... Rhinelander 6600!... Hello!... New Rochelle.... Twenty cents, please.... Will you pay at the desk, please?... Stuyvesant 3259. (*Plug*) Stuyvesant 3259!... Rhinelander 6600—the wire is out of order.... Excuse me, sir, it is?... I can't help it, sir.... It is reported out of order now.... Stuyvesant 3259 has been changed to Gramercy 6404.... Booth 8....

(*To Carrie*) He's better, Carrie.... Waked up?... Asked for me?... Gee! I wish I was there.'(*Plug*) Worth 7579.... Hello.... Worth 7579!... (*To a customer*) Telegrams? No, sir—in that far corner over there.... Morningside 937? Hello (*Plug*) Morningside 937!... Worth—.... The line is busy.... One moment, please.... Excuse it, please.... Morningside (*Handle*) Booth 1.... (*To Carrie again*) Carrie, that's a dandy little suit you've got.... You (*Plugs with pencil*)....You don't say!... That certainly is cheap.... *This*?... No.... Why it's terrible!... It's about five years old, but I guess I gotta make it go a couple of years more!... Hello, (*Plug*) still busy? Hello.... I will call them.... Hello—is that the Superintendent's office?... They're calling Mr. Jackson (*Handle*).... Is he there?... All right!... (*To Carrie*) I hear you had a grand time down at Coney!... Carrie, you're the gay girl! How was Herb?... Ain't he sly!... Well—I never!... You couldn't shake him?... (*To the office boy*) Say, Walter, go and get us a couple of glasses of grape juice.... Have one on me, Carrie.... Aw, go on!... It's awful cooling!... Go on, Walter.... Here's a quarter.... (*To a customer*) The Bureau of Information? Over there, by that big sign.... The right time? (*She looks at her wrist-watch*) Nine-forty-seven.... Not at all.... Good morning, Mr. Forster.... Yes.... What?... Oh, go on!... You don't say!... Aw, you can't put that over.... Certainly.... What?... Oh, come off!... Say—do you know the 9.50's been called?... Hello, (*Plug*) the what?... The Superintendent of Parlour cars?... (*Plug*) Oh, you want the Pullman office?... What (*Plug*) have you lost? Your watch?... Oh, you want the Lost

Articles Department!... Oh, you want the time?... I can give
you that: 9.52.... I guess he's lost his head by now!... (*Walter
returns*) Ah, here's the grape-juice!... Thanks, Walter....
Say, that looks good.... (*She sips*) 'Tis good!...

(*She turns to Carrie again*)

Carrie, did you hear about Annie?... Well, it seems that she
went out with that Mr. Masters, night before last.... And
what if he didn't take her to a movie that she'd seen three
times already, instead of the play—like he'd promised! (*Plug*)
Hello.... I can't tell you.... I'll give you the Bureau of Information.... So.... Hello.... Yes.... Just a minute.... (*To
Carrie*)—So, Annie was awful mad—she *hates* the movies
(*Plug*).... And gee! I had a laff when she was tellin' me about
it.... Well, it seems—... (*Into the mouthpiece. Katie has called
her from home again*) Hello.... Hello.... Katie—how's it
goin'?... You've been tryin' to get me?... Oh!... Well?... Oh,
gee!... Yes.... He's fainted again?... Oh!... What?... Stop
cryin', Katie—I can't hear you!... What?... Yes—yes.... Did
ye get the doctor?... Aha.... (*In anxiety she turns to Carrie*)
Carrie—take that call, will you?... (*To Katie again*) Yes—
well, call Mrs. Fisher now upstairs.... She'll come down and
help you.... (*Into the mouthpiece, to Katie*) Can't you get him
warm?... Oh!... Well, I'll come right over.... Yes.... I'll run....
Oh, about ten minutes.... Take that big shawl off my bed
and rub him, Katie.... D'ye hear me!... And give him some
brandy—it's on the bureau, back o' Mama's picture.... Gee!...

(*To Carrie*) Carrie—Billy's worse.... I gotta go!... (*She
takes off the head-and-neck piece and hastily puts on her coat
and hat, but still listens to the wire*) I'll try and come back in
a couple of hours.... She was tryin' to get me.... Ain't that
the limit!... Call up Central and they'll send you another
girl.... Hello.... Hello.... Chicago?... Ready?... Yes.... All
right.... (*To the customer who has been waiting*) Chicago
through, sir.... Booth 7.... (*She rises and calls to Walter*)
Walter, pick up my hat, will ye?... Thanks.... You can finish
my grape-juice.... Give me my purse—thanks!... Oh, I guess

he'll come through all right.... Only Katie is terribly scared!...
Goodbye.... Whew, my head!... (*To a customer*) Telegrams
—no sir.... In there—the far corner over there!... (*To Carrie
and Walter*) Goodbye.... I gotta run!

(*Seizing her purse and clutching her coat together, she runs
out of the office in anxious haste*)

A FRENCH DRESSMAKER

-»» ⊕ «««-

The couturière, a highly temperamental lady of a certain age, a high style, and an agitated, distracted manner, comes hurrying into the salon of her Paris establishment and greets two customers, an American lady and her daughter, who have just arrived. Several assistants hover about the room or come and go through the doors in a flurry of entrances and exits. The scene is one of much movement and distraction, and the dressmaker is continuously moving about, attempting to deal with a great many affairs at once.

Bonjour, Madame. Mademoiselle, bonjour!... Asseyez-vous, Madame!... Vous ne parlez pas français?... You will excuse me, Madame?... I speak very poor English.... (*To her assistant*) *Voyons, Pauline, ne laissez pas les tissus par terre comme ça. Vite, ramassez-moi tout ça....*
(*She turns smiling again to the lady*)
Pardon, Madame—something for Mademoiselle? Certainly, we make so much for *les jeunes filles....* I know so well what they require.... Won't you look at my models, Madame? Look everywhere, please!... *N'est-ce-pas qu'elle est gentille? Regardez donc cette petite taille!...* (*She turns again to another assistant*) *Ah, elles sont riches — mais oui — les Américaines, bien sûr!...* Pardon, Madame, I was just telling Hortense that white satin would be very pretty for Mademoiselle.... But she must have many dresses, many colours, pink, blue, lace, taffeta—for the theatre—for a walking costume.... *Oui,* Madame, we have everything.... (*To a third assistant*) *Ernestine, apportez donc le modèle Lumière Céleste...et le Baiser de Colombine....* (*To the lady again*) I show you something that will be perfect for Mademoiselle.... (*To a fourth saleslady*) Virginie! Show Madame those beautiful silks.... *Elles sont*

belles, n'est-ce-pas?... Regardez donc les magnifiques cheveux dorés.... Madame devrait avoir un portrait de Mademoiselle!... (*To the lady*) I was just telling Hortense, Madame, you should have a portrait of Mademoiselle.... *Oh, non, Madame — je ne suis pas flatteuse....* It is true, Madame.... I make Mademoiselle a beautiful dress—and you will be very glad to have a portrait of her....

(*An assistant comes to say that Mrs. Parsons has arrived for her dresses*)

Madame Parsons est là? Eh bien, faites vite descendre la robe de Madame Parsons — qu'elle n'attende pas.... Deux minutes et je serai là. Voulez-vous m'attendre au salon?... (*She returns to the lady*) Oh, yes, Madame, certainly we can make five or six dresses by the middle of June.... *Pardon!...* (*The assistant returns with a message*) *Le tissu de Madame Fauntleroy-Smith n'est pas encore arrivé?... Eh bien, qu'on aille vite le chercher chez le teinturier! Dépêchez-vous!...* (*Again she resumes talking to the lady*) And anything for you today, Madame?... Nothing?... Perhaps you let me take your measure and I make a toile.... So many American ladies do like this, and in a few weeks' time, you have your dress!... You get everything in New York?... Yes, I know—they have beautiful things in New York.... But then—it is not Paris!...

(*She is interrupted by another assistant*)

Qu'est-ce qu'il y a?... Oh, eh bien — répondez à Madame la Comtesse qu'elle soit sans crainte — que tout sera chez elle à huit heures ce soir sans faute!... (*To the lady*) You like these materials, Madame? (*To her assistant Pauline*) *Mais non, Pauline — ce n'est pas la qualité que j'ai choisie. Faites voir les autres à Madame.... Oh, ces jeunes filles — elles ne savent rien!...* ... (*To the lady*) Oh, yes, Madame—certainly, we shall arrange a price for Madame.... Leave that to me!... I will spoil Mademoiselle!... *Comment?...* (*She begins to supervise the measurements*) *Non, ma petite, ce n'est pas ça du tout!... Enlevez-moi ce col — et je l'épinglerai moi-même.... Et ôtez cette dentelle!...* (*She suddenly breaks off in distraction*) Madame,

I wonder if you will excuse me.... I have many people waiting for me and calling.... Hortense, my *seconde*, will remain with you, will take Mademoiselle's measure, and make an appointment.... Then, you choose the model.... And next week I will give you my whole attention, and we decide the details.... Oh, I shall have all the materials, and drape them on Mademoiselle.... *Oh, fiez-vous à moi, Madame*.... You need not worry!... It will be a pleasure to make something for Mademoiselle.... Trust me entirely, Madame!... Then you will excuse, Madame?... (*She moves towards the door, smiling but distracted*) *Bonjour, Madame*.... *Mademoiselle*....

(*She calls to her assistants in the next salon as she hurries out*) *Oui, je viens!*... *Je viens tout de suite!*... *Patience, j'arrive!*

CHRISTMAS EVE ON THE EMBANKMENT AT NIGHT

❖

The scene is the Thames Embankment in London. The night is dark and murky. A young woman of the London streets enters. She cowers and drags herself wearily. She wears a tattered shawl over her threadbare clothes. After wandering along the river and looking heavily into the stream, she moves towards a bench at the edge of the road, sits down, and speaks to a drunken man and his woman who are already occupying it.

Is this the way to the river?...

That's my affair, ain't it?...

Move up a bit, you old boozer, d'ye hear me?... (*To the woman*) What's wrong with you?... Hit ye, did he?... What's the use of blubberin' abaht it?... Why didn't ye bash 'im one?...

Home?... I ain't got no bloomin' home!... I'm sick of this blinkin' life....

My trade? Thievin' was!... Eh, we make a good job of it together—but it ain't no bloomin' use alone—and I'm quit of it, that's all.... 'Ave I ever been copped?... I've been in quod twice!...

Kids?... No, filthy little brats.... I '*ate* 'em!...

(*The man abuses the woman at his side*)

'Ere, stop that!... Leave 'er alone!... Cheese it!... Leave 'er alone, I say, or I'll call a copper, and 'e'll knock yer heads together!...

(*They rise to go*)

You off?... Naht! Stop at the gin palace down the road and 'ave one to cheer ye up....

(*She gets up and walks towards the river*) Jim—I'm comin'.

(*She hears a noise from a bundle under the bench*) Criky!... What's that?... A kid!... 'Ow come 'e's 'ere?... (*She takes up the bundle*) Stop yer cryin'! Some poor woman as don't want 'im and 'as gone on to the river.... Shut up, I say!... You little divil! I can't leave 'im 'ere to freeze.... Stop yer cryin'.... Ah...like it, do yer?... Warmer now, are yer?...

(*A gentleman passes, sees her, and speaks to her*)

Beg pardon, Sir?... My baby, sir!... I wasn't lookin', sir.... He's cold.... I ain't got no 'ome.... Would money 'elp? It would, Sir.... *Thank* you, sir!... (*She takes the money. He goes*)

A quid.... My Gawd!... Baby, come on.... We'll find a 'ome.... I'll warm ye...my baby...my little Jim!

(*She exits, singing*) 'Hark, the herald angels sing....'

VIVE LA FRANCE!
1916

A young French peasant woman comes walking slowly
down the street of a village near Verdun. She plods onward
wearily yet with persistent expectation. The village around
her is half in ruins; it is the second year of the war of 1914–
1918. She wears a peasant dress of black, with a dark
shawl around her shoulders and a white cap on her head,
and in her arms she carries a baby, muffled in another
shawl. She speaks tenderly to the child to quiet it as she
makes her way along the road. Presently she sees a friend
among the passers-by, then others.

Chut! Mon enfant, nous attendons ton père…. Chut! Ne
pleure plus…. (She greets another young woman in the street)
Ah, bonjour, Marie — le régiment arrive bientôt…. J 'entends les cris au bout de la rue…. Ah! Quelle peur horrible
je sens!… Merci, Marie!…
(She stumbles against a man passing by)
Oh, pardon, Monsieur…. Oui, Monsieur — j'attends le
régiment…. Oui, Monsieur, j'attends mon mari…. Il est au
régiment…. J'espère qu'il est au régiment…. Oh, non, Monsieur — je n'ai pas de nouvelles — je n'ai rien entendu depuis
son départ…. Il y a huit mois maintenant…. Non, Monsieur
— pas un mot…. Rien!… Oui, Monsieur, c'est mon bébé —
il a quatre mois. Il est gentil — c'est le portrait de son père….
Il dort…. Oh, oui — je connais beaucoup de garçons au régiment, des garçons de ce côté-ci — de braves garçons….
Mais oui, Monsieur…. Douaumont — Vaux — Verdun….
Ah! Quelle horreur! Ah, c'est affreux!… Monsieur le Curé
m'a raconté de telles histoires!… Oh, merci, Monsieur….

Oui, j'ai peur — mais j'espère toujours.... Merci, Monsieur — adieu!... (*The man passes on*)
(*She meets a little boy*)
Ah, petit Paul — tu cherches ton frère? Où est ta mère?... Mais non, tu n'es pas perdu — la v'là! Je la vois.... (*She sees the boy's mother and calls to her*) Louise!... Louise Vernet!... Voici ton petit, ici.... Cours, chéri.... Cours vite auprès de ta mère!... Par là!... Tu vois?... C'est ça!...
(*She meets another townswoman, Madame Blondat*)
Bonjour, Madame Blondat, qu'est-ce qu'il y a?... Vous avez peur pour Louis?... Ah, il ne faut pas pleurer, Madame.... Mais il y en a qui reviendront — pourquoi pas lui?... Courage, Madame — courage!... (*Madame Blondat goes on*) Ah — la pauvre!...
(*The village priest passes by*)
Bonjour, Monsieur le Curé.... Oui, ils viennent bientôt.... Je les entends déjà.... Merci.... Priez pour moi!...
(*She bends down her head to speak to the baby in her arms*)
Ah — tu ne dors plus?... Ah, ces beaux yeux — les yeux de ton père!... La bouche riante.... (*To a neighbour who passes*) N'est-ce-pas qu'il ressemble à Antoine?... Tu vois?... C'est vrai!... Ah, mon petit soldat — tu seras grand...brave, comme ton père!...
(*She suddenly becomes alert and eager as a file of soldiers comes up the street*)
Oh!... Ils viennent!... Ah, oui — enfin!... Oh, Hortense — regardons bien maintenant — si nous les voyons.... Oh, comme ils sont braves!... Oh, qu'ils marchent bien!... Mais comme ils sont maigres — fatigués.... Ah, les pauvres!... Oh, Monsieur!... Non, Monsieur — pas encore.... Je ne connais pas ceux-là.... Peut-être bientôt viendront les garçons de notre côté.... Oui, Monsieur — n'est-ce-pas qu'ils sont braves!...
Oh, Hortense!... V'là ton frère!... Oui — c'est lui.... Vite! Cours!... Prends des fleurs!... Non, Monsieur, c'est le frère de mon amie.... Ah, Dieu merci — il est là.... Maintenant ils

commencent, les nôtres.... Oh! Voilà Pierre Breton — un
ami d'Antoine!... Son camarade!... Son meilleur ami!...
Peut-être qu'il aura des nouvelles.... Est-ce qu'il me voit?
(*She calls to her husband's friend as he marches past*)
Pierre! *Pierre!*... Antoine?... Quand?... Où?... Une
charge?... Enterré?...
(*She cringes in her shock and grief, then stares in dull
incredulity as she continues to speak to Pierre*)
Va — oui.... Je comprends.... Mais, Pierre — viens me
voir ce soir si tu peux.... Et me dire tout ce qui s'est passé....
Merci!... (*She sobs in anguish*) Oh — Antoine!...
(*She now speaks to her child as she stares at the passing
soldiers*)
Viens, mon enfant! Salue les camarades de ton père!... Ces
héros.... Vainqueurs....
(*As the flag of France approaches she suddenly looks up at it
and cries out in involuntary exaltation*)
Oh! V'là le drapeau!... Vive la France!... *Vive la France!*

LE RETOUR DE L'AVEUGLE
(*The Return of the Blind Soldier*)

⋙ ✦ ⋘

A Frenchwoman of some thirty years comes out of the door of her house in a countryside of France and looks about the terrace for her three children—two girls, Louise and Adrienne, and a small boy, François. As she calls to them they come up on the terrace to her, and she then tells them that their father, a soldier in the French army, is returning home from the military hospital blinded. She speaks earnestly and compassionately, with deep gravity and as if for the first time asking the children to share the responsibilities of her life. The scene remains quiet throughout her monologue, but grief and anguish hover over it. The time is towards the end of the war of 1914–1918.

Louise — Adrienne!... Où est François?... Ah, le voilà. Viens ici, mon petit. C'est ça.... Mes enfants, écoutez: je voudrais encore une fois vous faire bien comprendre ce que je vous ai dit hier à mon retour de l'hôpital, après les semaines passées au chevet de votre père.... Vous comprenez, n'est-ce pas, mes petits, que papa est complètement aveugle?... Oui, chérie — pour toujours.... Et il faut que *vous* soyez ses yeux!...

Il faut que vous pensiez à chaque instant comment vous pouvez l'aider, l'amuser, lui faire plaisir...que l'un de vous soit toujours auprès de lui...prêt à lui rendre des petits services...chercher tout ce qu'il peut bien vouloir...deviner ses désirs...ses pensées.... Enfin, être ses yeux!

Surtout, mes petits, ne le laissez pas sentir que ça vous fait de la peine de le trouver changé, après cette longue absence... que ça vous attriste, de le voir ainsi, souffrant.... Pensez toujours combien nous sommes heureux qu'il soit vivant, et

PLATE XX

Doctors and Diets
Photograph by Trude Fleischmann, New York

PLATE XXI

At an Art Exhibition in Boston
Photograph by Trude Fleischmann, New York

puisqu'il ne voit pas vos yeux, montrez votre amour par vos actes et vos pensées...par vos caresses et le toucher de vos mains.... Racontez-lui tout ce qui vous intéresse — demandez-lui son aide pour vos leçons.... Faites-lui prendre part à vos jeux — comme avant, autant que possible.... Enfin, aimez-le plus que jamais!... (*As one of the girls starts to cry she clasps her closely*) Ne pleure pas, ma chérie! Embrasse-moi....

Soyons gais, et toujours gentils ensemble.... (*She pauses to listen as a motor-car is heard outside*) Ah, voilà l'auto déjà!... Non — restez ici! Je veux aller seule à sa rencontre....

(*She goes to the door of the house; then, after greeting her blind husband, she leads him forward to where the children are waiting on the terrace*)

Julien!... Me voici.... Oui, nous sommes sur la terrasse, les enfants sont là.... Sortons — par ici.... Attention! Voici les enfants.... Louise — Adrienne.... Et ton fils.... Viens, par ici... (*She leads him to a chair*) Assieds-toi dans le vieux fauteuil.... Non, j'apporte une chaise auprès de toi.... (*She places a chair near her husband's and sits down, the children beside her*) C'est ça!... Alors tu as fait un bon voyage? Tu n'es pas trop fatigué?... Comme tu as bonne mine — n'est-ce pas, Louise?... François — viens. Monte sur les genoux de papa.... (*The boy climbs on his father's knees*) Il est lourd, n'est-ce pas?... Oh, oui, il va bien — ils vont tous bien.... Tu ne trouves pas que Louise a grandi?... (*She beckons one of the girls to approach the father*) Approche-toi, chérie.... Tiens-toi droite que papa puisse te mesurer.... Elle vient à peu près à mon épaule! Tâte donc ses bras — forts, non?... Et Adrienne! Les joues grasses comme des pommes!... Quoi, chéri?... François veut que tu tâtes ses jambes.... Dures comme du fer, n'est-ce pas?... Et brunes!... Oh, il court toute la journée au jardin.... Il travaille beaucoup.... Oh, oui, il a des carottes, des épinards — toutes espèces de légumes que tu vas manger.... Ils ont tous leur propre jardin!... Oh, ils ont un tas de choses à te montrer, n'est-ce pas, mes petits?...

(*She rises to ask her husband if he cares to walk in the garden*)
Veux-tu faire une petite promenade au jardin?... Tu préfères rester ici?... (*She sits down again*) Adrienne, le coussin
rouge pour papa.... C'est mieux, merci.... Va maintenant,
chérie, emmène les autres.... Oui, elle est belle, elle est ravis-
sante, la petite — vraiment jolie.... Oh, elle n'entend pas —
elle est loin déjà.... Oh, ils sont adorables — ils deviennent si
intelligents!... Si tu savais comme je suis contente que tu sois
là pour m'aider à répondre à leurs questions!
(*She leans back in her chair and sighs*)
Qu'il fait bon ici, — et tranquille, n'est-ce pas?... L'air est
si doux. On respire le silence.... Tu entends toujours l'obus?...
(*She leans forward and speaks to him earnestly, pleadingly*)
Oh, Julien — il faut oublier, maintenant que nous sommes
ici ensemble.... Tranquilles pour toujours.... Loin de tout
ça. Que veux-tu?... Que puis-je te donner?... Tu n'as qu'à demander — les enfants et moi nous sommes ici pour te servir....
(*The girl Adrienne returns with a bouquet of flowers*) Ah, voici
Adrienne qui t'apporte des fleurs — des roses et des jasmins.
Sens...quel parfum!... (*The boy François comes with a butterfly
he has caught*) Et voilà François qui a attrapé un papillon....
Quoi, mon petit?... Il veut que tu touches ses ailes — comme
du velours, n'est-ce pas? Bleues et noires, avec de petits pois
jaunes. Comme il est joli!... Laisse-le voler, chéri — il n'aime
pas ta petite main chaude.... Ah! Le voilà échappé!... Cours
après lui.... Sauvez-vous, mes enfants — allez vous amuser....
(*The children run off*)... Oui, ils sont beaux, toujours gais,
toujours rieurs — comme des papillons eux-mêmes — en
bleu et en jaune!...
(*There is a long pause*)
Veux-tu manger, peut-être?... J'ai complètement oublié!
Veux-tu quelque chose à boire?... Rien?... Veux-tu que je te
lise quelque chose? J'ai un tas de livres amusants.... Tu es
bien ici?... Moi? Je suis bien.... Mes mains froides? Oh, mes
mains étaient toujours un peu froides — tu ne te souviens
pas?... Tu préfères rentrer? Alors viens. (*She rises to guide*

him back into the house)... Mais non, je ne suis pas fatiguée.... Je ne me fatigue jamais.... Oui, j'ai toujours mes couleurs fraîches — tout le monde dit que j'ai bonne mine.... Ma robe?... C'est la rose.... Celle que tu aimais toujours.... Mes cheveux?... Oui, toujours pareils — luisants, châtains. Pas un seul de gris — je te le jure!... Mes yeux?... Ils ne sont pas changés.... Oui, pleins de gaieté.... Mes étoiles...qui brillent?... Suis-je belle comme avant?... Mais oui.... Je suis belle — je serai toujours belle — pour toi.... (*Her voice breaks as she cries out in grief, at the point of tears*) Oh, Julien!... Je ne peux plus!

(*In anguish she embraces her husband and clings to him despairingly. Then after a moment she speaks to him in desperate resolution as she tries to recover herself*)

Donne-moi de ton courage!

(*They move slowly together towards the door of the house*)

IN COUNTY KERRY

❖

*The scene is Ireland, the year 1919. An elderly Irish-
woman of County Kerry stands in the doorway of her cottage as two young American girls ride up on their bicycles.
She wears a black woollen shawl around her shoulders, and
she speaks in the brogue of her country.—This sketch derives
from a true incident during a summer cycling trip that Ruth
Draper made with a friend through Ireland in 1919, just
after the first World War.*

Good-day.... Good-day!... Will ye come in?... Sure it's only
a shower, but ye'll be drenched if ye stand there.... Oh, ye
can leave yer bicycles under the tree.... Sure an' they'll be
safe there entirely—there's no harm will come to them at all,
at all.... That's right.... Run, now, quick!... It's lucky I saw
ye!... Come in now by the fire and dry yerselves.... Is it cold
ye are?... And is it far ye've come?... From America?...
Glory be to God—sure an' it's a great way ye've journeyed!...
And are ye Irish?... And are yer parents Irish?... Mercy
me! And you've come *all* this way to see Ireland?... Well,
well—think oɩ that!... Now, aren't ye the grand young
ladies!... And is it over the whole world ye're going on your
bicycles?... Ye must be worn out—coming so far....
   (*They enter the cottage*)
   Sit ye down, now—and rest yerselves, and dry yerselves....
Will ye take a sup of milk?... Sure an' there's plenty.... Oh,
ye'll not have water if ye like milk.... Maureen!—bring the
jug of milk and two glasses for the ladies.... Tell me, now—
do ye know a place in America that's called Boston, Mass.?...
Boston, Mass., U.S.A., is the name of the place.... Ye *do*?...
Ye've been there?... Well, now, whatever do ye think of that?
(*She sits down*)

D'ye know—I have three girls there, I have.... They've been there two years and more, now...and I'm afraid they'll never be coming back at all, at all...to the old country. Oh, they like it fine...and they write me long letters telling me all about it.... They do be enjoying themselves.... It must be a grand place, indeed...and maybe I'll be goin' myself one day.... Who knows? My daughter, Maureen—she's fourteen years of age, going on fifteen, and when she's sixteen years of age she's determined to go to Boston, Mass. and join her sisters there, so I suppose I'll be going along. I'd not like to be left alone.... Here's Maureen, now.... She's fourteen years of age, she is.... She's tall for her age—all my girls are tall.... They're *all* tall.... Pour out the milk...careful, now...don't spill it. Fill it up—oh, ye can have all you want—it's good for you—that's right.... Now, the other lady—careful, now don't let it drip.... Whatever do ye think, Maureen? These ladies have been to Boston, Mass., and they know the place well!... And is it from New York ye are?... Or maybe California?... New York—ye live there?... Surely the whole world must be in New York entirely.... And it must be a strange and lonesome place ye find Ireland after the great crowds on the other side of the sea!...

An' will ye be goin' back to America?... Sure an' I'll write the girls you're coming, and ye might make their acquaintance...an' tell them ye were here in their home!... An' d'ye like Ireland?... Ye *do*?... I'm glad—there's parts is very fine.... It's true there's parts that's beautiful.... An' have ye been to Donegal? An' ye've seen the cliffs of Sligo? And the mountains of Connemara, with the heather on the hill? An' ye've seen the sea, and the silver strand—the green fields, rocky roads, and the bog?... Ach, ye've seen it all! An' ye like it?... I'm glad!... This place?... Sure an' it's a small mean place...but it does us fine...the two of us here alone, now...an' my boy, he was killed in the war, he was....

Oh, it was a terrible war!... With weeping and pain over the whole world.... Well, it's a good thing it's over, now, and

I hope there'll never be another war! (*Turns quickly to look to the right*)

Och, Maureen—there goes the pig!... Quick!... I seen him go round the corner of the house.... Chase him, now!... and drive him back in the pen!... Och—that pig!... He has me distracted with the mischief that's in him, and me temper destroyed on me altogether.... We shut him up twenty times a day...and he finds his way out.... Heaven only knows how. We never see him go, but he wanders away across the fields, and he's as thin as a whippin' post, and he's eating his head off the whole day long! I bought him at the fair three weeks ago.... I paid two pounds for him, but I'd be glad to be rid of him for ten and six.... Sure an' he's no pig at *all*, I'm thinkin', an' that's the truth I'm tellin' ye now.... I do believe that he's a fairy...or some creature bewitched.... I've never seen a pig act like that.... (*To Maureen*) Have ye got him?... Well, put up the top bar...and put the three sticks across the way I showed ye...an' roll the barrel against the bars...and the big stone, too—and the old piece of tin.... He'll never get out of that, now—the creature!... He's a very peculiar pig.... (*Resumes talking to her visitors and seats herself on a kitchen chair*)

My boy? Oh, I was goin' to tell ye.... James was his name —we called him Jim—and he went off to the Dardanelles.... I suppose ye read about it in the papers?... The poor fellows were crowded on the ships.... They'd no notion at all where they were goin'... and they sailed for days and days across the sea...an' they come to a place...that's called Gallipoli... strange word.... Wait, now—there was another place—where he wrote the first letter.... Maureen! Whatever was the name of the place that the ship come in, that time that Jim went out to Gallipoli?... Suvla Bay!... That's the place where the ship come ashore, an' Jim wrote me a long letter tellin' me all about it.... An' it seems the heat was terrible, an' the poor fellows couldn't wait to get down off the ship, an' some went in the little boats, an' some were swimmin' ashore.... An' they never knew that the Turks were on the hill.... An' they were shootin' down on them in the water as they swam ashore, and the bullets was fallin' around them like rain...an' there was many killed that way. But Jim come through fine.... He was a grand swimmer—he was a very strong lad.... An' he come through fine.... An' he was there for weeks fighting the Turks on the hill.... I had three long letters telling me all about it.... Well, Jim was always a lucky boy...an' I always thought he'd come back to me.... I never had any fear at all, but now I'm goin' to tell ye....

One night I was sitting here...in the very place ye see me now...in front of the fire.... I was alone, and it was late, and of course, I was thinking of Jim.... And sudden-like a terrible fear come over me...that he was dead.... In me mind's eye, I saw him fall...and he never got up again.... And this terrible fear come over me...and nothing would drive it from my mind...and no word of comfort.... With the worry I was distracted entirely.... And in the nights the sleep never came to me at all.... And in the days, I had no peace.... So I went to the priest, to see if he would write a letter to the War Office in London, to ask if they would give me any news of my boy...where he would be?...and how?... But it's nothing he could learn.... He'd no answer to his letter, an' weeks went by...an' I went my way with a great heaviness in me heart... an' weeping continuously, I was.... The whole day long, weeping, and grieving, and worrying.... An' in the nights, too—always weeping....

Well, I had a little statue of the Blessed Virgin...a little small statue by the side of my bed. An' one night, I was praying and I was asking her, for the sake of her Son who was crucified—would she give me news of my boy...only to know if he was alive or dead...and I would be satisfied...only to know the truth, was all I asked.... An' as I was kneelin' down by the bed...suddenly, I looked up an' I opened me eyes... an' there on the other side of the bed...standing there, all pale...with a great light in his face...was Jim.... He was!...

An' I cried out to him an' I said, 'Jim—is it you?... An' is it alive or dead ye are?' An' he said, 'It's me, Mother...an' it's dead I am, with a wound in me side.' An' he lifted up his shirt an' he showed me the wound.... And I rose up then with a great cry to go to him, an' he laid his hand on me shoulder, an' he said, 'Give over weeping, now, Mother, or me wounds will never heal.' So do ye see, a great peace come over me then...an' I never cried any more.... From that day to this, I never shed a tear. Because that's what he said to me.... An' I knew then that if only I would cease to grieve, that he would be safe with the blessed Saints in Heaven.... But I never saw him again.... Ah, but ye see...I *knew*...an' I was satisfied!...

Well, now I'm goin' to tell ye something very strange. The very next day after—would ye believe it?—I had a letter from the War Office, London, telling me all about his death.... An' it seems he died the very time I told ye that terrible fear come over me.... Oh, it was weeks before.... But I knew the very day.... An' they told me that his Captain said that he was very brave.... Oh, I knew Jim would be brave.... An' they sent me a message of sympathy from the King.... I have it.... I could show it to ye—a personal message of sympathy from the King to me!... An' the pension comes regular now.... It does.... I have a grand pension—comes to me from the War Office, London, the first of every month...regular...an' I had a beautiful mass for his soul....Oh, thank you.... He was my only son.... He was a grand lad, twenty-two years of age, an' never a bit of trouble the whole of his life long.... Well, it's God's will, I suppose, an' there were many like me... but I hope there'll never be another war!... (*The young ladies rise*)

An' must ye be goin' now?... An' wouldn't ye stay for a bite of supper?... We'd be pleased if ye'd stay.... I have a little piece o' fresh fish I'll give ye...an' I'll make ye a loaf of soda-bread...an' ye'll have tea...an' honey, too, an' butter made this morning.... A little more milk, maybe?... Ye must be on yer way?... Well, the shower's past—it's a soft evening.... An' have ye far to go?... Oh, ye'll be havin' a grand ride.... Sure, it's downhill the whole way.... An' the sun will be shinin' along your road an' the wind blowin' after ye.... It'll be light for hours yet an' ye'll enjoy yourselves.... An' will ye be comin' back to Ireland?... Well, it's welcome ye'll be if ye pass this way again.... You, and yer husbands, too.... Sure an' it's not alone ye should be wandering through the length and breadth of the world always.... Goodbye to ye! Good luck to ye!... An' God be wi' ye as ye go! Be careful, now, goin' down the hill—an' come back again! Goodbye— goodbye! (*She stands in the doorway watching them ride off*)...

America!—*all* the way from America!... How strange. (*Suddenly breaks off and shouts*) Oh, there's that pig!... Maureen, he's out again, the creature!... Come now, and chase him!... Ye divil!... (*She dashes into the farmyard*) Be gone wid ye! However did ye get out at all?

THE CHILDREN'S PARTY

❖

A young mother enters, guiding her four young children into the room where a Christmas children's party is in progress. Her monologue shifts continuously from anxiety to delight, distraction to seriousness, throughout its duration. The children and their mothers fill the room around her with their holiday cries and excitement. She leads her four children—Herbert, Emily, Christopher, and Baby—forward and presently greets the hostess.

Come, Herbert—take your fingers out of your mouth!... And, Emily—don't forget your curtsey!... Now, children, will you *please* remember your manners, and say 'How-do-you-do' with a sweet smile?... Come on—come on! All keep together and follow me. (*She walks forward*)

How do you do, Mrs. Clark?... I'm *so* glad to see you—and how *sweet* of you to let me come with all my flock.... We're a perfect *army* when we get together.... The children are *so* excited.... Herbert, dear—Herbert!... Come, darling—take your fingers out of your mouth, and say 'How-do-you-do' to Mrs. Clark.... Do you know this is your dear friend Bobby Clark's mother?... Oh, Herbert! He *is* your friend.... I know that they were great friends last week!... Emily—come, darling.... And where's our curtsey?... Christopher—say 'How-do-you-do' to Mrs. Clark.... The *other* hand, dear—you know better than that—the *other* hand.... Baby! Come, darling—you mustn't run away!... Come here, say 'How-do-you-do' to Mrs. Clark.... This is our first real party, and we're very much excited....

Oh! Children!... Will you *look* at that tree! Isn't that a *marvellous* tree?... But, darling—it's *much* bigger than ours.... What *are* you talking about?... Now, Mrs. Clark, please don't have us on your mind! I know it's going to be the *most* perfect afternoon. You have so much to think about.... I shall hope to see you for a word, perhaps, later—but don't bother about us, because we're all going to be very happy, I know!... Thank you so much!...

(*She smiles, then suddenly looks severely at her son*) Herbert! Come here, dear—Herbert!—Come here! Listen: will you *please* take your fingers out of your mouth, and *keep* them out —and don't let me speak to you about it again. And remember all the things that I told you.... Oh! Herbert—I *did*, dear —I told you not to knock over the babies.... Be gentle with the little girls.... Step aside when older people pass—don't get your suit dirty—don't get your hair rumpled—remember your fingers.... And have a happy time! Now, run along....

Emily—come here—come here, Emily!... Now, stand still, and look at me! Do you remember what you promised Mother?... Then, *don't* let me see that expression—*on*—*your* —*face*!... I know you didn't, darling—but you're *here*, and you must make the best of it!... Well, perhaps nobody wanted to come—perhaps they'd *all* like to go—but they're *not* going.... Because they're going to behave—and that's what we *all* have to learn in life—we *have* to learn to *behave*!... And even when we're miserable we must pretend to be happy!... Now, smile, sweetheart—and go and play with those nice little girls over there.... But darling, we're *all* friends here—everybody's friends—you wouldn't be here at all if we weren't friends.... Now, listen, dear—smile—cheer up—keep going forward and never look back.... Think of others and forget yourself.... Smile and you'll be happy!... Run along.... (*To a lady*) She's very shy....

Christopher—come here!... Now, listen, dear: I told you not to show off—and the first thing you do is to stand on your head!... You're *not* so clever! Everybody can stand on their heads.... Yes, I *could*—when I was your age I certainly did.... I stood on my head very well.... But darling, we won't discuss that now.... You run along and watch what other boys can do.... They may be much cleverer than you are.... Other people may be more interesting than we are ourselves!... And we *don't* go to parties to show off.... Now remember what I said!... Baby—come here! Darling—you mustn't run away— you must stay with me.... Well, I'll find someone for you to play with—here's somebody now!...

How do you do, Mrs. Parker?... See, Baby—here's a little friend for you—just your age.... And is *this* the boy that I've heard so much about?... A *girl*?—Oh! I beg your pardon!... How stupid of me.... How do you do?... Will you play with my little boy?... Now, baby, be gentle, darling—remember she's a little girl.... Don't grab her tiger—don't kick her— don't pull her hair.... He *is* rather rough.... (*To the mother*) Are you nervous?... Well, I don't think he'll really attack her.... I think it's better if I don't watch him—he's some- times worse if he knows that I'm watching. (*She puts her hand over her eyes*) Tell me if he's smiling, because if he's smiling he's perfectly safe.... (*Watches between her fingers*) Oh, it's going to be all right—she's given him the tiger!... *Well*, he's a child who never gives me any trouble, Mrs. Clark, if—he— gets—what—he—wants. And he generally does. So I don't have to worry much about him....

Have you ever *seen* so many pretty children?... Who's that *lovely* child over there?... No—I mean that one with the blue bow—isn't she lovely!... *No*! Peter Harrison's little girl?... Sit still, my heart! I knew Peter Harrison a *thousand* years ago—we went to kindergarten together! He was the most adorable little boy and we absolutely *adored* each other.... Oh! I must *see* that child!... Come here, darling—come here and speak to me a moment.... Well, I want to talk to you, because, do you know—I knew your father when he was a little boy! Just about your age. And how old are you?... Six and a half? Oh, how lovely to be six and a half! Do you know, I was once six and a half—and so was your father—and we were great friends.... And I would like you to be friends with my little boys and my little girl.... So will you come to

supper some night?... Lovely! Now—tell me what's your name
so I can write you a little note, or telephone.... Cynthia? What
a pretty name! Cynthia Harrison.... What? It's not Cynthia
Harrison?... Cynthia Murphy?... Oh! I beg your pardon,
dear—I have the wrong child! No, never mind.... It's not
your fault.... Goodbye.... (*She turns back to Mrs. Clark*)

They all look so much alike these days.... But I wonder
who she is? Cynthia Murphy—do you know any Murphys?
Are there any Murphys?... My dear—do you know who I
think she might be? I wouldn't be one bit surprised if she
were the grandchild of old Mr. and Mrs. Murphy!... Oh, yes,
they did—don't you remember the summer we all spent on
the North Shore?... There was a *dreadful* little boy with
freckles—the most *poisonous* little boy! Well, that was Charlie
Murphy. He probably grew up, and it's perfectly possible
that that is *his* child....

What?... Going to play a game? What fun!... What?...
Get them in a circle?... Yes indeed!... Oh, I'd *love* to....
Herbert, dear—take your fingers out of your mouth! Listen:
we're all going to get into a big circle and play a game.... Tell
the boys.... Emily—come, darling—now's your chance—
join hands with those nice little girls over there and bring
them here.... It is going to be *great* fun. Smile, darling....

Hello, my Christopher!... Are you having a lovely time?...
What?... You saw the man take a rabbit out of a hat? No!...
And he found a *lemon* in your ear?... What a *wonderful* man!...
You go and stand over there—come, Barbara—will you
go next to my little boy?... Over there, dear—that little boy
in the blue suit.... Hello—what's *your* name?... Tommy—
Tommy what?... Tommy Woods?... Oh, I know your father,
Tommy—he's an old friend of mine....

Christopher—leave your socks alone, darling, and take
Barbara's hand.... You must *always* take a lady's hand when
she wants it.... Hold it softly and don't pinch.... Isn't this
going to be *fun*?... I don't know yet—Mrs. Clark is going to
explain to us how to play—*Shhhhh*!... Wait a minute—she's

going to tell us now.... (*To Mrs. Clark*) But—Mrs. Clark—I
don't *think* that's the way we used to play that game.... You
mean the one that ends in a tug-of-war?... I think they used
to call it London Bridge.... But don't you think that's rather
rough?... They always fall down, and they never know what
to choose.... Why don't we let the children choose a game?...
They may know something they'd like to play.... (*To the
children*) What would you like to play?... You don't *know*?...
What would you like?... You don't *care*?... They don't know
and they don't care—but we *must* do something!...

Herbert—can't you help Mother think of something,
darling—some nice game we could all play?... Wait a minute,
children—it's going to be such fun.... Now—there *was* a
game.... Oh! What *was* that game?... Don't you remember,
Mrs. Clark? We *always* used to play it at parties.... Everybody played it.... I remember there was music, and there
were chairs, and—you sat down and there wasn't any—chair.
It was marvellous! Such fun!... What dear?... It sounds like
'Going to Jerusalem?'... *That's* it! 'Going to Jerusalem!'
That's exactly what it is! 'Musical Chairs' or 'Going to
Jerusalem'! Oh, I remember it perfectly, now—it all comes
back to me! Mrs. Warner—can you play for the children?
We need some music.... Oh! Never mind if you're out of
practice.... Chopin's 'Funeral March'? Yes, that would do
perfectly. Oh, I adore it, don't you? I heard Horowitz play
it last week....

Wait a minute, children—don't run away!... It's going to
be such fun!... Fine, Mrs. Warner! Just play a little and
stop!... Well, the whole point is to stop—just begin, and
keep stopping.... Come on, children—Herbert, dear—help
your sister.... Emily—come, darling.... Smile and *throw*
yourself into it.... Herbert—take your fingers out of your
mouth.... Keep the chairs in a straight line—one one way and
one the other.... *Don't* take the armchair.... Now, children—
get in single file, one right after the other and follow that big
boy with the red hair.... All right, Mrs. Warner—they're

ready to start—off you go—keep in line—don't push the
chairs—sit down when the music stops....

What's the matter, Christopher? *What's* the matter?...
Well, darling, don't cry—you're not hurt.... Who kicked
you?... That little girl? Kicked you in the stom—Now,
listen, Christopher, you must not cry, darling—just because
a lady kicks you.... You *mustn't* cry.... Because in one way or
another everybody gets kicked.... Certainly—we *all* get
kicked. Daddy gets kicked and *he* doesn't cry.... No—*I* don't
kick him.... But somebody else may.... You're going to be
kicked all your life, but you mustn't cry.... Now you go and
find your nice trick-man and find me some more lemons....
(*To another mother*) He's a little young for this game....

Oh, Hello, Eleanor!... My dear—what a beautiful baby!...
Hello, sweetheart—have you got a little smile for me?...
Have you got a *little smile* for me? Oh! You *sweet* thing—you
look as if you thought I were an old idiot—yes, you do—agoo
—agoo—can you play peek-a-boo? *Peek*-a-boo!... My dear—
if only they'd *stay* that age!... Oh, yes—I have four, but mine
are all monsters!... No, I have no more babies. (*She pretends
to cry*) Oh, you *sweet* thing—that makes you laugh, you hard-
hearted little creature!... Oh, here's my boy, Herbert....
Come here, darling! This is my son.... He's ten and a half—
take your fingers out of your mouth, dear—and say 'How-
do-you-do' to Mrs. Porter.... *Herbert!*—*Look* at your suit!
How *did* you get so dirty?... Look at your *hair*! Covered with
cinders!... And your tie is all under one ear.... Oh! *Herbert*!...
But *where* have you been to get so dirty?... In the cellar?
Darling—you had no *right* to go to the cellar!... It *can't* be
more fun in the cellar!... Well, you must *not* wander over
people's houses, dear—you must play with the other children....Where are you going?... To supper?... Now—Herbert,
please don't eat too much! Remember what happened last
week!... Well, it will happen again—and worse—if you're
not careful.... No, dear—I said, '*No*'. Nothing but a glass of
milk and one chicken sandwich, and *very little* ice-cream, and

no cake—nothing more.... No chocolate sauce—no, dear. Now run along and do as I say.... (*She sighs heavily and turns to one of the mothers*)

Oh, these parties! Shall we sit down and have a moment's peace?... My dear—I'm a *wreck*! We've been to five parties this week—I believe we have four more to go to. I don't know *how* the children stand it! I'm perfectly *exhausted*!... They have had twenty-seven invitations to parties during the holidays.... Of course, I think it's *all wrong*—I think it's just as *wrong* as it can be!... But don't you think that nearly everything is wrong?... And the point is, what *are* you going to do about it?... Are you going to make your children different from other people's children? Are you going to give them a miserable youth to remember, and deprive them of pleasures which they consider normal—or are you going to swim with the stream?... Well—I'm swimming, but I expect to *sink* very soon!... You know—I don't think that we were ever intended to lead the lives we lead today!... And I feel that sooner or later there is bound to be a reaction.... (*She breaks off and talks to a baby*) What do *you* think about it, you sweet thing? What do *you* think about it? Do *you* think there's going to be a reaction?... You look so *wise*! Won't you tell us what to do? We don't know anything about anything....

Oh, my dear—I'm so glad to see you for a moment alone, because I want to talk to you about Walter.... I suppose you've heard?... Well, you know—it's true!... Yes, my dear, it *is*—it's true!... I can't tell you who told me—that's something I never do—because I never want to get other people in trouble.... But I can only say that I have *heard*—on *absolute* authority—that our dear Walter has *definitely* decided—yes, my dear, *definitely* decided...to...

(*Breaks off*) Christopher!—Come here to Mother! Come *here*!... What *have* you on your face?... Whipped cream? Why?... You put it there?... What for?... To be funny? What was funny about that?... What? That's the way Daddy looks when he shaves?... Now, darling—that is *not* funny! If

PLATE XXII

The American Tourist in *In a Church in Italy*

Photograph by Trude Fleischmann, New York

PLATE XXIII

The Italian Woman in *In a Church in Italy*
Photograph by Trude Fleischmann, New York

it were funny, I would be laughing—Mother loves to laugh....
Mother is *not* laughing—therefore it is *not* funny. Now—
stand still—it's all dripping.... Well, of *course* it's dripping....
Your face is hot and the cream is cold.... Look out!...
Stop laughing, Christopher—you'll spatter it all over me—
look out!... Don't put your hands on your face—you'll
get it on your suit, Christopher!... How *could* you do such
a silly thing?... It's very, very *naughty*, and very *silly*,
and there's nothing *funny* about it!... Stand away—stop
laughing!... Now go and wipe it all off—take a towel and
wipe your face.... (*To a maid*) Would you kindly help my
little boy wash his face?... Stop laughing, Christopher!
There is *nothing* funny about it.... (*Laughs*) Have you ever
heard anything so funny in your life? Oh! That child—he's
a perfect circus! He's got *such* an imagination!... (*To the
baby*) Isn't that a *funny* boy?... Isn't that a *funny* boy?... (*To
the other mother*) I think he's going to be an actor—or a
writer. Sometimes I think I'll not send him to school—but
just let his individuality develop....

Well, my dear—to get back to Walter.... I feel that something *can* be done.... I don't agree with you, my dear—I
don't think it's too late.... I think something *can* be done—
I think something *must* be done.... And I think that *you* or *I*
are the only ones to do it.... Of course, I feel that *you* will do
it far better than I.... Oh, my dear, I *do*.... I've always felt
that you had more influence with Walter than I.... However,
I'm perfectly willing to try.... I'm heart-sick about it.... I've
spent hours and hours wondering what was the best way....
And I've come to the conclusion that in life, generally, the
simplest way is the best way.... And I think that the thing to
do is just to *go* to Walter, and just say to him quite simply,
'Walter, Walter, old man—do you realize that....' EEEH!

(*She jumps up with a wild exclamation*) Look out! The lamp!
Herbert—you've knocked the lamp over!... (*To her friend*)
My dear—the lamp has crashed!... Mrs. Miller—is it broken?
Are you hurt?... How ever did you catch it? I saw my boy

rush by.... I saw his foot catch in the cord, and I knew the lamp was going but I couldn't.... Well, thank heavens, it isn't broken.... And I hope you're not hurt!... Well, you're very sweet to be so kind about it—you evidently understand children....

Herbert, dear—take your fingers out of your mouth and go and apologize to Mrs. Miller!... Tell her how sorry you are that you knocked the lamp over.... Thank you again, Mrs. Miller.... I hope my boy apologized.... I think I'll take them home—they're all getting so excited!... Herbert, dear!... Herbert! Listen, darling—will you *please* calm down?... Did you apologize to Mrs. Miller?... Well, go and get your toys together, because we're going home.... Because I *say* so, dear—don't argue.... Get all your things together and meet me here....

Emily! Come here, dear—come here!... How *did* you get so untidy? Look at your sash—all undone!... Well, darling—you must *not* let the boys pull you about like that.... It's not ladylike.... And I told you not to take chocolate sauce, and you've got it all over your lovely dress that Grandmother brought you from Paris.... Stand still, darling—let me wipe it off!... Stand still! Now, listen, dear—will you *please* calm down, because we are going home.... Because I *say* so!... Oh, I know you don't want to go. You didn't want to *come*, you didn't want to *stay*, and now you don't want to *go*.... But you're going! And not another word about it, dear.... Now I want you to go and find all your lovely toys and bring them here.... *What?*... *Emily!*—What do you mean by *saying* such a thing?... You're a spoiled, selfish ungrateful child! The trouble with you is—you go to so many parties—you have so many presents—that you don't appreciate anything!... Well, I'm just *ashamed* of you! Now, listen: you're not to take one thing with you, after what you said. You're to leave *every*thing behind, and maybe some child more worthy will be given all your lovely presents.... No, you can't trade with anybody, because you won't have anything to trade *with*....

Now, go and find the baby, dear, and bring him here.... Not another word!...

Christopher! What *is* the matter?... Well, your nose is *not* bleeding! Stand still, darling—stand still!... It's *not* bleeding.... Blow, and I'll show you.... Who struck you?... Freddie Warner?... That little boy?... Mrs. Warner, may I speak to your son?... Freddie—will you tell me, dear, whether my son, Christopher, struck you, or teased you, before you struck him?... *What?*... He grabbed your engine, and your boat, and hit you on the head with a stick?... *Christopher!* Aren't you *ashamed*? And Freddie's a smaller boy! Well, I wish he'd struck you *harder*—I'm *ashamed* to have such a coward for a son!... And look at Freddie giving you his horse.... Thank you, Freddie—you're very sweet to give Christopher your horse when he treated you like that.... What, dear?... You didn't want the old horse anyway?... Well—you come to my house tomorrow, Freddie, and you may have any toy of Christopher's that you like.... And you'll get the engine and the horse, and the boat back again.... (*To Christopher*) He certainly *will*, and you'll give him anything he wants— your favourite toy, if he wants it....

(*She prepares to leave*)

Goodbye, Mrs. Warner—goodbye, Freddie, dear.... Come on, Baby.... What?... Well—we're going right home.... Now, children—will you *please* remember your manners? Say 'Goodbye' nicely, and *quietly*, and thank Mrs. Clark for the *lovely* time you've had, and for all your lovely presents.... Never mind, dear—just *say* so.... We *all* have to do that.... And wish her a Happy New Year.... Keep together, now....

Goodbye, Mrs. Clark! I'm afraid that we must tear ourselves away.... Oh, the children have had the most perfect time! It's been the *most* marvellous party! I assure you we will remember this for days.... I'm sorry, but I'm afraid the moment has come.... Herbert—come, darling, take your fingers out of your mouth, and say 'Goodbye' to Mrs. Clark!... Thank her for all your lovely presents, and wish her a very

Happy New Year.... Emily wants to say 'Goodbye'.... Say 'Goodbye', darling.... Where's your curtsey?... Oh, indeed— you've given her *most* lovely things.... Everybody's happy.... Say 'Goodbye', Christopher—the other hand, darling.... You know better than that!... Say 'Goodbye', Baby.... Well— we don't *say* very much, but we *mean* a great deal.... And thank you again, Mrs. Clark—it's been the *most* perfect after- noon.... We've just *adored* every minute of it.... Well—I don't take them to too many parties, and I think in that way they appreciate things more.... Goodbye!... Wave goodbye, children. Goodbye!... Thank you again....

Come, my angels—come, my darlings.... Haven't we had a *lovely, lovely* time?... (*She turns suddenly, scowling and speaking severely*) Emily!—Emily, put that down.... I *saw* you take it! Put it down!... No, you may *not* have it!... Come on.... Christopher, look where you're going.... Herbert—take your fingers out of your mouth!... Come on, Baby.... Come, children.

(*She gathers her children together and shepherds them out of the room*)

A DALMATIAN PEASANT IN THE
HALL OF A NEW YORK HOSPITAL

❖

A haggard young Dalmatian woman moves along the hall-
way of a large municipal hospital in New York City. She
wears a black shawl and a kerchief on her head, and holds
in one hand a small folded bit of newspaper. In her other
arm she carries a baby under her shawl, and she leads a
small son by the hand. Her English is spoken with a heavy
foreign accent, and the Dalmatian with which she inter-
sperses it is here composed of sounds resembling the Slavic-
Latin languages. She advances among the people waiting in
the hall towards one of the benches that line the walls. Her
voice is timid, quavering, hesitant, and her expression
anxious and bewildered.

Sh—cula dop vansko jubin corisponvitan—shh....
Good morning—please—I like to see my husband—he's
here—his name, Maurico Valusto.... *Eh?* I don' understand
—I no speak English—please read paper—here—please....
(*She waits for the attendant to read the notice in newspaper*)
Rico, duba klensgorifa.
Sh—Shall I come wid you now?... You want I come?...
Eh? Wait—ya, I wait.... Eh—(*Confused, she looks to one side*
and sees a chair) Oh—sit down and wait! Ya, I understand....
You come back?... I wait here? You come and take me to my
husband?... Understand. Thank you!...
Rico—loma dupski vorja brenje.... (*She sighs and sits down,*
folding the paper; she looks all about, then notices a woman on
the opposite bench, and speaks shyly) Good morning. You speak
my language, maybe? I come from Ragusa—in Dalmatia....
No...you speak Italian?... No.... You read paper? (*She holds*

out the paper to her boy) *Rico, dali costazu pinglobju....* Eh?
You don't read! You don' read. I don' speak.... Oh, few
words understand, but no speak good.... My husband—he
work in de street—make a road. He go out every morning—
come back, night. Last week, he go out, an' he no coma back
—Monday—Tuesday—everyday—whole week, he no coma
back.... Oh! I go crazy! I dona know how find my husban'.
I dona know where go, who help me find my husban'.... A
woman in de house where I live—she live upstairs, I liva
down—she speak Italian, an' she read newspaper. She find
newspaper tella story of man got hurt in de street—ambulance come, taka de man to hospital.... Give name of de man
—Maurico Valusto—dat's my husban'. Oh! So I come now
find my husban'—dat man come back, take me see him....
    Your husban'?... Your husban' here?... Your baby?... Oh
—don' cry. Very bad sick?... Cut de head?... Ear?... Oh,
don' cry—he get well—good come here—know how take care
baby.... Sorry!... (*She looks tenderly towards the woman and
then turns her head and sees her little son*) Dat's my boy—four
years old—nice boy. *Rico, crande jova gulisan....* (*She calls
him to her and bids him speak to the grieving woman. He is shy
and turns away, and his mother is angry*) *Ah—stiko rame fisdu
mock....* (*Turns to the woman*) He's 'fraid strange people.
(*Speaks to the little boy, pointing to the woman*)
    *Rico, doniparfuga la mama—couda bimba in ospidal—clok a
bittu vanya trib bava guli—remshi grande venlipar.* I tell him
about your little boy.... (*Murmurs something to the boy*) He
says he's sorry your baby sick—he hopes your baby get well....
Nice boy.... Dat's my baby! (*Bends her head, opening her
shawl to show the baby to the woman*) Three weeks, two days—
small baby, dona like take out—too cold for baby.
    How long in dis city?... Four months, one week....
Friends?... Nobody.... Oh—dat woman, my friend. (*Holds
out the bit of newspaper*) She so kind. She help me when my
baby come—she take my boy, make no trouble me—she keep
her place—she help cook for my husban'. She likes my little

baby. She don' have baby, poor t'ing.... Money?... You tink I got money?... I got fifty cents—buy milk, bread—my boy, five cents, car fare go home—den I gotta no more. If Maurico no come back to me, I dona know where I go. I could work—I'm strong—but I canna leave my baby. (*She controls her tears, then sees the boy running off and speaks to him sharply*) *Rico, dumba struskipal no ginchek druba.*

(*She looks sadly about at the visitors passing through the waiting room*) Who all dese people?... Friends?... Friends all de sick people?... Many people come here—big place, many people gotta trouble. Everybody gotta trouble.

(*Her face lights up as she sees the attendant coming*) Dat man come now. He take me to my husban'.... Goodbye—hope your baby getta well. Rico—(*Reaches out her hand to the boy*) *Rico, boligar ne trupje Dada!* (*She speaks to the attendant*)

You find my husban'?... Eh?... Transferred?... What a mean 'transfer'?... Moved?... Where?... Nudder hospital?... No in dis place?... Where you took my husban'?... Bellevue Hospital?... Why?... When you took my husban'?... You dona know how he was when you took?... Oh—t'ank you.... (*Turns despairingly to the woman*) He's no here! Took away nudder place—was here—but gotta moved.... Bellevue Hospital—do you know where is dat place?... Up de city?... Down?... Twenty-six Street?... West Side?... East Side?... By de river?... Big place?... Through stone gate?... T'ank you.... Aw—mus' go on—maybe I find him dere! (*She clutches the baby in her arm and seizes the hand of her little boy*)

Rico, grimma duli vanja Dada—Bellevue Hospital—gluda jimaden—oh, miserdrenka lonifarga dreksh maloucha—(*She goes out, pulling the little boy, with a sob of agony*)

A MINER'S WIFE

I. IN THE COTTAGE: MORNING

The wife of a miner in the colliery district of Scotland runs into the mean kitchen of her cottage, where a cradle stands at one side. She is panting with anger as she breaks away from her husband with whom she has been quarrelling and flings him off. It is early morning of a dark day in winter.

Leave go—ye brute! Leave go, I say!... No, I'll not forgive ye.... Why should I forgive ye?... It's happened once too often—see! I warned ye—and I've stood it long enough!... Haven't I given ye chance after chance?... Well, I never seen ye really try. I've asked ye again and again to give me the money when yer paid, instead of goin' off and wasting it on drink. Ye lost two days last week—same as this.... How can ye expect to keep a family not working full time?... And I know where else some of the money goes.... Oh, ye needn't turn your head away.... I know yer wench.... You can buy *her* a fancy frock it seems.... And ye can't get boots for yer bairns. Shame on ye!... No. I *won't* let ye speak!... There's no explanation.... Ye can get along now. Yer late already— and maybe a bit o' hard work'll bring ye to yer senses....

(*She brings a cup of coffee to the table*) There's some black coffee I made ye.... Drink it—it'll maybe clear yer head!... I've too much to do without talking to ye. So be off with ye— and ye needn't come back for all I care. I'm through with ye —be gone!... Oh, shut yer bloody mouth! No words can help, for I'm deaf to all ye have to say.... Be off with ye!...

(*The husband goes off to work. She then turns to the cradle*) Sh-sh—there, there, don't cry.... Did I wake ye?... Poor wee lassie!... Jamie—run to the shop and get a bit of toffee

for baby. There's a half-penny in yon green saucer.... Lizzie
—Annie—Sheila—time for school!... Hurry up, now—you'll
be late.... Charlie and Rob have gone a while already. Hae
ye got yer books?... Yer pencils?... Oh, Sheila, yer a careless
girl—yer always losing yer pencil. I canna afford to be buying
ye any more.... Never mind, now.... Take that one in the
china cup.... On the shelf, stupid!... But mind ye bring it
back!... Get along, now! And mind ye come straight home
after school. (*She takes up a broom and sweeps the floor*)

(*The boy Jamie comes back presently*)

Well, did ye get the toffee?... Good boy! And ye had a suck
off it yerself. (*She turns to the cradle*) There, my pretty....
There—now lie still while I do a bit o' work.... Jamie—pick
up all yon papers and trash, and put them in the basket....
Save the good bits—they'll do for sums....

(*There is a knock on the door of the cottage*)

Good mornin', Mrs. McTavish!... It's a fine mornin'....
Will ye come in?... Do come and sit down a while. It's early
yet for market. (*Mrs. McTavish takes a chair*)... I didn't see
ye at kirk yesterday. And were ye to the wake last night?...
No—baby was ailin' and I couldn't leave her.... (*She sits
down wearily*) Donald was there—an' come home roarin'
drunk at three o'clock, so I got little sleep. I was awfu' mad
wi' him, because he was only just about again after two days....
Oh, he's been terrible lately.... Really, I'm fair put out....
It's been Tuesday or Wednesday before he's fit to work
again. They've been layin' off men at the mines, it seems, and
I warned Donald that they're sure to take them off that don't
put in a full week's work reg'lar!... Jamie! Baby's dropped
the toffee. Give it to her.... There, on the floor!...

Oh, Mrs. McTavish—what shall I do with him!... I was
awfu' angry this morning and I told him I was through with
him—that he needn't come back.... I did mean it—and he
might come to his senses if I gied him a good fright.... Oh,
maybe I could go to my mother for a bit—in the Highlands—
if I only had the money for the journey.... Well, I might get

a few days' work if I could find someone to mind the bairns....
Schools close soon, now—I'd have to wait until the holidays are over.... How ever I'm goin' to feed them I don't
know.... Ye see, they get their dinner now at school.... It
helps a lot, for I canna gie them meat.... Meat!... Why, I've
not seen a bit o' meat in this house for a month.... Oh, these
are terrible times! It's goin' to be a bad winter, all says. The
prices of everything appear to be goin' up all the time....
Wool is awful high.... I've been ripping up old socks of
Donald's that's more than half holes, to make stockings for
the bairns.... Jamie—take yon jug. The milkman's at the
door....

(*She turns back to Mrs. McTavish*) Then look at the place
we're living in. There's not a penny for repairs.... The damp-
ness soaks through yon cracks in the walls, and it's only in
bed we're warm.... Too bad Annie lost her wee girl.... They
say it was a starvation disease she died of.... She has five left.
Angus has been out o' work a month, now.... Well, he looks
like he had the silicosis.... Jamie—come awa'!... Don't touch
that! Take the wee brush and sweep the dust into the grate....
Oh, it's a terrible life for the men—for them that are no as
strong as oxen.... Look at Colin Moore and Gordon McClure
—wrecks they are, and not yet forty!... But something seems
to keep them at the mines. I've begged Donald again and
again to try and find other work, but he won't consider it at
all.... Sure, his father and his grandfather, three uncles, and
two brothers were all of them colliers—and it's proud of it
they were.... He'd no give it up.... No—ye can't drag them
from the mines!...

Oh well, it's prisoners we are, Mrs. McTavish—no better....
And just to have the strength to do my work is all I ask....
There's some worse off than I am, I suppose.... If only it
wasn't for the drink.... Oh, the curse of it!... And Donald's
an awful brute. He beat me with a stick last week.... My back
is sore yet.... I'm often 'feared for the bairns.... And the
language he uses!... I hate for them to hear it.... If it wasn't

for the bairns, I'd have left him long ago.... I'd leave him
now, if I could.... Care?... No!... I *don't* care!... How could
I care?... Aw, I've no feeling left.... Only contempt and hate
—aye, hate!...

(*She suddenly starts up*)

Hark! What's that?... Could it be the hooter?... The
alarm signal at the mine?... Oh, God!... An explosion,
maybe?... (*She runs to the door and looks down the road*)
Here comes Nell McClure and Mrs. Burr.... What is it,
girls?... Are ye sure?... It *is*—an explosion?... Which
mine?... She doesn't know—I must go.... Are ye comin', Mrs.
McTavish? (*She throws a shawl over her head and shoulders*)...
Jamie—be a good boy. Don't run out, see?... And mind baby
till I get back.... I'll not be long.... The others'll be home
from school soon.... Tell them to bide in the house.... Don't
go near the fire.... Come on, Mrs. McTavish—we'll follow
the others!... Up the hill to the right is the shortest way....

(*She runs in panic out of the door*)

II. AT THE PIT HEAD: LATE AT NIGHT

*She stands now among a crowd of women, wives and relatives
of the miners who have been trapped in the mine by the explosion.
They have gathered in suspense and anxiety at the pit head,
awaiting the results of the efforts at rescuing the men. It is late
at night. She strains anxiously and clutches her shawl around
her head and shoulders as she talks to the other women.*

Whew—this coal dust!... Like a fog.... Ye can hardly see....
And it gets in your throat.... De ye ken the time, Mrs. Burr?
Ye best go and get a cup o' tea. The Salvation Army lassie's
over there.... I'll try and get Annie Cameron to come over—
she's dazed-like with cold and fright and I can't get her to
speak.... Annie—will ye come to the nice fire over there?
It'll do ye good to walk about a bit.... Well, stop there, and
I'll bring ye a cup o' tea.... (*She goes to the Salvation Army
girl*) Lassie, can I have two cups?... One for a girl over there

—her husband's in the mine.... Aye, in Butt Three, where they're trapped.... She's only four months married.... She comes from the south and knows naught of such places as this.... No, my husband is in Butt Nine, but I have my friends in Butt Three, and in the rescue party.... Thank you —this'll do her good. (*She returns to Annie with the cups*) Here, Annie—drink this.... Then ye'd better walk up and down—ye'll be frozen if ye sit so still.... Ye've got to keep yer strength, ye know—so ye'll be of some use when the men are brought up.... Perhaps we can help the doctors.... They're all right so far, ye know.... The minister said they heard tapping on the walls, and they're driving in fresh air, so the first report said.... So ye mustn't worry too much—he'll be all right.... They're putting up a new bulletin now.... I'll go and see what it says....

Come, Mrs. Burr.... Come, Katie.... There's a new bulletin.... Christina, come.... I can see.... I'll read it for ye.... (*She goes up to the posted bulletin and reads haltingly*) 'The rescue party are making good progress on the seventh level working toward Butt Three at the end of the gallery, where it is believed twenty men are trapped. They have met considerable carbon monoxide gas, but the pumps are working well, and it is hoped to penetrate the Butt shortly. Women are requested to stand behind the ropes when the men are brought out to avoid confusion.'

(*She turns back to the women*)

Aw—why would they no let us help?... Are ye cold, Mrs. Burr?... It's the gas. It's awfu' hard to breathe—makes ye kinda sick.... Think o' the men working in those masks.... Yer husband was wonderful the way he led the rescue party.... Seemed like he gave them all courage.... He had a wonderful look in his face when he asked for volunteers.... I hated to see wee Charlie McGraw go down.... He's only fifteen.... But his father's in the mine.... He's the eldest of eight—a grand little lad he is.

(*She walks over to Christina, who is weeping*)

Cheer up, Christina.... I believe they'll be all right.... Nell McClure went home. She's got an awful sick boy and daren't leave him any longer. She's coming back as soon as she can. Poor Nell!... Yes.... Why, her father was lost in that terrible disaster in Gurroch when she was a girl. We came from the same village.... I'll never forget that.... There wasn't a house that hadn't lost a man.... They were trapped for thirty hours.... I lost an uncle and two cousins.... They were all lost—the rescue party as well.... The lamps went out, and the black damp choked them all.... Have ye seen the list of the men in Butt Three? The minister should have it.... Have you seen the list, Christina?... (*She listens to Christina, then exclaims*) Who?... Where?... Oh, may I see it, please? (*She reads the list which Christina has handed her*) 'Colin Moore, Georgie Cameron, Bill McClure, Jamie McPherson, Allan McKee, Tom Fraser, and Alex and Bob Anderson, Keith Morgan...' Keith Morgan—that's Donald's boy.... But Keith was with Donald in Butt Nine last week—he never told me he was moved!... Aye, Keith worked with Donald—so if he's in Butt Three—(*She breaks off in fear*).... I must find Lizzie Morgan.... (*She calls among the crowd of women*) Lizzie!... Has anyone seen Lizzie Morgan.... She might know.... Lizzie! Lizzie!... Christina—have ye seen Lizzie Morgan?...

They're coming up now.... We must get behind the rope.... Annie—come!... We must do as they say.... Come on!... Those are the doctors, dear, and they have oxygen tanks.... (*She peers anxiously at the victims as they are brought up*) It brings life back to the men who are unconscious from the gas.... Has Nell got back?... There's Alex—he was with the rescue party!... Any news, Alex?... Oh—! Georgie Cameron and Bill McClure?... Unconscious, but alive?... Don't tell Annie yet—leave it to me.... Here they come.... Oh, the fumes from their clothes—just soaked with that awful gas.... Stand back!... Let them have air.... Annie, take my hand!... We must get behind the rope now.... Come!... Here, Nell, stand by me.... I've not heard yet—they say we must wait....

But the doctors are there.... Yes, Lassie?... Ye want us to sing? Now?... Aye, we know it. Come on, girls, Kate, Christina—come, Annie—you know the hymn—sing!... Don't push.... Hold my hand.

(*She joins the other women in singing the hymn*)

> O God our help in ages past,
> Our hope for years to come.
> Our shelter from the stormy blast,
> And our eternal home.

Don't push!... It's hard to see....

> Beneath the shadow of Thy Throne
> Thy saints have dwelt secure....

(*Suddenly she breaks off singing and screams*)

Oh, it's Donald!... Ooooh!... Donald!... It's my husband, and he's dead!... Oh, save him!... (*She throws herself towards the body being carried on a litter*) Donald—it's me—it's Maggie! Say my name, Donald! I didn't mean what I said this morning—I didn't mean it!... Does he hear me?... (*She is pulled away by the others*) Don't take me away—let me stay by him!... Let me stay—don't take me away!... Donald!... Donald!... Donald!

A SOUTHERN GIRL AT A DANCE

She looks up eagerly as her hostess comes to speak to her, and she answers in the soft, melting, caressing voice of the American South, all her arts as a young coquette immediately evident. The scene is a corner of the dancing room at Mrs. White's large home, where a party is in progress.

I beg your pardon, Mrs. White?... Would I like to meet Dr. Porter? I certainly *would!* Shall I wait right here? (*She waits a moment looking at the dancers. Then Mrs. White comes up with Dr. Porter*) How do you do, Dr. Porter! I certainly am *pleased* to know you.... Well, if you don't mind.... I'd rather sit down, and have a little talk.... I'm about exhausted.... I've been dancin' and dancin', and I'm just about ready to drop!... I told Mrs. White I wanted to go home, but I just wasn't goin' to leave this party until I'd met you!... Shall we sit here? (*They sit down*)... No—that's the truth!... I declare, it *is* the truth.... Well, I'll tell you *just* how it happened.... Then maybe you'll believe me!... I was dancin' around a little while ago and...and I noticed you as I passed by, talkin' to a mighty pretty girl in blue.... And I said to Mrs. White, 'Who is that man over yonder, talking to that pretty girl in blue?'... And she said, 'Why, that's Dr. Porter. He's a risin' physician in this town!... And I said—you don't mind personal remarks, do you?... And I said, 'He's certainly got the most *beautiful* eyes I ever saw in my life, and I'd like to meet him.' So—here we are!...

So you're a doctor?... Is that so!... How wonderful!... Well, I declare!... *All* your life?... Do you know what I've always said?... I've always said, if I were a man, that's the *only* profession I'd choose!... I think it's the finest thing a man can do.... I think it's so *noble*, and so *unselfish* to give up

your life helpin' other people.... Takin' care of sick people....
And makin' everybody well and strong.... Stoppin' pain and
misery.... Gettin' up nights—cold nights—at the risk of your
own life maybe—to help someone who's in trouble.... I'm
sure you must *love* your work, Dr. Porter.... And I reckon
you do about half your curin' with those eyes!... No, I'm *not*
foolin'—I'm mighty serious! I'd rather talk to a man about
his work than anything.... To begin with.... 'Cause then
you're sure you've got him—anyway, for a little while.... Beg
your pardon?... Come and *see* me?... I certainly would love
to see you again.... Wednesday afternoon?... I was going
home on Wednesday.... But I declare—if you come and see
me, I'll put it off till Thursday.... Have a little waltz?... Yes
—I'd love to!... (*They rise*) No—I'm not a bit tired.... I was
only foolin'.... Oh, sugar! There's Mrs. White calling me!...
I can't dance with you now...I've got to meet somebody
else!... Well—I'll be waitin' for you Wednesday afternoon!...
Goodbye.... No, indeed!... I won't forget!... Thank you
kindly.... Goodbye! (*Dr. Porter goes*)

(*Mrs. White comes up with Mr. Arlington and introduces him*)
    How do you do, Mr. Arlington—I certainly am pleased to
know you!... I beg your pardon?... Well, if you don't mind—
I'd rather sit down and have a little talk.... (*They sit down*)
I've been dancin' and dancin' till I'm just about *dead*!... I
told Mrs. White I wanted to go home.... I was *so* tired out—
but I said I wasn't going to leave this party until I'd met you....
No, that's the truth! Well—I'll tell you how it happened....
Shall we sit down here? I was dancing around a little
while ago, and you were sittin' in that corner, over yonder,
talking to a mighty pretty girl in yellow.... You were talkin'
mighty seriously.... I didn't hear what you said.... But I only
heard your voice—and I said to Mrs. White, 'Who's that
man over yonder, talkin' to that pretty girl in yellow?' And
she said, 'Why?' And I said—you don't mind 'personal
remarks, do you?—and I said, 'He's got the most beautiful
speakin' voice I ever heard in *all* my life!'... I love a great

deep voice like yours! It goes rumblin' right through you!...
And she said, 'Why—that's Mr. Arlington.... He's a risin'
young lawyer in this town.' And I said, 'Well—I've *got* to
know him—that's all!'... So here we are!

So you're a lawyer?... Is that so?... *All* your life?... How
wonderful!... You know what I've always said?... I've always
said, if I were a man, it's the *only* profession I'd choose....
Oh, I think it's the finest thing a man can do.... I'm just
crazy about justice—there's so much injustice in the world....
Then, you're always helpin' people that are in trouble and gettin'
them out of it, and getting 'em divorces, and fixin' income
taxes, and everything.... And telling us what's right and what's
wrong.... And helping people out of holes they get into—
maybe just through being stupid.... I declare, I think lawyers
are *wonderful*!... You must have a lot of *brains*!... And I'm
sure you love your work, Mr. Arlington, and I reckon to
come to Court—and hear you pleadin' for some poor soul in
trouble.... What?... Come to Court?... Do you *mean* it?...
You got a *case* on?... When?... Thursday morning?... Oh, I
was goin' home on Thursday—but if I can come and hear
you, I am goin' to put it off till Friday.... Shall we have a
little waltz?... (*They rise*) Yes—I'd *love* to!... No—I'm not
a bit tired—I was only foolin'.... I just wanted to talk to
you!... Oh, sugar! There's Mrs. White calling me.... I can't
dance now...I'm mighty sorry!... How will I get to the
Court?... Will you come and fetch me? I'll be ready—ten
o'clock.... Waitin' at the door!... Oh, I'd go *any*where with
you!... Thank you kindly!... No, indeed. I won't forget!...
Goodbye! (*Mr. Arlington goes*)

(*Mrs. White comes up and introduces Mr. Noland*)

How do you do, Mr. Noland—I certainly am pleased to
know you!... I beg your pardon?... Well, if you don't mind,
I'd rather sit down and have a little talk.... I've been dancin'
and dancin'—I'm about dead.... (*They sit down*) I told Mrs.
White I wanted to go home, I was so tired out, but I said I
wasn't going to leave this party until I'd met *you*...because

I heard you were an artist!... Do you know that I guessed you were?... I *did*!... That's the *truth*!... I noticed you a little while ago, standing in that doorway, talking to a pretty girl in white, and kinda gesticulatin' with your hands.... And I said to Mrs. White—do you mind personal remarks?—I said, 'I'm sure that man is an artist, he has the most *beautiful* hands I ever saw.'... And she said you were a sculptor, and that you played the piano, too.... And I said I wanted to meet you.... So here we are!

Oh, I'm just crazy about art!... I'd rather be an artist than anything in the world!... I certainly do *envy* you.... You know—I feel so sorry for some men.... Well, I've just been talkin' to two professional men—a doctor and a lawyer.... Now, can you tell me *what* drives a man into that kind of work?... I don't see how they *stand* it!... I'd go plumb crazy.... Imagine spendin' your life thinkin' about sick people, and *sad* people, and *bad* people, and all the sin and sorrow in the world!... But you—you certainly are lucky!... Because you can just think, and dream, about beautiful things, and then make them with your own two hands! And make music, too.... How I would *love* to see your sculpture—and hear you play.... I beg your pardon?... Come to your studio?... Do you *mean* it?... When?... Friday afternoon?... Well, I was going home on Friday, but if I can come to your studio, I'm going to put it off until Saturday—maybe Monday!... I wouldn't miss that for *any*thing!... Shall we go in now, where it's nice and quiet, and dark?... And we can talk about art, and everything.... Come on!...

(*They go off arm in arm*)

FIVE IMAGINARY FOLK-SONGS

→≫ ✲ ≪←

Ruth Draper devised these folk-songs as jeux d'esprit *or exercises in* pastiche *and created synthetic or imaginary equivalents of five foreign languages for them, each one then being sung and dramatized in an appropriate costume of a sketchy or suggestive kind. They are given here as part of the record of her performances even though their printed form can convey little of the skill of humour, sentiment, or parody she gave to their rendering. The tunes to which she sang them were likewise* pastiches *of native folk music, and much was made of native mannerism and character, each song becoming a small vignette of the race or country it depicted.*

I. A SLOVAK LULLABY

Liedeloo liedo loo
Bamba luda liedo loo
Drubje cando plotz forla
Penje quechvo pras morda
Flaschne buva drub sorga
Bamba liedo loo.
Cranba volyen plotz slotera
Chez ne pungo lash volan
Dais ne lunyad non flobera
Brusta nogloo
Plaida ramoo
Drenga madroo
    Liedoloo!

II. A COSSACK LAMENT

Domba struski
Blosh malyfak

Bronya dnoplo davdadien
Crash en pityoff
Fluda nanyak
Pendrosh flamba
Bloyshobrien
Muy glubstandu
Muy mlifangu
Kluzak piotrob
Mlas banyo.

III. CORSICAN LOVE SONG

Niena, niena, ma poldestu
Cambi stredavi, ma clustaben,
Palga faresti rotto staru
Slenza la vuta mi pledaren
Velia lanzo perandola rema,
Storasti munto bellena fandro
Stela bespunta col tembalo fema
Stringe me cura che tila canzo,
Rosto tangedo,
Blaschenko crena,
Fluba fellona ta gista talu
Mena las blocati frische starena
Alda voluba,
Tramende daru.

IV. A SWEDISH POLKA

Flöten ponye stuba top
Bluge fisten ya,
Rasche molden linke yop,
Kätal stinka da.
Bube rexen köste ben
Klöre möde ke,
Tote yüppe lodye fen
Rüb es mendel frey.

Poste fende mü
Glübe sende glü,
Rex misten fess tren en
Venga svensken du
Yasse truben sku
Dreb morshen kless es fen
Melle blüb des grün
Yolle yüp des yün
Freya net loss pet es bey,
Nötye klos drag skur
Blubse tu häng kvur
Katel plüt hopp drenken drey.

V. ARABIAN BEGGAR'S CHANT

This wordless chant was improvised each time it was performed, and it was sung in an improvised language resembling the Arabic. The costume was that of a street-beggar in
one of the cities of the Near East.

Another of Ruth Draper's monologues, on her programmes from early years, resembled the above folk-songs
in being spoken in an improvised Balkan language. It was
'Love in the Balkans', sometimes listed under the title 'A
Serbian Woman and her Husband'. This was a melo-
dramatic-comic episode of Balkan love and passion, alternating a mood of violent peasant drama with exaggerated pathos
and fervent absurdity. Ruth Draper did not leave a manuscript of this sketch; it is mentioned here as one of her
improvisations in synthetic speech and exotic mannerism
comparable to the above songs.

IN A RAILWAY STATION ON
THE WESTERN PLAINS

⊱⟫⟫✦⟪⟪⊰

*The girl comes into the railway station of a lonely town on
the plains, rubbing her hands and shivering; it is deep
winter on the Western American prairie, and a blizzard is
blowing outside. The waiting-room of the wooden station-
house has a lunch-counter at one side where the girl works
and where Sadie has been doing duty until her arrival.
Night is coming on as the girl runs in from the storm. She
pushes the door shut against the wind and takes off her coat,
muffler, and overshoes as she greets Sadie.*

Hello, Sadie. Hustle up and get your things on—Joe's comin'
down the road.... (*She rubs her hands briskly*) Whew—it's
cold! Nice and warm in here.... Wait till you see what's goin'
on outdoors!... The snow's comin' down so fast you can't see
your hands in front of yer face, and the wind's blowin' about
eighty miles an hour. We'll be snowed up by morning!...

Say, did Jim come in to fix the leak in the coffee tank?...
That's good! Had me scared last night—made such funny
noises, I thought it was goin' to explode.... Did the baker
bring in the apple pies?... Any better? We had to throw away
half a dozen last week. They was like old wet flannel.... Snow
plough gone by?... She'll be comin' soon—the tracks are
covered, now....

(*Joe enters*)

Hello, Joe! Come on in. My, what a night!... Come over
and warm up.... Sadie's gettin' her things on—she'll be right
out.... Big storm—an' it come up so sudden.... We're in for
a big blizzard, all right.... Stoke up the fire for me, will you?...
(*She turns towards the door*) Listen!... Snow plough? Sure!...

(*Buz comes in*) Is that you, Buz?... There's my boy—just in time!... I want to send some coffee out to the boys on the plough. Leave yer coat on.... How many fellers on the plough, Joe?... Five?... Buz, get five big ham sandwiches and five sinkers, and put 'em on the tray here.... I'll give yer the coffee—I got the cups.... You put in the sugar and milk and stir it up.... They don't want no spoons. (*She fills five imaginary cups and puts them on an imaginary tray*) Is them the biggest sinkers you can find?... Now, go easy—don't hurry.... They'll wait for you.... Don't drop that load in the snow.... Hold the door open for him, Joe, will ye?... (*Buz goes out with the tray*) Sure they're stoppin'.... They know I won't forget 'em. That'll warm 'em up good!...

Well, Sadie, you for the big sleep?... Better tie that scarf around yer neck.... Tie her up, Joe!... You'll need all the hands you've got to keep you on yer feet!... Look out for the wind at the corner—there's a drift about four feet high. I thought I was goin' to be blown over.... See you in the mornin', Sadie. I'll be down to the store about noon.... I seen you had a nice piece o' blue satin.... Thought I'd make me up a new blouse. I seen a pretty pattern in the paper—with little diagonal tucks.... Well, so long—sleep well.... Goodnight. (*Sadie and Joe leave*)

(*She tidies the counter and shelves, whistling. Presently Buz returns*)

Well, Buz—drink it all up?... Send me their love?... Guess they was glad to get it!... Now, let's have one o' them pies—one's enough. There won't be many gettin' off tonight.... Umm—nice an' brown an' crispy.... Joe and Sadie?... Happy? They sure are. Nicest couple in town.... Why don't *I* get hitched?... Well, Buz, I can't decide. Who do you advise me to marry?... Danny? No.... Oh, he's just like my brother. We was raised together.... Sure he's fine—but I don't want to marry him.... Who?... Jerry?... *Now*, yer talkin'!... What put you in mind of him?... Ye seen us?... Where?... An' ye decided we was goin' to be married?...

Well, Buz—you guessed right. I *am* goin' to marry Jerry!...
An' ye never told nobody?... So nobody knows? We're goin'
to tell the folks next week.... Buz, you're a good little friend—
will you keep the secret a little longer?... (*She sweeps crumbs
from the table into her hand*) Open yer mouth an' I'll give yer
something good to keep it shut! (*She pours some of the crumbs
from her hand into Buz's mouth*)... (*Munches the crumbs*) Umm
—good pie! I love pastry crumbs!... (*Schneider comes in*) Hello,
Schneider.... Oh, Buz an' I just havin' a little chat.... Snow
plough's just gone by.... Joe and Sadie's gone home.... An'
here comes the crew of Number Nine!...

(*The men of the railway crew come in*)

Good evenin', everybody!... Hello, Mr. Raggles—coffee?...
Coffee for you?... (*She counts heads*) Nine coffees, Buz....
Gather round the stove, boys, and warm yourselves!... Hello,
Charlie—how's Minnie?... How's the baby?... You promised to bring me his photograph and ye never did.... You've
got one?... You have?... Lemme see it! (*She takes a snapshot
from Charlie, exclaiming*) Oh! Isn't he *lovely*!... Ain't he *cute*!
Look at the dimple.... Looks just like Minnie.... But he's got
your eyes. Goin' to break all the girls' hearts—just like his
dad!... Ah, ye did, an' ye know it. You were *terrible*.... Show
him to Mr. Raggles.... Oh, go on—ye know yer proud!...
Mr. Raggles—look at Charlie's baby—isn't he lovely?...

(*Danny comes in at the door*)

Hello, Danny, you're late. What happened? (*Startled, she
sees he has hurt his hand*) Holy smoke!... How did yer come
to do that?... Jammed it in the coupling?... That old dirty
handkerchief won't do it no good. (*She seizes Danny's hand*)
Lemme fix it for yer.... I'll wash it with hot water and dis-
infectant and bandage it up for yer. Come over here.... Gee!
That must hurt like sin.... Here, drink this coffee. (*She pours
water from an imaginary boiler into an imaginary bowl*) Buz,
give me that package of absorbent cotton. (*She reaches for a
bottle on a shelf and pours medicine into a bowl*) Good stuff!...
I don't know what it is. (*Reads the label*) 'Stops bleedin', stops

infection, stops pain.'... Smells good, anyhow!... Now, stick yer finger in—it ain't too hot! (*Tests heat of the water*) I swear it ain't.... Is it?... (*She helps bathe Danny's finger*) Did it bleed much?... (*Winces*) Sorry—but I want to get the dirt out.... (*She speaks to an onlooker*) Excuse me—I'm engaged.... Givin' some first-aid treatment. Tryin' to mend a smashed finger.... What's *your* trouble?... Heart?... Oh, that's in the advanced course. I ain't took that yet!... Now, Danny—that looks pretty clean. I'll bind it up for yer. Buz, gimme that roll of bandage.... There—in my box. Looks like a spool.... Can you hold yer arm stiff, Danny? (*She rolls the bandage around his finger*) Too tight?... Just give you some protection, and kinda hold it together. Buz, gimme that little pair o' rusty scissors hangin' on the nail.... Well, then look in my box.... Got 'em? Thanks (*Cuts the bandage*) I'll cut it up a little way.... Give me something to tie it with. (*She cuts the bandage in half with great difficulty*) Might be sharper!... There—keep yer arm up, if you can.... It won't throb so bad.... And, Danny—go to the doctor tomorrow an' get a good sterile dressin'.... Ye might get a bad infected finger—clear up yer arm.... Hope you get some sleep.... Goodnight.... Wish I could stop the pain!... You're welcome—goodnight, all.... Goodnight!... Goin' out to throw the switch, Schneider?... Want Buz to help yer?... Go on, Buz. Don't stay long out there—you'll freeze!

(*The men go out into the storm. She turns back and sees snow on the floor*)

Oh, look at the snow all over my clean floor!... (*She takes a broom and sweeps, singing 'There's a long, long trail a'windin''. The telephone rings*) Hello, the telephone—at this hour?... (*She goes to the wall telephone*) Hello! Hello! Oh, hello, Mr. Mitchell—nice to hear your voice. How've yer been keepin'?... No, I'm alone...Schneider's out at the tracks, throwin' the switch for Number Four.... You got bad news—what d'yer mean?... Oh!... (*She speaks in shock and horror*) No!... Lot o' people killed?... Oh!... Sendin' the injured here?...

But we ain't got no hospital.... Yes—we've got a doctor.... They're on their way, now?... How many?... Thirty—whew!... Yes, I understand.... We'll do the best we can.... Sure—I get you. I'll tell him.... Goodbye. (*She rings off, then cries out*)

Jerry! Jerry!... Buz! Wait! Go back and tell Schneider to throw the switch over and let the local come through on the express track.... Do what I tell you—and hurry!... Number Four is wrecked!... (*She returns to the telephone*) I gotta get help.... Hello—hello!... Say, Rogers—did ye hear what Mr. Mitchell told me?... Number Four is wrecked!... And there's a lot of people hurt bad.... And they're sendin' 'em here.... We gotta get ready for 'em.... Call the doctor.... I seen his light as I come by.... Tell him what's happened, and to hurry over.... Then, get Joe and Sadie—they just left here.... You'll catch 'em before they turn in.... Tell 'em to beat it back and bring blankets, and if they got any bandages and first-aid stuff.... An' tell Joe to bring the bottle of whiskey Uncle Jimmy gave him for Christmas.... Then call the dance-hall and get hold of Rosie—and explain to her. Tell her not to tell everybody—we don't want a crowd.... Get Sam, and Sallie and Charley, and Bill and Molly—they all live close.... And they can stop at their houses and pick up blankets an' towels an' first-aid stuff and disinfectants, you know.... Tell 'em to hurry over as quick as they can.... Be sure Rosie comes—she's got a good head and she's strong as a horse.... Goodbye!... (*She hangs up*)

Jerry.... (*She cleans up the counter as she speaks in tones of terror and despair*) Oh, Schneider—ain't that awful?... I dunno —he couldn't tell me.... Yes, I got the doctor, and Rogers is gettin' some of the boys and girls to help.... They're all at the dance-hall. I guess the doctor'll want to work in there. Pull those benches out from the walls so he can work both sides.... And so they'll get some heat from the stove.... (*She turns to Buz*) Don't ask me no questions—I can't tell yer nothin'.... And listen: you got to keep your head. It's goin' to be terrible.... You go over to the livery stable and wake up old Mike.... Tell him I sent yer.... Tell him what's happened.... Tell him to harness up the horses an' take his big sled down to the track by the freight station. Tell him to put a lot o' straw in the bottom and take all the horse-blankets and rugs he's got. He'll have to pull in close to the tracks so the injured can be loaded in, and taken to the village. We're tellin' everybody in the houses to be ready for 'em.... Tell him to hurry!...

(*She goes to the telephone again and rings*) Schneider—that's fine!... Now, let's call Mrs. Hall.... Ring twice—she's got a 'phone next to her bed.... Tell her what's happened and she'll get everything organized.... Tell her to notify everybody— tell 'em to turn their lights on an' get their extra beds ready, and all the blankets they got.... And things to eat and drink.... Somethin' hot, you know.... (*She waits*) She's probably asleep. Keep ringin'.... You'll get her.... Tell the Millers, the Jacksons.... The Brown children went to see their grandmother in Denver, so they'll have four or five beds there.... And that couple from the East, in the corner house—they've got a lot o' room.... The Macphersons—(*She interrupts Schneider as he talks to Mrs. Hall*)—about thirty beds.... Soup, eggs.... Tea, hot milk.... Hot-water bottles.... Did she understand?... Oh, Mrs. Hall is wonderful—we couldn't get along in this village without Mrs. Hall.... I bet you she'll have everything organized.... Can you think of anything we can do?... The trouble with this place is that there's nothing to do nothing with.... Nobody's ever ready for an emergency.... Did you ever *see* an accident?... Guess I won't be much use.... I felt kinda funny when I was fixin' Danny's finger....

(*She hangs up the receiver, then sees the doctor entering*)

Oh, Doctor—my! It's good to see your face.... Don't feel so scared with you around.... Just tell us what you want— we'll do the best we can.... I did—they're comin' as fast as they can, bringin' blankets an' towels an' first-aid stuff.... Some empty pails?... Yes, sir.... Lots o' hot water? Yes, we

have.... We got some little bowls and pitchers, too.... Boilin'
water?... Yes, sir.... Buz—did you tell Mike?... Good. Say—
did the laundry come back?... We got plenty o' towels,
Doctor.... And paper napkins.... Listen, Buz—I want you
to stay right here an' wait on the doctor.... He wants those
big pitchers filled with hot water.... An' the empty pails....
And get those little bowls on the shelf, there, that we used
for soup.... Put boilin' water in those pitchers.... Then, put
some towels here, and take the rest in to the doctor....

(*Rosie comes running in*) Oh, Rosie—my! You were quick!...
Lucky you live so close.... Isn't it *terrible*?... How did you
carry that load?... The others comin'?... (*Sadie comes in*)
Hello, Sadie.... In there.... Doctor, Sadie's brought a bottle
of whiskey.... Open up the blankets, girls, and spread 'em
over the benches.... They'll get warm by the stove.... Sally—
you take the counter and get the cups ready.... Tea or coffee,
Doctor?... Black coffee, he says.... Are the boys out there?...
(*Shouts*) Sam—listen: don't let everybody come through
here!... They'll want to come where they see the light, and
we'll be in a jam if they all come in.... Just bring them that
has to see the doctor. Any with light injuries'll be better off
goin' to the village.... All the neighbours is notified and Mike
is bringin' the big sledge down to the tracks so they can get
right off and get to bed and get some hot food.... Tell the
other boys out there.... Get yer coffee goin', Sal.... They're
comin' in, Doctor.... Hurry with the hot water, Buz.... Did
Mike go by?... Good! Here comes Sam, now....

(*The men now begin to bring the victims of the wreck into the
station*)

(*She runs forward to help an injured girl*) Just lean on me....
Your arm?... Maybe it ain't broke. We've got a good doctor
here.... We think he's the greatest doctor in the world....
He's an awful kind man—he does everything for us.... Don't
talk about it, now.... You'll be better when you get warm....
The girls will give you some coffee.... This way, please—
doctor's in there.... Take this towel for your head. (*She runs*

with a towel to an injured man) Doctor—look after that gentleman!... (*To a woman*) Let me take your baby! Look at him sleepin'!... Didn't get hurt a mite.... You've got a nasty cut—lucky it didn't go in your eye!... You've got a lot to be thankful for!... That so? Seems like a miracle!... Rosie—take this little feller. Don't wake him.... He was thrown right out of his mother's arms and she found him in the snow—not even scratched.... (*To another woman*) Will you sit down here, please?... The doctor's awful busy, and you can rest here.... I'll give you a nice cup of coffee.... Don't talk.... Will you sit here by your friend?... (*She brings the coffee*) Drink this.... Must have been terrible, waitin' in the cold.... Lights went out?... Take this towel for your hand.... You'll be all right when you've had a good sleep.... We'll get you to the village as soon as we can....

(*She turns to Sam, who comes in carrying a girl*) Lay her down, Sam.... Did you carry her all the way? Fainted, I guess.... (*She kneels down with the girl's head on her arm*) Give me some cold water—cold water—quick!... (*She dashes a little water in the girl's face*) You're all right, girl.... You're with *friends*. Have a little sip of water. Open your lips. Don't move—just lay there. You're safe—you're with friends.... (*She rises and turns to Buz*) Buz, come here.... See if you can find out any news of Jerry.... See if anybody knows what happened to the engineer.... Sam, you'd better take her in to the doctor.... She looks bad.... Lay easy—we're goin' to take you where it's warmer.... Don't do nothin'.... He'll lift you—he's strong.... Rosie, fix some pillows and blankets on the floor for this girl.... (*She helps lift the injured girl*) Got her?... Just let yourself go.... I'll stay with you.... Lemme get my arm out.... Your mother's fine. Don't worry—you're with friends.... We'll take care of you.... Doctor—look out for that girl!... She's just frozen!... Put some hot blankets on her, Sadie.... What, Doctor? A piece of stick for a tourniquet?... More towels?... Yes, sir—and more hot water?... Sally—take the doctor some more hot water.... Molly—

gimme that hammer. The handle will do.... Can I have your towels?... They've give out.... Yes, Doctor—I'm comin'....

(She suddenly turns and sees Jerry come in)

Jerry!... Jerry!... *(She runs into his arms)* Lemme look at you!... Are you all right?... Sure?... You jumped?... *(The doctor calls her)* Yes, Doctor! Lemme go, Jerry—the Doctor wants me to help him set an arm.... Thank God you're safe!... *(She breaks away from Jerry and turns towards the inner room)*

Yes, Doctor—I'm comin'.... I'll help you now.... What do you want me to do?...

(She runs off breathlessly to help the doctor)

DOCTORS AND DIETS

※⊕※

A lady enters a large restaurant in company with three of her friends, who have just met her for lunch. She carries an enormous handbag, wears green gloves, and has on her head an absurd hat from which two long green feathers project at violent angles in opposite directions. She talks in a rapid, flustered manner as she pushes her way through the patrons about the entrance and makes her way towards the tables, looking distractedly for the head waiter. For a moment her guests—Miss Laprune, Mrs. Noflaw, and Clara—fall behind; then, after the waiter has indicated their table, they join her and sit down.

I *know*, my dear—but *what* doctor said it?... Yes—but don't you know, Clara, if *that's* what she's got, that is *not* the doctor she should be going to.... Oh, no, my dear—she should be going to *my* doctor.... Well, I happen to know that that is his specia—Now, wait a minute!... We mustn't get to talking before we get our table.... Where *is* the head waiter?... (*She looks around the restaurant*) Well, he *should* be here!... You know we're half an hour late.... Hello—there's Fanny over there. This place is always full of friends.... (*She sees the head waiter*) *There* he is! I see him.... 'Way across the room— surrounded by women.... You see, the trouble is, I'm afraid he's going to give up our table.... We're so late—they're probably clamouring for tables.... He may have assumed that we were not coming.... (*She motions agitatedly*) Oh! If only I could make him *see* me!... I think the only thing for me to do is to go over there.... You wait here.... Oh, no—don't follow me—I'll come back—or I'll wave.... I'll let you know where I am—you stay where you are....

(*She edges her way through the tables, bumping into chairs and people*)

I'm *very* sorry.... May I get through, please?... I *beg* your pardon—may I pass?... Oh! I'm *so* sorry—I hope I didn't hit your hat.... Excuse me—may I pass?... May I get through?... I beg your pardon.... Thank you.... Excuse me.... (*She seizes the waiter's attention*) Oh—waiter! Oh, waiter —good morning—I am Mrs. Grimmer—Mrs. *Grimmer*.... G—R—I—M—M—E—R.... Yes—I ordered a table for four at one o'clock.... Well—I couldn't seem to catch your attention.... I've been waiting at the door for a quarter of an hour and I was so afraid I'd lose my table, as I know I'm late.... I saw you were very busy over here, and I thought I'd better come and tell you that I had arrived.... Yes, my friends are waiting.... Table for four.... Yes.... Mrs. Grimmer.... Yes, I *am* Mrs. Grimmer—I was here yesterday about eleven o'clock.... You put my name down.... Perhaps you'll just look in your book....

(*She sees a friend at a table nearby*) Hello! Hello, dear— where *did* you come from?... I had no *idea* you were back— did you have a wonderful time?... I'm *so* embarrassed—I feel that everybody is looking at me.... I've been waiting for nearly twenty minutes and I can't get my table.... I saw the head waiter over here, so I came to speak to him—and he doesn't seem to know *anything* about it!... You look *so* well.... Crazy about your hat!... (*She turns to the waiter*) Yes—I was here at eleven o'clock.... I had on a different hat—perhaps you don't recognize me.... But I come here *very* often.... Yes, I ordered a table for four—at one o'clock.... Mrs. Grimmer.... (*Turns to her friend*) How's Charlie—did he go to Guatemala?... Why don't you call me up some day, and we'll have a nice little party?... Haven't seen you for an age!... Let's get together.... (*Turns to the waiter*) Well, perhaps you'll let me look at your list.... Yes, I imagine.... So many people *must* claim tables.... This is such a very popular place and the food is so delicious.... Oh, I come here very, *very*

PLATE XXIV

At the Court of Philip IV
Photograph by Feyer, Vienna

PLATE XXV

Opening a Bazaar
Photograph by Trude Fleischmann, New York

often.... Yes, I know you put my name down on the right-hand page.... Oh, I'm *sure*.... It's dreadful to be late, but I was unavoidably delayed.... (*She murmurs names as she reads the list*) Here I am—GRIMMER!... This table? Oh, thank you *so* much!... Well, I knew you would.... I *thought* you'd recognize me.... Don't trouble—I'll find my way quite easily.... (*To the friend*) It's all right, my dear—he's got it.... Don't forget—call me up! Love to Charlie!... (*She beckons to her friends and points to the table, working her way back*)... May I get past, please?... I *beg* your pardon—I'm sorry!... Can I get through?... I *beg* your pardon.... Excuse me—I'm sorry —did I hit your hat?... Thank you *so* much—may I pass, please?... (*She recognizes another friend at a table*) Hello! I never saw you.... My! That looks good!... *Love* your hat!...

(*To her lunch party*) Well, girls, I thought I was *never* going to get here.... Yes, it's all right.... He didn't recognize me, but he's been keeping this table for us.... Now, let's sit down quickly before anybody else tries to claim it.... Well, it's *such* a pleasure to have you here.... Let's be quite informal.... (*She indicates the chairs*) Mrs. Noflaw—will you sit opposite?... Clara on my left.... Miss Laprune—will you sit on my right?... My! This *is* nice!... I've been looking forward to this little luncheon for *days*.... Now, I hate to start with an apology, but unfortunately, Mrs. Noflaw, I'm on a diet.... And I'm not going to be able to join you in these tempting dishes, but I want you to feel perfectly free to order anything that you like.... *A la carte*...or the *plat du jour*?... Everything is very good here—I think it's the best restaurant in town....

What?... You *are*?... Oh, what a pity!... Well, never mind.... I am, too, so I understand how you feel.... Well— we'll just show the others how much *character* we have! We will enjoy vicariously—is that the word?—the delicious meal that they are going to eat!... Now, Clara, dear—Mrs. Noflaw and I are both on diets, so order whatever you like, whatever you fancy most.... You can have my portion, too.... *What?*... You're *not*! My dear, since *when*?... *You?*... Of *all* people!...

Clara, do you *mean* it?... Well, isn't this *too* ridiculous!... Miss Laprune, do you realize that you are the only one here that's going to be able to eat this delicious luncheon?... We three are *all* on diets....

Now, what shall we have her eat?... She must have the *specialité* of the *maison*!... That delicious shrimp soufflé.... Oh, my dear...and the squab in jelly with vegetables is the *most* delicious.... (*To Miss Laprune*) *What*?... I don't know whether to laugh or cry! *She's* on a diet too!... Really, this is ridiculous!... Here we are at the very best restaurant in town and none of us can eat!... Well, surely you'll take something?... What is your 'régime', Mrs. Noflaw?... What? A cold boiled—did you say *turnip*? Why—I hadn't heard of *that*!... Full of Vitamin Q?... I hadn't got that far down the alphabet!... And what does Q *do* for us?... It *does*? How *marvellous*!... Did you hear what she said? Q makes *brains*! (*She turns to the other ladies*)—brains—brains!... But why isn't the whole world eating them?... Do you mean to say the old turnip that we used to just throw in the soup, they now find in that particular form goes right to the *head*—and actually becomes *brains*?... Oh! Aren't doctors *marvellous*?... What is yours, Clara, dear?... What?... Oh! You're going to that raw carrot man?... Clara, Clara—I hear there's more than carrots in that cure.... (*To the others*) Have you heard about the raw carrot man?... Oh, my dear—they say he has *so* much magnetism!... (*To Clara*) Well, you certainly *look* well! I've never seen your eyes so bright—is that *only* carrots?... Now, Clara!... (*To the others*) Oh, I always tease Clara— she's one of my oldest friends.... And what is yours, Miss Laprune?... The juice of *eleven lemons*? Oh! How *can* you?... (*To the others*) Did you hear what she said?... She's on the hundred-lemon cure.... You mean you had *ten* for breakfast?... And are having *twelve* for supper?... One more at every meal until she reaches one hundred.... And then what happens?... Oh—then it's *all over*!... And then you're immune for the rest of your life?... Marvellous!... Oh, I think you've got such courage!... But it's worth it!... You certainly look well!...

Now, if we can get a man—not always the easiest thing. (*She looks about and tries to hail a waiter*) Waiter!—would you?... *Could* you?... They seem to look right *through* you.... Nobody pays the slightest attention....(*Calling*) Would you?... They *all* look so preoccupied.... Could you?... Waiter!... Oh, *thank* you. Is this your table?... No, not very long....

Waiter, these ladies, unfortunately, are all on diets.... Do you think you could get for me some rather special dishes?... Well, do you think you could possibly find a perfectly plain, cold, boiled turnip—just *one*?... Just one!... Oh! You have them?... Funny, I hadn't heard!... Well, will you find a very attractive turnip, please?... Make it a personal choice.... Then I want some raw carrots.... *Raw carrots....* (*To one of her guests*) My dear, he's French and doesn't understand.... Do you happen to know what carrot is in French?... *Carotte*?... Oh, I *envy* you your French—*where* did you pick up so much?... *Cru? Carotte cru!*... (*To the waiter*) What?... Oh, I understand him now. He says he makes a *very* attractive carrot salad.... Grated carrot on a slice of ham, with a touch of mayonnaise.... You don't *care* for them that way?... You mean you prefer the bunch?... Oh, yes, dear—have it just as you like!... Yes, I *see*.... You want them *washed*, and you want the green *left on*?... You eat the *green*, too!... Certainly, I'll just explain.... (*To the waiter*) The lady wants the bunch— the *whole* bunch and nothing *but* the bunch.... So wash them and dry them and leave them *alone*.... With the green left *on*, please—*just* as they come from market....

And how do you like your lemons? Squeezed—strained?... And do you like hot water, cold water, Vichy water, soda water—*what* sort of water?... *No* water?... And do you care for granulated sugar, powdered sugar, or syrup?... No? You don't *take* sugar?... And you don't take *water*?... You mean you drink it right down?... My dear, how *can* you?... Waiter!... Yes. The lady wants the juice of eleven lemons—yes,

please—served in a *large* glass—a pitcher, if necessary....
Thank you!... No, I don't take anything, thank you.... No,
I don't *eat*.... Well, that's not quite true.... I *do* eat.... But
I only eat at night, you see.... I eat once a day.... But I don't
think it could hurt me to eat now instead.... It would be more
congenial!

Waiter—I'll just add to that order, please.... Bring me
three chocolate éclairs.... Yes, please—*three*.... (*To her guests*)
Well, my dears, you may think it's peculiar, but you can't
imagine *how* they're helping me.... You see, *all* my life I've
had a very peculiar craving for éclairs.... In my childhood I
wasn't allowed very many, and I don't ever remember *not*
being *hungry*.... No other food attracted me at all.... And
since I've grown up I've made a tremendous effort to control
my appetite for éclairs, but I was rather worried, and I heard
about this doctor who has made a study of the things that
people crave, and he feels that people *should* eat whatever
they fancy most.... But they mustn't eat anything else—
that's the point—so I went to him and I explained my
trouble and he just looked at me, and he said, 'Mrs. Grimmer
—the miracle to me is that you are alive at all!' He said I was
the most sensitive person he'd ever seen—that I belonged to
the hyper-hyper type and we *rarely* survive! Of course, I was
examined, and so was the éclair, and they found that the
éclair contains *every*thing my system lacks. So I take three a
day and I feel like a new woman!... Isn't it marvellous?...
And he gave me *such* encouragement—he said such a wonderful thing to me.... He said, 'Mrs. Grimmer, don't worry—
the fact that you are alive indicates to me that you are probably *going to live*.' And, my dear, I went out of that office
walking on air!... Just feeling like a million dollars—and I've
felt so ever since!... Oh, he's a *genius*—and he knows everything...and so *few* people do! His eyes seem to look right
through you.... He's certainly solved my problem.... And I
wish I could make all my friends go to him.... I wish I could
persuade Lola to take Alfred.... I *know* he could cure him....

Have you seen Alfred?... Poor old Alfred!... Oh! My dear, you wouldn't *know* him.... I don't think Alfred is with us for long.... I was very, very fond of Alfred.... I'm going to miss him terribly.... Oh! I know that he's not dead yet—but you wait, my dear, and see if I'm not right!... I *know* that my doctor could cure him—and I told Lola so.... But she's not even interested.... Well, she likes *her* doctor!...

And Isabel—there's another person I've tried to help.... My dear—she looks twenty years older than we do. You wouldn't *know* her.... Oh, she's lost her hair.... That's not *her* hair—oh, no! She lost *her* hair years ago.... And she's lost all her looks.... And she's going to lose Ned—that's what worries me.... Oh, he's out dancing every night.... And so often that's the way trouble starts.... And I went to Isabel and I *begged* her to get away—said I'd gladly keep an eye on Ned for her.... But she won't go. Aren't people *queer*?... Poor Isabel—she really is a fright!... I was very sweet and tactful—I didn't want to hurt her feelings.... I wouldn't hurt *any*body's feelings.... And I'm sure she understood.... But I felt *some*body must tell her, so I just said, 'Isabel, dear—you know I love you, but you are a fright, and I know my doctor could help you.' But it didn't seem to do any good at all—she refused to go!... It's *so* difficult to help people—because I feel they don't really *want* to be helped!...

(*The waiter arrives with the dishes*)

Oh! Here's our delicious luncheon!... The carrots to *this* lady, please.... Yes.... (*She indicates the guests*) The turnip there.... The lemonade this side.... Thank you. Oh! *Look* at my éclairs.... Now, I'm perfectly happy!... I feel better already—just *look*ing at them! (*She begins to eat*)

Oh, girls—it's such fun to have you!... Aren't we having a good time?... By the way, speaking of these things—have you heard about Flora?... You don't know my friend Flora, Mrs. Noflaw?... An old friend of ours.... Did you know she was worse?... Oh, no, she wasn't better, she was worse!... *Much* worse—she was getting worse and *worse*.... This friend of ours, Mrs. Noflaw, seemed to be just fading away and nobody knew *what* was the matter.... She's rather a peculiar girl.... She never wears anything but *green*.... And she was getting greener and greener.... And so she went to this doctor —it seems he examines you in regard to the way you react to colour—he is what they call a Colour Analyst. My dear, you'd better be careful.... It seems you should never wear a dress or associate with people who wear bright colours.... Or decorate your house, until you have been colour-analysed, because some colours can have the most *dreadful* effect on people—like poison—and some do wonders for you!

(*She turns to greet a friend*) How d' you do?... (*To her guests again*) Listen: let me tell you what happened to Flora. She went to this doctor, and she was put in a dark room.... Black as pitch.... With the doctor, and a machine which registers your reaction to colour.... Something is attached to you, and something is attached to the machine, and something's attached to the doctor. He presses a button, and colours are flashed on a screen—and your reaction is registered on a dial.... Suddenly, the machine nearly exploded, and the doctor was hurled across the room, and as he went, he said, 'Miss Idgett, you need purple. Your system is *starved*.' And he said he would not account for the consequences unless she got purple into her without any delay. So she didn't even stop to telephone her mother.... She took a taxi and she flew to the sanatorium.... And she was rushed right up to the fourth floor—that's the Purple Floor—and there—... Do you *know* what they did?... Didn't you *hear* what they did?... (*She sees a friend*) Hello, Lily—how are you?... I love your hat—most becoming—call me up some day!... Love to Joe!... (*To her guests again*) The first thing they *did*, my dear—she was stripped, and hurled into a pool of purple liquid, and told she had to soak there for three hours, and they left her alone in the pool!... Well, she happens to be a very good swimmer, so she swam for an hour, and then she floated for an hour, and then she said she thought she was going to sink, so she called. And they came, and they pulled her out and laid her on an amethyst slab, and wheeled her into a little cave where she is just immersed in purple light—night and day, my dear.... Oh, you *can't* get in.... Oh, no—she *can't* get out.... No—nobody can see her.... Oh, no.... She has to *lie* there, just as God made her.... The purple has to permeate *every* pore, and reach the very *marrow* of her bones.... It's the only way to save her.... (*She sees another friend*) How do you do?... It's nice to see you—love your hat—call me up some time.... Let's get together.... I'd *love* to. Goodbye!... (*To her guests again*) And, my dear—she's not allowed to touch a thing or think a thought that isn't purple.... She swims every morning in the purple pool, and eats purpleized food, and she's surrounded by flowers—she has pansies, violets, heliotrope, lavender, orchids, wistaria, and lilac.... She wrote me the *sweetest* letter on mauve paper with purple ink—and of course we use three-cent stamps, so that's all right.... And she says this purple peace seems to penetrate her soul.... And she has never felt so well in her life.... She's coming out on Friday, and the doctor said she must wear mauve for the rest of her life and redecorate her house completely. Otherwise, she's cured!... Aren't doctors *wonderful*?...

(*She glimpses another friend*) How do you do?... Did you see who I bowed to then?... Mrs. Pincher.... Over there in the corner—to the right.... (*She murmurs, smiling and bowing*) We're looking at you—we like your hat!... Pretty woman, isn't she?... Oh! But what she's been *through*!... Oh, my dear—you didn't know about Mrs. Pincher's operation?... Everybody's been talking about it.... They say there's never *been* such an operation in the *whole* history of surgery.... Well, she's been going to doctors for thirty years, and they all gave her up!... Oh, yes—she kept on living, but they all gave her up, so she got rather discouraged, and she went to this new man called Doctor Delvin, and he said that she didn't have what the others said she had.... But I never *do* remember what it was he said she had.... But anyway, he said he would have to operate—and he did, and, my dear, they say that the operation lasted for *eleven* and a *half* hours!... No, no—not seven—*eleven*!... I heard it on absolute authority that it lasted eleven and one-half hours, and the incision—did you hear about the incision?... Didn't you *hear* about the incision?... (*She sees another friend passing the table*) How do you do? It's nice to see you—my love to Harry—call me up some time.... Do!... Fine! *Crazy* about your hat!... (*To her guests*) My dear, the incision, they say, was *fourteen* inches deep!... They thought they'd *never* get there.... But she's cured!... It was a *complete* success!... The only trouble was, it killed the doctor!...

You know, girls—we're having such a good time, but we're going to miss the matinée if we don't hurry!... When you talk about worthwhile and interesting things, time just flies—doesn't it?... (*She hails the waiter*) Waiter, have you my bill?... Please.... (*To her guests*) Was everything *just* as you liked it?... Feel better?... (*She puckers her lips, referring to the lemon juice*) Oh! Did you get that *all* down!... Ooh!... (*To the waiter*) Thank you—I'll just sign.... I have an account here.... Everything was very nice.... Yes, we enjoyed our luncheon very much.... And this is for you.... Thank you.

(*They all rise from the table*)

Oh, girls—before we break up—... Speaking of doctors, I want to ask you to go on Thursday with me to Madison Square Garden to hear this new man!... Oh! My dear—haven't you *heard*?... He's *marvellous*!... Well, I think he's probably going to be the *greatest* doctor in the world.... You see—he's got a perfectly new idea. He never sees his patients. He's not interested in individuals, he prefers to treat a crowd. And he's organized these mass cures.... And he cures thirty thousand people every Thursday. It only costs a dollar and it really is a wonderful experience.... You see, he really *knows* what he's talking about, because he's spent his *entire* life trying to find out what it is—the cause of all the trouble in the world.... And he's *found* it, my dear.... *That's* the

point—he's *found* it!... Just wait till you hear him!... (*She
sees another friend*) Oh, hello—hello—why, Penny, dear—
how *are* you?... I haven't seen you for *ages*! I'm *crazy* about
your hat.... Well—call me up.... (*To her guests*) Come on,
girls, we must run or we're going to miss the play. Come on!

(*They make their way through the tables and out of the
restaurant*)

AN ENGLISH HOUSE-PARTY

➤➤➤⊛⬅⬅⬅

THE HOSTESS

The hostess, the mistress of a country-house in England, enters her drawing-room. She is a tall, shrewd, self-possessed woman. She finds that one of her guests has already arrived for her week-end house-party, and after greeting her she sits down near her in a chair, next to a tea-table. She speaks in a cultivated, somewhat worldly-wise, but cordial and amused English voice.

Oh, Emily, my dear! I *am* glad to see you! You're looking *very* well! I never saw you looking better, dear!... Will you have a cup of tea? It's here.... I've had mine, actually, but *do* have one.... I'm well, thank you, but I *am* rather tired.... I've been up in London all day and feel quite exhausted.... Do help yourself to bread and butter.... And I rather wish I hadn't anyone coming for the week-end.... It's a *very* odd party—I really can't think how I managed to get such an extraordinary 'mixture' together....

Well, to begin with, I have my little niece, Rhoda Milton, coming—she should be here any moment, now.... You didn't *know* I had a niece?... Dear me, yes—I have a great many little nieces. I have a brother, you see, and he's a parson, and he has eight children.... Isn't it *dreadful*?... Oh, they're very nice children—but eight *is* rather a lot, with very little money.... Rhoda is the eldest. She's about eighteen, and she's my god-child—but I'm ashamed to say she's never been here before. I've asked her often, but she's quite invaluable at home, and can't be spared! I finally persuaded my brother to let her come away for a month.... She's one of those unselfish girls who, I'm afraid, is rather *put* upon, and has no life of her own. She's not been to any parties, or met any men, or had any fun. I expect she's very shy, but I shall try to give her a happy time and perhaps later take her to London.

Then, I've got my dear Fergus Fox-Seton.... You've met him here, surely! He often comes—he's a perfect poppet.... But his *passion* in life is butterflies, moths, and beetles, and insects of all kinds—he does not like people very much.... He's apt to disappear—he wanders about with a butterfly net, and creeps out of the house at dawn in search of a particular spider.... He forgets to come in for meals, and has to be sent for—and he's not what one might call a very helpful guest, though I'm devoted to him.

Then, my old friend, Lord Vernon, is coming, with his daughter, Vivian—a very spoiled, very bored young woman who spends most of her time on a horse—and talks and thinks of little else.... I was very fond of her mother and I'm devoted to her father, so I ask her every year—rather hoping she'll not come!... However, I've got a young man coming who's said to be very devoted to her, and that will help, I hope!... I shall do everything I can to further the romance—as he's also very keen on horses and hunting.... Well, that is *one* basis for marriage!...

Then, I picked up in Venice last summer a young American artist, named Joe Wharton—a very talented young man.... I bought one of his pictures.... He's an odd type, but amusing.... I had a talk with him one day, waiting for a gondola at the hotel, and he said he was coming to England and longed to paint this part of the country.... So I said—as one does—'You must let me know when you come.' So he did—and I felt bound to ask him.... And I don't know what to do with him.... Let him paint? How *wise* you are, dear—I will....

Then, Captain Morton, the explorer, is coming, and though he's a most distinguished scientist, I find him *rather* difficult.... I expect you've read about him in the papers?... Oh! I've known him since he was a boy—he was a school friend of my brother's—and I've always followed his career

with interest, though I can't say I understand very well *what*
it is…. Surely you've heard of him?… My dear, he's *very*
famous—he's just returned from a long and most *perilous*
expedition—looking for something…something *frightfully*
important…. I only know he found what he went for…. I
believe it's a small bit of stone that definitely proves that the
earth is *millions* of years older than they thought it *was*….
And though he's considered one of the greatest scientists of
the day, and has been made a member of the Royal Society,
and has been honoured and fêted and asked to go to America
on a lecture-tour, he *never* speaks—*never*. So he is not a great
contribution to the gaiety of the party….

Then, Flora Fitzgerald—my *darling* Flora—is coming….
I know, you've always missed her…. Well, you have a treat
in store. She's from Virginia. She married a Guardsman—a
friend of my Percy's. He was drowned very tragically in a
boating accident…. Oh, some twelve years ago, now…. She
returned to the States, but she comes over every year, and
always comes to me…. I'm devoted to her—she's very gay,
never stops talking, and leaves one rather breathless—but
she's a darling!… She's always very vague about her plans—
but I believe she has recently flown over from America and
has been stopping in Paris. I heard from there only this
morning, saying she was arriving this afternoon—I don't
know *how* or *when* she's coming—but she'll suddenly appear!

Then, I have one prize! Whom do you think I saw in
London last week?… You'd never *guess*!… *Who*?… No….
No…. Oh! No, dear—long forgotten—what made you think
of *him*?… I wonder what became of him?… No, you'll never
guess—I shall have to tell you….

Sir John Herter! I *was* surprised—I'd not seen him for
over a year, and I thought he was in the States where he'd
been sent on some mission…. And there he was in Bond
Street on Thursday!… I noticed a very good-looking man
coming towards me, and suddenly realized it was he!… I said,
'What—you, Sir John?' And he said, 'Rather—here I am!'

And I said, 'When are you coming to me?' And he said, 'This very week-end, if I may.'... I rapidly thought of my party and realized it was rather a *strange* collection of people, but I was so enchanted that he should want to come that I said, 'Oh do come!' And he said, 'Well, I will.' So he's coming!...

Oh! Isn't he?... The most distinguished creature! What hasn't he got—brains, looks, position—and such charm!... I think he has a great future before him.... I wonder he doesn't marry.... He always seems rather indifferent.... He likes his independence, I expect, and he has a very interesting life....

(*She pauses suddenly and listens*)

I think I hear someone arriving—probably my little niece.... Excuse me—I must meet her.... No, stop there, dear— I'd like you to see her.... (*She leaves the room, and her voice is heard outside the door*) I expect she'll be *very* shy, and you're always so nice with the young.

(*She is heard greeting her niece*)

Rhoda darling!... Is that you?... How are you, dear child? I *am* glad to see you!... Are you very, very tired?...

RHODA

Rhoda enters, following her aunt. She is a shy but eager young English girl, visibly out of a country parsonage. She speaks in a low, soft, modest voice, gently but with suppressed excitement.

No, thank you, Aunt Ivy, not at all tired—it was a lovely journey.... Sit here?—but isn't this your chair?... (*She sits down*) No, thank you—no tea! I had some, thank you—in the railway carriage.... I got one of those jolly little tea-baskets.... A very good tea, thank you—bread and butter, a bit of cake and a biscuit—lovely!... No.... (*She turns to the other lady*) I have never been away before.... Yes, I did, most awfully— I had a book but I'm afraid I didn't read—because I was looking out of the railway carriage windows all the time....

(*To her aunt*) Thank you.... Mummy is quite well, yes,

Daddy, too.... Millicent and Muriel had the 'flu.... They were rather bad but they're better, now.... And Johnnie fell downstairs last week—didn't Mummy write you? He got the most frightful bump on his eye.... It was cut just here, and he had three stitches taken!... He's frightfully pleased, because he's going to have a scar—and it will be the *best* scar in the family!...

Ivy is quite well, thank you.... (*To the other lady*) Ivy is my little sister! She's nine.... She went to Manchester last week, Aunt Ivy—and had such a jolly time!... She went to the dentist!... She loved the drill!...

(*To the other lady*) I beg your pardon?... A large family?... Yes—I have seven brothers and sisters.... We're eight—ten, counting Mummy and Daddy.... Great fun—I *love* a big family.... Oh, *did* you?—then you know what fun it is!...

Parish work? Oh, not very much.... I have a Sunday school class—little boys.... Oh! They're darlings—they *are* rather naughty.... But we have great fun. I'm afraid we have more fun than religion! I *love* little boys.... Then, I have a sewing class of little girls.... Yes, they are *very* nice.... They sew beautifully.... Oh, yes—I *do* like them—but I've never liked little girls as much as little boys.... I don't know why.... Then, I read to the old ladies of the parish once a week.... I love old ladies!... We are reading *Barchester Towers*, Aunt Ivy—and they enjoy it *very* much. They want to read all of Trollope!... So it's lovely having the set you gave me for Christmas....

Oh! Aunt Ivy—I've a lovely surprise for you! I'm taking piano lessons!... Mummy discovered that the Vicar's daughter in the parish next ours plays the piano quite beautifully, and she kindly agreed to give me lessons for two shillings an hour!... Isn't it sweet of her?... I go twice a week on my bicycle.... Oh, it's only fourteen miles, and it's downhill all one way.... Lucy is such a nice girl, Aunt Ivy—her name is Lucy Violet.... She's a little older than I am, but we've become great friends.... She's got an aunt in London, and she went to stop with her last year for three weeks.... She had *such* a wonderful time.... Her aunt lives in Gower Street, near the British Museum, and Lucy went to the British Museum seven times!... She also went to the National Gallery, the National Portrait Gallery, the Royal Academy, the Tate Gallery, the Victoria and Albert Museum, and the Zoo...and to see the Wax Works.... And she went to Kew, and Hampton Court, and Windsor—and Eton, and she saw the meadow of Runnymede where the Magna Carta was signed.... And then, in the British Museum, she saw the Magna Carta! *Fancy*!... She brought back one hundred and twenty-five picture post-cards.... Oh, yes—I've seen them all, several times.... So now, I feel I am a little bit prepared if ever I'm lucky enough to go to London.... Oh, no!—I've never been. I've never been anywhere....

I am studying Greek and Latin with my father.... We're reading the *Iliad*, now.... Oh, it's glorious. My father reads Greek very beautifully—doesn't he, Aunt Ivy?... I hope to go to college one day—if I'm not wanted too much at home!...

Aunt Ivy—what do you think?... Daddy has given me the most *lovely* new frock...for typing his sermons for a year. Isn't it dear of him?... It's a little grey voile that Mummy got in Manchester, and it has got a little frill of real val lace at the neck that belonged to her grandmother.... And it's cut a tiny bit low, and I wear the topaze brooch you gave me.... And it has a rose-coloured sash!... (*She pauses*)

I beg your pardon, Aunt Ivy...but may I go and rest?... Mummy said I was to, before dinner—though I'm not a bit tired, and I'm longing to get out and see the garden.... It *was* so sweet of you to ask me, Aunt Ivy.... I shall enjoy it so— I'm enjoying it already!...

Such a *lovely* house!... (*She rises*) Oh! Don't bother—I'll find the children—they'll show me my room.... Is dinner at eight o'clock?... Half past eight?... That *is* late!... I shall be ready—and I shall wear my new frock!... Goodbye.... Oh! Thank you *so* much!... (*To the lady*) Oh! I should *love* to come and see you—thank you.... Goodbye.... (*She goes*)

LADY VIVIAN

She enters slowly casually, very bored and making no effort to conceal it. She is tall, horsey, supercilious, and speaks in a laconic, indifferent manner. She remains standing.

Hello, Ivy, dear! How are you?... How do you do?... No tea, thanks—no, really—but I expect Father will have a cup of tea.... Don't be foolish, Father.... You know you're frozen!... Give him some, Ivy.... Yes, we motored down—and it was rather cold.... And my father said he'd sell his soul for a cup of tea.... Yes, it is—very chilly.... I don't mind—in fact I prefer it—it's very much better for hunting, you see.

Hello, Reggie—when did you arrive?... By train? Your car still broken down?... But why didn't you come with us?... Didn't Father telephone? I asked him to telephone you to come along with us. (*To her father*) Father? Did you forget to tell Reggie to come along with us in the car?... No, I *told* you his car was broken down.... Oh.... (*To Reggie*) Sorry—he forgot!

(*She takes a cigarette*) Why weren't you out on Thursday?... Most awfully good run!... Yes, it was—who told you?... Oh! He knows nothing whatever about it—he was miles behind.... I saw him at the meet on his spavined old crock—but then he disappeared.... No wonder!... Di got a nasty spill.... No, not serious—broke her collarbone and cracked two ribs, got some nasty scratches and wrenched her wrist rather badly—nothing serious.... She fell in a briar and her hair caught and pulled away a bit of scalp.... And as I came by, I saw a long strand of red hair, and I said—there's Di, hanging on the briar—and she was groaning in the ditch.... Frightfully funny....

My new young horse carried me magnificently.... Glad I bullied Father into buying him for me.... He sailed over a high-post trail, and a couple of fences, and I gave everyone a nice lead...and held it all the way!... Didn't you know I had two new hunters?... A chestnut and a black.... Beauties!...

PLATE XXVI

The Private Secretary in *Three Women and Mr. Clifford*
Photograph by Nickolas Murray, New York

PLATE XXVII

Mrs. Clifford in *Three Women and Mr. Clifford*
Photograph by Dorothy Wilding, London and New York

Father?... Birthday?... Rather!... I'll give you a mount next week, if you want.... You may have all my horses, for I shan't be here.... I'm going abroad.... Paris.... No, not long.... I dunno—rather tired—bored, actually.... I shall buy a hat, I expect.... I'm hunting with the Quorn the first week in December, and I want to be very fit....

Stroll in the garden?—How long before dinner? All right —I don't mind.... I'll tell you something frightfully funny! Do you know that Russian Prince we met at Badminton in October? What's his name? You know—he looks like a walrus. Rides like one, too.... That's it! He appeared at the meet on Thursday, mounted on my old grey hunter—you know, the one I sold last year....

By the way, I want to ask your advice about my brown mare. I'm afraid I'll—(*She exits while speaking*)

FLORA

She is first heard speaking outside the room, then comes sailing in breathlessly and with immense cordiality, her arms spread wide in greeting. She speaks in the broad, soft accents of Virginia—a Southern American voice but with nothing timid or hesitant about it. She exudes enthusiasm, friendliness, good fellowship. She embraces her hostess before greeting the other guests with great hearty gestures.

Ivy—here I am!... Ivy—darling! How are you?... How'd I get here?... A friend dropped me at the door—he was motoring this way.... (*To a guest*) How *do* you do—excuse my rushing in like this!... Oh, Lord Vernon—how *lovely*! I am *so* glad to see you!...

No, thanks, Ivy—no tea—too near dinner-time.... *My*! It's *good* to be here again!... Yes, I flew from Paris this morning.... I flew from New York three weeks ago!... Lord Vernon, please sit next to me at dinner tonight, I want to hear *all* the news!... Fergus, how *are* you? *My*! You look *well*!... I hoped I'd find you here...because I've brought you a present, and I can't wait to show it to you!... A Brazilian Luna moth!... The most *beautiful* thing you've ever seen! It's about eight inches across—and the most *divine* colour!... I remembered you wanted one for your collection.... Well, I have a friend in Rio, and I asked him to send me the *finest* moth he could find!... Just *wait* till you see it! I've had it framed in a double glass frame of pale green enamel.... Have you added a lot to your collection? I want to hear about *every*thing!... I'll never forget that time last year—when I fell in the swamp and lost all your precious butterflies! What fun we had!... Oh, do *let's*!... Tomorrow morning, before breakfast.... You *bet* I will—I'd *adore* to. Do sit next to me at dinner and we'll arrange it—and I'll bring down the moth.... (*She swings around to Captain Morton*)

Captain Morton!... How *wonderful* to see you again—back safe and sound—after your *marvellous* journey!... It must have been thrilling! I read about your great discovery!... Can't you show me a little piece—just to hold a few billion years in my hand?... My! You must be *proud*!... Have you got your diary and your photographs with you?... I can't *wait* to see them!... Ride?... Tomorrow? Oh! I'd *love* to! I just feel like a gallop along the top of the Downs after two weeks in Paris! That's a *perfect* idea—try and sit next me at dinner and we'll ask Ivy—and bring down your pictures! *Please!*

(*The hostess's children have come in to say good-night*)

Oh! Children—*must* you go to bed?... *Just* as I come?... Listen, come to my room while I'm dressing.... I'll be there in about five minutes.... I've got *lots* of presents for you in my bags.... Don't forget—I'll be waiting for you!... (*She waves the children off, then sees the young American painter*)

Joe Wharton!—I don't believe it! *Kiss* me! What a *lovely* surprise!... Ivy wrote me she'd met you in Venice and just loved your painting.... Isn't she *adorable*?—I'm so glad you met.... What *luck* to find you here! Sit down a minute....I saw your mother just before I left—and Cousin Kate— and Fannie Lou, and little Peach.... And everyone sent you

all kinds of messages.... They're afraid you'll never come
home.... *My*! It's *good* to see you again!... Let's make a plan
for tomorrow.... We might go off for a picnic and do some
sketches.... I know the loveliest places to paint!... My plans?...
I expect to be here for a while...and perhaps, later, go to
Italy.... I'd like to go to Venice—no, I've never been. I've
just always been waiting for the right mo—

(*She breaks off, hailing Sir John Herter*)

Oh! How *do* you do, Sir John!... Do you know Mr.
Wharton?... Sir John Herter—Mr. Wharton. I come from
the same place at home—we were raised together.... Ivy?
She's gone up—*everybody* has gone to dress, I guess—it's
late.... See you later, Joe—sit next me at dinner and we'll
plan our picnic!

(*Pauses*) Johnnie!... Listen, darling—I'm going to do just
what you said, but we've got to be practical.... I simply *must*
tell Ivy.... I'll go and tell her right now! It's going to be
quite a shock.... No—you see, she doesn't know we met in
America—she doesn't know we flew over together.... She
doesn't know you motored me down.... So I'll have to break
it to her gently. Then she'll help us, 'cause we don't want all
the others to know!... Try and sit next to me at dinner, and
then we can make plans for tomorrow and get away from
everybody.... No, not *now*!... *No*, Johnnie!... *No*—there
isn't time—*no*, not *one*! Let me *go*!...

(*She breaks away from him and goes off to dress*)

AT AN ART EXHIBITION IN BOSTON

➨ ❦ ⬅

The lady who enters the exhibition hall of the Boston Museum wears glasses, a long grey coat of the 'duster' type, a scarf at her throat, and a flat 'sensible' hat. She carries a large roomy handbag. Accompanying her are several old friends—there is Kate, perhaps a cousin; there is Mrs. Walker; there is a child, perhaps a niece, called Mary. She moves slowly along the walls of the exhibition, from picture to picture. She speaks in a New England voice.

Come on, girls—here we are.... Now, let's keep together. We'll enjoy them so much more!... Oh!—oh! Look at them all! I never *saw* so many pictures!... Now—wait a minute.... Let's find out which way we go.... Do we go from right to left, or left to right?... It's very confusing, if we don't follow the order in which they are hung.... Well, I think I'll ask that lady—she looks pleasant and she's probably been around.... (*Speaks to a strange woman*) I beg your pardon—would you kindly tell me which way the pictures are hung? Does one go from right to left, or left to right?... They start in *this* corner?... Thank you so much. I hope you've enjoyed the exhibition—it looks very interesting.... Come on, Kate, we start over here!... The lady was very nice and she didn't mind my asking at all!

Now, who has the catalogue?... Mrs. Walker, won't you give little Mary the catalogue? She reads very nicely and this is her first picture exhibition—isn't it, Mary?... This is a catalogue, darling, and it will tell us the names of all the pictures. You see, the numbers on the pictures correspond to these numbers, and beside each number is the name of the picture—what the artist meant it to be.... One doesn't always know!...

Come on—let's keep together.... Now, everybody look for
number one—look for a little brass disk, darling, with number
one on it.... In the corner of the picture.... Don't look at the
pictures until you've found the number.... Number one—
number one—where are you?... *Here* we are! Oh! I've found
it—and you needn't look it up! Easy to see what that is, isn't it!
An 'Old Red Barn'.... Isn't that pretty?... Come on, Kate...:
'The Old Red Barn'.... Oh! I love that.... That's what I
call *Art*, Mrs. Walker.... It brings back nature, and represents a familiar scene—certainly to a New Englander there's
nothing more familiar than an old red barn. See the green
door and the old shingled roof—moss on it. Reminds me of
Grandmother's barn in Vermont....

When cousin Kate and I were little girls, darling, we used
to go up and spend part of our holidays with our grandmother
in Vermont.... We came from Salem, but our grandmother
lived in Vermont, and she had a great big barn just like that,
and on rainy days we used to play in the hay-loft.... Remember the time that Freddie Bruce pushed me out of the swing?...
And I fell where there wasn't any hay?... And oh, what
a bump I got!... Those were happy days.... See the clover
field! That lovely mauve—one can almost smell that warm
sweet air.... Oh! Don't you *love* it?... I hope they keep bees....
Oh! They must—they're very stupid if they don't....
Think of all the lovely honey they might have.... I imagine
the beehives are behind the barn or maybe in the apple
orchard to the left.... Wouldn't you think so, Mrs. Walker?...
Look for the hives, Mary.... Well, we can't *see* them, darling,
because they're probably behind the barn and the artist
couldn't see them either. Artists can't paint what they don't
see.... That wouldn't be honest.... But I'm sure they're
there!...

What a lovely June day!... See the clouds floating in the
blue.... hmmmh.... You can just *smell* that sweet hot air and
all the apple-blossoms.... I wonder if Freddie Bruce ever
married that fat Hickson girl?... I wonder what became of

them?... Oh, Oh, there's a cow! We had a cow named Daisy, and we used to ride on her back while she munched the grass. Why, they've tied that cow to the apple tree.... *We* never tied Daisy!... Sweet—sweet—sweet!...(*She moves on*)

Heavens! What's *that*?... *That* one—up there!... Well, it's one of those very modern things.... Sometimes if you get well away from them, something emerges (*Backs away*).... I beg your pardon! (*She speaks to another stranger*) Did I tread on your foot? I'm *so* sorry.... I hope I didn't hurt you!... (*To her companions again*) And sometimes, if you creep up on them with half-closed eyes.... I can't make head or tail of it.... D' you know what it looks like to me?... It looks to me as if the artist had accidentally sat down on his palette, and then sat down on the canvas!... Well, my dear—there's no *form* to it.... Just a whirl of colour.... Have you ever *seen* such colour?... Oh—look at that scarlet—right next to the magenta.... And then the shrimp pink.... And what do you suppose the purple spots signify?... D' you know, those colours set my teeth on edge.... Heavens! That reminds me! I have a dentist appointment on Tuesday.... I'd forgotten all about it.... Isn't it lucky I saw that picture? I go to Dr. Parker and he charges you whether you go or not!... Look it up, darling—see what it's called.... Number seven.... What's it *meant* to be, dear?... A 'Study'?... It doesn't say what of?... Well—that's an easy way out for the artist....(*She moves on*)

Oh! There's a picture of the ocean!... What a marvellous picture!... Look at the sea, darling.... That's a seascape.... A picture of the ocean.... Oh! What a rough, rough sea!... Yet it's painted so smoothly.... How *can* they do it?... Oh! Those wild, tempestuous waves!... Aren't the artists brave to go out and paint a sea as rough as that?... I don't see how he kept his canvas dry.... But that *can't* be painted from the shore, Kate.... You don't see those giant waves unless you get well out to sea.... I suppose he had tarpaulins and umbrellas to keep the spray off. (*Starts to sway*) It's a remarkable picture...almost too realistic! I can't help it, but pictures of the sea make me think of just one thing.... Oh, I'm the worst in the world. I've never found *any* remedy that helped me. (*Moves slowly on to the next picture*)

Look at that man up there!... What a *face*!... Why, I've never *seen* such an ugly man! He's not only ugly—he looks *evil*.... That's an *evil* face.... He looks to me like a criminal— almost a degenerate. Poor thing—I wonder why the artist wanted to paint anyone who looked like *that*?... He must have been a morbid man to choose such a type.... My dear— I just had the most dreadful thought!... Don't you see a slight resemblance to somebody we know?... I hate to say it —but to me it looks a little bit like our dear friend, Charlie Miller.... Don't ever tell him I said so!... Look it up, darling.... See who the poor thing is.... Three hundred and forty-four.... 'Portrait of Mr. Charles B. Miller'.... Heavens! It *is* Charlie Miller! Why—it's a libel!... It's no more like Charlie.... I never would have known it in the world!... Charlie's got such a frank, sweet face.... And he's got a heart of gold!... Oh! I think it's *dreadful* to hang such a picture—without con- sultation with the family or friends.... Poor old Charlie.... He's such a dear—I hope his mother never sees it.... It's not one bit like him!... (*Moves on*)

Oh! There's a lovely picture!... Look at the balloons, Mary—see the balloons? Aren't they adorable?... All those strange shapes.... I've always loved balloons.... See them floating in the blue!... Aren't they pretty?... What?... They're *not* balloons?... What *are* they?... 'A Bowl of Fruit'?... Oh, well.... I think I see what you mean...Maybe you're right.... How funny!... Yes—it could be...could be bananas and pears and peaches and cherries...in a large blue bowl.... I see what you mean.... But to me they still look like balloons.... Well—Mary will tell us.... Now, Mary—this is where we want the catalogue.... Tell us who is right and who is wrong. Cousin Kate says it's a bowl of fruit and Auntie says that it's balloons.... Number three twenty-four.... Three twenty- four.... 'Nymphs Bathing'?... *Well*!—did you ever?... Well,

I can't tell dear, because I've never seen any nymphs.... And if that's what they look like, I don't *want* to see them.... *Most peculiar!...* (*Moves on*)

Oh! Look at that picture of the willow-ware tea-set! Isn't that pretty?... Did you ever know my old aunt Agatha, Mrs. Walker?... She was my grandfather's sister—my great-aunt Agatha.... She lived with him in Salem, and when we were children, we used to go to tea on Sundays.... There were fourteen grandchildren.... Do you remember Aunt Agatha's cookies, Kate?... I was looking through the old family Bible last winter, and glancing through Elijah, when out fell Aunt Agatha's recipe for cookies—right out of the middle of Elijah!... My grandfather was a sea captain in the China trade, and he had brought back beautiful things from China, and he had a willow-ware tea-set with a huge platter—just like that one.... And there would be a mountain of cookies, which we demolished.... How we loved those Sunday afternoons in the old house!... (*Moves on farther*)

Oh! Here's a pretty picture of a forest!... Mary, see the forest, darling?... Well, it's just a forest.... Beautiful green trees—pine trees—birch trees—it's what they call a grove.... It must be near sunset—at dusk.... See the golden light filtering through the trees?... Oh! What a peaceful, quiet place... cool and lovely...deep—*deep* in the forest...a little secret grove.... Wouldn't it be lovely to wander down the path?... What, dear?... Something going on in the corner?... *Is* there?... (*Abruptly, taking the child's hand*) Mary—come with Auntie!...

Come here—I want you to look at this picture.... *This* one.... This is a picture they call 'Still Life'.... And it is a picture of a dead fish.... See!... Isn't that funny?... Well, there's a dead fish, and an onion...and an oyster, and a string of pearls...and a silver cup, and a bottle...and a big piece of ice.... See all those lovely cool grey and silver tones.... (*Grasps little Mary's hand more firmly, leading her on*) No, no —darling—*not* that one....

See that picture of the little tiger cubs.... Oh! Don't they look sweet, like kittens?... That must be in a zoo.... I don't suppose he could paint in the jungle.... Isn't it pretty?... And, my! What a variety of things!... There's a picture of a young girl reading a letter.... Oh! She's had bad news—poor thing!... There's his picture on the table.... I believe he's forsaken her, Mrs. Walker.... He has a very weak face, hasn't he?... She's reading a letter—see the tear? How well that tear is painted.... Isn't that a pretty way to do her hair?... You know, Kate—I think you could do something with Charlotte's hair like that...just run the ribbon through the curls and tie it around.... And see her little slipper in the fire-light.... Look it up, darling—see what it's called.... Number twenty-nine.... What's it called?... 'Forsaken'.... I was right!—it's called 'Forsaken'.... Poor child! Still—she's young—she'll get over it.... And I don't believe he was good enough for her!... I love those story-pictures.... They always appeal to me.... (*Again she moves on to the next picture*)

Oh! That must be an eruption of Vesuvius!... Let's get well away from it.... What a dramatic picture!... See that great band of red and the wild black clouds.... It must be—that must be the lava.... Well, it was a mountain, darling, and the mountain exploded, and out of the mountain poured a material called lava—which was really a sort of molten metal... and it buried a whole city.... It was a dreadful disaster!... How fierce and terrible Nature can be! I hear it's still smoking....I've always wanted to see the Bay of Naples, but I don't believe it's safe.... Look it up, dear—see if it isn't the eruption of Mount Vesuvius.... Number sixty-nine.... What is it?... 'Sunset in Vermont'!... Well!—It's not like any *I've* ever seen.... But you know, I think artists see things differ-ently—don't you, Mrs. Walker?... (*She turns to her friends*)

I think we must go now.... I have to take the four-forty trolley back to Jamaica Plain.... Well—it's an interesting exhibition...all except those nudes.... Why, I think it's dreadful to hang pictures like that in rooms with people you

know…. *Look* at poor Charlie Miller!… I think Art is wonderful—and artists are wonderful…but I think that artists,
like everybody else these days, are going *too far!*… Come,
Mary. (*Mary has apparently tried to go back to the forest
scene*)… Didn't you hear Auntie say *no?*…

(*Seizing Mary firmly by the hand she leads the party out of
the gallery*)

IN A CHURCH IN ITALY

※»⊛««※

*The church is in Florence, and the scene is a spot below one
of the altars, above which rises a painting of the Virgin—*
La Madonna della Misericordia. *The nave and aisles
around are stirring with wandering tourists and local folk,
and in the immediate foreground, as the curtain rises, there
is discovered an Englishwoman busy with her paints, one of
the legionary race of painters and water-colourists who once
thronged the scenes and pensions of Italy.*

THE ENGLISH PAINTER

*She sits before a portable easel on which her canvas rests,
making a copy of the Madonna. She wears a linen smock, a
wide-brimmed English hat, and a scarf. Another Englishwoman
sits near her, similarly occupied.*

I'm *so* discouraged—I simply cannot get it!... Oh, it's frightfully bad—it's the very worst thing I've done.... You see, the
trouble is I started all wrong, and it's so terribly difficult to
get a thing right if one starts all wrong. It's very badly drawn
and I started to paint too soon, and now it's too late!... No,
you see—it's all so *flat*.... There's no perspective at all....
Those mountains should be miles and miles away—and I've
got my mountains under my arch.... And the colour's frightful!... Let's have a look at yours.... Oh, it's *lovely*! Darling,
it's *lovely*!... I say—that's jolly good! I wish you wouldn't
touch it—it's really terribly good, and you might spoil it! Do
leave it alone!... Oh, no—your highlight is exactly right....
Your sky is perfect.... Your mountains are *miles* away. I think
it's the very best thing you've done!... Terribly clever!... Oh,
my dear—there's *no* comparison. (*She studies both pictures*)
Of course, you've got in all your yellows, and that *does* change

the values.... I want to put in Saint Barbara's skirt, but I find I've not got any chrome.... Could you lend me some? (*She takes the tube*) Oh, thank you.... I'll give you some to-morrow.... What a lovely fat tube! I never get tired of squeezing paint.... I'm going to use my favourite brush.... It always brings me luck.... I think I shall sketch it rather roughly.... That big splash of yellow may pull the whole thing together!... (*She dabs, steps back to look, her head turned sideways; then takes more paint on brush, steps forward slowly, and puts a bit of paint on the canvas*) No better! I shall give it up.... Everything I do makes it worse.... I shall begin a new one tomorrow....

(*She begins to pack up her painting gear*)

Come on—I'm going to drag you away.... I'm so afraid you'll spoil it! I wish you'd leave it alone!... It *is* lovely.... Aren't you tired?... Well, *I* am.... We've done a good three hours work.... Come on—let's hurry.... Here comes that horrible old beggar—she's always here.... Everyone gives her pennies—I'm sure she's got a fortune tucked under that shawl.... And my dear, I wish you could see what's coming up the nave.... About twenty tourists!... Let's escape before they start staring.... I can't *bear* the way they all watch you while you paint.... They really seem to prefer to look at the copies....

I've got a lovely plan for this afternoon.... Don't you think it would be fun to go to Fiesole for tea?... I thought we might ask those American girls.... They're rather nice.... And they paint jolly well.... I've seen some of their sketches.... And then I want an excuse to buy one of those lovely rich chocolate cakes in the Tornabuoni!... We'll have four of everything in our tea-basket, and we can have an enormous tea, sitting under the olive trees.... And then, we can do the valley as the sun goes down!

(*She begins to walk out of the church, carrying her equipment*)

I can't bear to leave this place.... Haven't we had a lovely

holiday?... Do you know what I long to do next?... If I can
finish this, I'm going to start on Botticelli's 'Primavera'....
Well, we've got ten days more.... I ought to be able to do it
in ten days....

(*She and her friend leave*)

AN OLD ITALIAN BEGGAR-WOMAN

*She enters, wearing an old, ragged shawl that covers her head
and shoulders and falls down over her dress. She is stooped and
obsequious, and speaks in a cracked and aged voice. Bending and
soliciting, she approaches a group of tourists who have come up
the nave.*

Buon giorno, Signora.... Signorina.... Ha visto la Madonna,
Signora?... Ecco!... *La Madonna della Misericordia* — la più
bella Madonna d'Italia.... Sì, Signora — molto conosciuta —
a tutti i forestieri piace molto questa Madonna.... Sì, Signora....
Americana lei? Inglese? Parla bene Italiano!... Signora ha
qualche cosa per la povera vecchietta, un soldino prego —
per l'amor di Dio.... Per carità, Signora.... Sono molto
povera — molto vecchia...conosco ben la miseria.... (*She
takes the coins from the ladies*) Grazie, Signora — grazie,
Signorina...quanto è buona!... Tante grazie.... Dio la benedica sempre.... Buona fortuna la segua.... Arrivederla,
Signora...grazie....

    (*She goes to another group of tourists*) Buon giorno, Signora....
Signorina.... Ha visto la Madonna, Signora?... Ecco!...
La Madonna della Misericordia — la più bella Madonna
d'Italia.... Ha visto le cartoline postale...nel mercato?...
Signora, un soldino prego — per carità.... Sono molto vecchia, molto povera.... Non ho niente da mangiare.... Ho
cinque bambini a casa.... La mamma è morta.... La mia
figlia è morta.... Ha lasciato cinque piccoli bambini che pian-
gono sempre — siamo senza pane per tre giorni.... Abbiamo
fame!... (*She takes the coin*) O, grazie, Signora...tante grazie....

Non dimenticherò mai, quanto è buona. Pregherò per l'anima dei suoi cari morti.... Dio la benedica sempre — tante grazie....

(*She moves to a third tourist*) Buon giorno, Signora.... Ha vista la Madonna — si chiama la *Madonna della Misericordia*?... La più bella Madonna d'Italia?... Prego, Signora — per carità.... Sono molto povera, molto vecchia.... Un soldino prego — per l'amor di Dio.... (*The tourist brushes her off and refuses*) Ah — che brutta gente....

(*She goes off muttering angrily*)

THE AMERICAN TOURIST

She enters with a group of fellow-tourists, ladies from America. She wears a long grey travelling coat and a plain flat hat, and carries an umbrella and a volume of Baedeker in its bright red cover.

Come on, girls—let's keep together—come on.... Oh, my feet! Whew!... Nice and cool in here.... Oh, that market! Those stones are the *hardest* stones I have ever walked on— they just seem to bore right up through the soles of my shoes!... Now, don't let's get scattered, girls.... Mrs. Bloomer—don't look yet!... I'm going to read!...

I know, dear—but *what's* the use of looking if you don't know what you're looking *at*?... Well, I've got the book all marked here.... I'll tell you in five minutes and you'll enjoy it so much more....

Don't get scattered—I can't shout.... Ethel, can you hear? Nora, can you hear?... Everybody ready? Bessie? Fanny?... Mrs. Bloomer, won't you come a little closer? Everybody ready? (*She reads*)

'This church was erected about 1436 on the site of a Romanesque church of the Ninth Century which was destroyed by fire.' Oh, isn't that a shame—the church was destroyed in the Ninth Century!...

Well, I'd rather have seen the Ninth Century church.... I

like the old things best.... (*She returns to her guidebook*) Oh! There are some remains.... That's good! Girls, there are some remains of the old church.... We can see them when we go out.... They're incorporated in the walls of the south transept—remind me, Bessie! (*She resumes reading*)

'Traces of a pagan temple were discovered in draining the crypt in 1904.' They must have had a flood—isn't that interesting!... Mrs. Newton, did you hear what I read about the temple?... I know you went to Greece and you were crazy about the temples.... Well, you needn't have gone so far.... There was one right here!... It seems they had a flood, and they were draining the crypt, and they came on the remains of an ancient pagan temple in the mud.... Well, it's very interesting, dear, because it shows the deeper you dig, the more religions you find.... You see, everything gets covered up.... And then it gets uncovered again....

(*She reads from the book, and points with her umbrella*)

'The dome'— that's the dome up there—'the dome was added in 1537 and restored in 1879 by the architect Spizzo, having been cracked by the earthquake of the preceding year.' Oh, *why* do they tell you so many things!... When was that earthquake?... Well, never mind—they had one.... And a man named Spizzo mended the crack.... You can't *see* the crack? I guess he did a good job, so probably he wanted the credit for it.... These people have a lot of hard luck, don't they?... Well, they had a fire, and then a flood and an earthquake.... And they've had a lot of wars.... But they keep right on building, and making beautiful things....

Now, 'In the pavement to the N.E.'—whatever does 'N.E.' stand for?... N.E.—it sounds familiar.... Oh, North-east— of course!... That's over there.... Now, let's get hold of Ethel.... Ethel!... She always wanders off just when you want her.... Ethel!... I can't shout.... Ethel! Bessie, poke Ethel.... Ethel, will you look around where you are standing, dear, and see if you can find a little piece of brass inlaid in the mosaic floor?... Well, it's important.... It's in the book, and we

ought to find it.... She'll find it—she finds everything....
Hot, isn't it?... *Very* warm. Do you think it's hotter today
or yesterday?... But I think you feel it more today.... Have
you got it?... She's *got* it!... Put your foot on it.... That little
slab was placed there in 1611 for the purpose of making
observations through a corresponding aperture in the dome....
Oh, my goodness—now we've got to find a hole in the dome!...
Come, everybody, and look.... *I have it—right there!*...
Follow the line of my umbrella.... See it? Isn't that wonderful?... That little hole is over three hundred years old! Now,
take your foot off, Ethel.... What do you see, dear?... Nothing?... Oh! I thought that was the whole point.... Well,
never mind!... Don't let's quarrel—we're having too good a
time!... Well, it's in Baedeker, the best book that's published.... Something important must have happened through
the hole once, or they wouldn't have written a whole para-
graph about it....

'The attic story' (*She points with the umbrella*)—that's the
attic story—'supporting the barrel vault'—that's the barrel
vault—'is pierced by fourteen windows.' Let's see if that's
right!... One, two, three, four, five, six, seven, eight, nine,
ten, eleven, twelve, thirteen. That's perfectly true—there *are*
fourteen!... 'And supported by thirty-six columns!'—don't
bother, Nora, it's too late—'on which the architrave rests.'
Well, I'm glad *some*thing's resting.... Now is your chance to
learn what an architrave is—it's that flat piece that lies under
the cornice, resting on the capitals.... Wait a minute—wait!...
I'm not through yet.... There's a whole half-page more....
Do you want me to skip? (*She turns and asks Fanny*) Do *you*
want me to skip?... Well, I'll skip, if you want.... I'd like to
read it all, but I'll skip....

We ought to go to the roof.... 'There are four hundred and
seventy-six steps to the upper gallery.... Entrance left of the
North transept door.... Fine view, worth a visit, best at sunset.' Well, that lets *us* out.... We'll come back some evening
when it's cool....

Now, let's finish the chapel.... Up there to the right, there should be a bust—have you got it?—of the learned Marco Savozza.... Never heard of him.... The book says to be¯sure to note the way the eyes appear to flash.... (*She stares sharply at the bust*) Well, you know, they *do*!... If you look at that man, he seems to be winking at you.... Why, you old rascal—don't look at me like that! Is he looking at you, Bessie?... Is he looking at you, Nora?... You see—the eyes follow you wherever you go.... I bet he was a gay old boy.... My! But these people can carve.... They take a lump of stone, and make a man look alive.... I call that art!

(*She reads again*)

'To the left is the monument of General Carlo Trembolo who fell in the battle of Scaputra in 1427.' Bessie, you're the girl for battles, do you know that one?... Never mind, I'll look it up in my battle-book.... I have one at home. 'His little dog, said to have followed him on the battlefield, lies at his feet.' Oh, what a sweet story!... I must tell Mrs. Newton.... Mrs. Newton—did you hear what I read about the little dog?... That little dog up there loved his master so much in 1427 that he followed him on to the battlefield, and the poor little fellow was killed. Isn't that sweet—they memorized the dog, poor little faithful friend!... I bet that makes you home-sick for Laddie!... Fanny, do you know Mrs. Newton's little dog Laddie?... You *don't* know Laddie Newton?... Oh, he's the *cutest* dog.... How many tricks is it you've taught him?... Seventeen! Tell them about the banana—that's the one I love.... Oh, go *on*—tell them!... Well, I'll tell you—she's so shy—it really is unique. Well, this dog of hers loves bananas, and she comes into the room holding.... (*She breaks off*) What do you say?... Oh! *All right*.... (*She resumes reading*) 'There are some fragments of frescoes on the walls, possibly an early work of'—Oh! I *can't* pronounce his name!... I never heard of the man.... They're freely restored.... And they're not sure they're his...so let's leave them alone.... (*They move along*)

Now, girls, we must do the altar-piece.... It's the most important thing here.... Well, you're sure to like it, dear, because this is by that man we all like—Giacomo Palli.... We love all his things, and this is considered his masterpiece—it says so.... (*Reads*) 'Undoubtedly the finest Giacomo Palli in the world. Considered generally to be his masterpiece, and in a state of remarkable preservation.' (*She gazes at the altar-piece, amazed. She looks at all her friends to see their reaction*) Marvellous! Takes your breath away! Mrs. Bloomer, you'd know it was a masterpiece, wouldn't you—even if you never had read one word about it?... Oh, yes you would.... Bessie?... Well, it's hard to explain, dear...if you don't *feel* it.... But there's always something about the really *great* things that just gets you.... And *that* picture has *got* it!... You see the effect it had on all of us—nobody said one word!... You don't want to speak—you just want to look, and try to re-member.... Marvellous!... Look at the colours. Fanny, just see how the colours glow!... About five hundred years.... (*She turns to the other members of the party*) Five hundred.... Five hundred.... And see the whole composition of it!... Look at that sky—did you ever *see* such a blue?... Then, way off in the distance...those mountains.... And the little flowers in the grass.... And couldn't you just *touch* that marble?... See the way it's carved? And what beautiful fabrics their garments are made of...those velvets and brocades...and the golden embroidery.... And look at the trees against the sky.... And aren't they fine-looking people! Look how they hold their heads! Portraits, I guess.... And then, your attention goes up and up, and *there* she is: the *Madonna of Mercy*. *Misericordia* means mercy—I looked it up in the dictionary.... (*She turns again to other members of the party*) Mercy!... Mercy!... *Isn't* she lovely? Look at those outstretched hands —seems like she's sorry for everybody in the world.... Oh! And look at the little angels!... Aren't they darlings!... Mrs. Bloomer, did you see the angels? Aren't they *lovely*?... They look so gay, flying around in the sky.... I bet you those angels

are good.... (*She searches hastily in the book*) They *are*!...
They're double-starred! That means they're very, *very* good....
Well, everything is starred: the church is starred—the
altar-piece is starred.... But the angels are double-starred!...
I love to guess right—it makes you feel good!...

I wish I knew more saints.... I hardly know a saint.... Oh,
there's St. Lawrence with his grill.... Well, he was broiled
as a martyr, dear, and in the pictures he always carries a
grill.... I want to get a postcard of him.... Mrs. Bloomer—
did you ever know my mother's cousin, Effie Brown, from
Omaha?... Well, her son was Larry Brown, and we called
him Saint Lawrence because he used to grill steaks for us
when we went on picnics. We'd make a little fire on the edge
of the lake out of pine cones and twigs—a nice hot bed of
ashes—and then Larry would come along with his old grill
and cook steaks! *My*! They *were* good!... So juicy and nice!...
Well, never mind.... They have art over here and that's what
we came for.

(*She reads again*) Now, 'there's a famous fresco over a
door, and some handsome bronze gates, a couple of candlesticks, and an angel on a font'... (*She claps the book shut*) But
I say, let's go!... (*Apparently there are some protests*)

I *know*, dear—but if we're going to do the Pitti this afternoon we ought to do two or three more churches before lunch....
Let's go out this way.... I want to see the Romanesque
remains that are incorporated out there.... (*She pauses at a
question from one of her companions*)

Oh, all right—I'll wait for you.... (*To the others*) She wants
to sketch an angel. She's *always* sketching angels.... By the
way, Mrs. Newton, did I hear you say you wanted a shampoo?... Well, I know a place. I met a friend of mine named
Josie Stubbs yesterday, in that shop where we were buying
chocolate, and she knows some American girls who've started
a beauty-parlour over here, and they brought everything from
America. They've got American soap, American methods....
They've got *Harper's Bazaar* and *The New Yorker*. She was

there yesterday, and she said she had the best time since she's been in Europe.... So I thought I'd go. You can get a dandy shampoo for only forty liras....

Bessie, don't let me forget to ask you where you got those little boxes.... Do you remember the address?... The second turning to the left after you cross the bridge? I want to get some, because they're just ideal for souvenirs.... Well, my dear, I've got to take *forty-three* presents home, and I must find some very *small* things.... My suitcases are full now.... I know Mrs. Bloomer's in the same fix I am about presents.

Mrs. Bloomer! Mrs. Bloomer—did you see Bessie's boxes? I said, did you see Bessie's little *boxes*?... I thought you might like some.... They're different coloured leathers, tooled in gold.... They're no bigger than a quarter, and you could just scatter them through your suitcases and never know they were there.... (*She turns to Fanny*) What?... That's just what I was telling her—that they *were* small.... Smallest boxes I ever saw.... I imagine they're the smallest boxes in the world.... No, I was thinking last night—what could you put in those boxes? Well, I thought of one thing: you know what they'd be perfect for?... A cough-drop to take to a concert!...

Come on—let's go.... Oh! *Look* at that little boy! What a beautiful child!... Have you ever *seen* such eyes?... Hello, Sonny.... Did you step right out of that picture? You look like one of those little angels.... *Isn't* he beautiful? I'm going to give him a soldi.... Oh, it doesn't hurt to give—unless they ask.... Well, he didn't ask—he's no beggar.... *Look* at that smile!... Isn't that worth a soldi? Here, little boy—this is for you.... But listen, it's not *all* for you.... (*To the ladies*) What do you suppose 'divide' is in Italian? Do you know what I think it might be? *Divido*.... I'm going to try it, anyway.... (*To the boy*) Listen: you *divido* with an *amico* and then it won't hurt you.... Nothing you divide will *ever* hurt you.... (*To the others*) He knows we're talking to him—he's just as bright as he can be.... I bet you he understands.... And he said, '*Grazie*'

—that means 'Thank you'.... Well, I've picked up quite a lot
of Italian.... Goodbye, little boy! Oh! I *love* these children!
They're so friendly and they're so beautiful—and they're so
intelligent.... Oh! They *are*, Mrs. Newton, they learn this
language when they're little bits of things....
(*She moves on with her friends as they leave the church*)

AN ITALIAN GIRL

*She runs in quietly, searching for someone. She wears a black
shawl over her shoulders, a lace scarf on her head, and carries
a red rose. After looking anxiously around the church, she
finally sees the young man and runs eagerly towards him, smiling
and panting for breath.*

Eccomi, amore mio...eccomi.... O, che corsa ho fatto.... Ho
fatto il giro della chiesa, per scappare la mamma.... No, non
t'ho visto, in nessuna parte...sono entrata da questa porta....
E poi, ho cercato, ho cercato e non t'ho visto...dove stavi?
Dietro alla colonna?... No — due minuti soli...perchè la
mamma è fuori al mercato, e devo ritornare a casa subito —
subito.... No — amore mio, per stasera non sarà possibile,
perchè la mamma non esce stasera!... Non posso mai lasciare
la casa.
Allora quando?... Domani sera?... Sì!...perchè la mamma
esce domani sera!... Ho sentito dire che va a far visita a mia
zia, in campagna.... Allora — verso le nove posso uscire!...
Dove c'incontriamo?... Dove?... No!... Non mi piace —
perchè è troppo lontano — sì — dieci minuti da casa mia...
così perdiamo tempo...aspetta!... Pensiamo un po' — aspetta.
Penso io.... No — no — ah, ci ho un'idea.... Il cortile del
palazzo — sì lo sai!... Nell'angolo del cortile, a sinistra...la
piccola porta nel muro, è sempre aperta la notte.... Sì — va
bene?... E dopo, possiamo andare sulla collina?... Nel giar-
dino della villa?... Ci sarà la luna domani sera.... La novella
luna! O che bellezza!... Come?... Non voglio dirlo; perchè

già l'ho detto; ma sì...tu lo sai bene...te l'ho detto mille, mille volte!... Non voglio dirlo più!... Ma sì — sì ti amo — ti adoro! Sempre — sempre, tutta la vita, te lo giuro...devo andarmene adesso.... Sì, due minuti sono già passati, è pericoloso di rimanere di più.... Allora addio — e fai tu una piccola preghiera alla Madonna...per domani sera.... Arrivederci!...

(She crosses herself before the altar and prays a moment. Then she crosses herself again, and with the end of the gesture raises her hand to her lips, and looking back at him, runs off silently)

A GERMAN TOURIST

She wears a green Loden cape and a pointed Bavarian felt hat as she enters, peering about the church through her glasses and then slowly approaching the altar. She carries a cane, a large purse, and a number of bundles that hang on strings from her arms. She motions to the other members of her party to gather round and look at the Madonna.

Gretel — Gretel!... Ich hab's gefunden!... Hier ist das Bild!... Dort oben! Ich bin ganz sicher... Ich hab' so oft davon Fotografien gesehen... In der ganzen Welt ist es bekannt!... Überall findet man Fotografien davon!... Wo ist denn Willy?... Willy — Willy — such' nicht weiter... Hier ist das Bild!... Jawohl...ich hab's gefunden... Kinder — kommt...ihr müßt das Bild anschauen...guckt mal dort oben, was für ein hübsches Bild... Das muß euch für das ganze Leben vorhalten... Siehst du die Jungfrau, Elsa?... Sie sieht ein bischen wie die Tante Anna aus — nicht wahr?... Und dort oben die süßen kleinen Engelchen!...

Was willst du haben?... Schokolade?... Hier, in der Kirche?... Ich werde mal suchen... Nein... Es gibt kein Stückchen mehr... Morgen bekommt ihr was!... Sch — sch — Paßt mal auf!... Hört mal!... Die Tante wird uns ein

bischen vorlesen aus dem Buch... Was sagst du, Frieda?...
Der Kaiser war hier?... Ah so!... Und Goethe auch?...
Hörst du, Willy?... Einmal war der Kaiser hier — und
Goethe auch... Denkt euch mal!... Er hat das Bild riesig
bewundert!... Ich muß mir Ansichtskarten kaufen zur Erin-
nerung!... Aber das ist wunderschön...Ganz prachtvoll...
Fabelhaft!... Wie viel Uhr ist es, Willy?... Schon viertel
vor Eins?... Ach, es ist spät!... Wir müßen uns beeilen!...
Die Anderen werden schon auf uns warten — im kleinen
Restaurant neben der Alten Brücke...weil sie gestern dort
echtes Münchener Bier gefunden haben... Und ich glaube
vielleicht könnten wir etwas Deutsches zum Essen kriegen...
Ach! Diese italienische Küche gefällt mir gar nicht!...
Schmeckt es dir, Kätchen?... Du hast das auch gern?...
Nein, mir *gar nicht*!... Immer die ewigen Macaroni!...
Spaghetti!... Jeden Tag, Macaroni! Macaroni! Macaroni!...

*(Shaking her head and beckoning to the others to follow,
she moves out of the church)*

AN ITALIAN PEASANT WOMAN

*A woman in a long black shawl enters and crosse sherself as she
passes before the altar. She pauses and then moves forward
slowly, gazing up sorrowfully. She crosses herself again and
sinks to her knees in deep and concentrated prayer, eyes closed
and hands clenched, head bowed, with an expression of deep
anguish on her face. Gradually she opens her hands in supplica-
tion, her head raised, her eyes still closed. Relieved of suffering,
a look of peace and serenity slowly comes over her face. The lights
go down and the curtain falls.*

CURTAIN

SHOWING THE GARDEN

An English lady of somewhat advanced middle age guides her visitor into her country garden, and as she talks they move down the pathway from one bed of flowers to another, pausing at each as she explains.

Come, Mrs. Guffer, do come. I am longing for you to see the garden.... Tea is not quite ready—and I'm so afraid you are going to run away the moment we've had our tea that I am determined you should have at least a *tiny* glimpse of the garden! I won't take you far.... Happily it's very near.... I always feel that I am most fortunate in having a part of my garden into which I can fairly *tumble*.... Here we are already!

Oh, do you?... How very sweet of you!

As a matter of fact, you know I am rather sorry you should see the garden now, because alas! it is not looking its best.... Oh, it doesn't *compare* to what it was last year.... We've had a very poor season, I think.... Oh, it's been very much too dry.... I think everyone has suffered....

For example, take my Pomonas—these are the *Pomona Grandigloras*.... The blossoms should be as large as a small saucer, and you see, mine are *tiny*.... And as for my poor *Glubjullas*, they never came up at all!... I can't think why, because I generally have great luck with my *Glubjullas*. I am particularly fond of them, and I have a *great* variety.... People come from far and wide, and they all agree they have *never* seen finer *Glubjullas* than mine.... I take no credit for my success, because I happen to have particularly fine *Glubjulla* soil, and I *do* think in the case of *Glubjullas* everything is in the *soil*!... I can't *think* what happened this year....

Next week my *Funnifelosis* should be in bloom.... They will completely fill that corner that is all bare now with their huge foliage and tall blue blossoms.... They will make a most lovely mass just there—where it looks rather sad just now, I'm afraid!

I'm so sorry those wretched creepers are completely hiding my *Lummylosias*. It *is* a pity—because they are all out.... If only we could see them!... See—there *is* one!... Just at the top of the wall.... I must see if I can find the gardener and ask him to cut away the creepers.... There he is! You don't mind if I call?... I have a rather piercing voice, I'm afraid.... (*She shouts*) Diggum! Diggum!... He hears me!... Diggum—will you please cut the creepers? I am very anxious for my friend to see the *Lummylosias*. It is a pity they grow so fast—they smother everything.... Cut them well away, Diggum.... I think we shall see them before you go....

(*She sees a dog*)

Oh! Where *did* that wretched dog come from? Chase him away, Diggum!... How did he get into the garden?... Oh! You nasty little dog! Go away! Go away!... (*She suddenly turns at an interruption from Mrs. Guffer*)

Oh! I *beg* your pardon.... Is he *yours*?... I *am* sorry!... Will you forgive me! I'd no idea you'd brought your dog. But why didn't you bring him to the house? I'm *very* fond of dogs.... Come here, you sweet puppy—come here, you darling!... What's his name?... Brownie? Come along, Brownie!... A *dear* little dog! (*She strokes the dog's head*) And what a friendly creature, to run to me when I spoke to him so brutally!... You *are* a darling!... No, really, Mrs. Guffer.... Please believe me.... I am really *very* fond of dogs, and am most happy to have him!... But you see, sometimes stray dogs manage to get into the garden.... And they do scratch rather.... Oh! But he couldn't hurt anything—those soft little paws.... Oh, no!... He's most welcome in my garden.... And how pretty he looks—running in and out among the flowers!

(*They move along to another bed*)

Now, Mrs. Guffer—I am longing to show you something

which I propose to do.... And I want you to persuade my husband that it's a *very happy* plan!... My husband—like so many men—is hopelessly conservative.... He never wants to change *any*thing.... Whereas *I* think that part of the fun of having a garden is to make some little change each year— some little improvement. And I am always full of ideas, which he regularly sits upon, I may say!... Now would you mind coming over here? I think we can see it from here.... No, I believe it would be better if we went over there.... Yes —now I think I can show you what I mean.... Do you see that group of cypress trees there—the dark Italian cypress?... Then, you see to the right a group of smaller, rather insignifi- cant trees?... That's it! You're looking right.... Do you know what I propose to do?... Cut them down!... Yes—take them all out!... There are five, I think.

It *does* seem rather drastic. But really, do you know—I am rather sorry that I haven't done it before.... I think it is going to be an enormous improvement.... It's going to give me a little *vista*, which will be rather exciting, I think!... I shall see more sky—which is always desirable. And on a clear day I hope I shall see the horizon—which would be *very* jolly!... Then, I shall have a sense of space—of distance.... A little glimpse into the *beyond*—as it were.... I think a vista always gives one a feeling of mystery.... And I always think it's *very* exciting.... When one opens something up, one never knows what one may find....

Then, it's going to solve another problem. When I was in Venice some fifteen years ago, I picked up the most enchant- ing little statue—a little marble boy on a pedestal.... And I have *never* been able to make up my mind where to put him.... So the poor darling has been in my garage for fifteen years, hid under a bit of tarpaulin.... And now, I know what to do!... I shall bring him out and put him in the gap, and I think he will be very *happy* there, don't you?... Standing on his pedestal.... With his little arms outstretched against the sky.... He should feel very much at home. It will seem like a little bit of Italy.... Creamy marble and a cypress tree—they suggest Sunny Italy! A very happy thought, I think—on our gloomy winter days!

Then, too, I am trying to induce my husband to let me cut down that tree, and put in a little marble pool!... I agree—it is a very nice tree, and I am very, *very* fond of trees.... But I want to break this mass of green.... And then, I think water is *so* enchanting—don't you?... The way it always reflects things.... It does—doesn't it?... And I think it would be so delicious suddenly to stumble on the crescent moon, just *there*.... Or a pink cloud drifting by.... Or a star....

Then, on *this* side—(*She swings her arm to the right, pointing*) Oh! I *beg* your pardon!... I hope I didn't hurt you!... I propose to extend my hardy border.... I feel I must have more colour, and I propose to put in a mass of perennials.... Which will give me colour all summer long!...

And on that side (*She points to the left*) I propose to continue my old brick wall, and cover it with ivy.... I think it makes a *very* happy background—don't you?...

(*They move along*)

Oh, look at my *Seccalikums* just coming up!... Diggum—have you seen the *Seccalikums?* They're all up—doing beautifully.... Oh! Don't you *know* them? They thrive in dry weather! You see.... They're pushing their way through the very dusty soil, and appear to be quite happy.... I hope they're going to be yellow.... (*She stoops over the flowers*) Are you going to be yellow, my pets?... I *mean* them to be yellow!...

But my poor *Dampfobias* are not doing well at all, alas!... They need continual rain and damp.... They never thrive unless it rains every day.... And one can hardly wish for that!

I am sorry my *Schimonas* are over.... They were particularly fine this year.... I think it was a very fine *Schimonas* year.... *Every*one was talking about their *Schimonas*.... They are great favourites of mine.... Strange to think that was a mass of pink a week ago! There is only one left.... That little brown bell.... What a pity to think we shan't see them for another year!

(*Again she moves along*)

And my *Nosellas*, too, alas, are just over.... I am *very* fond of *Nosellas*! They're perfect poppets—most accommodating little chaps—and all that they need is a little *blood*. I gave them a little this year, and they throve on it!...

Oh, I am sorry! I wanted to cut you a *Mrs. Huntley Buncum*, but I'm afraid they are all about to fall!... There were five perfect buds last night—and now, alas, they are full blown!... Oh, I *do*!... I think *Mrs. Huntley Buncum* is my very favourite rose.... But the pity of it is—she fades so soon!

Oh, do you? How very sweet of you.... That border was a dream in June, and it's going to be nice again in October.... Could you possibly come back in October?... June and October are *the* months for that border.... Just there, where it is rather bare now, I had a mass of *Marinbellas*.... One is told to plant them at least fourteen inches apart.... And do you know what I did?... I put them in very close together—and the result was a *pool* of blue!... You can't *think* how lovely it was!... And behind my *Marinbellas*, I put *Mloops*.... White *Mloops*!... Oh, no! I shouldn't put any but white, Mrs. Guffer. *Mloops* come in very peculiar colours, not always desirable.... They're rather treacherous.... One can never be sure of a *Mloop*. But with white one is always safe, I think.... Blue and white are safe in everything!

Then, I had a mass of yellow *Glypsafantums*—then, some mauve *Bosanias*. A delicious combination!... And in and out and all along the entire length of my border, I had a carpet, Mrs. Guffer—no exaggeration, a *carpet*—of those darling little pale pink *Punnyfunkums*.... You don't *know* the *Punnyfunkums*?... Oh, Mrs. Guffer!... You will never know peace until you discover the *Punnyfunkum*! It is an annual—and *such* a comfort! Anyone can have it.... Do put it down.... You have your little book?... I always carry one.... And a pencil?... (*She dictates as she watches Mrs. Guffer write*) Pale pink

Punnyfunkum, penny a packet.... Sow them freely in your border, and you can't think what a happy result you'll have!... Because, I think, we've all had the experience that in a border, something *always* disappoints one.... *Some*thing fails!... And when you have your *Punnyfunkum*, it really doesn't matter.... Nothing matters!... Because wherever there is nothing else, the *Punnyfunkum* goes! It creeps in and out and fills all gaps.... And the *great* advantage of the *Punnyfunkum* is that it does well in *any* soil, and appears to bloom at *all* seasons!... I can't think why there are none out now.... I have *never* known it to fail before!

(*They move on*)

Here is rather an interesting plant, Mrs. Guffer—something I am very proud of.... It's a great favourite of mine.... It's called *Missayearea Idowtans*.... It blooms every second year. This *was* to have been its year.... But, alas!—the wireworms have got it, and I am *afraid* there will be no flower....

I am sorry my *Millasquiffaglorians* have not done as well as usual this year.... We had a touch of frost last Thursday, so I fear they will not recover!...

Oh, here's my Arthur to take us in to tea!... Arthur— Mrs. Guffer highly approves of my plan of cutting down the trees and putting in the little pool. Now, Mrs. Guffer—you *must* tell my husband what you said to me!...

Oh! I beg your pardon!... I see a caterpillar on your hair. May I pick him off?... He's caught in a curl.... I have him!... I can't think where he came from! (*She squashes the caterpillar with her foot*) We *never* have caterpillars—do we, Arthur?...

But you *must* come again, Mrs. Guffer, and see the garden when it's really looking its best.... Because this is not our real Fairhill weather.... No—indeed!... The sun should be shining and the sky should be blue.... And if you come in October, I shall be able to show you a second blooming of my *Mloops*... and possibly pick you a *Mrs. Huntley Buncum*....

Shall we go in to tea?... I think it's ready now!

A COCKTAIL PARTY

―»» ✿ «««―

A middle-aged woman, smartly dressed and hatted, has just entered a large room where a cocktail party is going on. She looks about confusedly at the throng of guests, then suddenly greets a woman she recognizes. Throughout her talk she shifts, turns, greets now this person, now another; and there is much crowding, pushing, and shoving as her chatter proceeds. She carries a handbag which she juggles from one arm to the other as she handles her cocktail glass and the food.

Hello, Isabel! Haven't seen you for *ages*? *Where* have you been hiding yourself! Egypt?... You *have*?... How marvellous! (*She turns and speaks to a strange woman*) How do you do?...

(*To Isabel again*) Who *is* that woman? No—the one with the crazy hat.... Tell me about your trip!... (*She turns suddenly*) Why Kitty! How *are* you? *Nice* to see you! Going to be here for a while?... How's everybody in Boston? (*She turns again*) Gloria!... I was hoping I'd find you here!... My you look *well*! *Divine* dress! Smart!... (*To a servant*) No thank you, not just yet.... (*To Gloria*) By the way, what's the latest news of Penelope?... (*To the servant*) Oh, I can't resist those chicken livers—thanks—mmmmm.... (*To Gloria*) Twins!... Heavens!... How many does that make?

(*To another lady*) How do you do? Of *course* I remember you! It *is*!... *Years*! You live in California now, don't you?... Florida?... Oh, I knew it was somewhere!... You haven't changed a bit!... Oh, yes I have!... Look at my grey hair.... You haven't got *one*, that I can see!... You *do*? I never would have guessed it! You must have an awfully good man.... I remember you all so well that summer!... Will you ever forget that horrible picnic, and the storm? I don't know what I should have done without your husband on that slippery path, in the ravine! He was such an angel!... He practically carried me, I was so terrified of falling!... How is he?... Oh, I'm *sorry*!... I hadn't heard.... Whom did he marry?... Really?... I went to school with her.... One of the most *un*attractive girls I ever saw!... Please forgive me!... I must have been away and no one told me about it.

Hello Jean!... My dear you've lost *pounds*!... Call me up!... I suppose that adorable boy of yours is at Harvard by now?... Yale?... Oh, I know it is—a wonderful college!... I'm just prejudiced, I suppose.... My husband was captain of the football team when he was at Harvard.... They won that year!... And that sweet little girl who seemed to live in a dream world?... I remember she told me she was going to marry a fairy prince!... A missionary in Africa? How wonderful!...

(*To a servant*) Is this a martini?... Thanks.... (*To Jean*) Goodbye! Nice to have met you again!... (*Sips*)

Hello, Maud!... My dear, I've just made the most *awful* break!... (*Sips, then bumps someone at her right*) Clarence!— if this isn't the *luckiest* thing!... I've been *dying* to see you!... Do you know Miss Doolittle?... Of course, how *stupid* of me!... I forgot you were cousins.... How's Genevieve? (*To the servant*) May I have one of those? (*She shifts her glass*) They're the *best* things!... I know.... But if you can get Parmesan cheese they're even better.... I have the recipe.... Clarence, I must know if it's true about Jim and Caroline?... (*She bumps someone at her left*) I *beg* your pardon.... Grab an olive for me, will you?... But don't you think he still cares for Pam? (*Eats the olive*) I'm terribly worried about it—I really am—absolutely *sunk*! And yet.... One never knows....

Maud, be an angel and stay where you are so that I can face this way!... Stand still!... I see someone I want to avoid.... That Ruggles woman.... I'm so afraid she'll see me.... If she speaks to me, I shall probably scream!... Oh, haven't you heard what she did?... Well, my dear—I can't tell you now, but I've never in all my life been so tempted to *murder* anybody!... She's coming this way.... Watch me cut her!... (*She does so, then turns with a smile to a man who addresses her*)

Yes, I am.... You mean Bunny Bloomer—I always call him Bunny.... He is indeed—one of my oldest.... Really?... Well, he's talked to me a lot about *you*!... I saw him last week, fatter than ever!... I *adore* him!... What *can* I do with this olive pit?... How about the azalea? (*She hands the pit*)... Thanks....

(*Turns left*) Darling—hello! You *cute* thing!... How's the baby? Oh, I beg your pardon.... I didn't realize you were talking.... (*She bows to the stranger*) How do you do!... Oh, don't let me interrupt!... About Russia?... Oh, do let me hear what you were saying!... How *interesting*!... *Really*?... But what *is* going to happen now?... Oh, I must have one of those little sausages! Could you put this down for me? (*She hands her glass to the servant, then eats*) Thanks.... Go on.... Yes.... I see perfectly!... (*She bumps someone*) Excuse me.... Exactly! But doesn't that put us in an impossible position?... (*She cries*) Oh, all over my glove!...

Oh, there's Jumbo! Jumbo!... Jumbo!... Hello!... When did you get back?... Have fun?... How's everything?... Do let's sit down—I want to hear *all* about your trip!... Now, tell me everything!... (*She lights a cigarette*) Thanks.... Oh, such a day as I've had!... I went to the dentist, and then I had a permanent, and after a very *boring* luncheon, I went to a *ghastly* meeting!... Then I talked to Bill in Paris.... He called from the Airport.... Just off to Baghdad!... (*To a servant*) Martini, please. (*She shifts her cigarette*) Didn't you *know*?... Oh, he'll be back in two weeks.... Oil.... And then I came on here, and now I must go home and dress, and go to the Opera!... My, it's nice to see you!... (*She puts out her cigarette*) Tell me all about yourself!... (*To the servant*) Is that egg?... (*She shifts her glass*) No, but I *adore* those little

fish balls!... (*Eats*) Wish I had a napkin!... Got a hanky?...
Thanks.... Jumbo—I suppose you've heard about Pauline!...
Quite a situation!... What?—But it's all her own fault.... I
know, but do you suppose he's *really* a Communist?... (*She
breaks off*) Glory—is that the right time? I *must* be going....
No honestly I *must*! Let me go—no really—I *must*—if I can
get through this crowd!...

(*To a stranger*) How do you do?... Of course!... Yes, I've
often heard Bill speak of you. In college together, weren't
you? Goodbye, Jumbo!... *Wonderful* to see you.... I want to
hear more!... So do call me up!... Yes, he's just come back
from Europe.... He says the situation is really *very* serious—
he says the trouble *is*.... (*She turns to another guest*)

Hello!... Excuse me.... Listen, Charlie.... Will you and
Peter come to dinner on Thursday?... Canasta?... I'll try
and get Flora.... No, Bill's in Baghdad.... I beg your pardon?...
Well, call me up!... He says the *real* trouble is.... What?...
Yes, do!... No, don't dress.... The real trouble is there
just isn't anybody who knows....

Hello, Sally.... Heard you had the mumps!... Good!...
Anybody who knows...excuse me...who knows *what to do*!...
So he feels rather hopeless.... Oh, *terribly* interesting...
and, of course, Jumbo is a man who's *had* a lot of experience,
and knows what he's talking about.... They say he really
ought to be Secretary of State.... (*She sees an old friend*)

Admiral!... How lovely to see you again!... Wonderful!...
Alas, I'm just going.... You look *blooming*!... Oh, thanks—I
am.... Better for seeing you! I wish I could, but I'm just off!...
Do!... Anytime. I'd *adore* it.... Where's Dolly?... I
haven't laid eyes on my hostess!... Oh, *there* you are!... My
dear—*what* a lovely party!... I never saw so many nice people...
and such *interesting* people.... How *do* you find so many
men?... And such *food*!... Those are the best little cheese
things!... Wish I knew how to make them!... I must run now,
alas.... Going to the Opera!... Goodbye.... Thanks!...

Hello, Bertie!... You off, too? Got your car?... Divine!...

Will you really?... Angel!... Hello, Mabel!... No, can't!...
Just going!... (*Louder*) What?... Can't hear!... *Dead*?...
Who?... *Really*?... Never knew him!... Too bad!... Oh, I
must have one more of those chicken livers.... Coming,
Bertie!...

(*She elbows her way through the crowd*) May I get through,
please?... Gladys!... Oh, dear!... You're just the person I
wanted to see!... No, just going! I hear you know all about—...
(*She bumps into someone*) Excuse me.... Well, call me in
the morning! If not, I'll see you at Milly's cocktail party—
and we'll have a good talk!... Coming!... Bye!... Going
where?... No—wasn't asked!... So long!... Opera.... What?...
Tristan! (*Walking off*) Or maybe it's *Carmen*—I forget—
I don't really mind. They're both good.... Bye!... Hello!...

GLASSES

—»» ✤ ««—

*An elderly lady enters. Her glasses are pushed up above her
forehead, on her hair. She sits down in an armchair near a
table. She takes a spectacle-case up from the table and finds
it empty. She looks up perplexedly, then rises, crosses to the
door, and calls upstairs to the right.*

Has anyone seen my glasses?... Mildred!... Mildred!... Did
I leave my glasses in your room?... Just look on the bureau,
dear, or on the desk—or perhaps on the mantelpiece.... I
think I may have left them there when I stopped and spoke
to you.... (*She crosses to the left and calls down*) Annie!... Will
you see if I left my glasses downstairs—look by the telephone
in the library, or in the little red chair by the fire, where I
was reading the newspaper.... Or possibly I left them in the
kitchen!... (*To Mildred again*) Find them, Mildred?... Now,
where could I have left them?... I read the paper, then I went
to the kitchen, and I stopped to telephone in the library—
oh, dear! (*She stoops over a chair and turns the cushions. The
glasses fall off her head into the chair*) Here they are!
   I've found them, Mildred.... All right, Annie.... I have
them—they were here, just in the chair!... (*She settles down
to read, polishing the glasses on her skirt*)
   Annie, just close the door, will you? I feel a draught....
(*Someone knocks*) Come in!... Who?... Oh! Of course—come
in, dear Mrs. Moon. What a pleasant surprise!... Not at all....
I'm delighted.... I was just sitting here reading.... Do sit
down.... I'm particularly glad to see you, because I want to
talk about Henrietta, whom I know you've just seen.... Will
you smoke?... Oh, you're knitting.... So am I! Now isn't this
cosy?... I *had* my glasses.... Don't bother!... I'll find them....

I think I dropped them when I got up to...(*She looks all over the floor and under the chair*) greet you. (*She finds them in the chair*) Here they are.... Now, are you comfortable? Enough light?... That fire might be a little brighter. (*She gets up to poke the fire*)... There! (*She settles down again in the chair to knit*)

Now—tell me.... When you saw Henrietta, how did she seem to you?... (*She takes the glasses off*) She *did*?... Well, that surprises me! (*She puts them on again*) I mean, that you didn't notice the change in her?... Why yes—I *did*.... A great change.... Well, it's hard to explain—if you don't sense it.... And of course it all depends on whether you think she did or she didn't.... Oh, bother! I've dropped a stitch!... Exactly—that's what I mean.... No, not with Albert.... Poor old Albert—oh, no!... Why, with that Mexican singer!... Well, many people *think* so.... Yes, I suppose one should.... But haven't you always thought Henrietta was rather— (*Mildred interrupts*) Yes, dear?... Excuse me.... Yes, Mildred?... Too long?... Well, come here and show it to me.... You don't mind if my little granddaughter interrupts us for a moment?... Yes, the children are staying with me—the two youngest. Their mother has gone to Texas to see my son.... Yes, Donald's in the Air Force—a Colonel.... I had a wonderful letter from him which I took to read to some friends at a bridge party I went to yesterday.... It's a great joy to have the children—but it's rather strenuous at times.... Somewhat changes the pattern of one's life....

Mildred—this is Mrs. Moon.... Mildred's going to a little party this evening, and she's having trouble with her slip.... Now, what's wrong?... Well, dear, if we take a tuck just above the knees we won't have to change the shoulder-straps.... Come here and I'll show you!... (*She gets down on her knees*) Excuse us, Mrs. Moon, if we do a little dress-making?... Did you bring some pins? Now stand straight!... Give me a pin.... Don't look down—turn around.... Not too fast.... Stand up.... And turn.... There! That will be right.... Now,

pull me up.... Look out! My glasses!... Now take if off carefully, dear, so the pins won't fall out.... Yes, I'll do it.... Oh,
it won't take long—I promise to have it ready.... She's *so*
excited about the party.... (*To Mildred, who goes out*) Shut
the door!...

(*To Mrs. Moon*) Well, to go back to Henrietta.... Yes, but
don't you think she's quite capable of losing her head?... And
given the circumstances, I always say—*given* the circumstances.... Yes, of course, that's true—dear me, how true!...
Alas—too true!... Oh! the telephone.... (*Into the telephone*)
Hello? Yes, Mrs. Crumpet?... Did I lose a pair of glasses?...
No.... You found a pair on the table after bridge yesterday?...
Have you tried Estelle? She's always losing hers.... You'll
probably find they are hers.... Not at all.... I would have
been so grateful if they had been mine, but I know I brought
my bridge glasses home! Nice of you to call.... (*She hangs up
and turns to Mrs. Moon*)

Poor Mrs. Crumpet—some careless person left their
glasses, and she's already called five people, but no one
claims them.... People are *so* absent-minded.... I'm sure it's
Estelle.... Do you have trouble? I used to, but I have a
system now. I keep them *all* in special places.... I have these
—my near glasses—with me always!... I'm blind as a bat—
I'm lost without them for reading.... Then I keep my far
glasses and my street-walking glasses with my gloves, so I
won't forget them when I go out.... Then I keep my theatre
glasses with my opera glasses—an old pair that came from
Paris in Eighteen-seventy and that belonged to my grandmother.... And I keep my bifocals there too, because I only
use those on trains—so I can read and look out of the window
at the same time.... You can't use yours at all?... Well, they
are dangerous.... The first time I used them I thought I was
about to have a stroke—the ground seemed to swim right up
and hit me.... They made Sally Slawson sick, she said.... But
one can *learn* to use them.... It's better never to walk with
them on, particularly on stairs—they're really dangerous....

Then I keep my bridge glasses in a little blue dish on my desk, next to my engagement book.... And my piano glasses on the piano.... So I don't think I have as much trouble as most people!... Well, to go back to Henrietta.... I was about to say that when you think of her background, it's not surprising if.... She certainly *has*, my dear—a very definite inheritance.... Do you mean to tell me you never heard the story of her old grandfather, General Trufitt, and the Russian masseuse?...

Excuse me, the telephone!... (*As she gets up, she sticks the glasses in her belt*)... That seems incredible!... (*Into the telephone*) Hello!... Yes, dear.... No, I don't know it, but I can look it up.... No trouble—it's right here in my little book.... You'll have to be a little patient as I haven't got my glasses.... Don't bother, Mrs. Moon, I left them somewhere in the chair, but I can manage.... I am rather proud—sometimes I can see without my glasses.... (*She consults the little book*) Let's see—here it is, if I can make my arm long enough.... It's Regent 5–3958.... No, it's 3–3953.... How's Pauline? That's good. Did she have her permanent?... Broke a tooth? Oh, poor thing!... Same old tooth?... Oh, well, give her my love and tell her not to bother with her hair, but to get a permanent *tooth*! Goodbye.... 3953, I said. (*She rings off*)

Now, *where* did I put my glasses? (*She finds them in her belt*) Here they are! Had them all the time! What a fool I am!... (*To Mrs. Moon again*) Now, what were we talking about?... Oh, yes.... Well!... Years ago—it must have been when I was about nine—no, before that. I couldn't have been more than seven.... I remember we spent the summer in the Blue Ridge Mountains and old General Trufitt was there— charming old man, a friend of my mother's—and one day he fell down on a mountain path and wrenched his knee quite badly....

(*Four boys suddenly come in*)

Hello, boys!... Mrs. Moon, this is my grandson, Donald.... Say 'How do you do' to Mrs. Moon, dear.... These are his

friends, Jerry, Peter, and Toughey.... Well, boys, what are
you up to?... Playing commandos?... Oh, well.... Don't get
too riotous and wreck all the furniture.... And keep out of
my bedroom, please, and my bathroom, and go quietly.... Remember commandos go very quietly, sometimes!... Donald
—remember you have your homework!... No, dear—the
boys *can't* stay to supper.... And the doctor ordered the
General to bed and recommended massage.... (*To Mrs.
Moon*) Having difficulty?... Just turning your heel?... So
am I.... Want some help?... (*She starts to get up*) I'd be delighted to show you.... I *love* turning heels.... Well, you come
over here, then. Sit on the arm of my chair and you can watch
me. It's really awfully easy!... Now—you start on your purl
side, and you purl two beyond the middle, then you take two
together and one more, and turn, then slip that first one—
the one you just took—and knit plain for four, then slip one,
knit one, and slip the slipped one over the knit one, and take
one more, turn and repeat. It's perfectly simple.... See?...

Well, where was I?... Oh, well, there was a very pretty
little Russian waitress at the hotel—I can see her now.... She
was blonde, with a lovely voice, and she came and told the
manager that she'd been a masseuse in St. Petersburg.... I
believe she went so far as to say she'd massaged the Czar!
And she told the manager that if it would help, she'd love to
rub the General's knee.... (*Someone knocks*) Come in!...
(*Mildred comes in*) What's the matter now?... Grandpa's lost
his glasses?... Where did he lose them? I've not seen them.
(*Calling*) I've not seen them, dear.... Did you take them to
the office?... Look on the hall-table.... Mildred—run up to
your grandfather's room and look on the table next to his bed,
and on the bureau in the bathroom where he keeps his
shaving things.... (*Calling*) Did you look on the shelf in the
coat closet, Charles?... Well, you sometimes leave them
there when you go to get your hat.... Annie—will you help
Mr. Cary find his glasses?... Where did you last have them?...
Well, try and think.... Look by the telephone, and in the

little red chair by the fire where you read the paper.... Donald —stop playing, dear.... You and the boys go and look for grandpa's glasses.... Where? *Everywhere!*... Well, you can go on being commandos.... Just pretend you're on a dangerous mission....

(*Mrs. Moon rises*) Oh, Mrs. Moon—must you go?... I'm so sorry!... It's been lovely to see you and have a cozy chat.... I'm sorry for the interruptions, but I'll finish the story another time.... It's a long story.... And I always thought the old General's—shall we say, temperament?—accounted for a great deal in Henrietta!... Goodbye!... (*To the boys*) What? Soldiers marching by?... Where?... Oh, come quickly—let's look (*Rushing to the window*) I hear them, but I can't see a thing! (*Squinting*) Well, I haven't got my glasses.... Oh, these aren't the right ones, dear—these are my reading glasses.... I need my far glasses.... Never mind—it's too late now.... They'll be gone by the time you find them!... (*She sees her husband enter*)

Well, dear, haven't you found your glasses yet?... Well, I'll come and have a search!... Why do you *always* lose your glasses?... These? No, they're mine, of course!... What makes you think so?... But I see perfectly with them. I've been using them all morning.... I think I know my *own* glasses.... Are you sure?... How do you know?... A crack in the rim? (*Examining the glasses*) So there is!... All right—I suppose they *must* be yours.... There they are! (*She throws them into the chair*) But I wonder where *mine* are?... (*She sees Mildred enter*) Yes, he's found his, but I've lost *mine*.... So I can't fix your slip till I find them.... (*The telephone rings*) Answer the telephone, dear.... Annie, will you see if you can find my glasses? Who is it?... Cousin Estelle?... (*She takes the telephone*)

Oh, hello, Estelle! Did Aggie Crumpet call you about your glasses?... They were yours?... Oh, good—I told her I thought they were—that you had a way of losing your glasses.... What?... You've got *mine*? What do you mean?... You picked them up from the bridge table thinking they were yours?... But I know I brought my bridge glasses home, dear—I always keep them on my desk, and they're there now.... What?... I used my *reading* glasses?... When?... Oh, when I took Donald's letter from Texas out of my little bag to read it to you all? Oh, I guess I did!... Yes—those must have been my reading glasses.... You're quite right—I remember now. I put back the letter and forgot the glasses, and you picked them up thinking they were yours.... I see. Well, I hadn't missed them until this moment.... I'm *so* grateful to you!... No—don't bother, I'll send little Donald for them. Thanks again.... I'm glad you have yours....

Donald, Donald—listen, boys—listen, commandos—see who can go fastest to Mrs. Savage's house and bring back my glasses.... Yes, she has them.... I'll give a prize to the one who gets there first! And Donald—why don't you ask the boys to stay for supper as soon as they get back? I'd love to have them.... Now, Mildred—I'll fix that slip.

Annie!... I've found my glasses! Miss Estelle took them by mistake.

(*She goes off with Mildred, very pleased with herself*)

THE ITALIAN LESSON

⇢⧫⇠

A New York lady is seated on a chaise-longue in her boudoir. She is a 'society lady', of Fifth Avenue, Park Avenue, or another street of the upper East Side. She wears a silk peignoir, trimmed with feathers at the neck. She has a book in her hand which she has been casually scanning. There is a small table at her side, with a telephone. The door of the boudoir opens and she looks up brightly, speaking in a high-keyed, somewhat strident, emphatic New York voice to the person entering—a lady teacher of Italian.

Come in!... Oh! Good morning, Signorina, good morning! I'm *so* glad you've come!... Oh, Signorina, I can't tell you how excited I am—to think we have arrived at Dante at last!... It's almost too good to be true!... I am really *very* proud... Yes, I have the book here, and I must confess that I read a little last night, just before I went to bed.... And I find I understand *quite* easily.... So I think we are going to *skim* right through it!... You have the book?... Shall I start and just read a few lines at a time, the way we always do?... This *is* a great moment—Dante at last! (*She reads from her book, in Italian*)

> *Nel mezzo — del cammin — di — nostra — vita*
> *mi ritrovai — per una — selva — oscura*
> *che la — diritta — via — era smarrita!*

Wonderful!... Now, let's see.... *Nel mezzo*—just means 'in the middle', doesn't it?... *del cammin*—'of the road'—'in the middle of the road'. That's not very poetical. In English I don't think one *could* begin a poem with 'in the middle of the road'. We needn't be absolutely literal—don't translators always take certain liberties?... One could say, for instance, 'midway along the pathway'—or 'midway along the roadway of our life'. That sounds better, I think...*mi ritrovai*—'myself I found'. Of course we say, 'I found myself'.... *per una selva oscura*—'in a forest dark'. We say 'a dark forest'.... *che*—what's *che* doing there?... Oh! I see—short for *perchè*.... 'found myself in a dark forest' because the *diritta via*—'direct way'—*era*—'was'...*smarrita*...wait a minute—don't tell me!... Such a funny word.... *smarrita*...(*Searches for meaning*) I know.... It means 'lost'—doesn't it?... Rubbed out—obscure.... I imagine the path was overgrown, and they probably couldn't see their way!... Such a picture—those two men—Dante was with Virgil, wasn't he?... And I suppose they were just stumbling along together.... Marvellous lines! They're so wonderful, Signorina, because they're so *true*! That's what's so extraordinary—to think that those lines were written literally hundreds and hundreds of years ago—and yet they are so applicable to life today!... Don't you think that's what happens to people in the middle of life? So often one becomes confused, and can't see where one is going.... Of course he was a genius, wasn't he—like Shakespeare?... He and Dante seem to have known *every-thing*...known what would always be true.... I imagine we're going to find this *full* of quotations!... (*Starts to resume reading, then abruptly breaks off*)

Oh! Goodness—is that half-past nine?... Will you excuse me one minute, Signorina, while I call up a friend? I have to catch her before she goes out.

(*Into telephone*) Hello! Plaza 3-7674.

It's something rather important.... (*Speaks to a little girl whom she sees entering*) Hello, my sweet!... Gently, darling—don't pull me over.... Say good morning to Signorina, Nancy, and then run along, because Mother is having her Italian lesson....

(*Into telephone*) Hello! Is Mrs. Norton there?... May I speak to her, please?... (*Cupping the mouthpiece with her hand, she speaks to her little daughter*)

What, sweetheart?... Can you? You mean, 'may' you go to the movies this afternoon?... No, darling—certainly *not*— you never go to the movies in the middle of the week, and you have your dancing-class today, anyway....

(*Into telephone*) Hello, Mabel—How *are* you?... Mabel, my dear, I had to call you up to know what happened yesterday afternoon after I left.... Well, I saw there was going to be a row, and I was dying to stay, but I had my Bible class and had to fly.... Well, what happened?... (*Turns impatiently to the child*)

Darling, please don't interrupt—Mother can't discuss it now. I said: no!... That's enough. Run along and close the door. Goodbye.

(*Into telephone*) No, I wasn't saying goodbye to you.... I was getting rid of a troublesome child.... Yes, I saw that.... Yes. And then what happened?... What?... She *didn't*?... *Real* hysterics?... What did you do?... You *didn't*!... A whole glass of water?... What nerve!... Well, I've always *heard* that's the thing to do for hysterics, but never heard of anybody *doing* it.... Didn't it ruin her hat?... My dear, how *awful*! What a situation!... My dear, it wasn't your fault. I thought you were most tactful—after all, one *must* discuss things. One must co-operate on any committee—and compromise.... One doesn't behave like that.... Of course, I've always thought her the most im*poss*ible person.... Abso*lu*tely!... and I've always been slightly suspicious that.... What?... You *have*?... No, I've never *heard* it, but I've always *thought* it.... But if that's the case, I think we must just quietly get rid of her.... Exactly—that's what I mean.... Yes, I agree with you.... Mmmm—yes.... I do indeed....

(*Speaks to the baby whom she sees entering*) Baby—put that bottle down! Naughty! Don't touch!... Signorina—would you keep an eye on the baby?...

(*Into telephone*) I'm sorry, dear—the baby was sucking the top of my perfume bottle.... I thought it would poison her....

(*Speaks quietly to the cook whom she sees entering*) Good morning, Jane.

(*Into telephone*) No, the cook just came in.... Well, I can't discuss it now, I'm in the middle of an Italian lesson and can't take the time.... But I'll see you tomorrow at luncheon at Gertrude's.... Aren't you going?... Good—then let's sit together and we can thrash it out.... Meantime keep it under your hat.... It's not going to be easy or pleasant, but we must devise a plan.... I feel strongly that.... Exactly!... Absolutely! I agree with you.... Yes.... All right.... Well, then, goodbye, dear—I'm sure you handled it beautifully.... And I wish I'd been there—I mean, to help you out!... Goodbye! (*Hangs up receiver*)

(*To the children*) Children, if you are going to play in here, you *must* be quiet.... Barbara, don't tease. You know he doesn't like it.

Excuse me a minute, Signorina—I want to order dinner.... I won't be a minute.... (*Turns to the cook*)

Now, Jane. We are going to be eight for dinner, tonight— and I want a very simple dinner.... Have you some clear soup?... Then let's have clear soup—put something *amusing* in it.... I don't really mind what. And then we might have that fish soufflé that I like.... You know—it's white and fluffy and easy to eat.... In that low silver dish—with cheese on top, and brown.... It isn't fish? I always thought it was fish— it tastes like fish, it looks like fish....

(*Hears telephone and picks it up*) Hello? Oh! Hello, dear.... (*She speaks in a bored and listless voice to her husband*) What do you want?... Your bag packed with your golf clothes, and your clubs?... Sent to meet you at the 12.10 train?... All right.... No, it's no trouble—Morris will take them.... I have the other car.... What?... You want your brown tweeds?... All right.... No, it's no trouble—I'll tell James.... Morris will be at the gate of the train at five minutes past twelve.... (*Turns violently and cries*)

Look out! Billy—get off that chair *at once—get down*! Look out—you'll fall.... Be careful! Stay where you are—let Barbara lift you down....

(*Into telephone*) No, he didn't fall—he *never* does.... But he must *not* climb all over my furniture.... Oh, he was climbing on top of the bookcase by way of the high-backed chair.... What did you say?... A new driver?... I don't know anything about it.... I'll ask him....

(*To the child*) Billy, do you know anything about a new driver of Daddy's that came from Spaulding's?... You do?... Well, go and get it and put it in his golf-bag right away.... Don't do anything else on the way—just keep your mind on that one thing till you get it done....

(*Into telephone*) Yes, he knows...it's probably broken by now.... (*Turns to greet the governess who enters*)

Good morning, Mademoiselle....

(*Into telephone*) Yes, I will. Don't miss the train.... Goodbye—have a good game.... I said, have—a—good—game.... Goodbye!...

(*To the cook*)

Then, Jane—we might have a little leg of lamb.... I'm rather tired of lamb.... Oh! I know what I'd like: why don't we have those pigeons, Jane?... You remember that nice recipe I had?... That I got in France?... For *pigeons en casserole*?... You've *lost* it? *Oh, Jane!*... Well, I remember it, I think.... You put in eight little pigeons.... And you put almost everything in with them.... There were little browned onions, and bits of apple—and tiny potatoes, browned.... And peas, and carrots, and mushrooms.... All swimming about in a divine sauce.... I don't know how you make the sauce.... I think there was red wine in it.... You cook it slowly with the cover on, the old woman told me.... (*The telephone rings*)

(*Answers telephone*) Hello?... Oh! Good morning, Gladys—good morning, dear.... How nice of you to call! I was about to call you, anyway, to ask whether the children's dancing-class was meeting at your house this afternoon.... Oh! Then Mary has not got chicken-pox?... That's good news! They said she had chicken-pox and I was going to offer this house for the class.... I'm *glad*!... Then the children will be there as usual at three.... Thank you for calling up.... Goodbye!... (*Turns to the little girl*)

Nancy! *Nancy! What* did you say then?... Tell Mother *exactly* what you said.... Nancy—my dear child! You should be *very glad* she hasn't got chicken-pox—you'd probably get it yourself if she had it, and you deserve to get it for having such unkind thoughts.... Anyway, darling, we don't say such things—even when we think them, we don't say them.... (*Resumes talking to the cook*)

Then, Jane—we might have tomato salad.... One of those rings of tomato jelly with things in the middle.... And I rather feel like a Camembert cheese.... Why not?... Dessert? Oh! Surprise me, Jane—I like to be surprised.... How about fruit? Just fruit and coffee—that should be enough for anybody.... About eight-thirty—you know how late they always are.... (*The cook leaves*)

(*Speaks to Miss Nealy, the seamstress, who now enters*)

Oh, good morning, Miss Nealy—I'm so glad to see you.... Did you get my telegram?... Can you give me three days?... What luck!... (*To the Signorina*)

Will you excuse me a moment?...

Now, Miss Nealy—it's about this fancy dress ball. They have suddenly decided that I have to be in some tableau. I have to represent the figure of Hope, and it shouldn't be difficult.... It's a very famous picture, and fortunately I have a copy.... You'll find ten yards of blue chiffon up in the sewing-room.... Barbara—will you do something for Mother, please?... Put that down! You can't do two things at once, dear.... On the edge of the mantelpiece, just back of that vase.... Look *out*, darling—don't knock it over—no, that's an engraving.... The *blue* picture—that lady, dear, blindfolded, listening to something, sitting on a ball.... Let Miss Nealy see it, dear—you've seen it fifty times yourself.... It's a famous picture by an English artist, Miss Nealy.... Do you think you can copy it?... We will have to invent some way of making the chiffon cling around the legs.... Do you think if you spray me with glycerine in a perfume-atomizer it would help?... We shall have to do that after I get on the ball.... You see, it should *cling*, and not look like a dressing-gown.... Well, all right. If you'll cut it out, I'll try it on before I go out—in about half an hour....

(*Miss Nealy leaves. Resumes speaking to the governess*)

Now, Mademoiselle—it's rather complicated about this morning. I'm taking Nancy to the dentist, so leave her home. Then Billy has his riding-lesson and Barbara her gymnasium.... Then will you take the baby for a turn in the park, because I told Nurse she could go to Hoboken to see her aunt—who has something in the hospital there?... Then stop at Sherry's and get some *marrons glacés*, and chocolates, and mints, and bring them all back for luncheon—I mean the children—and the candy for dinner.... Then, this afternoon the little girls' dancing-class will meet as usual at three.... And Billy has his carpentry-lesson—hasn't he?... And while you're waiting to pick up the children, I'm going to ask you to do a few things for me.... I will explain at luncheon. Thank you, Mademoiselle.... (*The governess leaves*)

(*Calls to her daughter distractedly*)

Barbara, get the baby, please—she's in the scrap-basket!... Well, pull her out. Come, children!—hurry along!... Billy—did you get Daddy's driver?... Good boy!... Come, Nancy—I've told you twenty times not to touch the things on that table.... Well, just make up your mind that you're not going to do it, and then you won't—because that's what minds are *for*....

Run along, children—get out as quickly as possible.... Do what Mademoiselle tells you, and don't come back! Good-bye! Be good! See you at luncheon. Shut the door!... (*The children leave. She turns back to the Signorina*)

Now, Signorina—I think we'll run through those lines again—just to get into the spirit of it.... *Nel mezzo del cammin*.... (*Telephone rings*) Oh, this telephone! I'm afraid it's important, or they wouldn't call me....

PLATE XXVIII

Mrs. Mallory in *Three Women and Mr. Clifford*
Photograph by Angus McBean, London

PLATE XXIX

Vive la France: 1940
Photograph by Angus McBean, London

(*Into telephone*) Hello!... Who?... Miss Pounder?... Oh! Good morning, Miss Pounder. Miss Pounder, I was going to ask you to come and see me, but I think I can explain on the telephone. It's about my little Billy.... I'm sorry to hear that Billy is doing badly in his Mathematics.... Well, I'm dreadfully sorry, Miss Pounder, but I've been thinking it over, and I've decided we will just have to give up Mathematics.... You know, Billy is a very sensitive child.... He's a *peculiarly* sensitive child—I'm afraid he is not quite like other children, and he simply *hates* Mathematics.... Well, he doesn't seem to know *what* he's doing. I find him sitting, chewing a pencil, and he doesn't get anywhere.... And *what is the use* of going on with a thing when one doesn't get anywhere?... And I find it's affecting his health.... He's not sleeping well. He has a strange dream—a sort of nightmare, really—every night. He dreams of falling into a pond, and the pond is full of fish, and the fish are all numbered.... They chase him, and bite him, and he wakes up screaming.... The psychoanalyst tells me that that is a very dangerous symptom and I must try to remove the cause, which is *undoubtedly* Arithmetic.... Well, I really can't discuss it with you, Miss Pounder.... I know you've had more experience than I—but after all, I *am* his mother.... I think I know what's best for my boy.... Yes, we will give up Arithmetic entirely, until I think he is strong enough to go on.... Goodbye, Miss Pounder—I'll let you know.... (*Hangs up. A maid knocks at the door*)

Come in.... Who?... The—Oh! I forgot her! Signorina, my little manicurist has arrived—I meant to put her off and forgot.... You don't mind if I have my nails done? She's very quiet about it.... Yes, Nelly—ask Miss Mary to come up. (*Resumes reading*) *Nel mezzo del cammin di nostra vita....*

(*Sees children at door*) *Children!*—I told you not to come back! Now, darlings—run away—please don't bother me again.... What?... The new puppy?... Oh! How *exciting*! I'm sorry, Signorina, but the children have a new dog—and we've been waiting for days for him to arrive from the country, and they want me to see him.... He's only a puppy—he won't be long.... Come on—bring him in quickly.... Oh! The *darling*! I never saw anything so sweet! Billy—don't hold him so tight, dear—you'll choke him!... Put him on the floor and hold him, and let the baby pat him.... Pat him on his *head*, sweetheart—that's his *tail*.... He won't bite you.... Gently!... Now let him go.... Look out! Better not let him get under the bed—keep him out in the open.... (*The manicurist enters*)

Good morning, Miss Mary.... Look at our new puppy—have you ever seen anything so *sweet*?... Isn't he a *darling*!... Quick, Billy!—don't let him get my slippers!... Come here, puppy—come here, you sweet puppy!... What shall we call him, children?... We must find a name.... Do you know what I think?... I think it would be *lovely* if we called him *Dante*, because he came in the middle of my Dante lesson.... Oh! Dante was a famous man.... We can call him Dan for short.... Come on, Dante old boy—you darling Dante!... (*Strokes his head*) Yes, you *are* a precious Dante!... Can you manage, Miss Mary? (*Extends her hand to be manicured*)... Hush, children! The telephone....

(*Into telephone*) Hello!... Oh! Good morning, Count Bluffsky, good morning.... Yes, I left a message because I wanted to tell you that the portrait has arrived.... Yes, it's hanging in the drawing-room in the place that you selected, over the piano—the light is lovely on it, and we're *crazy* about the frame.... Everyone admires it.... But I was wondering if you would let me make a few tiny suggestions.... Well, my husband and I were looking at it last night. We put the child up on top of the piano, on a level with the picture, and we both think that you've got her a little bit *thin*.... Do you think you could make her a little fatter?... Then there is something not quite right about the mouth.... Do you think you could change the mouth and give her a little smile?... Then, I forgot to tell you that in summer, when she plays and gets very hot, there's a lovely wave in her hair—and little curls about her temples.... Do you think there's any objection to painting her as though she were *hot*?... Then, when may I bring her in, Count Bluffsky?... On Tuesday at two?... And please don't think we don't like the picture.... Oh! It's a *real* work of art, and I think it will be absolutely perfect if you make those little changes.... Goodbye, Count Bluffsky—I look forward to coming to your studio again! Goodbye!...

(*To the child*) Oh! Darling, don't grumble—he's only going to take about half an hour....

Now, children, run along. Take the puppy to the kitchen and give him a little water but nothing to eat—I'll see about that later. And don't come back!... (*The children leave with the dog*)

(*Resumes reading*) *Nel mezzo del cammin*—(*Looks up suddenly as the clock strikes*) Oh! Miss Mary—let me go! I'd no idea it was so late—I thought there was plenty of time—I'm so sorry—they're not too bad—I'll call you in a few days—Goodbye! (*The manicurist leaves*)

Signorina—I *am* dreadfully disappointed, but I'm afraid I'll have to stop! You don't know how sorry I am!... I care more for this than for *anything* I do, and I can't bear to have my lesson interrupted.... Let me see—when will you come again?... Not Tuesday or Wednesday.... But Thursday—yes, I know I'm free Thursday. Come early—at a quarter-past nine, and we will have a *nice, long, quiet* lesson! Goodbye!... Oh! I think it is thrilling—so beautiful and so profound! I can hardly wait to get on.... Goodbye! (*The Signorina leaves. Calls maid*)

Marie! Marie!... (*Rises from the chaise-longue*) I must be out of the house in fifteen minutes! I want my black cloth dress with the braid, my fur jacket and my three-cornered hat.... Has the car come yet?... (*The secretary enters*)

Good morning, Miss Swift! Thank heaven you have arrived! You will find a mountain of papers on my desk.... I wish I could stay at home and help you.... I'll be back about half past twelve and can give you a few minutes before lunch.... But first, before you do anything, will you try to get me some men for the opera on Monday? I have a box, but I have no men.... There's a Russian lady coming and I ought to have somebody who knows something about Russia.... Is there anybody?... You might try Mr. Fisher—I don't *like* him, but he speaks Russian—he spent a week there once, and thinks he knows everything—he can talk to her.... Then, try for little Mr. Miller—he's always free and he likes everybody and everything, and always gives me a feeling of hope.... I put him on a scrap of paper and tucked him in the blotter—hope he didn't get torn up.... Sir Basil Something.... Look in the scrap-basket—pink paper.... Have you got him?... That's it! Sir Basil Rood.... He's at the Ritz, I suppose. They generally are—to begin with.... Well, try those three, and if you can't get any of them, just take my list of possible men and run right through it.... Get anyone you can as long as it's a man....

(*Answers telephone*) Camilla—darling! How nice to hear your voice! When did you get back?... I didn't expect you so soon.... Had a good trip?... I'm dying to see you!... No, I'm not busy.... Well, why don't you lunch with me today?... Just me and the children, and we'll have a cozy time.... What?... Oh! Do *tell* me—did you hear the whole story?... Was it what we thought?... Much *worse*?... *What*?... *No*!... Heavens! Do they know where they went?... Is anyone going after her?... What a situation! I can't wait to hear.... Well, that's not for the children's ears, so I'll meet you at the Plaza at one?... Fine!... No, I can't this morning.... Well, I'm rushing out now—I have to get to a funeral in twenty minutes.... Oh! I've been up for hours—I've already had my Italian lesson.... I'm reading the *Inferno*.... Oh! It's divine!... I'm quite far along.... Yes, I read pretty easily now—I've always kept up my Italian.... Whose funeral? Poor old Daisy—wasn't it *sad*?... *Awfully* sad! And yet I'm not so *sure*.... I never thought she was.... I don't see how she *could* have been.... I never *liked* him, did you?... Well, that's *that*.... No, dear, I can't. After that I have to take one of the children to the dentist.... This afternoon? Perhaps I can.... Let's see— (*Speaks to secretary*) Miss Swift, what have I this afternoon? Just look at my engagement pad—to the right.... (*Into telephone*) Was Mexico wonderful?... Did you get to Guatemala, too?... No, dear, I can't.... I have an important hospital committee at two—I'm the chairman, so I must be there.... Then what?... A Philosophy class at three—awfully interesting, I wish you'd join.... And then?... A Contract lesson at four—I'm awfully stupid about the new rules.... Now, I must run.... Goodbye, dear.... I'll see you at one, at the Plaza.... So glad you're back! Thanks for calling me!... (*Hangs up*)

Now, Miss Swift—will you take these notes while I dress?... (*Begins dressing*) Will you please write to the ladies on a list which I think I left under the bronze hand to the left of the blotter—and ask them if they will serve on a committee to raise twenty thousand dollars by the end of May for the furnishing of the new Day Nursery?... Don't care how we do it—but we *must* have the money by the end of May.... I'll help in any way I can.... And please send ten dollars to the appeals under the silver frog, and five dollars to those under the jade egg.... Then, what concert tickets have we got this week?... The Philharmonic? Oh, *Lord*! That seems to come so often!... Is there anyone who likes music? Everyone says they do, but I never believe them.... I know—Miss Hattie Tufts, my old piano teacher—she adores it, and she takes her crippled sister. My seats are on the aisle, and they stumble in together.... Then, will you please ask the cook to send a basket of very nourishing and appetizing food to the nightwatchman's little boy at Roosevelt Hospital?... Oh! Didn't you know he'd been run over—very badly hurt?... But he's going to be all right—I talk to the surgeon every day.... She'll know—a little roast chicken, rice pudding, sponge cake, some soup jelly, and fruit—and get a toy from the nursery to put on the top of the basket.... Every day at twelve o'clock, to Jimmy Pike, Children's Ward, Roosevelt

Hospital.... Then, Miss Swift, will you see that Morris takes Mr. Clark's golf clubs and his bag to the station, and stands at the gate of the train at five minutes past twelve?... He wants his brown tweeds.... Marie, will you please tell James?... And there should be a new driver in the bag.... I don't know if Billy remembered to put it in.... (*Turns to maid who enters*) What is it, Nelly?... What?... The boiler has burst?...

Miss Swift—the boiler has burst!... Will you please send for the plumber, and get him to mend the boiler, for we *must* have it for dinner.... (*The telephone rings*) I'll answer—it's probably for me....

(*Into telephone*) Hello?... (*Stops suddenly, her hand over the mouthpiece, and turns to the maid*) Marie—leave my purse and gloves and that little parcel there—then will you get my grey flannel suit and have James put it in the car—I have to take it back to the tailor.... And Miss Swift—will you go to the library, and on the table between the windows, you'll find the minutes for the hospital meeting this afternoon—a black book with yellow papers stuck in it.... Please give it to James to put in the car.... Wait a minute!—on the sofa in the drawing-room is a very dirty lampshade.... And on the mantelpiece I think I left a pile of yellow taffeta samples.... One of them has a pin stuck in it.... Will you pin that to the lampshade, and have James put it in the car—it has to be re-covered.... Then come back, Miss Swift—I want to speak to you before I go out.... (*Miss Swift leaves*)

(*Speaks in telephone. Her voice now becomes soft, melting, seductive*) Hello!... Did you hear all that?... They are.... Yes, I was.... About five.... I'm all right.... No, I wasn't—what made you think so?... How are you?... No, I can't.... I'll tell you when I see you.... Nothing to worry about.... So am I—but what can we do?... Oh! Did you go?... Weren't they wonderful? I wish we might have gone together.... Yes, that's the one I liked best.... I knew you would....I must run now.... Yes.... All right.... Yes, I will—I promise. Goodbye. Don't be late.... (*Hangs up the receiver gently*)

(She calls to the maid)

Marie—will you tell James to have tea in the library and a nice bright fire?... About five.

Miss Swift—are you there?... Would you please telephone one of the bookstores—Brentano's or Scribner's—and ask them if they would send at once, by special messenger, a new book that's just been published, called *Our Inner Life*.... I don't know who wrote it, but I have to discuss it at the Book Club on Tuesday and I must glance through it first.... I know it's called *Our Inner Life. Our—Inner—Life.*

(Having put on her hat and coat while talking, she takes her gloves and purse from the dressing-table, hastily retouches her hair in the mirror, and hurries out of the room)

AT THE COURT OF PHILIP IV

※ ✦ ※

*A ball is in progress in the Royal Palace in Madrid. The
time is the Seventeenth Century, during the reign of
Philip IV. A lady of the court moves among the guests of
the King, greeting now one courtier, now another. She is
dressed in a sumptuous panniered gown of velvets, brocade,
and gold lace, in the style of Velázquez's portraits, with
ropes of pearls around her neck, a large fan of black lace and
a rich handkerchief in her hand, and an elaborate black lace
mantilla dressed about her hair. She sweeps through the
ballroom with a high bearing yet with an air of concealed
anxiety. Presently the Duc de Lisle, an emissary of the King
of France at the Court of Spain, approaches her. She bows
and smiles as he greets her.*

Ah — bonjour, Monsieur le Duc, bonjour!... Très bien, merci....
Oui, je viens d'arriver de Paris, où j'ai rencontré plusieurs de
vos amis qui m'ont priée de les rappeler à votre bon souvenir!
Oui, j'ai passé deux semaines à Paris, et une semaine à Fontainebleau, et là se trouvaient leurs Majestés, le Cardinal, le Duc
d'Anjou, la Duchesse d'Orléans et plusieurs personnes bien in-
téressantes. Et tout le monde m'a demandé de vos nouvelles!...
   Oh, il faisait le plus beau temps du monde — ah, quelle beauté,
la forêt de Fontainebleau! On était si gai — on s'est si bien
amusé.... Nous avons fait la chasse, tous les jours, et nous avons
dansé jusqu'à l'aube.... Et nous avons causé sans fin — sur des
sujets bien divers.... Oh, la politique, la philosophie, l'art.... Et
puis — l'amour.... Et le scandale! Ah, oui, tout le monde aime
le scandale!... Nous avons fait des pantomimes, toutes espèces
de jeux ridicules — et nous avons même joué à cache-cache dans
la forêt! Ah, Paris — quelle belle ville!... Oui, au Théâtre —

j'ai vu une nouvelle tragédie de Corneille — 'Le Cid.' Oh, c'est magnifique, et naturellement cela m'intéresse follement, puisque la scène se passe dans mon pays! (She curtseys as the Prince of Wales passes) *C'est le Prince de Galles — il vient d'arriver, en visite chez le Duc de Buckingham.... Il a beaucoup de charme! C'est Juana Pacheco qui est avec lui! Elle est belle, n'est-ce-pas? Il paraît qu'elle vient de commander son portrait à Velázquez — on sait bien qui le payera!... Ah, vous ne saviez pas?... Oh, il est très épris!... Quel joli bal, elle est exquise, la jeune femme de votre Ambassadeur, sa robe de soie brochée rose lui va à merveille!... Laquelle?... La dame en satin blanc?... Oh, c'est une amie intime à moi — la Duquesa de Alcala!... Mais avec plaisir.... Duquesa! Permettez-moi de vous présenter le Duc de Lisle. Nous danserons la pavane plus tard, nous vous prions de vous joindre à nous.... Alors — à bientôt — au revoir!...*

(She bows low as the Duc de Lisle leaves her, then moves towards another lady of the court and speaks to her in a low voice)

Beatriz—are you alone? I must talk with you, and we must speak in English so no one will understand! My dear, the most dreadful thing has happened!... I am in deep distress, and I come to you for advice, my dearest friend!... Well, yesterday my husband had gone to the chase, so I went to pass the day with my cousin Juanita. It was such a beautiful day that we decided to go to the forest for the afternoon. The Marquesa and her sister, Doña Teresa, and Marie Louise joined us. I sent my servant to your house to ask you to come, but you were not there.... Oh, it was so beautiful, and we passed happy hours. We played games—we lay in the grass— and we bathed in the stream, it was so warm! You must not tell! We told stories, we had many cakes, and oranges—and how we laughed!... They teased me, you know, because the King had been very attentive to me at the Ball on Friday.... Yes, he was—but you know how he is—only last week Doña Luisa was his favourite!...

But, my dear, listen: I was very tired after the Fête in the woods and I went very early to bed. Carlos was not yet returned from the chase. I was in my room, looking out of the window. Did you see the moon? Oh, such a night, so beautiful—and the air cool—sweet from the jasmine! I was standing there, dreaming, looking at the stars—and suddenly I heard steps on the terrace. I hid quickly behind the curtains, but I peeped through. And in the moonlight I could see a tall figure in a long black cloak—masked—passing behind the orange trees, and approaching my window. And he spoke my name! I became like stone, then he called softly. To my horror I recognized the voice of the King! It is true! You *must* believe me! I was cold with fear, wondering what I should do. At this moment I heard Carlos whistle, and his steps advancing quickly from the stables. In the moonlight, the dark figure of the King against the white wall was seen, before he could escape, and Carlos called out and challenged him! His voice was terrible! Then I heard a great scuffling on the gravel, and then I saw Carlos lashing his whip—furiously! I was trembling with horror!... Yes!... Imagine! His whip! It was soon over. His Majesty ran off, and Carlos came to me so angry I was terrified. But I soon convinced him that I had not expected the King. Then he was in despair—to have lost his temper! And also to ruin his career at the court!... Oh, it is dreadful!... Carlos will be banished—and we must leave Madrid!... Of course the reason will never be known—the shame is too great—but we shall be sent away! I am in despair—where shall we go? What can I do? Who can help me? To think I have been the cause of my Carlos's disgrace! Tell me, what do you advise? Who could help me?... Olivares?... Olivares!... Yes, I know, he is the only man who has power with the King.... But Beatriz, what will he ask for such a favour?... There is no time to lose and I must save Carlos!... But you are right. Yes—I could speak with him tonight. I am dancing the Minuet with him.... He is coming now?... Oh, my dear friend, pray for me!

(*She leaves Beatriz and turns to greet Olivares*)
¡ *Buenas noches, Conde Duque! ¿Comienza el minué ya?*

¿En qué cuadro estamos? ¿Aquí? ¡Muy bien! (She takes her place for the minuet and turns to greet the other dancers) *Bonsoir, Général!* Good evening, Your Highness! *Buona sera, Eccellenza!* (She begins the dance, speaking to each dancer in turn as she joins hands and turns) *J'apprends, Général, que vous partez bientôt pour les Pays-Bas? Quel dommage! Hélas! Toujours la guerre! Est-ce-que nous aurons jamais la paix?*

Good evening, Sire! And did you find the journey from London very fatiguing? I dream to go—but it is far! I would like to fly—like a bird! Perhaps one day!

Ho avuto una lettera, Eccellenza — da Roma, che parla di un uomo nominato Galileo, il quale ha scoperto che la terra volve attorno il sole! Che meraviglia! Credete che sia possibile? (Turns and curtsies to Olivares) *Me gusta tanto bailar — ¿es verdad? ¡Oh, gracias, muchas gracias!*

(She dances the grand-chain, ending with a deep curtsey. Then she turns, speaking to Olivares in a low voice)

¿Conde Duque — puedo hablar con vuesa merced un momento? ¿Aquí? ¿Los dos solos?... (They sit on a nearby divan) *¡Yo sé — usted sabe — todo lo ocurrido anoche! ¡Estoy desesperada! ¡Le ruego me ayude a salvar el honor de mi esposo!... ¡No tiene la culpa — porque se vuelve loco cuando está celoso!... ¡Es horrible! ¿No puede hacerse nada para obtener la clemencia del Rey? ¡Estoy muerta de angustia, y recurro a vuesa merced como el único que tiene influencia con Nuestra Majestad!... Sí.... Sí.... ¡Ah, sí!... ¡Vuesa merced me lisonjea!... ¿Es verdad que hace tanto tiempo que vuesa merced me ama?... Y si consiento.... ¿Se salvará?... ¿Guardará su cargo en corte?... ¿Puedo confiar?... Sí.... ¿Y cuándo le veré? ¿El miércoles que viene? Sí.... ¿Dónde? Sí.... ¿Cuándo?... Bueno.... Mi coche esperará a la caída de la tarde, cerca de la fontana al borde del bosque. Sí.... ¿Iremos a la Garcuella?... Bueno.... Entonces — no le retengo más.... ¡Ay!... Suena la marcha.... No, gracias, se la he prometido al duque inglés — ¡allí está!... ¡Buenas noches, Conde Duque! — adiós por hoy, y gracias...¡muchas gracias!* (He kisses her hand and leaves her)

(She smiles again as she greets the Duc de Lisle)

Here I am, Duke—yes, it is the march for supper. Will you forgive me one moment, I must speak with my friend? *(She hurries to Beatriz and speaks in a whisper)* Beatriz—it is arranged!... He has promised!... Oh, he is so powerful! He can do anything!... We shall remain in Madrid!... Goodnight, and thank you! *(She puts her finger on her lips)*

(She turns back to the Duke with high ceremony)

Now, Duke—I am ready.... And were you at the Corrida this afternoon? It was so beautiful! The young matador is a marvellous boy!... So brave! He is only nineteen, and has already killed twenty toros!...

(She extends her hand as the Duke leads her towards the procession that moves off to the hall of the supper)

OPENING A BAZAAR

꙳꙳❀꙳꙳

The scene is the terrace of a country house in England, arranged with stalls, exhibits, flower and food booths, a platform with chairs, for the annual summer bazaar. The elderly lady who enters—the mistress of the house, perhaps a lady of title—wears a large feathered hat, a lace scarf over her shoulders, various chains of pearls and ornaments and a feather boa about her neck, and she carries a reticule, a summer parasol, and a lorgnette which she uses freely for looking, pointing, and emphasizing her words. She enters smiling and bowing to the assembled friends, guests, and patrons of the bazaar who have gathered on the terrace. Her voice is English, cultivated and dignified, but very hospitable and friendly.

Good afternoon, Mrs. Carruthers. Good afternoon, Elizabeth. Isn't this the most *lovely* day?... How fortunate we *are*! Fancy if it had been yesterday!... We should all have been drenched—such a downpour!... Well, Mr. Floyd—here we all are.... What a splendid gathering!... Many old friends, I see—and many new ones.... Hello, children!... Good afternoon.... It is indeed—a most lovely day!... How fortunate we are!...

Well, Mr. Floyd—I think we might start. I see no occasion to wait longer—we have such an afternoon before us!... Quite. Then you will begin with a short speech—and a prayer to follow, of course.... Oh, rather—yes, indeed!... Then a few words of introduction, I suppose—and then my speech.... Oh, I have it here. *Terrified*, as usual! Isn't it ridiculous, Mr. Floyd, when you think of the number of years I have been doing this—and I'm *always* nervous!...

Why, Margaret! I am *so* glad you were able to come.... I hope you've brought the children?... I shall want to see them all later.... Oh, Harriet, aren't you going to sit with us? You *must* be with us on the platform. I'm sure there are places for you here.... I'll ask.... Are there two places?... Two?... Yes, Harriet, they have kept two for you and Lorna.... Is the baby better?... Oh, I'm *so* glad—you've had *such* an anxious time.... We must have a little chat afterwards.... Is my hat in anyone's way?... Shall I move a little? I don't want to obscure your view!... (*She takes a chair*)

(*Laughs as she listens to the Parson making the opening speech*) He's always *very* funny!... A splendid start—making them all laugh!... (*The Parson continues talking*)

(*Murmurs aside to someone*) So *true*! So *true*—what I was saying last week.... It can't be said too often.... Admirable!... (*Falls silent; a prayer is about to be said by the Parson*)

(*Rises, bowing her head in prayer. Then she listens in an amused and slightly embarrassed manner as Mr. Floyd introduces her. She takes her speech from her bag and steps forward, bowing to people on the platform and to the audience. She now raises her voice*) Mr. Floyd, Ladies of the Committee, Ladies and Gentlemen: I feel sure that you will agree—that we should rejoice together—that the rain has *stopped* and that the sun is shining, and therefore—that you will be able to enjoy the full beauty of the afternoon! I hope that everyone will feel *quite* at home, and at liberty to wander about the garden and park, after—if I may suggest anything so obvious—they have thoroughly visited every stall and table of the bazaar, and generously indulged themselves at tea.... (*Stops, turning to Mr. Floyd*)

Beg pardon, Mr. Floyd?... Speak a little louder?... I'm afraid they will not hear me under the trees—there's such a *wind* blowing!

(*To the audience*) I wonder if you would all mind coming closer?... I have a very poor voice. Come along, children.... I like to have you close about me.... That's better! (*She continues in a raised voice*)

I feel I voice the opinion of everyone here, when I say we are all deeply grateful to the ladies of the Committee who have organized the bazaar, and thereby given us a chance—if I may so express it—to thoroughly enjoy spending our pounds, our shillings, and our pence, as the case may be!... The cause is one which, I may say, appeals to *all* our hearts, for I am sure you will all agree that the splendid work so ably started by our late Vicar's sister is one that appeals to *all* our sympathies....

Dear Miss Caroline! How well I remember when she first came here, when I was a tiny girl, romping about under these same trees!... Everyone loved Miss Caroline, and it is in her dear memory that, I feel I may say, we are all happy to support the admirable work which she organized in our village....

Part of the funds raised today is for a new bicycle for our dear Nurse Stubbs. Where is she? (*Looks about*)... Ah, *there* she is!... And I am sure you will all agree that we heartily join in wishing her God-speed on her many errands of mercy! (*She consults her notes*)

Three pounds, ten shillings, and sixpence will be deducted from the proceeds to pay for the materials used in putting a new gutter on the roof of the Village Hall, the work having been done free of charge by the Boy Scouts of the village. (*Turns to look at boys and pounds with her parasol*) Well done, boys!... I am delighted to hear such splendid applause!... I know that we are very proud of the boys—who came to the rescue, and did such a very skilful piece of repair work, made necessary by the ravages of the recent storms....

I feel I have taken more than my share of time from this happy occasion, so with a renewed vote of thanks to all those who have so generously given of their thought and their time to organizing the fête today, I declare—the bazaar—open!

(*She bows. Suddenly she realizes she has forgotten the telegrams in her bag*) One moment, please, Mrs. Morrison!... One moment, children!... I am sorry, ladies and gentlemen...but

I have here three telegrams...*quite* the most important part of my speech.... Thank you, Mrs. Carruthers.... I forget everything these days. I sometimes think I am losing what little brains I have.... One moment please!...

The *first* telegram is from the Duchess, who regrets that owing to a sharp attack of gout, she is unable to drive over as she had hoped to do—but she sends her best wishes for the success of the afternoon.... Poor dear, I'm afraid she's *very* bad—I've begged her to go to Harrogate—but she never thinks of herself.... These unselfish people are sometimes very tiresome....

The second is from Dean Plumbridge, who says: 'Hearty good wishes for the success of the bazaar, and my blessing on my parishioners.' He never forgets us, does he—the *dear* Dean—and we never forget him!...

The third is from my son in India.... (*Bows shyly, as the audience applauds*) 'Thinking of you all today—best wishes to all my friends—good luck to the bazaar—Cyril.'... I should like to add that in his letters my son speaks of his constant thoughts of his friends at home.... He will be returning soon from his great journey, and I feel sure that the *happiest* moment of his homecoming will be when he receives your welcome....

And now, I must not take any more of your time.... *Thank* you for your patience! Let us all *rush* to the stalls and swell the proceeds of the bazaar to unanticipated proportions!... Thank you!... (*Her speech ends*)

(*She turns now to speak to her nearby friends*) They have been *very* patient.... I have such a poor voice, no one ever hears me.... However, what I say is of small importance!...

(*Takes a bouquet which a child brings up to her*) Are these for *me*?... *Thank* you, Charlie—What a *lovely* bouquet!... *Such* beautiful roses—from your mother's garden, I'm sure.... Thank you, dear, and I hope you will have a *happy* afternoon.

Now, Mary, if you're tired, do slip away.... Oh, I shall stay

PLATE XXX

Mrs. Hancock in *The Return*

PLATE XXXI

A Last Portrait: December 1956
Photograph by Roy Schatt, New York

until the end—I *always* stay until the end.... But there are people coming for dinner, and I don't want you to be tired, so please don't wait—you'll soon be bored.

(*Bends low to speak to an old man in a wheel-chair*) Good afternoon, Mr. Dew!... And how is the leg today? You look very *smart* in your new wheel-chair.... I *like* the red wheels—they're so cheerful! How well he looks, Mrs. Dew.... I'm *so* glad he felt able to come.... It *is* nice to see you about again—we have missed you in the village.... Mrs. Dew, has he tried the sunlight machine I sent him?... Oh, but he *must* try it!... There is no danger.... (*Bends and follows the chair across the terrace*) Mr. Dew—I beg you to try the sunlight machine.... No, it will *not* explode. Electricity *never* explodes, does it?... It might *burn* slightly—but do try it every morning.... It's helped me enormously.... I've had bad neuritis in my arm, you know, and I'm sure it will help your leg.... (*To Mary*) I think he's very skilful with his chair.... (*Calling*) Don't go too fast round the corners!...

Come on, Mary. Has that child gone? I really cannot be bothered with this bouquet. If you will observe, it's put together with picture-wire, and it weighs at least five pounds! I can't *bear* carrying a bouquet, and I must have my hands free. I don't want to hurt his feelings.... I shall leave it here—but don't let me forget it! (*Puts the bouquet on a chair*)

Good afternoon, Marjorie dear! Mary, I'd like you to know Miss Marjorie Dimple who always has a most delightful stall, full of such useful things!... (*They begin to move along the stalls*) See the aeroplane made of buttercups floating over the stall!... Now, *what* are *these* bright little things?... Iron holders? And what are they for?... To hold irons? How *clever*!... I *see*—to keep the hands from burning...made in the shapes of flowers from scraps of silk and velvet.... Delightful! Is that a rose or a tomato?... I'll have it, whatever it is—and the tulip, and the daisy.... My laundress will be delighted!... How *very* effective those gilded bulrushes are!... Yes, I will take them, please.... I've always thought bulrushes very decorative, but people do not use them very much.... Of course, they're twice as pretty when they're gilded.... Yes, thank you—I'll take the lot.... (*To Mary, sotto voce*) I know exactly where I shall put them!... Those painted tambourines are beautifully done.... Who did them?... Judy Flint! Ah, the dear child!... Mary—I must ask you to look at these tambourines done by a little crippled girl—a particular friend of mine. She's never walked, but she paints beautifully!... She made me the most charming teacup last year, covered with tiny violets, and she does Christmas cards and candleshades.... Would you like one, dear, for a souvenir?... Which one?... (*To the saleslady*) My friend will have the 'Houses of Parliament', and I will take 'St. Paul's'—a favourite view of mine—the dome through the trees.... (*Pointing with her lorgnette*) I'll take some of those sachets, please—six pink and six blue.... What pretty doilies! Exquisite crochet!... Like lace.... Who did these?... Mrs. Crow? Is she *still* doing that work?... Mary, those doilies are done by an old lady who is ninety-eight years of age.... Ninety-nine? Ninety-nine, Mary!... She has most amazing eyesight and works without glasses!... Marjorie, dear, will you put my things together, and I'll come back later.... I must get on to the other stalls....

(*Moves on*) Good afternoon, dear!... What? Will I take a chance on a scooter? Well, I don't really know what a scooter is, but I think I'll have to try it. I've tried most things in my life, and I don't want to miss anything!... Two shillings?... There you are!... I'd like number seven and number nine, if I may.... How very nicely he writes! I hope I win my scooter!... Come on, Mary.

Good afternoon, Mr. Huggins—and how are the rehearsals going?... Oh, you mustn't worry! You made such a success of *As You Like It* last year, and I'm sure *The Tempest* will be equally good. I haven't seen it for forty years, and I'm greatly looking forward to it. Who have you for Prospero?... Mr. Jebb, the grocer?... *Admirable*! I'm sure he'll do it *extremely* well.... And Ariel?... Emily Gulliver?... Is that Frank's or

George's child? I always get the little Gullivers mixed.... But isn't Emily the one who has a very bad squint?... Yes, she *is* a graceful little thing—I often notice her skipping about the village.... Well, I expect they will be looking at her feet—they won't notice the eyes!... Do ask my gardener to help you with the magic island. He will be very flattered, I'm sure. Let me know if you want to borrow any properties from the house. I shall be happy to help in any way I can.... (*She moves on*)

Come, Mary—we must get on.... I shall take you to a most dangerous table—Mrs. Bean's cake table.... Here we come, Mrs. Bean—to be tempted by all your lovely cakes!... Oh, how rich and delicious!... I have never *seen* so many pretty cakes—all made in the village.... They *do* look good!... Oh, I must have that *very* elaborate pink and white affair.... I shall take it home and show it to my cook—it will make her *madly* jealous.... What?... She *made* it?... Dear me—how funny!... In all the thirty years Mrs. Whippet has been cooking for me, I have never seen a cake like that on my table! She's been hiding her talents!... Oh, yes—I shall take it.... We shall have a good laugh.... I'd like the chocolate cake, please, and the Swiss roll, and that seed cake, and.... Oh! Do I see *cream buns*?... Oh, give me the lot! I have a great weakness for cream buns! When I was a child there was a baker in the village who made the very *best* cream buns I've ever tasted, and—Oh, here's my friend, Clarence!

Clarence, did you hear me talking to your mother about those cream buns? Do you know, I've bought them *all*, and I intend to *eat* them all, except possibly *one*—and who do you think is going to have that one?... Who?... *You!*... Would you like it?... Well, you shall *have* it, this very minute, without further delay!... May we have one, Mrs. Bean?... Now, Clarence—hold out your hand—I'll put it very lightly in the palm...so...now wait, until I tell you something funny about cream buns. They have a way of oozing out in the most unexpected places, so I advise you to take tiny nibbly bites around the edges, and when you come to a safe.... Good afternoon, Molly.... *Oh! Oh!* That *always* happens! Never mind! (*Takes out her handkerchief and wipes Clarence's chin*).... No, no! He was very polite, he said 'Thank you'—that was the trouble. He took rather too big a bite, and spoke at the same time!... *Quite* all right—but of course he didn't have a hanky!... I never bothered with hankies.... I used the back of my hand.... Is that what *you* do? It makes an excellent wiper, doesn't it?... Quite all right—no harm done.... I hope you'll enjoy the rest of it....

Yes, Mr. Floyd?... Oh, I agree—a cup of tea would be *most* acceptable.... Shall we ask the older ladies to join us? They look rather buffeted about, standing there.... (*She calls to the ladies*) Oh, Mrs. Jelliby, Miss Lucy, Nurse, Mrs. Jakes —won't you join us?... Mr. Floyd and I thought it would be rather a good idea to have our teas now—there's such a crowd, and when everyone has gone into the tent for their teas, we can come out and do the stalls more quietly.... Mrs. Jelliby, would you lunch with me on Friday? I'd like to talk to you about the Women's Institute before the meeting....

Oh, here come the Boy Scouts! I *must* speak to them. One moment!... (*Goes forward with outstretched hands*) Well, boys —how are you?... Good afternoon, Jerry! How do you do, Michael—and George! Dear me—you have *grown* since Wednesday!... And my little Fred, the smallest scout in the world—and the bravest, I'm sure. Jake—Martin—how do you do?... Now, let me look at you!... I must see your new uniforms. They *are* smart! Such *nice* material!... I wish I knew what all those little patches and badges—those signs and symbols of the scouts—signify.... I wish that one day you would come and tell me what they *all* mean.... And I hope you heard what I said in my speech! We are all *very proud* of you. You have done a *beautiful* piece of work, boys, and I'm sure you enjoyed doing it.... The fact is, we *all* enjoy doing things well! Now, remember that *all* your lives, and put your heart into whatever you do—just as you did when

you mended the gutter!... Now run along—don't waste your
time with me.... Have a happy afternoon, and don't break
your front teeth on all these funny things you are going to
do. I shall see you all on Saturday afternoon after the cricket
match. Goodbye!—thank you for speaking to me!... Remember
me to your mother, George—I was sorry to hear she was
not well.... (*Turns to the ladies*) They *are* darlings—and they
have done a most remarkable job.... The carpenter told me
that the gutter doesn't leak a drop....

Now, don't let me stop to speak to people. We really *must*
get on.

(*Suddenly she stops and looks through the crowd*) Is that
Buckle?... It *is*!... Why, Buckle—what a *very* pleasant surprise!
I had no idea you were here!... Is Mrs. Buckle with
you?... I shall hope to see her later.... I am *very* well, thank
you—I needn't ask how *you* are!... You and I are most fortunate—we
are indeed!... Thank you, I have good news of all
the family. They are scattered far and wide, but they're all
well. Pamela is arriving on Friday with her children, for a
nice long holiday, I hope, and as a matter of fact I was about
to write you a note, because in a letter from Pamela which
came last night, she says: 'The children give me no peace.
They are determined to see Buckle the *very day* they arrive.'
So do you think we might come to tea on Friday? I hope it
won't be too much for Mrs. Buckle—we shall be rather a
large party, I'm afraid.... We shall be nine!... They are impatient
to see you—just as we used to be.... They are dear
children—but they grow too fast! That's the only fault I
find.... There are so few little ones left. Little Pamela, my
youngest grandchild, is now seven.... Yes, Pamela, is seven—
just the age that I was, Buckle, when you first knew me! And
she loves climbing the big cherry-tree, just as I did!... Do
you remember the time I fell out of the tree and broke my
leg, and you carried me home and told me stories so that I
forgot the pain?... I've *never* forgotten the stories.... I've
brought up my children, and my grandchildren, and many

other children, on your stories.... And *how* you told them! *How* we used to laugh!... What fun we used to have in the old barn!... What happy days those were, Buckle—what happy days!... I don't think the cherries are nearly as sweet as they were in those days.... But it's always a pleasure to see you again, because you don't change!... You don't grow a day older! How *do* you manage it?... I'm afraid not, but we all do the best we can! Goodbye!... And I'll let you know definitely about Friday.... (*Calls as he leaves her*) Oh, Buckle, are you fond of salmon?... I've just had a beautiful salmon sent me from Scotland—and I shall be happy to share it with you. I'll send you a piece later in the day. Goodbye.... Goodbye....

One of the finest men, Mrs. Jelliby, that I have ever known —a *remarkable* character. You knew him too, Mrs. Jakes— we were all young together.... Buckle?... Oh, I thought you knew.... He was groom and coachman in our family for fifty-nine years.... He's known four generations of the family— brought us all up, and taught us all to ride.... I can so well remember my father saying that Buckle was a genius with horses and with children.... We brought him all our troubles, and I shall remember until the end of my life things I learned from Buckle as a child....

Now, ladies, we really must get on.... We can't linger like this, or we shall never get our tea!... Good afternoon, Mrs. Brown—isn't it a *lovely* day?

(*Bowing and smiling to all about, she walks away and off the terrace with her friends*)

THE ACTRESS

❊

*The famous actress enters the drawing-room of her private
apartment in an hotel in Paris. She is handsome and graceful,
of a consciously histrionic manner, with high-dressed hair,
and garbed in a long afternoon gown, jewels at her neck,
wrists, and ears—very decidedly an actress in her every
movement, gesture, and bearing. She is no longer a young
woman but her appearance flashes with presence and aplomb.
Her English and French are spoken with a marked foreign
accent: she is evidently of Central European nationality,
and the native speech she uses here is devised of characteristic
Slavic sounds and accents. She is smoking a cigarette
languidly and with a show of weariness and studied disdain.
She is about to take a chair when a manservant enters to
announce a visitor.*

*Entrez.... Oui?... Oh, eh bien, vous avez dit que j'étais là?
Alors — rien à faire.... Faites monter monsieur.... (The servant
goes to bring in the caller)*

*Ah, vieil idiot!... Il m'embête!... (She looks very bored, cross,
and tired, but looks up with a bright smile as her visitor, a portly
American gentleman, enters)*

Ah, Mr. Bumstead—what a pleasant surprise! I am so
happy that you came! (*She now exudes her charm and hospitality*) No, no, not at all—I was thinking of you. I was saying to myself, I wish now Mr. Bumstead would come....
Always you make me happy.... (*They take chairs*) Tell me
quickly, quickly—did you enjoy my performance last night?...
Really?... Oh, thank you—thank you!... It is true? You
were not disappointed after all that you have heard?... I was
afraid!... Oh, I am so happy. And Morowski—was he not

wonderful?... Oh, he is the *most* great actor in the world!...
Am I not fortunate?... Oh, for years we have acted together—
we have fourteen plays in our *répertoire*. Since children, we
have played together. His parents—my parents—were actors,
so we lived always in the theatre, you see.

And now, you leave Paris?... You see only two plays? But
you will see *every*thing in New York.... Yes, we play now six
weeks in Paris, then we play four weeks in London, then we
take the steamer to New York for our American *tournée*. Oh,
I am dreading this journey to America—this great ocean to
cross!... I am terrified!... No, I have never seen the ocean....
My only consolation is that you will be in New York to meet
me—my only friend in that great country!... And I am so
anxious to meet Madame, your wife—and your children....
Seven?... How wonderful—a real American family!... And
you will let me come to your house? And I will bring my
little dog, for the children to see.... Oh, Mr. Bumstead, were
you able to arrange my suite on the steamer?... Yes?... And
I may have my little dog in my cabin?... Yes! Oh, *thank* you!
I was told they would not allow my little dog—that I must
give to the butcher my Follette!... Oh, *thank* you, *thank* you
—you are *so* kind!...

(*She rises as Mr. Bumstead makes ready to leave*)

You must go? So soon?... About our party tonight?...
Yes, I have asked my friends—Blondaloff, my Impresario—
and Félix Morowski, you will meet. You will enjoy to talk to
him. He is very intelligent, and he speaks English very well—
more better than I speak. I am ashamed, I make many mistakes! Then, my old friend, the Comte de Gaparin, and the
new soprano of the Opéra Comique—a small party.... I
understand, and now you go to buy presents for Madame and
your children, and your friends. I know you spoil everybody
—like you spoil me! I am sure. And you have enjoyed your
first visit to Paris?... Oh, I shall miss you—you have been so
kind! I am coming tomorrow to the Gare St. Lazare to say
goodbye.... Of course, I come to say *Bon Voyage* to my new

kind friend! And then, you leave me your automobile—I will take it from the station?... I am *so* grateful!... I enjoy to drive—it is a rest for me, and fresh air—and I will think of you.... Goodbye!... I hope you will enjoy the play—I explained sufficient the meaning, I hope. It is my favourite role! *Au revoir — mille mercis et au revoir! A ce soir*—you will come to my dressing-room after the play? And then we go to our last little supper.... I shall be ready—*au revoir*!

(*Mr. Bumstead is shown out by the servant*)

Tiens, Follette! (*Picks up her little dog and caresses him*) *Nous allons partir en voyage, tu entends, et tu seras avec moi dans ma cabine. Ce vieux monsieur a tout arrangé!*

(*She suddenly looks up, surprised and pleased by the entrance of a young poet who has been ushered into the room by the servant*)

Cecil! I did not hear you come—you come like a ghost! Did you meet the old fat American gentleman in the hall?... You must not laugh—he is so kind. He is kind like he is fat, and he will be very good to me in New York. He has many cars, many children—he talks always of his wife, his family, his farm. He has never been to Paris, and he has never met an actress, and he has enjoyed it.

I will send away my little dog. I know you do not like Follette. *Marie, prends Follette. Monsieur ne l'aime pas. Ne le laisse plus rentrer!* (*The dog is taken out by the maid*)

Darling, sit down—you look tired. (*She sits down, the poet on the floor at her feet*) Tell me quickly, quickly—did you enjoy my performance last night?... Oh, I am *so* happy!... Really?... *Thank* you, darling. I played to *you*.... Yes, because I knew you would understand. You are a poet, you are an artist—you know what it is.... *Thank* you!... You were not disappointed? I was afraid you expect more.... I *am* happy!...

Darling, I read the play you wrote for me. In the Second Act, you *must* make my part more important.... Yes, yes, Morowski is a great actor.... But, darling, I can say to you— *I* am more great.... You must make me more always the centre. He is there; he makes me more great only, you see—

but *always*, I must be the most important.... You will see tonight what I mean. It is my greatest role.... Also his.... But always, I am the *raison d'être* of the play—you see?... (*She becomes restless*)

I cannot talk to you more now.... The most dreadful thing has happened! I am in despair. I will tell you.... Last night, when I returned from the theatre, I find a letter from Blondaloff, my Impresario, to tell me that he had heard from the American manager that they did not want Morowski— that they will not pay Morowski's salary—that they prefer one star—that is *me*—that they prefer a young man, and would like his understudy, who is a very fine-looking boy, but he is *not* a great actor—not like Morowski! Oh, I was *furious!*... I will *not* act without Morowski.... So I must now talk to Blondaloff, and tell him that I will break my contract, and will not go to America without Morowski! So you see, darling, I cannot talk to you. I must save my strength for tonight. My life is very difficult—always trouble, never peace. But this must be settled immediately, you see? (*She rises*)

Darling, thank you that you came. You know how I love you. You are like my child—and you are a great poet.... I know you will have a great triumph one day. *Au revoir!* To-morrow I have the automobile of the old fat American.... Yes, Mr. Bumstead is leaving me his motor-car. I will take you now for many drives—for picnics. We shall go to Chan-tilly—and the forest of Fontainebleau. And we shall laugh, we shall cry, and you will make me poems, and I will tell you many things—and you *are* my darling boy!... *Au revoir, cher!* I will play to you again tonight—and you will come to my dressing-room. I like to have you close. *Au revoir!* (*She embraces the poet and he leaves*)

Pauvre garçon! (*The servant comes to announce another visitor*)

Jean? Monsieur Blondaloff est là?... *Alors, faites le entrer!* (*She looks indignant and cold as she awaits the entrance of her Impresario*)

Ah, Blondaloff — me juta yen ablanoff kari pukta — chetiva. Dumba vanye luba dreb — carlanga kreh — Félix Morowski in America?

(*She asks for an explanation of his letter*)

Potta stuba duli gar in Paris. Frenje parnino gluka in London e imanya gluika crestiuka in America? Ah — me grastonipola stub!

(*She asks why Blondaloff refuses to pay as high a salary in America as in London and Paris*)

Bluyga drange.... Ah...ah... Keshinga plotz.... Vanya cruda illovi. Ah, Blondaloff, mi granye che dum vorka tresh ni var!... Cula liggitte drenga pluni voeta — kres ne punga kola eh — Sisteva!... Du gar ne flopakuva eh? Chi trackecha — Félix Morowski — ah?

(*She expresses her amazement that he has agreed to take the company to America without Morowski, and without recognizing his importance to the success of the plays*)

Mime kula blotze tor — Félix Morowski, eh? Cranba volyen plotz slotera carama vana Félix Morowski, eh? Polyno, grubafit, morona, killayak, pruitebo Félix Morowski, eh? Ah, Blondaloff — vonipar sillik nejuba vimtevo — e crunava im triompleo in America duba lanika posar!

(*With increasing anger, she builds up the argument in favour of keeping Morowski, and enumerates his qualities as an actor and the various roles in which he is supreme. She ends in a burst of fury and indignation, threatening to give up the tour and break her contract with him unless he accedes to her demands*)

Da, da, da, criam povlo vandu — gonava — cludo parta — grido fulba. Da, Blondaloff — Morowski e Marnova luda posar — gammado — trival....

(*He calmly goes over the points in the contract, agrees with her, and takes his leave*)

(When she finishes her tirade Blondaloff leaves, and she coolly bows him out)

Ah — là là!... *(She sighs, exhausted by the discussion, and picks up the telephone)* Passy cinquante-neuf-soixante-douze.... C'est l'Hôtel Impérial?... Monsieur Félix Morowski, s'il vous plait.... Appartement soixante-neuf....

Allô, allô!... C'est moi.... Oui.... Il vient de me quitter — à l'instant même.... Oui, c'était comme je te l'ai dit — il avait l'audace de me demander de jouer sans toi!... Alors, j'ai refusé net, c'est tout.... Non, j'étais tout ce qu'il y a de plus gentille — très calme, très complaisante, très amicale.... Eh bien, il a tout accepté!... Non, il était tout-à-fait de mon avis.... Tu auras un nouveau contrat. Tout sera arrangé selon tes désirs. Alors, ne t'inquiète plus, n'y pense plus — sois tranquille.... Oui, oui!... Moi, je suis morte de fatigue.... Mais je vais me coucher maintenant.... Je te promets.... Je ne verrai plus personne.... Je vais tâcher de m'endormir.... Et toi, aussi — repose-toi.... Et je te verrai au théâtre.... Et nous jouerons comme des dieux!... Oh, tu as été magnifique hier soir — tout le monde en parle!... Eh — gluba tuni vas kepula — drenga cuorla vanga dub tremorna. Ah, Félix!... Oui — je t'adore!... Au revoir...à bientôt.... *(She puts down the telephone and sighs heavily)*

Marie!... *(To the maid)* Voulez-vous préparer mon lit — je vais me coucher. Donne-moi la main! Oh, Marie, je suis complètement usée — morte de fatigue! Je n'ai plus de force — mes nerfs sont à bout! Cette vie me tue — comment jouer le rôle de ce soir? C'est le plus difficile de tous mes rôles.... Non, le coiffeur vient — et il faut que tu arranges le col de ma robe. Il y a quelque chose qui ne va pas — il faut que tu — *(She is interrupted by her manservant)*

Entrez! *(The servant speaks, announcing the arrival of a troop of callers)* Qui?... Le Ministre des Beaux-Arts, l'Ambassadeur de Pologne?... Oh! Une vingtaine de personnes?... Oh! Quelle horreur!... Je les ai complètement oubliés!... Alors, faites entrer tout le monde!... *(She is immensely flustered and frantically prepares to welcome her visitors)* Et Jean, préparez

vite le goûter. Vous avez de petits gâteaux?... Mon dieu!...
Marie! Vite, tenez le miroir — vite!... (*She hastily arranges her*
hair) Oh, *mes cheveux en désordre — rien à faire!... Il faut que*
je reçoive ces gens....

(*Abruptly she recovers her poise and becomes cordial and*
effusive as the visitors enter)

Entrez, entrez — quelle joie! Monsieur le Ministre! Mon-
sieur l'Ambassadeur! Quel honneur vous me faites! Que vous
êtes gentils d'être venus si vite.... (*She moves from visitor to*
visitor in greeting and with extravagant gestures) *Un succès fou,*
n'est-ce-pas?... Merci de ces belles fleurs — quelle merveille!...
Please come in, everybody — oh, I am so happy to see you!...
No, I was waiting, waiting, hoping always that you would
come....

How do you do!... Oh, Lord Fitzgerald, thank you for the
beautiful red roses!... And Miss Brown—I am so happy that
you came.... *Ah, ziago druva — banje kor —* Lord Fitzgerald,
may I introduce you to my aunt? She comes from very far to
see me act in Paris!... *Druika loota,* Lord Fitzgerald— *can-*
derouka glibinski por!... Please come in, everybody! Now, we
shall have some tea.... How do you do!... How kind you are!...
No, I am not tired—I am *never* tired!... No, I *never* rest!...
Je dis que je ne suis jamais fatiguée.... Tellement j'adore mon
art!... Tellement j'aime mes amis!... I say, so much I love my
art—so much I love my friends...!

Come now, we shall have some tea—some cakes—and
talk.... (*She leads them towards another salon*) No, I have
time.... No, I never rest!... I am so happy!... *Venez, main-*
tenant, prendre une tasse de thé.... Et nous allons reparler de
la soirée.... Vraiment, cette visite couronne mon triomphe!...
Venez — par ici!...

(*She goes out leading her visitors, with cries of excitement and*
delight and with large gestures of hospitality, to the room where
tea has been prepared)

THREE WOMEN AND MR. CLIFFORD

⟫✦⟪

I. THE PRIVATE SECRETARY

The scene is the office of Mr. Clifford in the Wall Street district of New York City. There are two large desks with chairs behind them—Mr. Clifford's to the right, Miss Nichols' at the left. Miss Nichols, the secretary, is sitting at her desk, writing and telephoning. She is a young woman of striking capability, charm, energy, efficiency. She speaks in an assured, self-possessed voice, by turns commanding, warmly sympathetic, and sharply perceptive, and is at every moment in complete control of the situation. Throughout the action she is continuously busy, alert, and indefatigable. As the curtain rises she is speaking into the telephone.

(*Into the telephone*) Yes, Mr. Wright.... Well, I'll explain the whole matter to Mr. Clifford, and you may be sure that he will understand.... Oh, Mr. Clifford understands *everything....* Don't worry.... Yes, I'll let you know tomorrow morning.... You are very welcome.... Not at all—it's a pleasure.... Goodbye....

(*She turns to one of her office assistants who has entered from the outer office*)

Lily, have you got those newspaper notices cut out yet?... Well, hurry up, and put them on Mr. Clifford's desk—he'll be in any minute, now, and I'd like to have them there when he comes in.... Did you ever *read* such articles?... Marvellous!... Did you see what *The Times* said?... Said it was a remarkable achievement and should be—

(*She looks up suddenly and rises as Mr. Clifford enters. Lily leaves*)

Oh, good morning, Mr. Clifford! I didn't know you'd come in.... I was just talking to Lily about the newspaper notices.... She's cutting them out for you.... I don't suppose you will even look at them—but we're all very proud down here.... Yes, Mr. Clifford, I did.... Well, Jerry said the best seats he could get for that play were in the eighteenth row, 'way over on the side, so he's going to try some other agents.... I'm *sure* he'll get good seats—he always does....

Yes, Mr. Haynes should be in any minute, now.... I gave him an appointment for ten-thirty.... Then, you have your Board meeting at eleven.... Yes, you're lunching out today, Mr. Clifford.... This is the day you said you would meet those South American gentlemen about the Chilean nitrates —at twelve-forty-five, at the Club....

Oh, I told Dr. Softer you would come in this afternoon at four-thirty to have your tooth filled.... Now, Mr. Clifford— I'm not going to let you put that off another day!... Well, you have already put him off three times, Mr. Clifford, and he telephoned and asked me please to remind you to go.... He said it would only take fifteen minutes, and he said he wouldn't hurt you—I asked him!... I know you do, Mr. Clifford—we *all* do—but we all *have* to go!...

I was going to call Anderson about your white flannel trousers.... Did you say you wanted them all let out an inch and a half?... And ready by Friday without fail?... Yes.... Mr. Clifford—(*She moves towards Mr. Clifford's desk*) Here is your aunt, Mrs. Randlett's list of securities.... If you have a minute, will you try and look them over—because she telephones nearly every day...and I'd like to be able to tell her you had been looking at her list.... She seems to worry so about those securities.... She is *such* a sweet old lady.... I hope her rheumatism is better.... No, nothing of any importance.... There's a very interesting letter from Mr. Hall at the plant in Hopewell—I left it on your desk.... It came yesterday after you'd gone.... He says he thinks there's going to be a strike.... The men are very restless and moody...many staying away from work...and he wishes you'd go down and give them a good talk.... He says you could straighten the whole situation out in no time....

(*The telephone on her desk rings*)

Hello?... (*She listens a moment, then turns to Mr. Clifford*) Mr. Haynes is here now, Mr. Clifford.... Yes—Lily, ask Mr. Haynes to step in, please.... You mean the pale yellow roses?... I think Wadley and Smythe always carry them—if not, I'll find them somewhere.... (*Rises as Mr. Haynes comes in*) This way, Mr. Haynes—Mr. Clifford has just gone into his private office.... (*Goes to Mr. Clifford's door and presents Mr. Haynes*) Mr. Clifford—Mr. Haynes.... If Mrs. Clifford should call, are there any messages?... Be sure and ask about little Patsy's foot.... Oh, yes, I will, of course.... (*She returns to her desk and picks up the telephone*)

Lily—will you please get me the St. Regis roof restaurant, Max Schling, and Wadley and Smythe, the florists?... Both, please—right away.... (*She hangs up the telephone, but in a moment it rings*)

(*Into the telephone*) Hello!... I'm sorry, Mr. Clifford is in conference. Who is it, please?... Oh, Mrs. Randlett!... Good morning! I didn't recognize your voice!... I am sorry, Mr. Clifford is very busy just now. Is there anything I could do?... About your securities?... Well, Mr. Clifford was looking at your list this morning.... It's lying on his desk now—and the very first thing he did when he came in was to look it over carefully—and he's very satisfied with everything that he's holding for you.... No—but Mr. Clifford feels that everything will improve in time.... It's just a question of time.... And you know, none of your dividends has been cut—which is rather exceptional.... So you mustn't worry.... Mr. Clifford keeps a sharp lookout on all your affairs.... He never forgets you—he was saying this morning he hoped your rheumatism was better.... Not at all, Mrs. Randlett.... It is no trouble—it's a pleasure.... Call me any time.... The children are well, thank you!... Oh, I'll tell him.... That's a very nice message, and I agree with you.... Goodbye, Mrs. Randlett.... You're very welcome.... Goodbye!... (*She hangs up*)

(*The telephone rings*)

Hello! St. Regis?... I want to order a table, please.... Seven-thirty tonight.... Mr. Anthony Clifford.... On the roof. I'll call later if there is anything special to order.... But please give Mr. Clifford the table in the corner.... That's the one he prefers.... Correct! Thank you! Goodbye!... (*Hangs up. The telephone rings again*)

Hello! Is this Max Schling?... Is that you, Mr. Charles? Good morning!... It's Miss Nichols speaking.... Mr. Charles— have you some very nice red roses?... Well, will you please send two dozen to Mrs. Clifford—to the house, please—the town house...tomorrow morning between nine and nine-thirty.... No card—just send the roses.... Thank you. Goodbye....

(*She turns to the outer door as Lily enters with the newspaper clippings*)

Come in, Lily.... Aren't they *marvellous*!... Put them on the desk, dear—will you?... Oh, Lily—will you give me a glass of water?... I think I'll take some aspirin.... No—not bad.... Just a little neuralgia, I guess.... I didn't sleep very well last night.... I think it's the heat.... This will knock it out.... It's nothing, anyway.... Thank you.... (*She takes the aspirin and drinks a glass of water*) Oh—I *hate* that taste!... Sure, I chewed it up—that's the way to take aspirin—didn't you know?... Chew it up and drink a whole glass of water— it acts quicker and it's better for you, anyhow.... Shut the door, dear, please—shut the door.... (*Lily leaves*)

(*The telephone rings*)

Hello! Is this Wadley and Smythe?... Will you tell me, please, if you have any of those pale yellow roses?... You have? And are they very fresh and lovely?... Then will you please send two dozen to Mrs. Mallory, 120 East 63rd Street, late this afternoon?... No card—just send the roses.... Charge to Mr. Anthony Clifford.... You have the address?... Correct. Thank you. Goodbye....

(*The telephone rings*)

Hello!... Oh, good morning, Mrs. Clifford—good morning!... Everything is *just fine*.... How are you, Mrs. Clifford?... And how is Patsy's foot this morning?... Oh, how lovely!... They *did*?... What a *relief*! Oh, I am *so* glad!... I'll tell Mr. Clifford—he was very anxious.... We were both so worried—we wondered.... Well, that's fine!... You are coming into town tomorrow morning, are you not, Mrs. Clifford?... Well, I thought I would meet you at the house.... There are a number of things I would like to go over with you.... I have all the information about your flight to South America.... Well, I made a reservation for you on the twenty-fifth, but there are planes almost every day.... Yes, I made all the appointments.... The hairdresser will see you at ten-thirty.... Bergdorf will give you a fitting at eleven-thirty.... The contractor will meet you at the shop at twelve-forty-five, and the electrician will be there with the fixtures.... Yes, the ladies will meet you at the Ritz for luncheon at one-fifteen.... They were *delighted* to come.... Yes—yes, Mrs. Clifford—I spoke to the man about the bicycle. It's coming on the four-twenty train, and I ordered a birthday cake—plain sponge—I thought they could all eat that.... Pink icing, and her name, and 'Happy Birthday', enough for thirty children.... And I got some nice little favours to put in the cake, Mrs. Clifford—I thought it would be amusing for them.... (*She listens*)

He is bringing her a puppy.... A puppy...a wire-haired puppy.... But that's what she wants—she begged her father for a puppy!... And he took a great deal of trouble about it.... He's got it up at the house.... He says he can't get to work in the morning—he's always playing with the puppy! It's the *loveliest* little dog you ever saw!... Oh, Mrs. Clifford—it would break her heart if you didn't let her have it!... But *why*, Mrs. Clifford?... Oh, but that doesn't take long—it's very little trouble...and I know you'll find him irresistible!... Well, you have to get used to so many things, Mrs. Clifford!...

Yes, I spoke to the man about your golf-clubs.... They
will be ready Friday. He said he could make the driver as
good as new, but he can't do anything with the mashie—it's
too badly broken—but Mr. Clifford has the pieces and he
was going to have it copied for you.... Well, he knew it was
your favourite club.... Well, that is just like Mr. Clifford, Mrs.
Clifford.... One inch shorter and suede wrapping so your hand
won't slip?... I'll make a note of that.... And could I *what*?...
Prizes for the party?... Thirty?... First, second, and third
prizes for boys and girls...between the ages of seven and ten?...
Yes, I could—perfectly—no trouble at all.... Four fishing-
rods...a new croquet set...ten pounds of candy...and some
more bathing caps?... I sent a lot last week.... They've lost
them?... Well, I'll send some more.... Some wool and some
knitting needles?... What kind of knitting needles, and what
kind of wool?... *All* kinds?... Very well.... Goodbye, Mrs.
Clifford.... Yes, I sent different sizes and colours and models....
They are very glad to have your order, and you can send
back what you don't require.... All right, Mrs. Clifford—call
me if you want anything, and I will see you in the morning....
Goodbye.... My love to the children.... (*She rings off*)

(*Lily looks in*)

Come in, Lily.... Who's there?... Oh, that nice little book
agent? I thought he was dead!... He's had pneumonia?...
Oh! Does he look very badly?... *Poor* little man!... I wonder
if he has anyone to look after him?... I think he told me once
he lived with his sister.... Tell him I'm very sorry I can't
see him now, but that we're glad he's well again.... And that
we are always wanting books.... And tell him to come down
and see us often.... There's a book we want right now—Mr.
Clifford was speaking about it yesterday—it's called *The
Psychology of Inflation*.... Never mind who wrote it—I guess
there's only one.... And then, I want a nice copy of *Alice in
Wonderland*.... Mr. Clifford was looking up some quotation
the other day.... He wanted it for a speech.... Something
from the Mad Tea Party—I couldn't for the life of me

remember it.... We ought to have a copy around the office, anyhow.... Tell him to send one down....

(*The telephone rings*)

Hello!... I'm sorry, Mr. Clifford is in conference.... Who is it, please?... Mr. Reynolds?... Mr. Reynolds of Boise, Idaho? Oh, good *morning*, Mr. Reynolds!... This is Miss Nichols speaking—Mr. Clifford's secretary.... Well, I've heard Mr. Clifford speak of you so often...and I'm sure he will want to see you.... But I couldn't very well disturb him now.... May I have him call you back?... And where may I reach you?... The Waldorf?... Room 1647.... What time would be convenient?... About two-thirty?... Oh yes, he'll be here then.... His children are in the country, now, but I'm sure he'll arrange it if possible.... I hope you'll be able to come down and see the office, Mr. Reynolds.... Oh, thank you?... Not at all—it's a pleasure.... Goodbye, Mr. Reynolds.... (*She hangs up. The telephone rings*)

Hello! Oh, hello, Jerry—have any luck?... What'd you get?... Third row, centre aisle?... Jerry, you're a wizard! I hear you can't get seats for that show for six weeks ahead.... That's *fine*!... Thanks. I'll send a boy up to the office some time this afternoon.... G'bye.... (*As she rings off she sees Mr. Haynes coming from Mr. Clifford's room*)

Good morning, Mr. Haynes. Someone will show you out. Good morning.... (*Mr. Haynes leaves. She turns to Mr. Clifford who has followed him from the inner office*)

Now, Mr. Clifford—you have about five minutes.... May I go over a few things with you?... I have some good news— Patsy's foot is perfectly all right.... Mrs. Clifford just called up.... Isn't that wonderful?... Well, they took an X-ray last night, and it seems no bones are broken at all.... Yes, the bandage is off and she's up and running around...and it doesn't hurt her any more.... Isn't that fortunate?... Mrs. Clifford?... She seemed very cheerful.... The boys—she didn't mention them.... I guess they're not up to any mischief yet!...

And then, your aunt, Mrs. Randlett, called, just the very moment you closed your door! Wasn't that lucky?... Yes— she was.... Yes, I did—I said just that.... I said a little more, and she seemed very satisfied—said she wouldn't worry— and she thanked you for asking after her rheumatism.... Oh yes, you *did*, Mr. Clifford.... She says she's much better and hopes to see you soon.... Oh, she sent you the sweetest message!... She said, 'Tell him I know my affairs are in the wisest, kindest hands in the world.' Wasn't that *lovely*?...

Then, your friend Mr. Reynolds called.... Mr. Reynolds? Oh, yes, you *do*, Mr. Clifford!—Mr. Reynolds of Boise, Idaho.... He was in your Company in France.... He had red hair and told funny stories.... You said he was one of the nicest men you ever knew!... Yes, *that's* the one—Mr. Reynolds. Well, he just called up to say he's in town, and on his way to Cape Cod with his seven children.... He seemed very cheerful.... No, Mrs. Reynolds is following next week.... He wanted her to have a little rest, so he brought the children.... Yes.... He would like you to call him at the Waldorf at two-thirty, this afternoon.... He sounded so nice on the telephone....

(*She opens a drawer in her desk, takes out three little boxes, and moves towards Mr. Clifford's desk*) Mr. Clifford—I have some watches here that I had sent down from Cartier, and Tiffany, and Marcus.... Well, you know—it's Mrs. Clifford's birthday tomorrow.... And I knew you wanted to give her a watch as she's lost hers.... I thought it would save you trouble...and the time was getting short.... Oh, there are so many to choose from, it's confusing!... Yes, of course—that is the most practical.... But I'm sure that *that* is the one Mrs. Clifford will prefer.... Well, it *is* the loveliest...and, of course, Mrs. Clifford always does like the best.... I think we know her taste by now!... Yes, I'll send it up to the house tonight.... Then, I ordered two dozen roses, Mr. Clifford, to be at the house first thing in the morning.... Mrs. Clifford is coming in to do some shopping—and the house seems to look so bare, with everything put away—so I thought a few flowers would make it more cheerful.... Well, you have so *much* on your mind—you can't think of everything....

The charities list? I have it all ready—but there's no time now.... Oh no, Mr. Clifford—it will take us at least two hours!... But you have two minutes, and I want to tell you about Jim Crosby.... Yes, everything is arranged.... I did exactly as you told me—I called the doctor at the Sanatorium, and he knew all about Fanny's case, as he's been in touch with the New York doctor. He was very much interested, and feels that six months will be all that's necessary.... He has a lovely room all ready, and he'd like to get her up there as quickly as possible.... Monday?... Jim to go with her?... And spend a week?... Oh! Mr. Clifford—how *wonderful*! You *would* think of that!... Yes, it will make all the difference if Jim can see the doctor and get Fanny settled.... You want to see Jim at two-thirty?... Would you mind if I speak to him first?... I'm afraid he's going to be rather overcome when he knows what you're doing.... He's an awfully sensitive boy.... (*A pause. She listens to him*)

No, Mr. Clifford—nothing of any importance.... I hate to tell you, but Mrs. Clifford has overdrawn her account again this month.... Well, it's all because of the shop.... You see— when Mrs. Clifford decided to re-decorate the shop, she took the money from her clothes account, and now, of course, the bills are coming in—for her South American clothes.... And there's no *money* there!... It *is*...and yet it seems so wise to put the money in the shop when Mrs. Clifford has made such a wonderful success of it.... She certainly *has*!... Everyone says it's the smartest hat shop in town.... Oh, she *does*!... She often speaks to me about it. She says she's never enjoyed anything so much.... And she seems so much *better* since she's had the shop.... Well, I guess work is good for everyone, Mr. Clifford.... It's a pity they all can't have it.... (*She suddenly breaks off and speaks urgently*)

It's time for you to start, Mr. Clifford.... Could you get a little rest after the dentist?... Shall I send Erickson?... Oh, Mr. Clifford—you know a massage rests you more than anything.... And you've been under such a strain.... Yes, about half past five?... Don't hurry, Mr. Clifford—you have plenty of time, and I'll be here when you come back.... (*She goes with him to the outer door as he leaves*)

(*The telephone rings*)

Hello!... Oh, good morning, Mrs. Mallory.... I'm sorry— Mr. Clifford has just left the office.... Well—he was a little late and he rushed off.... He'll not be here before two-thirty.... Yes, Mrs. Mallory—I know he's expecting you to dine with him tonight.... At the St. Regis, at seven-thirty, I believe.... And then you are going to see this new play called *Power*.... Oh, they say it's marvellous!... It *is*—but we got them!... Mr. Clifford generally gets what he wants, Mrs. Mallory!... I hear the play is remarkable—I hope you will enjoy it.... I'll tell him you called.... Goodbye, Mrs. Mallory.... I beg your pardon?... Oh, thank you.... Indeed I could!... Oh, I could find use for anything.... Yes, I have a number of friends...and I think they *are* about your size.... Yes.... I can understand.... One does.... Well, if it's convenient to you, Mrs. Mallory, I could come up some time, and bring a suitcase, and take the things, and tell you later who I give them to—if it would interest you!... Oh, I'll enjoy doing it.... And thank you so much!... Goodbye! (*She rings off*) What a wonderful woman!...

(*The telephone rings*)

Hello!... Yes, Mrs. Clifford.... Mr. Clifford has just this minute left the office.... I'm afraid I can't reach him...not before two-thirty.... You are motoring in tonight?... But, Mrs. Clifford—I'm afraid Mr. Clifford couldn't take you to the play tonight, because he's engaged.... No, it's an engagement he's had for some time.... I'm *sure* he couldn't break it.... Isn't that *too* bad!... Well, how about tomorrow night, Mrs. Clifford?... No, he's not coming to the country tomorrow. He has a very heavy day—a six-thirty meeting which will detain him—but he has nothing in the evening, and I'm sure he would like to go to the theatre. He always does when he's tired, and he will be *very* tired!... Exactly.... I was just thinking that you would really have more time than if you rushed back to the country after your busy day.... And then, if you went to bed early tonight, you would be more fresh for tomorrow.... Exactly!... Was there any play that you particularly wanted to see?... *Power?*... Oh, I hear that *Power* is really *very* poor, Mrs. Clifford.... Well, it *was* good, I believe—but it's not so good *now*.... There is a new play, Mrs. Clifford, called *The Question*.... It opened last night and was very well reviewed.... I know Mr. Clifford wants to see it.... Well, I think you are very wise, Mrs. Clifford.... It's lucky you thought of it, because I think it will be more satisfactory in every way.... Yes.... And I'll see you at the house in the morning.... Call me if you should want anything.... I will be here after two-thirty.... I will.... Goodbye, Mrs. Clifford.... You're welcome.... Goodbye.... (*She rings off*)

(*She at once picks up the telephone again*)

Lily, will you please ask Jim Crosby to come in and speak to me?... I want to get out to lunch, and I'm in a hurry.... Tell him I won't keep him a minute....

(*Jim Crosby enters. She greets him warmly and seriously*)

Hello, Jim!... Good morning.... Jim, I'm rushing out, and I just wanted to tell you that Mr. Clifford wants to see you in his office at half past two.... It's about Fanny.... Yes, he knows.... I had to tell him, Jim.... I know you didn't, but he said you looked worried about something and did I know what it was?... So I told him.... He said he wished he'd known before, but he said that you've got the very best doctor, and that you must do *exactly* what he says.... So he told me to get in touch with him, and make all the arrangements to get Fanny to the Sanatorium immediately.... The plan is for you to go up with her on Monday, and spend a week.... So you'll have a little holiday, and get Fanny settled, and see the doctor.... All the sanatorium expenses will be

paid from this office, so you won't have to worry about anything.... Now—so long and cheer up!... All your worries are
over!... Tell Fanny I'll come Saturday morning and help her
pack.... (*He leaves*)

Poor fellow!

(*She picks up the telephone*)

Hello! Worth 7–3259, please.... Hello! Is Mr. Hurley
there?... May I speak to him, please?... Hello, Charlie!...
(*Her voice now becomes soft and intimate*) Did you think I was
never going to call, dear?... Just got through.... I'm all right....
What?... Oh, no—it's gone—I took an aspirin, and we
had a very quiet morning, here.... I feel *fine*.... Where shall
we meet? The corner of Nassau and Pine is the quickest for
me.... And then we can go to that little French grill.... I've
got on my green hat.... What?... I won't *tell* you!... Don't
be *silly*!... Let me go—I'll be there all the sooner.... Yes, I
do. Goodbye....

(*She steps hurriedly to the outer door*)

Lily! Will you do me a favour?... I'm in an awful rush....
Will you call up Jerry and ask him to get two very good seats
for a play called *The Question* for tomorrow night.... And
then, please call the masseur, John Erickson, and tell him to
go to Mr. Clifford this afternoon at five-thirty, without fail....
I don't care *who* he's got, or *what* he's got.... He *must* be with
Mr. Clifford, at the house, at five-thirty.... And if anyone
calls, I'll be back in an hour. I'm just stepping out to lunch....

(*She has put on her hat and now hastens out of the office*)

II. MRS. CLIFFORD: IN THE MOTOR

*Mrs. Clifford stands at one side of the stage. She is waiting for
her motor outside a New York theatre. The play has just ended,
and the audience is streaming out of the doors of the theatre. She
wears a long rich evening robe, and as she waits, she moves or
staggers slightly as the people in the crowd push her about. She
looks at them coolly and contemptuously, and when she speaks*

it is in the cold, tired voice of unconcealed boredom and fatigue. Mr. Clifford stands at her side, looking for the car in the crowded traffic. She speaks first to the people against whom she is pushed, presently to a friend in the throng, then to her husband.

I *beg* your pardon. I'm *so* sorry. Somebody pushed me.... Tony—there's *no* use our both standing here—why don't you look for the car? I'll wait here.... (*She waits, but the pushing and crowding continue*)

I *beg* your pardon—I'm so sorry.... (*More pushing. Then she sees a friend*)

Hello, Elsie—I never saw you—where were you sitting?... Poor play, wasn't it? *Awfully* poor.... (*The pushing continues*) Excuse me—people keep pushing.... Elsie—are you going to be in town next week?... Well, I may come in on Thursday.... If you haven't anything better to do, why don't we have luncheon together?... I'll call you up.... Goodnight.... (*She calls to Mr. Clifford through the crowd*)

Here we are, Tony!... The car is coming up now.... Come on—follow me—hurry up!... (*She edges through the crowd*) I beg your pardon—may I get through, please? I'm sorry— my car's just coming up—excuse me—may I pass?... I *beg* your pardon.... (*She stoops to enter the car, seats herself, then settles back in the car and looks out of the window, yawning. Mr. Clifford has followed and now sits beside her. The car starts*)

Well, I can't say I think very much of *that* play.... Oh, I thought it was terribly poor.... Yes—it was rather well acted in spots—but I thought on the whole it was poor.... There certainly wasn't very much 'question' about it.... Well, I mean, the question was answered in the first act—one saw exactly what was going to happen.... I mean, one saw that his wife had neglected him—and that she was going to drive him straight into the arms of that soft and sentimental creature.... Oh! How I *loathe* that type of woman!... Pretty? Do you think she was pretty? Well—yes, if one *admires* that type....

(*Yawns*)... I suppose she *was*.... Well, I didn't enjoy it, any-way.... But I doubt if I could have enjoyed anything, even if it had been a wonderful play—I was so tired....

(*During what follows she stirs and sways slightly with the motion of the car*)

Oh, I've had a very exhausting sort of day.... I left the country very early this morning.... I got to the house just after you'd gone downtown.... Miss Nichols was there, and we went over a lot of tiresome things together.... I found your roses, which were lovely.... And the watch—it's a beauty— and it *goes*! Just what I wanted. Then, I started off on a dozen tiresome chores.... Oh, I had my hair washed and they did it very badly. Then I tried on a lot of clothes, and none of them fit.... They were perfectly hideous, anyway—I wish I'd never ordered them.... Then I had to meet the contractor at the shop and go over a lot of tiresome details about the re-decorating of the shop...choosing fixtures and things.... Then, I met Ethel and Joan for luncheon—we had the worst food I have ever put between my lips. It really was practi-cally uneatable.... Then I went downtown, on the subway, to a big wholesale place for some ribbon.... (*Yawns*)... Some *ribbon*. (*Loudly*)... Then, I came uptown and bought a lot of things I wanted—a lot of things I needed. Then, I went to the Club and ran into some women who had some very amusing gossip, so I lingered there, and got no rest at all....

Among other things I did this morning, I went over the flights to South America with Miss Nichols...and she's got something for me on the twenty-fifth.... That's about the time I meant to start, so I'll make my plans to go then....

Now, Tony, while I'm gone, you'll have to keep an eye on the children, and keep things more or less in order, because, I warn you, Mademoiselle and the tutor are absolutely *use-less*.... Mademoiselle?... She's an old *fool*.... Yes, she's *nice*— I know you like her.... I don't mind her.... The children love her, and she adores them.... But she has no real control over them—they do pretty much what they want.... They're much cleverer than she is, and as for the tutor—he's nothing but a boy himself—he needs watching as much as Peter and John.... Now, *please* don't spoil them, Tony.... Yes you *do*—you spoil them terribly.... You give them every blessed thing in the world they want.... Well, *that's* the way to spoil children.... That's the way to spoil *any*body...give them everything they want.... That's what you've always done—and you've *ruined* the children....

Well, anyway—please try and look after them a little.... And pay particular attention to John and that wretched boat you gave him.... Oh, I wish you'd never given him that boat.... Well, I don't think he's fit to have a boat.... You think he's so clever—and so plucky—and such a wonderful sailor.... I don't think he knows what he's doing *half* the time.... Did I tell you what happened on Thursday?... I don't know how I could forget—it nearly killed me.... It was the day of the race, and there was a tremendous wind.... All the little boys had two reefs in their sails—they all had another boy with them—and they all wore life-preservers. John wears no life-preserver—he says he's lost it.... He had no one to sail with him—he sailed alone.... He tells me that you told him that he could sail alone.... But you didn't tell him he could *race* alone?... Well, he *did*—and he carried full sail in that terrific wind.... Of course, he was miles ahead all the way—and they did tell me he had sailed a very remarkable race.... No—he *didn't* win it!... Now, wait—I'm speaking.... He *was* miles ahead and he *should* have won, but just before he reached the finishing line the mast was carried away!... The whole thing collapsed!... I wish you'd seen it! It was the most terrifying sight! I was quite far off—in a launch—and through the glasses I saw his little figure against the sky—and then apparently swept into the sea!... I went through ten minutes of absolute agony!... And they found him, if you please, all tangled in the ropes, covered with the sail—roaring with laughter!... Well, I *don't* think that kind of thing should be considered fun!... It's *far* too serious.... Something's going to happen to that child some day—and it's not going to be *my* fault!... I *beg* you to talk to him seriously.... I don't think he has *any* prudence—I don't think he has *any* judgement—and I don't think he's fit to have a boat! Well, I've had my say!...

And Peter's worse in his way, and it's all *your* fault.... Because you laugh at every blessed thing he does!... Oh, he's *not* so funny.... He made me so *cross* last week.... One night when you were in town I had some older people for dinner.... I wanted everything very nice and quiet.... The boys were supposed to be in bed and asleep.... And Peter had managed to crawl out on to the roof of the dining-room, and dropped an enormous bunch of lighted fire-crackers down the chimney on a string.... Go *off*?... Of *course* they went off—what do you suppose?... They made the most horrible noise and smell.... Old Mrs. Parker nearly fainted—Jackson dropped the potatoes.... And we had to finish dinner in the drawing-room.... Well, *I* don't think that's funny!... That kind of thing just *doesn't* amuse me!...

Now, please try and keep them at home, Tony....They seem to have got to an age where they think it's more fun to go out.... Well, why *should* they go out? They have every-thing in the world they could possibly want at home—*why* should they go out?... Well, I think that home is a place to stay in....

(*She sighs*) I honestly don't know *what* I should do if I couldn't get away for a little rest and change.... Oh, I don't know.... I'm just tired out.... My nerves are all on edge.... Oh, *I* don't know.... Just life, I suppose—everyday life—that's what gets you in the end.... I can't explain.... But you wouldn't understand—even if I could explain.... Because you *never* understand!... I'd like you to try my life for twenty-four hours and see how you feel!... I tell you, it's no joke—looking after four children, and three houses, and all the endless outside things that I have to consider from morning till night.... Besides my work—you never seem to think of *that*! You seem to forget I have the shop.... I sometimes think I'll give it up!...

Well—it's more of a strain than I bargained for.... It's a tremendous responsibility.... Yes, it's a success—a great success.... Yes, I enjoy it—I admit I enjoy it.... But the trouble with success is—it takes all your time.... And you can't do the things you really *want* to do!... Yet, I suppose I should miss it if I *didn't* have it.... What I really need is some very capable person to help me—that's the trouble.... I haven't got a really efficient assistant.... I mean—somebody who can take responsibility without being directed every minute.... Somebody like your Miss Nichols—she's exactly the person I need.... If you really loved me, you'd give me Miss Nichols—clever little thing....

I often wonder if Miss Nichols has any life of her own?... I bet you she'll never get married.... Well, I think she's absorbed in her work.... She's devoted to you—seems to be devoted to *all* the family.... She's always doing things for everybody—and seems to enjoy it.... She embarrassed me very much this morning when she asked me if I had any old clothes to give to some poor woman she knows, but I had nothing to give her at the moment, so I thought I'd just give her a cheque, and when I went to write it, I found I had no money in the bank!... So will you please put some in?... I know you think I'm very extravagant.... I suppose I *am*— but after all, one can only learn through mistakes.... That's the only way one learns anything, I suppose—through mistakes—and now I find that I made a very stupid mistake when I decorated the shop in French Eighteenth Century.... Why?... It's perfectly obvious *why*.... Because the Eighteenth Century is absolutely finished!... You'll never see it again!... Oh, no—one must be modern now if one expects to attract attention to a shop.... You simply *must* be modern— and I must say that the shop is going to be very attractive....

Well, the floor is black marble, and the ceiling and the walls are black mirrors.... And all the details—the fixtures, the furniture, everything—are steel.... The whole thing is just marble and glass and steel.... It's really adorable!... I wish you'd look in now and then, and see how things go on....

There are lots of things I want you to do while I'm away.... But I'm too tired to think of them now.... Oh, I think I'll be home by the end of the month.... I'd like to stay on...and fly over the Andes and come up the West Coast.... They say it's wonderful.... But I feel I shouldn't because then *you* won't get away—because you're so *stuffy* and conscientious.... You say you can't leave the children unless I'm at home—which is so silly.... Because Mademoiselle and the tutor are here... and they're perfectly capable of looking after the children!... After all—*that's* why we have them...to give us our freedom.... Well—I'll get Miss Nichols to look up flights tomorrow.... (*She looks, yawning, out of the car window*)

Oh, we're nearly home, thank heaven.... There's the old Museum! I'm ashamed to say I've not been inside the Museum for nearly a year.... Huh—I'll bet *you've* not been there for about *fifteen* years!... I remember we used to go sometimes...when we were engaged.... Oh, I remember when you were crazy about art, and music, and poetry.... (*Yawns*) But you seem to have lost it all.... Well, one *does*, I guess... lose things...lose one's taste for things.... We seem to be home.... Oh, I'm *so* tired—pull me up, will you?...

(*She rises in a bent posture, stoops, and steps out of the car. She stands waiting a moment, then asks with grudging curiosity*)

Where are you going?... For a walk?... Crazy idea!... Yes, it *is* a lovely night.... But I'm too tired—I'm going straight to bed.... Goodnight!...

(*As she walks to the house door she pauses and calls*)

Oh—Tony.... Will you please remember to leave your door open tonight?... Don't forget—it makes a nice draught through.... Goodnight!

(*She turns to enter the house, saying to the chauffeur*)

Goodnight, James.

III. AT MRS. MALLORY'S

A large upholstered arm-chair, in which Mr. Clifford is sitting, is turned with its back to the audience. On one of its arms Mrs. Mallory sits, looking down at Mr. Clifford as they talk. She is quiet, graceful, warm and gentle of voice, and wears a long beautiful scarf around her shoulders and over her evening dress. She bends gently and comfortingly above Mr. Clifford as she speaks.

Tired, my love?... But Tony, think what you've done in the last two days!... But darling, what a triumph!... And you must have such a sense of relief, as well as pride.... Oh, I wish I'd been there!... Standing among the men...watching their faces as they listened...seen their mood changing...heard them laugh when you told that story!... And in the end, they cheered?... Oh, I'm so *proud* of you!... Well, thank goodness that worry is over!... I wish all your worries would vanish as easily.... Do they?... It *is* peaceful here....

Oh, darling—before I forget.... Do you think you'll be in town next Thursday night?... There's the most lovely concert at the Stadium—would you like to go?... Wonderful programme—Brahms, and Schubert—and that lovely Debussy.... Yes, I have the tickets....

Am I tired?... No, why should I be tired?... I've had a lovely day.... I took a long walk this afternoon and stopped in at the Museum, and wished you were there with me when I looked at all our favourite things.... Then your Miss Nichols came in to collect some clothes I had for Jim Crosby's wife...and we had tea together.... And she made me roar with laughter—how *could* you forget to tell me about Peter dropping those fire-crackers down the chimney!... What a rascal!... And about Johnny nearly winning the race!... What a wonderful boy!...

Weren't you proud of him?... Oh, I *know* you were!... Oh, he'll be all right—don't worry!... But he's learned his lesson.... He'll not do such a thing again.... I bet you were

just as brave, and *just* as rash as Johnny.... And *just* as mis-
chievous as Peter...and that you drove *your* mother nearly
crazy!... You must have been the most adorable little boy....
I wish I'd known you when you were a little boy....

Oh, Tony—Miss Nichols told me about her engagement
and asked me to the wedding.... I was *so* pleased!... She
seems very much in love.... Do you know the young man?...
Is he good enough for her?... Oh, I'm *so* glad—then he has
a real future.... They ought to have a very interesting life....
Wonderful girl!... What *are* you going to do without her?...
(*She listens*)

What?... Oh, Tony.... Don't let's discuss it any more....
But darling, we're so happy—it's so perfect as it is.... But
darling—you know how I feel.... Some day...perhaps... (*A
pause as she listens*)

But Tony...think what we have.... And think what we
might lose.... Yes.... It is.... After all.... So different!...
How often we've said that.... You and I don't have to face
the challenge of everyday life.... Well, perhaps—someday...
when the children are older—when they don't need you so
much...and might understand....

Do you remember the time we stood on the shore and
watched the tide come in?... Remember what I said?... Well,
hasn't it all been true?... We *are*!... It *is*!... You *have*!...
Have I?... Oh, Tony!... *Have* I?

(*She falls into his arms*)

CURTAIN

VIVE LA FRANCE!
1940

-»» ✪ «««

*Night has fallen on a beach in Brittany in the autumn of
1940, but stars shine overhead in the darkness. A young
Frenchwoman comes up stealthily, speaking in a low cautious
voice to an old woman who follows her, the mother of her
husband Victor, who is planning to escape by night from
German-occupied France in a rowing boat across the Channel to England. She wears the garb of the Breton country
people—a black woollen dress, with a shawl tied about her
head and throat. Speaking at first scarcely above a whisper,
she cautions the old woman to follow her to the place
arranged for Victor's departure. Presently they sit down,
she on the sand, the Mother on a rock, to await his coming
with his companions. The air is ominously still and an
almost complete darkness covers the scene.*

Par ici, ma mère, par ici! Oui, c'est l'endroit, je suis sûre. Je
me rappelle, le rocher était là!... Victor m'a dit qu'ils em-
barqueront de ce côté de la plage—car entre dix heures et
demie et onze heures on est sûr de ne pas rencontrer la
patrouille allemande.... Oh oui, on est sûr.... Mon Dieu, on
a bien étudié tout ça.... Non, pour une bonne demi-heure
il n'y aura aucun danger.... Jean et Christophe viendront
de ce côté embarquer avec lui. Georges est avec Victor....
Ils sont en train de mettre les dernières choses dans le bateau
— en face de la maison du vieux pêcheur, tu sais — le vieux
Louis Breton, qui habite là-bas, où la plage est complètement cachée de la route.... Oh, on mettra l'ancre, et la voile,
et les ceintures de sauvetage — toutes sortes de choses
dont ils auront besoin pour le voyage.... Non, personne que

nous.... Victor a défendu à leurs femmes de venir.... Il ne veut personne — que toi et moi!... Nous pouvons nous asseoir ici — attendre le bateau.... Mets-toi là, sur le rocher.... Je vais me mettre ici sur le sable à tes pieds.... (*She sits down on the sand while the Mother sits on a rock*) Comme ça.... Non, je suis bien.... Non, je n'ai pas froid. J'ai ma jupe de laine et mon châle — j'ai chaud....

Oh, quelle nuit obscure — sans étoiles — aucune étoile.... Ça vaut mieux — il y aura moins de danger sans étoiles.... La mer est calme, mais il y a du vent au large — le vent du sud-ouest — le vent de terre.... Oh, c'est bien! Victor m'a dit que si le vent du sud-ouest continue il compte faire la traversée en deux jours.... Tu sais, maman, il paraît que nous sommes juste en face de la côte de Cornouaille.... Il paraît qu'il y a un petit promontoire tout près de Falmouth.... Victor m'a montré sur la carte.... C'est là que plusieurs Français ont déjà debarqué.... C'est là où il espère trouver des amis, et c'est là où il aura des renseignements pour prendre contact avec l'armée....

Oh, je me demande si j'ai pensé à tout?... Son sac était comble — il n'y avait pas un coin pour mettre davantage!... Eh bien, j'ai mis deux paires de chaussettes, les bleues que tu viens de finir — elles sont belles!... Et le vieux tricot de son père que j'ai raccommodé pour la dixième fois. Tellement il aime ce vieux tricot — et puis un cache-nez de laine bien chaud.... Il emporte des papiers très secrets, tu sais, que j'ai cousus dans la doublure de ses pantalons, et d'autres que j'ai collés entre les semelles de ses bottes.... Oh, oui, il porte deux pantalons, deux paires de chaussettes, un tricot, un cache-nez, des gants de laine.... Il aura bien chaud.... Ne t'inquiète pas.

Puis, j'ai mis son tabac, un bon morceau de fromage, une bouteille de vin que le curé m'a donnée.... Comme il est généreux!... Il m'a donné une bouteille de Bordeaux pour mettre dans le sac de Victor pour emporter en Angleterre.... Du pain? Ah, oui, il y a un grand sac de pain, et un peu de viande aussi, que le boucher m'a donnée.... Tout ça, il l'a caché à la maison du vieux pêcheur — tout ça il mettra dans le bateau avant de venir ici pour faire embarquer les autres....

Dis-moi, ma mère.... Quand ton mari t'a quittée, en dix-neuf cent quatorze, pour aller au front—au moment de l'adieu, tu as pleuré?... Crois-tu que je puisse être aussi courageuse?... Mimi a pleuré toute cette nuit.... Elle ne veut pas que Georges s'en aille.... Moi non plus.... Mais je lui ai dit : la guerre n'est pas finie.... Il faut se battre.... Et puis, je lui ai dit : veux-tu que tes enfants soient des Boches?... Et on n'a pas le droit de penser à soi-même?... C'est vrai.... Oui.... Je sais.... Tu as raison.... Au moment de la guerre, personne n'a le droit de penser à soi-même.... C'est Victor qui me l'a dit — il m'a dit presque les mêmes mots.... Oui, je comprends.... Toi qui as passé par là, tu m'aideras.... Oh, je ne pleure pas.... Nous avons fait nos adieux — et je lui ai promis de ne plus pleurer!...

Chut — tu entends quelqu'un?... (*She whispers anxiously*) Oui — j'entends des voix d'hommes.... Écoute!... N'aie pas peur.... Ne t'inquiète pas.... Ça doit être Jean et Christophe.... Reste là.... Je vais aller voir.... C'est toi, Jean? C'est toi, Christophe?... Ah, grâce à Dieu.... (*The two men come up*) J'étais un peu effrayée.... Quelle heure est-il?... Ah, déjà?... Il doit arriver bientôt. Chut — il me semble que j'entends des rames.... Oui, par là.... Non, plus à droite.... Tu entends? Par là, maintenant, toujours à droite.... Le voilà, le bateau — comme un spectre.... Ça touche le sable. Va l'aider un peu, Jean.... Va l'aider un peu.... Le bateau est là, maman, Victor vient d'arriver.... Non, il n'aura pas un instant.... Il m'a dit qu'il fallait partir aussitôt pour ne pas manquer la marée et le vent.... Il approche....

(*Victor comes up to them*)

Alors — ça va? Tout est en ordre? Il faut partir tout de suite?... Tu as tout ce qu'il te faut? Tu as pensé à tout?... Ta montre dans ta poche?... À droite?... La boussole? Où est la boussole?... Facile à prendre?... La lampe électrique

marche bien?... Tu as les deux — ah, tant mieux.... Tu as
bien mis le sac de pain pour qu'il ne se mouille pas?...

Mets ton cache-nez autour du cou... (*She winds his scarf
firmly around his neck*) Laisse-moi le faire.... Comme ça....
Tu as bien chaud?... Il faut partir tout de suite.... Alors —
tu trouveras moyen de m'écrire?... Bientôt, j'espère.... Je
tâcherai.... Oui, j'ai ton adresse.... Oh, ne t'inquiète pas pour
nous — nous nous arrangerons bien, ta mère et moi — et le
petit.... Il dormait quand j'ai quitté la maison.... Oui, je le
soignerai comme si tu étais là.... Je me souviendrai de tout ce
que tu m'as dit.... Je ne le gâterai pas.... Je te promets....
Il sera un brave garçon — il sera toujours ton fils....

Et je soignerai bien le potager.... Et le vieux cheval.... Et
le pauvre chien.... Il hurlait quand j'ai quitté la maison —
il sait que tu pars!... Et nos pommiers — et nos roses....
(*She tells him to say goodbye to his Mother*) V'là ta mère....
Va lui dire adieu — je te laisse.... Maman, Victor veut t'em-
brasser, il veut te dire adieu.... Va — va toute seule — je te
laisse....

(*She waits apart while Victor makes his farewell with his
Mother. Presently he comes back to her*)
Alors.... Oui. Oui — je te promets. Mais tu reviendras....
Je suis sûre!... Tu reviendras!... Oui, ils viennent.... Ils
t'appellent — il faut que tu partes.... Va maintenant!... Va —
je t'en supplie!... Que Dieu te garde!... Au revoir!... (*She
embraces him. He goes off in the boat*) Chut!... Non — il ne
veut pas.... Il m'a défendu d'approcher le bord de l'eau....
(*To the Mother*) Il veut que je reste avec toi.... Tiens ma
main.... Écoute — on ne voit rien. Écoute — je n'entends
plus les rames.... Il est parti.... Viens — rentrons à la maison.
Il faut que nous prenions la petite route pour éviter la
patrouille allemande.... Tu sais, le petit sentier qui passe par
les champs.... Je viens — va en avant.... Je viens, je viens....

(*As they go off, she suddenly stops in excitement, looking up
at the night sky*)
Maman, viens vite, viens vite! Des avions qui arrivent —

oh v'là un autre — un autre!... (*She points upwards to the planes passing overhead*) Non, ce ne sont pas des Boches.... Ce sont des Anglais — c'est la R.A.F.!... La R.A.F. — une escadrille anglaise!... Des bombardiers volant vers l'est!... Allez-y! Bonne chance, les gars! Vive la France!!

(*She waves her shawl wildly and cries towards the sky as the English planes fly towards the East through the night*)

THE RETURN

I. MRS. DREW

She enters the living-room of her house in the country, a dignified young woman in her thirties, wearing a grey flannel suit. She turns to speak to Mrs. Hancock, the village postmistress, who is following her and who has come to help her resume occupancy of the house after its war-time tenants have left it. The time is the end of the Second World War, and the place is England.

Oh, it's so lovely to be in the cottage again.... (*She turns, looking all about, then stops, her smile fading to a look of amazement*)... Mrs. Hancock—look what they've done! Have you ever *seen* such disorder?... When did the tenants leave?... Only last night? And did they just walk out leaving it like this?... But they've moved all the furniture—changed the pictures—everything! Why, I'd never recognize the room!... They might at least have put things back more or less the way they found them!... Is it *all* as bad as this? All the same frightful disorder?... Our room? The nursery? The kitchen? (*She looks into other rooms, exclaiming*) Why, they've just thrown things about.... Oh, dear!... And it's all so dirty— look at the curtains, all torn and filthy.... And look at our lovely table—scratched and burnt with cigarette-ends.... And the lamp—see, Mrs. Hancock, my favourite lamp—broken!... Oh, I wish I'd never let the cottage. I'd no idea tenants could be so destructive! Of course, I wouldn't mind so much if I had more time.... But I can never get it cleaned by Wednesday!... You see, I only got the telegram last night saying that Johnny was flying home next week.... So I rushed down today to see if you could find someone to clean the cottage—and you say there is really no one?... Everyone is worked to death and has no free time?... If only I could stay —but I promised the hospital I'd work until Wednesday, and I must get back and be on duty by five-thirty today.... Yes....

You see, when I got Johnny's first letter after his release, he said it would be the end of June before he got home.... So I notified the tenants, and planned to come down next week with little David, and work quietly getting the cottage in order, having it all perfect by the time Johnny arrived.... Then, last night comes the wire saying he's got a chance to fly, and is arriving on Wednesday!... I don't like to ask the hospital to let me off.... But even if I could come, I could never move all the furniture, and get the rooms cleaned in three days! It would take at least a week!... Oh, dear—I really don't know what to do!... Johnny will be broken-hearted.

You see, he thinks we're already living here. I got a letter only last Monday. (*She takes a letter from her pocket and reads*) He says: 'I'm so glad the tenants are leaving the cottage so that you can move down from London, for I count on meeting you and David there. I shall let you know just when to expect me, though I fear it will not be before the end of June, but please be there, standing in the doorway as you were when I went away—and as I've seen you—' (*She stops*) You see—in all his letters, ever since he was captured at Dunkirk —from all the prison-camps, he's written of the cottage and the garden, and said it's helped more than anything to picture it all. He said that often when he was sitting on a pile of dirt, looking at barbed wire, he'd imagine he was walking through the rooms, sitting in his big chair by the fire, reading, or watching me count stitches in the baby's jersey.... Or he'd pretend he was working in the garden with David at his heels, pulling all his flowers.... Then he said sometimes he'd imagine he was fishing with Mr. Jones—or playing darts with Jim and Billy Boots.... Or wandering into the pub, and talking politics and fertilizers with the men.... I know he'll want to do all those things as soon as he gets back.... And he'll expect to find everything the same, just as he remembers it—all lovely and clean and cosy and comfortable, with all the familiar things about.... And full of flowers!... Look at this mess! If I tell him, he'll probably want to come down and clean it with me!... But I know he shouldn't work.... Oh, his leg is still very bad, I believe. I know he needs a rest, and he does want to be here so terribly.... And little David counts on meeting his father here.... We had such lovely plans!

Oh, dear!... No—I'll just give it up. I don't think I can let him see it all this way.... We'll just wait at the flat—lucky we have those two rooms—and David will stay at his grand-mother's until you can find someone to do the heavy work and get it in some sort of order—at least clean—and then we'll come and do the little things ourselves.... Never! mind... It might be worse. At least we know we have a house to come to, so I shouldn't grumble. So just lock up again and keep the key.... I'll let you know what we decide.... Thank you for coming.... I know you are.... But, dear Mrs. Han-cock, you *couldn't* have known.... Don't worry. It can't be helped.... I must run—I have to take the three o'clock train—but I want to have a look at the garden—

(*She hears the telephone*) Hello—the telephone!... How funny—no one knows I'm here, except the porter at the flat.... I told him I was coming down for the afternoon.... The hospital knows—

(*She picks up the telephone*) Hello!... No one answers.... Hello! Yes, this is Mrs. Drew.... Trunk call? Yes?... Heavens—I hope nothing has happened—that he can't come after all.... Hello! I'm waiting.... (*To Mrs. Hancock*) Did they leave a list of the things they broke or lost, do you sup-pose?... (*Into the telephone*) Hello?... Yes?... *Johnny!* Where *are* you?... You're in *England*?... Oh, Johnny—I can't believe it!... You *flew*?... Are you all right?... Sure?... Yes, I am.... Yes, he is.... We are.... Oh, Johnny—does it?... So does yours.... How is your leg, darling?... Sure?... Yes.... Oh, it's lovely!... Yes—just the same.... Everything is just the same.... Where are you?... Actually?... But you can't get here tonight, darling.... There's no train.... But I'm coming up to London—now.... Yes.... I was just starting for the station when you called.... You arrive at seven?... Oh, I'll be there well before you.... Shall I come to Victoria?... You'd rather I waited at the flat?... All right.... Yes, David's there.... We'll both be there.... Oh, Johnny, it won't be long now.... Yes.... Yes.... I will!... Do be careful of your leg, darling.... Don't run for the train.... Yes, I am.... Goodbye.... I must go.... I will.... Yes—we'll be waiting.... Oh, Johnny!...

(*She rings off, then turns again to Mrs. Hancock*)

He's here! He landed in Westcott this morning and is coming up to London by the afternoon train.... Oh, I can't take it in.... Isn't it wonderful?... Oh, *nothing* matters now! I don't mind *where* we meet or *where* we live.... Just having him back is all that matters!... It was silly of me to take on so about the cottage. I feel rather ashamed.... I could laugh about it now—it seems so unimportant.... Oh, he won't mind. Johnny doesn't get fussed over things the way I do!... We shall be happy wherever we are—and I'll let you know when we decide to come down.... Thank you for coming here with me—I know how busy you are, and you must get back to the post office. And I must run for the train!... I'm so excited, I shall probably run to London if I miss it!... Bless you, darling Mrs. Hancock!... And thank you again!... Isn't it *wonderful*!... I will.... He'll be asking for you, I know.... Goodbye! Give my love to everyone in the village and tell them our news, and say that we shall be coming soon.... Goodbye!

II. MRS. HANCOCK

She is a cheerful, ample woman of about fifty, and as she enters, leading a group of other village women, she smiles and talks heartily. She has a plain low hat on her head, wears a large

*cleaning-apron that covers her arms and dress, and carries a
dust cloth as she guides the women into the same living-room she
and Mrs. Drew have recently inspected.*

Come in—come along, girls.... All ready for you!... I was
just doing a bit of last minute polishing.... D'you think it all
looks nice?... Yes, everything's in order now.... Just the tea-
things to get ready.... And I thought it would be ever so nice
if you girls did the tea, as you weren't here last night. Come
along, now—we haven't got too much time!... Put a match
to the fire, Maggie.... Oh, it's going to be a cool evening, and
I want it warm and cosy when they come.... I can't do much
walking with my bruised knee.... What a fool I was—falling
down last night!... Didn't you hear? When I was scrubbing
the kitchen floor! I thought I'd got it all done, but it seems
I left a little pool of soapy water.... And I came running along,
and slipped and fell, and thought I'd broke my leg.... Oh,
no! It's not broken—but I've got a bruise on my knee that
looks like a plum.... So I'll sit here and order you all about!...
Put the kettle on, Ethel!... No, it's not too early, and the
fire's burning nicely....

(*Mrs. Dodd comes in at the door with a bunch of flowers*)

Come in—oh, come in, Mrs. Dodd.... What lovely wall-
flowers! From your garden?... They *are* lovely!... Nellie will
arrange them. There's a pretty yellow glass vase, Nellie....
They'd look ever so nice on the table by the sofa.... Oh, and
let's put the yellow pansies Mrs. Moggridge brought in the
little blue bowl.... And then fetch a vase for the daisies Mr.
Jones left in a pail in the larder this morning.... He's gone
to the station to help with their luggage and I said I'd arrange
the daisies.... I nearly forgot them!... There on the table by
the Captain's chair.... Sit down, Mrs. Dodd.... Wasn't it
lucky I was home last night when the wire came?... Oh, you
didn't see it?... We missed you—but I knew you had to stay
with the baby.... Is he better?... That's good.... Here it is....
Maggie—show the wire to Mrs. Dodd.... Everyone's been

reading it…. Haven't you got your glasses?… Well, I'll read it to you. Everybody always brings things to me to read…. They forget their glasses—or have *lost* their glasses—or *broke* their glasses…. I am lucky—I don't need glasses!… I do hope I never have to use 'em….

(*She holds the telegram at arm's length and reads*) 'John insists on coming down after all. We shall be arriving to-morrow about six. Please leave the key in the usual place.'… That means under the mat…. So they'll be coming by the three o'clock train…. The tea-cloth is on the sideboard, Agnes. Mrs. Moggridge'll give you a hand with it. Get it nice and smooth, dearie…. It's not quite straight—the embroidered bits go in the corners…. That's better—*that's* it…. Beautiful, isn't it?… Her favourite, I believe. They brought it back from Italy where they went on their honeymoon. I know she values it very highly….

Well, you see, I was just home from the post office, Mrs. Dodd, and I was having a cup of tea, and Mrs. Barton and Mrs. Jones had popped in for a chat…. And I'd been telling them of the awful state of things at the cottage…. Come, girls —get on with the tea-table…. Put the bowl of roses in the centre, Ethel, then put the candlesticks on the table, close to the roses…. Be sure to get them straight…. They're not opposite…. *That's* better…. Now, fetch the cups and saucers and the plates, Emily…. Careful, dear!… You know, that tea-set belonged to Mrs. Drew's grandmother…. It *is* lovely!… Spode, I believe—Spode…. She never uses it, but I thought this was an occasion so I got it out….

Well, I never did like the tenants…. And you can't imagine how upset it all was…. Are you cutting the bread, Mrs. Grey?… So, the minute I read the wire, they said, 'Why not go to the cottage tonight and put it right to surprise them?… We can't let the Captain come back to such a home, after all he's been through'…. Think of it—five years in prison camps…. Not to speak of *her*, working in the London hospital all through the blitz…. So, when Mrs. Barton suggested going,

I was ever so pleased.... I had the very same idea, myself.... I could have cried yesterday when I saw her so disappointed.... I know they both had their hearts set on meeting here.... Oh! (*She turns to the girls*) There's a jar of strawberry jam on the piano, Maggie.... Put it on the table, on a plate, and with a spoon.... No—don't turn it out. That's wasteful. Leave it in the jar.... Mrs. Luke brought it in this morning.... Lucky —she just had half a jar left....

So we rushed out, you see, and told my husband and Mr. Jones and Mr. Barton who were smoking their pipes by the gate, and Mr. Jones said, 'It'll seem like old times to have 'em back. They can't come soon enough to suit me.' He and the Captain were always great pals—always chaffing each other and going off fishing together.... And Mr. Barton said how lucky it was the week-end, so we all had the time.... The children playing about the village were so excited when they heard the news, and ran along from house to house telling all the neighbours.... And we got Jim and Billy Boots right away, so we were seven.... Then we collected brooms and pails and mops and rags—and soap and powder, and we all came along....

(*She sees Mrs. Slater at the door*) Come in, Mrs. Slater.... Have you brought the scones?... Oh, look! They *are* beauties!... Fetch the muffin-dish, Maggie, and put them near the fire.... Sit down, Mrs. Slater.... I was telling Mrs. Dodd about last night.... How we *worked*! First the men moved all the furniture back in place.... And then we started in to sweep and scrub and scour and polish!... (*There is a knock*) Come in!... Is that you, Auntie?... Come along!... Now, what have you got under that cloth?... Oh! Look what Auntie's brought.... A cake!... Look, everybody!... Come and see the cake! Oh, what a beautiful cake—with raisins!... However did you get the raisins?... You got a parcel?... From New York?... Now, *who* sent you a parcel?... Oh, that American friend of Mrs. Drew's who was staying here before the war?... How kind of her!... Fancy her remembering!...

Fancy her thinking of us so far away!... Don't touch!...
Watcha' doin', dearie?... Well, you may smell it, but don't
touch!... What?... Oh—yes, you may have that little raisin
on the edge of the plate....

Sit down, Auntie dear.... I was telling Mrs. Dodd about
last night, for she missed all the fun.... Well, all the while
we was working, others popped in to help, and we had a
crowd in here.... Rushing about, bumping into each other
with pails and rags.... We was all talking at once.... Borrow-
ing the soap, laughing and giving orders and criticizing—and
doing things over that somebody had already done!... (*She
sees Mrs. Boots come in, carrying a bouquet*) Hello, Mrs.
Boots!... Oh, what gorgeous peonies—they're an answer to
prayer.... I saw them in your garden this morning and hoped
you'd bring them.... Agnes—fetch that tall white vase for
Mrs. Boots's peonies.... I should put them on the bookcase,
I think.... Did you bring the tea?... Splendid!... And sugar
too! Oh, lovely! We have so much sugar. Agnes brought some,
and Emily's mother sent some, and Mrs. Jones and Mrs.
Barton and I each brought a little.... The sugar basin must
be nearly full!... Put it all in together, dearie.... Mind! Don't
spill a grain!...

Well, Mrs. Moggridge, scrubbing the bathroom, started
singing old songs, and we all took it up.... You never *heard*
such a noise!... Getting the verses mixed up and everyone
singing off-key in the different rooms.... How we laughed!...
Is the kettle boiling yet, girls? The fire is going nicely now....
We might put on another small bit of wood.... Yes, there's
plenty—Billy Boots brought a basketful.... You see, with so
many to help, you'd be surprised how quickly we got everything in order.... How late did we work?... How late did we
work, Mrs. Moggridge?... Must have been a little past two....
Then, some of us came this morning and hung fresh curtains.... They *do* look nice.... Oh, she had a clean set put
away.... Mrs. Drew always had her house looking so nice—
she's a wonderful little housekeeper.... I always said her

house looked like Mrs. Drew.... Funny, isn't it?... Then, I
fetched the linen from the trunk, and aired it, and made the
beds.... By the way, Dolly—did you say you was bringing a
little milk?... Oh, good!... Put it in the jug now, dear....
There it is on the table.... Mr. Slater, the station-master,
saw the lights on his way home last night, so he stopped in
to see what was going on. I rushed at him with a rag, nearly
knocked him over.... Did he tell you, Mrs. Slater?... And he
got right to work and cleaned the grate and the kitchen stove.
He did a beautiful job.... He said he'd tell the Captain when
he saw him at the station this afternoon what a pity he was
coming home to such a dirty house!... What? Who did the
brasses?... Mrs. Barton!... They *do* look beautiful!... Mrs.
Barton's brasses are always beautiful.... No one can do
brasses like Mrs. Barton. She had a bit of old red flannel....
She wouldn't lend it to anyone for fear of losing it!... So I
whispered to everyone to bring her the brasses—and she was
sitting on the floor all night polishing brasses!... Then, I
fetched down some ornaments that had been put away, and
photographs of the family.... What I knew they'd like to have
about when they came home.... I do hope I've put them in
the right places.... I remember her mother was on that table
by the sofa, and her father was always standing on the bookcase with his horse.... And that one of the Captain as a boy
was over there, on that table with the little black elephant
beside him.... Isn't David the image of his father at that
age?... I never noticed the likeness before.... I don't know if
they're bringing the boy, but I got the nursery in order as
well as I could....

It must be nearly time for them to be coming.... There's
the church bells striking six. I think I'll light the candles
now.... I know it's wasteful, but they look so pretty!... They
had just four left at the grocery, and Mr. Barton brought
them over this morning. Give me a match, dearie.... Thank
you. (*She lights the candles*) You see, Mrs. Drew gave me her
silver candlesticks to keep safe for her, so I polished them up.

I thought she'd be pleased to see them again.... I believe they was a wedding-present from her brother....

Yes, Africa, I believe—wasn't it Africa?... The tanks.... Oh, he *was*!... Oh, they were—he often came here.... Here are the matches, dear.... It's the only box we have, so put them on the table by the Captain's chair.... Now—let's see! There's bread and jam.... Who put the honey here?... No, dear—I brought that for their breakfast—they can't have jam *and* honey too.... Put it on the sideboard.... Leave the scones by the fire—they'll keep warmer there.... Who brought the eggs? Three eggs! *Where* did they come from?... Your granddad sent them?... How lovely! Three eggs to boil!... Then there are four ginger biscuits, and Auntie's cake!... I wish we could have buttered the bread for a treat. But never mind.... We have Mrs. Slater's lovely scones. It's a gorgeous tea! It *does* look pretty.... See how the china shines, and see the little roses reflected in the silver!... What, dearie?... A rose for her dressing-table? Yes—take that one!... Pull it out carefully—that's right. Put it in that tiny glass vase.... They're waitin' for Mr. Slater and the luggage....

(*She looks about the room*) Oh, it *does* look cosy.... So cheerful and bright.... You've done the flowers beautiful, girls.... The azaleas on the piano are a picture, Ethel.... I hope we've thought of everything. I hope they'll be pleased.... Did you finish the bathroom, Mrs. Moggridge?... Is the plug working all right? Jimmy Boots was fussing over it last night.... Plenty of towels?... And the bit of soap? Mrs. Drew sent me a piece last Christmas.... Lucky I'd never used it. I always try and keep a bit of soap for an emergency!... Now watch the time....

Oh, Maggie—here's the key.... Lock the door and put it under the mat like she said I was to.... Now draw the curtains. They mustn't see the light as they come up the path, nor see us walking away.... No, leave them open on the garden side—the sunlight looks so pretty on the cabbages.... No, dear, you mustn't peek through.... No one must look but me!... I'll watch through a tiny crack in the curtains and tell you when it's time to start.... Remember, we're all to go to Mrs. Jones's house. She'll give us a cup of tea, and we'll talk it all over!... You'd better all gather at the kitchen door.... And don't talk until you're well away from the house. They mustn't see us, or hear us creeping away!...

(*She stands by the curtain, peering out over the audience*) Here they come!... They're coming up the road.... All three!... The Captain is limping badly.... It seems his leg never got right.... He broke it, you know, that time he tried to escape.... And then he had to walk some three hundred miles.... He seems taller than ever—but dreadfully thin.... He's got his arm around her.... Little David is running ahead.... He's got on his father's cap—he *does* look funny!... Now they're nearly at the gate.... Stand by the door now, and be ready to go—but don't start till I tell you.... Now they're coming up the path.... I wish you could see their faces.... I feel I shouldn't be looking.... The Captain's got the same beautiful smile.... She's looking up at him and laughing.... They're both laughing!... Oh, they seem so happy, I could cry my heart out!... Now they're almost at the door.... Little David's looking for the key. He can't find it!... Now he's got it.... Now remember keep together and go out quietly—and don't talk.... Wait a minute—not yet.... They're in!... I'm coming!... *Shh!*

(*She places the third chair at the table as she crosses the stage, limping, with her finger on her lips. Then she silently leaves the room*)

APPENDIX

I. *Stage Requirements for the Monologues of Ruth Draper*

The following properties were those Ruth Draper used in her performances of the monologues throughout her career. The stage or platform was otherwise bare, cyclorama curtains of a grey, light brown, or neutral colour forming the only background for the sketches. She kept her own sets of these curtains in New York and London for her theatre seasons in America and England, elsewhere using whatever curtains or background the local theatre, hall, or house provided. A few of the following properties—a limousine-seat for *Three Women and Mr. Clifford*, the Renaissance benches for *At the Court of Philip IV*, a chaise-longue for *The Italian Lesson*—were also part of her equipment when she went on tours of the larger theatres, but more often she used local properties supplied by her manager or sponsors. The monologues are here listed alphabetically.

The Actress
A drawing-room arm-chair with a small low drawing-room table at its side, and another plain or upholstered straight drawing-room chair.

At an Art Exhibition in Boston
No stage requirements.

At a Telephone Switchboard
A plain square table that can be used to suggest a telephone switchboard, with a straight wooden chair in front of it.

At the Court of Philip IV
Two long low benches matching each other, if possible upholstered and in the style of the sixteenth or seventeenth century.

A Board of Managers Meeting
A drawing-room table and a straight drawing-room chair.

A Charwoman
No stage requirements.

The Children's Party
A drawing-room chair with arms, and a small drawing-room chair without arms.

A Class in Greek Poise
A plain straight chair, and a small plain table.

Christmas Eve on the Embankment at Night
A plain low wooden bench, if possible of weathered appearance.

A Cocktail Party
A drawing-room chair with or without arms, and a low coffee-table.

A Dalmatian Peasant in the Hall of a New York Hospital
A plain straight office chair.

A Débutante at a Dance
A large roomy upholstered or overstuffed arm-chair.

Doctors and Diets
A small rectangular table to serve as a restaurant table, and a straight restaurant chair.

An English House-Party
An English or French drawing-room arm-chair.

Five Imaginary Folk-Songs
No stage requirements.

A French Dressmaker
No stage requirements

The German Governess
A plain straight chair

Glasses
An upholstered arm-chair with a soft cushion in it, and a small table at the side of the chair.

In a Church in Italy
A small straight wooden or rush-bottomed chair, such as might be used in an Italian church.

In a Railway Station on the Western Plains
A plain kitchen table, or a narrow long dark-wood table to suggest a lunch-counter in a country railway station.

In County Kerry
A plain kitchen chair.

The Italian Lesson
A chaise-longue, or a low arm-chair with a small bench or foot-stool to be used with it in the manner of a chaise-longue; a small low table beside this chaise-longue or arm-chair; and one straight chair to suggest a chair standing in front of a dressing-table.

A Miner's Wife
A plain wooden table and a straight wooden chair.

On a Porch in a Maine Coast Village
A kitchen chair or plain straight rocking chair.

Opening a Bazaar
A small straight chair.

Le Retour de l'Aveugle
A French arm-chair, if possible upholstered.

The Return
A square or round table, and three straight chairs that are alike and easy to move.

A Scottish Immigrant at Ellis Island
No stage requirements.

Showing the Garden
No stage requirements.

A Southern Girl at a Dance
A drawing-room arm-chair.

Three Breakfasts
A rectangular table to serve as a dining-room table, and straight chair to be used with it.

Three Generations in a Court of Domestic Relations
A plain office chair without arms.

Three Women and Mr. Clifford
'The Private Secretary': two plain square tables to serve as office desks, and two straight office chairs.
'Mrs. Clifford: In the Motor': a low sofa or love-seat that suggests the back seat of a limousine.
'At Mrs. Mallory's': A large low overstuffed arm-chair.

Vive la France! 1916
No stage requirements.

Vive la France! 1940
No stage requirements.

The furniture was placed on the stage according to simple diagrams given to the stage manager. The prefatory notes and stage directions in the monologues will suggest to the reader how the furniture was used. In most cases it was placed in the centre of the stage, the chairs facing the audience directly or at an angle. No special lighting was required by Ruth Draper for her performance of the sketches. In only two or three of the monologues (as indicated here in the text) was the curtain required to fall at the end.

II. *A Tabulation of Characters Portrayed and of Characters Evoked in the Monologues of Ruth Draper*

The number of characters portrayed in each monologue is given in the first column; the number of characters evoked or addressed is given in the second. When the phrase 'and others' is used it indicates characters in a larger group or crowd who are not specifically named, addressed, or otherwise individually evoked.

The monologue	Characters portrayed	Characters evoked
The Actress	1	10 (and others)
At an Art Exhibition in Boston	1	4
At a Telephone Switchboard	1	10 (and others)
At the Court of Philip IV	1	9 (and others)
A Board of Managers Meeting	1	11
A Charwoman	1	3
The Children's Party	1	19
A Class in Greek Poise	1	5
Christmas Eve on the Embankment at Night	1	4
A Cocktail Party	1	24
A Dalmatian Peasant in the Hall of a New York Hospital	1	4 (and others)
A Débutante at a Dance	1	3

The monologue	Characters portrayed	Characters evoked
Doctors and Diets	1	11
An English House-Party	4	11
Five Imaginary Folk-Songs	5	—
A French Dressmaker	1	7
The German Governess	1	7
Glasses	1	10
In a Church in Italy	6	(a) 1
		(b) 4
		(c) 11
		(d) 1
		(e) 3
In a Railway Station on the Western Plains	1	17 (and others)
In County Kerry	1	3
The Italian Lesson	1	18
A Miner's Wife	1	12 (and others)
On a Porch in a Maine Coast Village	1	3
Opening a Bazaar	1	25 (and others)
Le Retour de l'Aveugle	1	4
The Return	2	(a) 2
		(b) 11
A Scottish Immigrant at Ellis Island	1	13 (and others)
Showing the Garden	1	3
A Southern Girl at a Dance	1	4
Three Breakfasts	3	(a) 2
		(b) 2
		(c) 6
Three Generations in a Court of Domestic Relations	3	1
Three Women and Mr. Clifford	3	(a) 14
		(b) 6
		(c) 1
Vive la France! 1916	1	8 (and others)
Vive la France! 1940	1	3
Totals:	Portrayed: 54	Evoked: 330

EDITOR'S NOTE

The titles of some of Ruth Draper's monologues passed through a number of alterations in the course of their history. All titles as printed in the present volume are given as she gave them in her final manuscript of 1955–6, but for the benefit of those who wish to trace the record of her work in the future, a number of her changes of title are noted here. The monologue now called 'The Children's Party' was earlier listed in her programmes as 'A Children's Party in Philadelphia'. 'The Actress' was called 'Mlle. X. of the Comédie Française' or 'of the Théâtre Français' in her programmes of 1916–20, and on some occasions as 'A French Actress at Home'. 'Three Breakfasts' in its earlier and shorter version was listed as falling into two parts: 'First Breakfast on the Farm' and 'Breakfast after Fifteen Years'. 'A Southern Girl at a Dance' was called in 1911 'A Southern Girl at a Dance in the North', and 'A Débutante at a Dance' was then known as 'A Débutante in a Conservatory'. 'Love in the Balkans' (not printed here since no manuscript of it exists) was once listed as either 'A Serbian Scene' or 'A Serbian Woman', and on occasion as 'A Roumanian Lady'. 'At a Telephone Switchboard' was first titled 'A Switchboard Girl', and 'At an Art Exhibition in Boston' as 'In a Boston Museum'. In addition to the early monologues listed in the Foreword to Part II of this book, of which no complete manuscript was made by Ruth Draper, a number of others appeared on her early programmes of 1908–20: 'An Afternoon Call', 'Adopting a Child', 'A Fashionable Wedding', 'Dressing for Dinner', 'A Runabout Drive', 'A Philadelphian Visiting'; and 'Three Generations in a Court of Domestic Relations' was then called 'Three Generations of Russian Jews'. The monologue known as 'A Class in Soul Culture', not printed here because the manuscript is incomplete, was presented as a sequel to 'A Class in Greek Poise', and it presented the same speaker and characters. It must also be emphasized again that the wording of the monologues varied greatly over the years, and that recordings made by Ruth Draper in the last years of her life show many incidental changes from the texts as printed here and based on her own final manuscripts, though the basic theme and sense of each monologue were usually preserved. All texts and titles as now printed follow Ruth Draper's approved and final typescripts made in 1955–6.

All details in the memoir of Ruth Draper in Part I are based on written and printed—in one case on tape-recorded—documents except in the passages indicated as deriving from personal information or memory. The basic sources were R. D.'s own archives: her letters sent or received, record-books and diaries, address-books, theatre programmes and records, and her large collections of newspaper clippings, reviews, and press-notices; but these have been supplemented by consulting the files of newspapers and magazines concerning her career, contemporary theatre histories and reference-books, and accounts by her relatives, associates, and friends. One difficulty in using personal documents was the habit of Ruth Draper and her friends of omitting yearly dates in their correspondence. Month and day usually appear, but the year of writing seldom; in her files of clippings precise dates are also frequently lacking. I have generally avoided using references when exact dates are missing, unless these could be otherwise ascertained. When specific dates are not given in the memoir, as in the letters quoted in Part XII, it is because they are missing in the manuscripts, and such omissions are allowed here only in the case of documents which, though relevant, do not refer to specific events or dates in her life.

The account of Dr. William H. Draper and his family in Parts II and III is based on contemporary year-books, on the obituaries that appeared at the time of his death on 26 April 1901, on the proceedings of the New York Academy of Medicine, and on family information. The sketch of Charles A. Dana, besides using similar works of reference, relies primarily on the *Life of Charles A. Dana* by James Harrison Wilson (1907) and *Dana and the Sun* by Candace Stone (1938). The account of Paul Draper, while using newspaper records and obituaries, is based chiefly on a short memoir found among R. D.'s papers, evidently written by her at the time of his death in 1925; the manuscript is typewritten but it shows additions and corrections in her own hand. Muriel Draper's *Music at Midnight* (1929) has also been used here. The records of the Spence School and the *Spence Alumnae Bulletin* have been followed in the account of R. D.'s attendance at that institution.

The material concerning Henry Adams and Henry James in Parts V, VII, and VIII of the memoir derives mainly from the documents or books indicated in the text and footnotes. Leon

Edel's edition of the *Complete Plays of Henry James* (1949) has been followed in the account of the monologue James wrote for R. D. in 1913. James's sentence on the 'Persian carpet', variously worded in other reports and interviews quoting R. D., is given here in the version quoted by Mr. Edel (who tells me that he took it from a note written down by Mr. Simon Nowell-Smith at R. D.'s dictation) and corroborated in personal conversation. In Part VI, R. D.'s statement on the major influences in her career comes from the *New Yorker* interview of 6 March 1954. The short account of Beatrice Herford derives from various articles in New York and London newspapers, from obituaries at the time of her death on 18 July 1952, and from the serial volumes of *Who's Who in the Theatre* and similar theatrical annuals or reference-books. An article on 'The Legend of Oliver Herford' by Julian Street in *The Saturday Review of Literature* for 26 June 1943, has also been useful; it is reproduced in *The Saturday Review Gallery*, selected by Jerome Beatty, Jr., and the editors (1959). The details on Paderewski are taken from his own *Memoirs*, from other books on his career, from various interviews of R. D.'s, and from family information, but the quotations by R. D. come from the interview published in the *New Yorker* for 6 March 1954, as preserved in her scrapbook. The account of Cyril Harcourt's play *A Lady's Name* as produced by Marie Tempest in 1916 derives from New York newspapers of that year as well as from a prompt-copy of the play.

The discussion of Lugné-Poe and his theatre in Part IX is based on his letters to R. D., on R. D.'s record-book, on Lugné-Poe's own books as listed in the text, and on various histories of the modern French theatre, particularly Gertrude Rathbone Jasper's *Adventure in the Theatre: Lugné-Poe and the Théâtre de l'Œuvre to 1899* (1947) and two books by Jacques Robichez— *Lugné-Poe* (Paris, 1955), and *Le Symbolisme au Théâtre: Lugné-Poe et les Débuts de l'Œuvre* (Paris, 1957). Lugné-Poe, born Aurélien-François-Marie Lugné, added the name of the American ancestor of the French symbolists to his own surname, thus becoming Lugné-Poe. The name later came to be printed or written frequently as Lugné-Poë, even in certain of his own books and in some of his later letters, and it is preserved in that form on the memorial plaque on his theatre in the Cité Monthiers, rue de Clichy, in Paris; but it is given here in its original and authentic form, without the diaeresis. In quoting R. D.'s diary in Part IX, I have felt free to emend her rapid notes in the abbreviations she used, repetitions, and incidental slips of her pen.

The chief sources used in the accounts of Edward Sheldon and Lauro de Bosis in Part XII are given in the text and footnotes. Besides personal letters, Eric Woollencott Barnes's *The Man Who Died Twice: The Biography of Edward Sheldon* (1956) and the manuscript of *The Three Fates* have been followed. The account of Lauro de Bosis follows R. D.'s own translations of and prefaces to his *Icaro* (1933) and *The Story of My Death* (1933), Gilbert Murray's foreword to the former volume, G. M. Trevelyan's foreword to De Bosis's *The Golden Book of Italian Poetry* (1933), R. D.'s file of letters from Romain Rolland (the originals of which she gave to the Harvard University Library), and numerous personal letters and contemporary newspaper reports (some acknowledged specifically in a footnote), though the controversial aspects of his career and death, and Giuseppe Prezzolini's dealings with these in his *Italiano Inutile* (1954), are only slightly indicated in what is written here.

As previously indicated, R. D.'s own record-book and her collections of newspaper and magazine clippings form the basis of all references to her public career, engagements, and travels, but these have been further verified through newspaper reports, theatre programmes, and other records wherever possible. It must again be emphasized that the account of R. D.'s friendships in America, England, Europe, and other parts of the world in Part XII of the memoir is admittedly selective and fragmentary. It has been found impossible in this short record to do justice to all the friends who figured in her life and correspondence, and apologies are made to those who have been necessarily slighted, unmentioned, or inadequately treated. R. D.'s statements on her work and art in Part XIV derive chiefly from a tape-recorded interview for Station WFMT in Chicago in February 1955, but a number of printed interviews as well as personal recollections have also been drawn on. Since she often objected to the inadequacy or unreliability of printed interviews, the oral evidence of the Chicago discussion has been taken to be as authentic as is possible in such matters. Bernard Shaw's words at the end of Part XVI were variously reported in R. D.'s interviews; they are given here as quoted by her in an interview for the *Washington*

Post in 1952, preserved unchanged in her scrapbook. The short account of her work for the Keats-Shelley Association of America is based on several letters she printed in the New York newspapers, on the issues of the *Keats-Shelley Memorial Bulletin*, on her typewritten reports of the work of the Association, and on Neville Rogers's *Keats, Shelley and Rome: An Illustrated Miscellany* (1949 and 1957). The awarding of the honorary degrees at Edinburgh in 1951 and at Cambridge University in 1954 follows the printed programmes of those ceremonies. The final pages of the memoir, relating to the events of the year 1956, are based on R. D.'s record-book, on her last newspaper clippings and letters, on the obituaries that appeared in the international press after her death on 30 December 1956, and, necessarily, on personal and family information.

M. D. Z.